TO POISON A NATION

TO POISON
A NATION

*The Murder of Robert Charles and the Rise
of Jim Crow Policing in America*

* * * *

ANDREW BAKER

NEW YORK
LONDON

Requests for permission to reproduce selections from this book should be made through our
website: https://thenewpress.com/contact.

Published in the United States by The New Press, New York, 2021
Distributed by Two Rivers Distribution

ISBN 978-1-62097-603-6 (hc)
ISBN 978-1-62097-604-3 (ebook)
CIP data is available

The New Press publishes books that promote and enrich public discussion and understanding of the issues vital to our
democracy and to a more equitable world. These books are made possible by the enthusiasm of our readers; the support
of a committed group of donors, large and small; the collaboration of our many partners in the independent media and
the not-for-profit sector; booksellers, who often hand-sell New Press books; librarians; and above all by our authors.

www.thenewpress.com

Composition by Westchester Publishing Services
This book was set in Garamond Premier Pro and WTC Mader

Printed in the United States of America

10 9 8 7 6 5 4 3 2 1

Contents

Note on Race and Language

Racial distinctions in turn-of-the-century New Orleans were complicated, but broadly reflected a three-tiered society in which access to socioeconomic power correlated to physical appearance. This included a white majority, which had largely overcome antebellum divisions between English- and French-speaking populations, but which remained highly divided between native-born Americans and foreign-born immigrants. The substantial black minority included "Creoles" or "Creoles of color" with African-French ancestry, along with lighter-skinned individuals with significantly mixed African and other European ancestry. Related differences in color frequently, although not always, corresponded to social and economic status. To reflect these divisions, I have used the adjectives "white," "black," and "colored" to generally define each group. I use "white" to collectively describe the racial majority, although I reference ethnicity in cases where it played a significant role, as with the tensions surrounding Italian immigrants. I use "black" to collectively describe the racial minority, but I use "colored" to distinguish elite leadership and professionals, whose influence and self-definition distanced them from the community's working and underclasses. During Reconstruction and its aftermath, the New Orleans black community resisted marginalization in many ways, including by capitalizing the word "Negro," commonly written as "negro" by white authors who capitalized "Caucasian" and "Anglo-Saxon." I have replicated these dual capitalizations in quoted sources to preserve the resistance or degradation implied by the choice. For the same reason, I have not censored racial slurs.

Modern activists and academics have made compelling arguments for capitalizing "Black" in contemporary usage. In the context of this book, I have chosen to stylize all racial groupings as lowercase in order to maintain analytical consistency while directly engaging the constructed nature of these contested sociohistorical categories. Because I am writing specifically about late nineteenth-century New Orleans, I have chosen the lowercase to emphasize the fragility of these categories at a time when they were being reaffirmed as foundational.

TO POISON A NATION

Prologue

SHORTLY AFTER ONE O'CLOCK ON MONDAY AFTERNOON, May 23, 1892, twenty-seven-year-old Robert Charles and his brother Henry marched toward the depot in Rolling Fork, Mississippi, a sleepy railroad crossing where tensions were running high.[1] The Charles brothers worked for the railroad as common laborers, maintaining the tracks that crisscrossed the countryside—and they knew all about the troubles. Days before, a black co-worker had been executed for killing a white company foreman. News of the racially charged murder had sparked outrage across the South, traveling more than two hundred miles to the railroad terminus in New Orleans, where big-city reporters covered the crime story to its grisly conclusion. They put a positive spin on seventeen-year-old William Knight's agonizing strangulation, describing how the young man calmly walked to the gallows and suffered a lengthy torture before asphyxiating "just seventeen minutes after the trap sprung."[2] The judicial lynching was intended as a warning for black men everywhere in the region to mind themselves—which the Charles brothers were currently disregarding. They were moving forward on a dangerous mission to recover a pistol stolen by another railroad employee. Both men were carrying rifles as they walked through the restless town.

The Charles brothers approached a freight train that was preparing to leave the station and confronted the young black man whom they suspected, but he claimed that a white flagman had taken the weapon. The flagman overheard the exchange and jumped down from the train, pointing the stolen weapon at the brothers. Then violence exploded in the muggy afternoon. The white man opened fire—but missed the brothers, who returned a salvo that sent him scrambling around the locomotive. Hightailing it toward the caboose as the train began to steam away, he glanced over his shoulder and was stunned to see them following close behind, undeterred and quickly closing the gap. Unscathed by the exchange, he decided to give up his loot rather than his life. He tossed the pistol away and hopped aboard as the train gathered speed, relieved to see his pursuers turn aside to retrieve the gun, before retreating toward the western swamps outside town. Outraged white citizens formed search parties and followed the fugitives, but the hounds were unable to catch the scent in the surrounding forests. They quickly gave up hunting. Robert Charles and his brother had disappeared into the dismal swamps that once concealed runaway slaves.[3]

In New Orleans, the shootout went unnoticed. The bloodless scrap was unimpressive by the violent standards of the post-Reconstruction South—and besides, reporters there were busy with a different sort of railroad trouble, covering the contentious negotiations as business leaders unsuccessfully pressured the mayor to deputize civilians as special police officers and crush a streetcar conductors' strike that was disrupting citywide transportation. Eight years would pass before anyone made the connection between a black man in a backwoods railroad crossing and troubles brewing in the South's great commercial metropolis. But unseen threads, causality and contingency, slowly tightening, bound Robert Charles to the volatile city. When the snare finally closed, New Orleans faced an explosive crisis that seemed to threaten its future—and maybe even spark the genocidal race war that many white Southerners believed would be the inevitable end of emancipation.

It was a steamy Monday night in New Orleans, July 23, 1900, when three police officers confronted Robert Charles and his roommate, who were sitting on a doorstep in a working-class neighborhood. While the precise course of events would be shrouded in controversy, the violence that followed was undeniable and shocking. After wounding one patrolman and eluding capture, Charles ambushed a police squad outside his one-room apartment in the early morning hours, brutally executing two officers with the same Winchester rifle that his brother had been carrying when they marched through Rolling Fork almost a decade before. As the largest manhunt in the city's history unfolded, white mobs took to the streets, brutalizing adults and adolescents, murdering at least seven black residents in cold blood as civil authorities and deputized citizens desperately fought to restore peace over three days of bloody racial violence. When two officers stumbled across his hiding place, Charles gunned them down. Finally cornered, he exchanged gunfire with hundreds of besiegers in a spectacular daylight shootout witnessed by thousands. Before dying in a blazing finale, he evened the score, killing seven white men—four police officers and three civilians—and wounding maybe twenty more, the wildest one-man rampage the South had ever seen.

Anonymous in life and suddenly notorious in death, Robert Charles took his secrets with him to an unmarked grave, leaving behind a gaping void at the center of an unbelievable story. Conspiracy theories swirled as reporters doggedly chased down leads, reassuring and alarming shaken residents as they uncovered the sordid details of his criminal past and radical doctrines. Portraying the assassin as a fanatical villain and a remarkable physical specimen, they crafted an origin story for the "archfiend of the century," but produced a character study that was far more fiction than reality.[4] In response, civil rights activists compiled a sympathetic counternarrative, describing a martyred antihero who resisted police brutality and singlehandedly defied a lynch mob.[5] Researchers have since contributed to this more nuanced understanding of Robert Charles, combing through the few available sources from a forgotten episode— newspapers, court filings, correspondence, and more. Yet the historical record is mostly bare and the figure who emerges is ambiguous, appearing in only glimpses that require subjective interpretation of fragmentary and problematic evidence. Because he created virtually no surviving archive before his controversial final moments, Charles is a character imagined by the reader's sympathies, somewhere between the dangerous black radical who murdered police officers and the peaceable black citizen who defended himself against unlawful violence. But by broadening our perspective to the troubled city that consumed him and his legacy's enduring consequences, Charles becomes something more than the villain or hero in a true crime yarn. Instead, his archive tells the story of a black man whose life should not have mattered to the regime that murdered him—and why it mattered so much.[6]

* * * *

ROBERT CHARLES was born a world away from the bustle and sometime chaos of New Orleans, but its central role in the changing political and economic landscape of the postwar South shaped the winding course that brought him to the place where he would die. Conceived in slavery, the fourth-born son of Mariah and Jasper Charles entered a new world of precarious freedom on the banks of the Bayou Pierre, a minor tributary in southwestern Mississippi, one stop in the massive river system that brought cotton to the South's commercial emporium: New Orleans. The natural landscape—fields, rolling hills, and pine forests— was the backdrop for ugly postwar realities as planters violently resisted social change after emancipation.[7] Although black sharecroppers faced daunting challenges, the Charles family overcame these obstacles to sustain themselves. Tending eighteen acres on a cotton plantation alongside the waterway, they purchased a few animals and necessary farming implements. Unusually, Mariah and Jasper also managed to provide a rudimentary education for their children. Like his brothers, Robert began working during his early teenage years—but he was already reading and writing.[8]

Despite his family's modest homestead on the edge of the Bayou Pierre, his childhood and adolescence were harsh. Political violence was everywhere in the Reconstruction South, as white supremacist paramilitaries targeted black men who tried to make good on voting rights. Jasper Charles was among the sharecroppers who registered—and almost certainly among those who armed themselves in self-defense as assassinations and massacres took place with chilling frequency.[9] The bloody death of Reconstruction in the 1870s brought a fragile cease-fire, but the situation in southwestern Mississippi worsened during the early 1880s, as poor farmers explored interracial alliances, threatening the local political dominance of established planters. Cannon fire and the brazen assassination of a Republican organizer by white paramilitaries during one campaign season forced black families to hide in the swamps. The violence prompted a federal investigation based in New Orleans, where terrorized witnesses could testify in relative safety. But the proceedings were a partisan farce that produced a 750-page report and nothing more.[10]

Robert Charles was seventeen years old when the white rebellion negated his soon-to-be voting rights. He had grown tall and strong, hard farm labor adding muscle to his six-foot frame. His older brothers had already left home and he was also preparing to leave rural Mississippi, where good jobs were rare, but trouble was common. Given recent events, there was no chance that the situation would improve. Shortly after terrorists crushed the interracial farm alliance in its infancy, Charles relocated to Vicksburg, a railroad boomtown thirty miles from home. There he found steady work as a section hand working for a line nicknamed the "Mississippi Valley," which boosters promised would return prosperity to a chronically depressed region by sending crops to markets in New Orleans faster than any steamboat could manage.[11]

By his early twenties, Charles had been drawn from the fringes of the Deep South cotton economy and closer to its center in New Orleans, just one among countless black laborers whose sweat was fueling its long-awaited renaissance. Although their lives and sometimes deaths were shaped by its fortunes, most would never set foot in the great metropolis. Like his parents, many remained in sharecropper cabins dotting the countryside, while others filled its bustling satellite towns to maintain the growing transportation system that sprawled outward like steel tentacles. Hundreds of railroad workers serviced locomotives in Vicksburg's machine shops and repaired tracks in the surrounding area—exhausting and dangerous work done mostly by black migrants from outlying rural communities.[12]

Arriving in Vicksburg in the late 1880s, Charles spent four years working in the company buildings clustered on the riverfront. Laboring and socializing with black co-workers in the rowdy world of railroad men, he was anonymous to white observers—almost. Toward the end of his time in Vicksburg, a five-sentence blurb appeared in the newspaper there, one that would take on retrospective significance. As reported, a town constable approached "Robert Charles, a negro charged with threatening the life of one of his acquaintances," who dismissively muttered that the warrant had nothing to do with him and kept walking. Charles was taken at gunpoint and supposedly "behaved very rudely" when he appeared before a judge, but there were no follow-up stories on his case, suggesting it amounted to nothing. Maybe it was based on bad information, as Charles protested, or witnesses refused to cooperate, or authorities decided against prosecuting a verbal dispute between black laborers— regardless, the episode showed that he was willing to nonviolently resist an arrest he considered unlawful.[13]

During his four years as a section hand, Charles provided only this premonition that he was destined for notoriety. But there was no hard evidence—at least, not until May 1892, when the unexpected shootout at the Rolling Fork railroad depot forced him to abruptly give up his job and leave the area. After the bloodless gunplay, Charles returned to his childhood home as a fugitive, if not an especially wanted one. But he would not stay in southwestern Mississippi long, soon packing up his few belongings and moving to New Orleans, a place where he could be truly anonymous. Traced over three decades, his journey from a cabin on the Bayou Pierre to the largest city in the South had taken him through diverse scenes in the changing regional economy: from sharecropping plots, to railroad boomtowns, and finally to the metropolis that consumed and exported produce from this fertile hinterland. Along the way, he had become someone who was capable of extreme violence—at least in self-defense, but perhaps also in more questionable circumstances. In any case, he was no more dangerous than countless others in his world. Like other black men in the post-Reconstruction South, his experiences had been shaped by brutality in many forms. In adolescence, Charles had survived white terrorism by hiding with family members in the swamps near his childhood home. Now in adulthood, he bore physical and psychological scars inflicted by a hostile world: he walked with a noticeable limp, caused by a serious ankle injury that never quite healed; his front teeth were discolored and decaying; he drank regularly, although rarely to excess; he was sociable, yet prone to depressive episodes; he could be restrained, but when he was comfortable enough to speak earnestly, the words flowed in torrents.[14]

For all these characteristics, Charles drew no particular attention when he reached the urban heart of the agricultural economy. To white observers, he was only a black workingman from the countryside, joining a class whose numbers were a growing source of concern to those whose fortunes depended on them. Like its newest citizen, New Orleans had been scarred by violence—and it could be combustible. But it was primarily a place of commerce, where the seasonal chaos of Mardi Gras and the more general rowdiness of public life complemented the workaday rhythms of the waterfront and warehouse. Reaching his thirtieth birthday, Charles was drawn there by the ordinary rather than the extraordinary, hoping to keep his head down and find steady work in a marketplace that needed men like him. Thousands had already taken advantage of those possibilities, quietly living and laboring without encountering trouble. The convergence of a man and a city with histories of violence would be disastrous, but at the time, there was no reason to predict an explosion.[15]

* * * *

WHEN HE ARRIVED in New Orleans during the mid-1890s, Robert Charles reached a city on the edge, suspended between a tumultuous and disappointing history and dreams of a remarkable future. Envisioned as a world-class American emporium since Thomas Jefferson purchased the expansive Louisiana Territory with eyes on "the one spot on the globe" that would assure his country's prosperity—an environmentally improbable urban marketplace, springing from a topographical soup bowl, surrounded by noxious swamps, semi-protected by a natural levee, but perpetually threatened with destruction by encroaching floods—New Orleans had not quite lived up to expectations.[16] Its antebellum boosters weathered depression, disease, and more, only to watch Yankee railroads siphon produce and profits eastward more efficiently than the Mississippi River could steam it down to them.[17] But the far greater catastrophe was the hurricane brought on by secession.[18] While the Confederacy held strong over four terrible years, New Orleans fell within twelve months, suffering a humiliating federal occupation and a severe postwar depression, locally—and wrongly—attributed to "carpetbagger misrule."[19]

Yet as the new century approached, decades of broken promises were being swept away, nostalgia sweetening the painful memories and exciting developments promising to brighten the years to come. As local authors wrote romantic eulogies to the chivalrous Old South and gave rise to a growing tourism industry, an emerging generation of merchants, financiers, attorneys, and civic reformers planned improvement projects that would solve the problems that prevented antebellum New Orleans from reaching its potential.[20] To outsiders, the city was marketed as a charming anachronism blending Old World sophistication and Dixieland hospitality, a languid oasis from the jarring speed of the modern world.[21] For its business-minded visionaries, the city was a blistering commercial hub, connected with American and European ports by overlapping trade and social networks. They were participants in a progressive revolution that was speeding commerce and remaking the world's greatest cities, while admittedly struggling with a uniquely Southern challenge: black freedom, commonly known as the "negro problem."[22]

In New Orleans, the problem was a long-standing one. Home to the largest antebellum slave markets in America, at its most unforgiving, the city was a ghoulish factory where human beings were processed as saleable commodities and planters acquired the "hands" they worked to death on cotton plantations carved from the Deep South's killing fields.[23] For those bought and sold in auction yards and in world-class hotels where masters enjoyed the fruits of their laborers, the city had a bone-chilling reputation. It was an abyss that consumed the living, a place where loved ones from the slave-exporting states were reduced to painful memories. "New Orleans was called Nigger Hell," one former slave remembered. "Few who went there returned."[24] Yet among thousands of slaves who lived and labored there, the most fortunate could find rare opportunities in the urban economy and in white households, purchasing freedom and securing manumission.[25] In freedom, they joined a distinctive population dating to the city's French colonial origins, when fluid conditions allowed *gens de couleur libres*, also known as Creoles, to establish themselves as artisans, merchants, and professionals.[26] Creoles were the most prosperous non-white population anywhere in antebellum America, a multiracial colored elite whose relationship to both free and enslaved blacks was always strained and sometimes hostile—particularly because many were slaveholders themselves, although never accepted as equals by white society.[27] These unresolved tensions contributed to a complex and combustible society, one that simultaneously epitomized and subverted white supremacy while paradoxically embodying the brightest dreams and darkest nightmares of black Americans—and that was *before* the Civil War came along and made antebellum New Orleans seem downright orderly by comparison.[28]

Emancipation was a red-hot torch in the social powder keg, as struggles over the meaning of black freedom made New Orleans the most dangerous city in postwar America. Confederate veterans and leading private citizens joined paramilitaries to win on the streets what they lost on the battlefield, waging a bloody insurgency targeting Republican authorities and black civilians who tried to make good on their constitutional rights. Dozens were killed and hundreds injured in five major urban battles and one-sided massacres.[29] Spectacular violence influenced the rise and fall of Reconstruction nationally and reshaped social dynamics among white residents locally. As previously quarreling Anglo-Americans, French speakers, and Irish immigrants came together to oppose black rights, their alliance seemed to unify the white community as never before.[30]

Meanwhile, black residents faced deadly threats and found unprecedented opportunities, navigating long-standing culture and class divisions to unevenly construct a shared community. Established free blacks and colored elites both cooperated and clashed with the former slaves who flooded New Orleans during Reconstruction as they fled extreme violence in the outlying countryside and sought opportunities in the urban economy.[31] Civil rights activists successfully campaigned to desegregate public schools and transportation, contested victories that generated political momentum and promoted solidarity.[32] Black colleges, newspapers, churches, and clubs opened and thrived, enriching social life but also frequently reinforcing divisions corresponding to color and former status. These ambiguous outcomes made postwar New Orleans as bewildering as it had been during the antebellum era, both an unparalleled hub of regional and national black resistance and a place where colored elites seemed to practice segregation nearly as scrupulously as many white residents.[33]

New Orleans emerged from Reconstruction with conflicting prospects, socially fractured and economically battered by postwar devastation in the 1860s and nationwide depression in the 1870s, yet seemingly on the verge of a long-awaited renaissance.[34] Although its growth had been slowed by geographic challenges and short-sighted development strategies, it still ranked among the nation's leading ports—and its boosters were finally starting to act that way.[35] Since the antebellum period, white business leaders had been accused of sitting back and waiting on the surrounding waterways to bring them easy profits as rivals in other cities energetically improved. But they were more ambitious and aggressive by the early 1880s, plotting infrastructure projects, staging a world exposition, and competing for outside investors with newfound energy, "aroused and awake to the future possibilities of this great city."[36] As they grew more aroused, these merchants and professionals embraced a more cohesive identity, building on the success of the New Orleans Cotton Exchange, founded six years after the war to share information, standardize practices, and settle disputes in the city's most important trade.[37] Other sectors soon followed its successful example, and the organizing boom culminated with the New Orleans Board of Trade, created in the late 1880s to coordinate action and lobbying among the commercial exchanges.[38] Business elites pointed this progressive surge in other directions, founding civic organizations, cultural institutions, and charities. Restoring themselves as patriarchs of post-Reconstruction New Orleans, they imagined both a revolution and a return to normal: sweeping modernization spearheaded by a traditional ruling class that had been temporarily dislocated by secession and occupation.[39]

But that was the problem. If the struggle for racial supremacy had collapsed distinctions between white men during Reconstruction, those who had formerly been pushed to the margins were less interested in returning to the antebellum status quo. As federal troops withdrew from the South and social elites in New Orleans celebrated the beginning of a sure-fire golden age they called Redemption, some paramilitary organizers were busy transforming the opposition's political wing into a prototypical urban machine. Officially known as the Crescent Democratic Club, but more often called "the Ring," they capitalized on growing union organization to build a formidable grassroots base among white laborers, both native and foreign-born.[40] Although common elsewhere in urban America, machine politics was unprecedented in New Orleans. Its un-expected emergence forced businessmen and middle-class moralizers to counter with a series of reform organizations, each one short-lived and styled as progressive, but representing socially conservative allies opposed to the working-class machine and its alleged corruption. By the early 1880s, the unity that had defined the fight against Reconstruction was giving way to a more worrisome political reality: white residents were loyal Democrats in state elections, but citywide contests were bitterly divided along class lines.[41]

The outcome was a white nightmare. As evenly matched machine bosses and reformers swapped the mayor's office back and forth in alter-nating elections during the 1880s, black voters played a decisive role. They composed roughly one-fourth of the electorate in New Orleans and followed patterns comparable to those of their white counterparts: collectively backing statewide Republicans, but generally splitting along class lines in municipal elections. Colored elites and professionals sided with reformers, while black laborers more often supported the working-class machine. But with such high stakes—and with so little bargaining power in other arenas—they were flexible enough to provoke false charges that they sold their votes to the highest bidders. Inevitably, they would be easy scapegoats to the losing side and underappreciated, but absolutely critical allies to the winners. As control of New Orleans switched hands, white observers worried that Redemption was a false dawn. Although the occupiers were gone and statewide Republicans were vanquished, the path to power in the South's most important city ran through black voters. And perhaps even more disturbing from the business perspective, by the early 1890s, there were signs that working-class electoral politics were evolving into something even more threatening: interracial labor solidarity.[42]

As the twentieth century approached, class struggle confounded race politics in the South's leading metropolis, where machine bosses clashed with aristocratic reformers and white laborers tentatively reached across the color line. Similarly divided and precariously balanced on both sides, the black community in New Orleans was bound to come under fire as racial hostility intensified across the region—but there was reason for cautious optimism. Its colored elites were more than ready to leverage respectability and capital to preserve the relative standing they had protected for generations, with resources unrivaled by any comparable group in the country. Meanwhile, disadvantaged black laborers were energetically reaching out to white counterparts, working to build something even more disruptive. Although they shared the same dark horizon, black residents in New Orleans were better prepared to resist the coming storm than anyone else in the emerging Jim Crow South—and perhaps even transform the city into a polestar for a new revolution, one that would finally make good on the promise of freedom.[43]

* * * *

IF THE SOUTHERN architects of Jim Crow looked toward New Orleans with concern during the early 1890s, those outside the struggling region also had good reason to pay close attention, particularly as black refugees fleeing violence and disenfranchisement gradually began to trickle northward. After all, the city was the rural, underdeveloped South's big exception. No other city in the former Confederacy had more than one hundred thousand residents and none was among the nation's top thirty by population. Purchased in less divisive times as the commercial outlet for an expanding young country's great watershed, it had survived a century of American prosperity and calamity. Its national significance had peaked when speculative booms made it arguably the second-largest city in antebellum America, but it remained the second-richest export hub in the country and among the world's busiest ports, with the size, infrastructure, and problems to match.[44] Triple the size of its closest competition in the South, New Orleans was the twelfth-largest city in America, boasting nearly 250,000 full-time residents and a population that supposedly doubled during the winter business season.[45] Beyond merchants and cotton brokers, it was home to roughly fifty thousand white laborers, similar to Pittsburgh, Milwaukee, and other growing Midwestern manufacturing centers. And while wrongly dismissed, both then and now, as too culturally distinct to compare directly with other American cities, it was a place where hardening racial attitudes were quickly replacing more nuanced cultural divisions with color lines that reflected an emerging national standard, at least now that the "Indian problem" was finally solved: whites, questionably white immigrants, and blacks.[46]

But one thing did make turn-of-the-century New Orleans unique among its peers. At a time when more than 90 percent of black citizens lived in the South, heavily concentrated in the countryside as exploited agricultural workers, the black community in New Orleans was oversized compared with nearly every other major American city. With the exception of the nation's capital, it was home to more black residents than any city in the country: eighty thousand souls representing nearly one-third of its overall population. Aside from Washington, DC, and Baltimore, nowhere else in the top fifteen cities did the black population share approach double digits—across the remaining urban areas, it averaged one in forty residents. Although it was less than one-tenth the size of its antebellum sister city, New Orleans was home to twenty thousand more black residents than New York City.[47]

If anything made New Orleans unique in the late 1800s, it was being a big city with a big black population. Confronting problems with crime, sanitation, and corruption shared by all fast-expanding cities in the late 1800s, local authorities blamed these uncommon demographics, citing the large number of black residents as an extraordinary challenge to progress. But while these complaints were rooted in the racial politics of the emerging Jim Crow South, they also represented anxieties that would spread widely as the Great Migration dramatically reshaped the demographics of urban America. By this measure, late-nineteenth-century New Orleans was hardly a city mired in the antebellum South's toxic legacy. With its large black population, it was really just ahead of schedule, confronting one of the twentieth century's most significant policy dilemmas a few generations ahead of its peers. Demographically, New Orleans trailblazed an urban America that would come into existence during the 1950s and 1960s, when black residents in Detroit, Chicago, Cleveland,

Philadelphia, St. Louis, and other major American cities finally surpassed one-fourth of the urban population and gave rise to the "inner city" as a modern "negro problem" in national discourse. Although they imagined themselves dealing with the unwanted consequences of slavery and emancipation, white residents in early Jim Crow New Orleans were actually encountering—and shaping—the American city of the future.[48]

Turn-of-the-century New Orleans was an American premonition rather than a symptom of the South's blighted history—one that foreshadowed police violence, mass incarceration, and structural racism in our own time. Just as slave pens, plantations, and paddy rollers in antebellum America were forerunners of today's racialized prison state, Jim Crow New Orleans—with its declining labor radicalism, self-serving alliances between crooked politicians and businessmen, and exploited yet resistant black underclass, repressed by intensifying police brutality—was on the bleeding edge of law and order in urban America.

It did not have to be that way. Beginning with the most audacious strike in American history, this book follows a successful campaign by businessmen in New Orleans to undermine black and white solidarity and reframe the resulting labor violence as an urban crime problem. They viewed themselves as the city's masters, but the path to victory took a winding course, shaped by strong opposition from below. As competing visions of interracial cooperation, white supremacy, and black resistance were contested on the streets and in the press, the outcome was never certain. During the 1890s, New Orleans seemed to career between class and race warfare, unleashed by forces that nobody could easily control. The stakes were never higher than in July 1900, when police officers confronted Robert Charles and sparked a crisis that was decades in the making, but unfolded over a single business week.

This is the story of the crisis and its consequences. It is about a hopeful city where histories of violence and visions of progress were hopelessly entangled and where an anonymous black workingman became a notorious "negro fiend," gunned down and stomped into the muddy streets by white avengers determined to destroy him and the broader danger he represented. They failed, at least partially. Through his fierce resistance, Charles exposed the overwhelming challenge of enforcing Jim Crow's hardening racial order in urban space. Yet his actions also gave authorities a mandate to strengthen that system. And when the dust settled, those who had so abysmally failed to protect black lives came through not only unscathed, but also empowered. White residents scarred by decades of racial and labor violence embraced a unifying narrative advanced by editors, politicians, and the business community, coercing black leaders to reframe the crisis as the turning point when law-abiding citizens rose up against criminals on both sides of the color line. Closing the chapter on a bloody history and looking toward a bright future, they forged a new order from violence they had precipitated, guiding New Orleans away from its destructive past of paramilitaries and white mobs and toward a more profitable form of racialized violence: modern policing. That regime would transform the city in profound and deadly ways, but it would soon extend beyond its limits.

This book is not just about how ruthless men reshaped New Orleans in Jim Crow's image. It is about the street-level power structures they pioneered and the stories they told to legitimize them, about violence that would spread like a sickness in the blood, beyond the city and South to poison a nation.

1

Fortunes

AROUND ELEVEN O'CLOCK ON SUNDAY MORNING, November 6, 1892, thirty-four-year-old James E. Porter and fellow union representatives climbed the steps and passed between the marble columns of City Hall, across from Lafayette Square, where municipal authorities and merchants anxiously prepared to begin last-ditch negotiations to stop an economic catastrophe.[1] Porter was unique among those scheduled to attend the meeting, which made his presence on the labor delegation especially notable. Born on a Mississippi cotton plantation, the former slave had relocated to New Orleans as a child, growing up strong to become a longshoreman and taking on a central role organizing black dockworkers.[2] Highly respected on both sides of the color line, Porter was one of the five men chosen to represent the most ambitious labor alliance in American history—roughly four dozen affiliated unions and thirty thousand members, black and white, skilled and unskilled. His purpose was as simple as it was daunting: reach a settlement with business leaders in a months-long wage dispute that had spiraled into a crisis.[3] Reporters covering the contentious talks were outwardly positive that both sides would reach a breakthrough, but as Porter and his comrades filed through the doors and disappeared into the imposing building, everyone realized how desperate the situation was becoming.[4]

The short-term origins of the problem dated to the late spring, when municipal authorities refused to crush the streetcar conductor strike, eventually forcing transportation executives to accept wage increases, ten-hour workdays, and a "closed shop" with hiring preferences for union members. It was an electrifying victory that energized workers across New Orleans, jump-starting a movement that had been slowly gathering momentum since the end of Reconstruction. During an exhilarating summer organizing boom, thirty chapters representing everyone from barbers to clerks received charters from the American Federation of Labor and officially joined the nation's largest union affiliation. With little warning, the South's greatest commercial metropolis became the fastest-growing labor stronghold in the country, setting the stage for a confrontation between conservative business leaders and radicalized workers. Emboldened by success, a triple alliance—teamsters, packers, and warehouse workers—gave employers an ultimatum at the beginning of the "business season," the make-or-break period beginning in early autumn, when merchant houses stacked fortunes shipping cotton and produce to American and European ports. The choice was simple: better pay, shorter hours, and union recognition, or face economic ruin. Directors from the New Orleans Board of Trade coordinated the business community's response and refused to concede anything, declaring, "The merchants must not yield."[5]

In late October 1892, workers followed through and went on strike, but found themselves up against tenacious opposition. For more than two weeks, the merchants held strong, bringing in strikebreakers and trying to divide the triple alliance along racial lines. Promising to negotiate with the majority-white packers and warehousemen, they refused to bargain with the teamsters, which included a significant minority of black drivers. Managers openly discussed the strategy, describing the benefits of hiring scabs to drive the low-sided wagons that hauled goods between wharves and warehouses. "We're spared the humiliation of having a man at our side on payday, watching to see whether the correct amount is given," one boss explained, adding, "especially when the man appointed to supervise our weekly payroll is a big, black negro."[6]

Despite the campaign of racial division and sensational rumors that black workers were attacking white strikebreakers, the triple alliance stayed the course, calling on the city's newly organized labor movement to support the cause. The response promised to be revolutionary. Following days of unproductive negotiations, Porter and the other leaders were finalizing plans for an audacious counteroffensive: a general strike enlisting *all* union members in New Orleans, roughly one-third of the city's entire workforce—more than enough to choke business and force merchants back to the bargaining table. "The gauntlet has been thrown down by the employers that laboring men have no rights that they are bound to respect," Porter declared, repurposing the memorable phrase from the U.S. Supreme Court's most infamous pro-slavery decision to invoke a new age of domination.[7]

Desperate to avoid a shutdown, authorities summoned both sides to the mayor's office on Sunday morning for brokered negotiations, but the meeting was basically fruitless. Businessmen demanded the alliance end the strike before they would agree to arbitration; the labor organizers rejected a precondition that would leave them with no leverage, but agreed to a temporary delay when they learned that the governor of Louisiana was arriving on the midday train from Baton Rouge. Porter and the others headed out to update the rank-and-file gathered at Three Brothers Saloon, a downscale French Quarter barroom that served as union headquarters. Meanwhile, the business delegation retreated to the famous St. Charles Hotel, located only a few blocks away. For more than thirty-six hours, messages flew back and forth between the dueling camps. The merchants reluctantly conceded arbitration on wages and hours, but rejected hiring preferences for union members.[8] Organizers recognized that it was a fool's bargain. Without a closed shop, employers would undermine the labor movement by hiring competition from outside the ranks, starving out the union and its members. On the eve of the presidential election, workers made the decision: the strike would go forward.[9]

As voters streamed to the polls on Tuesday morning, November 8, 1892, bustling scenes along the Mississippi River suggested a normal workday. Roustabouts and longshoremen guided heavy cotton bales aboard the motley fleet of tramp steamers and oceangoing cargo ships bobbing along the levee. Despite Porter's central role in negotiations, dockworkers had voted to remain neutral for the strike's duration. It was a serious blow to the labor alliance, but elsewhere in the city, the sunrise revealed stunning images of the South's busiest metropolis, unmoving. Streetcars parked in stables, wagons unhitched, shops deserted, industries shut down, and more than thirty thousand posts unmanned—New Orleans had stopped working. On street corners, paperboys sold a pitiful, four-page edition of the city's most popular daily, half the usual length, comprising advertisements and reprinted articles. "The *Picayune* appears this morning, without news and in distress," its publishers apologized. "Our printers, all members of the Typographical Union, have joined the general strike."[10]

Leading up to the work stoppage, the business community had loudly demanded the deployment of state militiamen and deputized citizens, predicting a one-sided bloodbath between strikebreakers and union thugs. Some even claimed that Porter was threatening violence.[11] Now the shrill warnings were proving completely false. Police responded to a few scuffles and some other minor disturbances throughout the day, but nothing approaching the worst-case scenario anticipated by alarmists. Peace reigned, perhaps even more frightening to conservative observers denied a pretext to demand intervention. What would have been unthinkable only a year before was becoming an undeniable reality: hard-pressed workers were wresting New Orleans from its wealthy patriarchs and commanding its fortunes.[12]

Among those watching the unbelievable scenes unfolding, few were more frustrated than the bad-tempered editor pacing inside the *Times-Democrat* building, a four-story complex on the edge of the downtown business district, smack-dab in the middle of the famous Camp Street row where reporters from competing dailies raced each other for scoops. Page M. Baker had been spending recent months in a state of righteous indignation, but striking typesetters were enough to push him over the edge. With an aquiline nose and piercing gaze that gave him the appearance of a goateed bird of prey, the fifty-two-year-old publisher was an imposing figure even when he was relaxed, which was seldom.[13] Semi-affectionately nicknamed "King" in reference to his esteemed reputation and patrician sensibilities—not to mention his authoritarian managerial style—Baker was best known for reading and re-editing his newspaper every morning, "marking the most glaring errors" and then delivering "a stormy sermon," mostly curses, to his cowering staffers.[14]

The explicit approach was also effective. After more than a decade in the news business, the former Confederate artilleryman was among the

South's most famous editorialists. His salvos combined admiration for business and its men with contempt for anyone who opposed them, which included organized workers. Leading to the strike, the second most popular newspaper in New Orleans had been roasting union leaders on more than economic grounds.[15] Jeopardizing prosperity was bad enough, but as a proud champion of white supremacy, Baker was even more disturbed by interracial solidarity among workers. From his perspective, white laborers were race traitors, choosing James Porter's low cunning and chasing financial gains over the responsible leadership exercised by the city's bright commercial minds. "The very worst feature seems to be that the white labor organization appears to be under the domination of Senegambian influence," he grumbled, citing the West African region where 40 percent of Louisiana's imported slaves originated.[16]

If successful, the New Orleans general strike jeopardized the socioeconomic foundations of his adopted hometown, but officials were showing no shared concern. Baker watched as they rejected the business community's pleas for preemptive intervention, his frustrations mounting as the mayor's office pointedly refused to deputize right-minded citizens as special police officers who could bring the strike to a decisive—though likely bloody—conclusion. His reporters were exaggerating the few instances of violence and fabricating attacks by black union members on white strikebreakers, unconvincingly attempting to reframe interracial labor solidarity as a race riot in reverse—one that threatened to undo the order that had been restored by Reconstruction's bloody street battles. As he worked on the next morning's editorial, Baker surveyed the peaceful streets—and declared war on the new administration, headed by a machine boss who represented the antithesis of his aristocratic values. "Citizens of New Orleans, your mayor has failed to perform his duty," the editor seethed, "and the police, infected by his weakness, are not prepared to protect your lives and property."[17]

* * * *

MAYOR JOHN FITZPATRICK scanned the front page of the *Daily Picayune* early Wednesday morning, satisfied that the city's most popular newspaper was providing more balanced coverage than its conserva-

tive rival.[18] But although things were calm, Fitzpatrick understood that peace in the streets was only part of a more complicated picture. Even for an administration that enjoyed strong backing from the strikers, the pressure to resolve the situation would intensify with each passing day. Joint negotiations had produced no breakthrough and more unions were joining the strike. As business suffered and the pain spread, violence could escalate. Moderate voters could be persuaded by skewed coverage. And there would be long-term consequences, economic and social—how bad was anyone's guess. Not to mention the harm to his own political prospects.[19]

More than anyone in New Orleans, the forty-eight-year-old mayor understood how tough it was to hold on to power in his hometown. Born to an Irish blacksmith and raised by the sisters of St. Mary's Orphan Asylum, he grew up tough to become a larger-than-life figure in the city's overlapping worlds of labor and politics. As he rose from newsboy to apprentice to craftsman, Fitzpatrick built a reputation through leadership positions in blue-collar mutual aid societies and civic organizations, but he commanded respect the old-fashioned way. Now a burly, mustachioed man with a silver-haired cinderblock for a head, he had a taste for violence, whether refereeing John Sullivan's bareknuckle prizefights or trading punches with political rivals who grudgingly admired his moves. "Fitzpatrick was a man of great ability," one blue-blooded contemporary conceded.[20]

For an aspiring politician in late-nineteenth-century New Orleans, proletariat credentials, boisterous charisma, and a boxer's chin were all valuable assets. After Reconstruction, an urban machine composed of professional grassroots organizers and a working-class base faced down a series of progressive reform organizations, mostly conservative businessmen and middle-class do-gooders.[21] Bosses from the city's seventeen wards competed for influence in the machine, formally known as the Crescent Democratic Club, but they universally viewed the opposition as effeminate "silk stockings," dilettantes whose governing delusions came from reading too much Roman history, without a clue how to run the everyday operations of a modern city. Reformers countered by framing "ring" bosses as corrupt masters to enthralled workingmen, practicing the lowest political arts with support from the degraded masses. Although neither stereotype was entirely accurate, both hardened over a decade's worth of bitter campaigns as ringleaders and reformers swapped the mayor's office back and forth in alternating elections.[22]

But one thing was consistent in New Orleans politics. Regardless of which side held the advantage, "Captain" John Fitzpatrick always seemed to advance his position. After earning his first appointment as a clerk in the criminal courts, the ambitious young politician was elected as a Louisiana state representative before heading the Orleans Parish Criminal Sheriff's Office in the late 1870s. By his mid-thirties, he was a rising star of post-Reconstruction politics and the "Big Boss of the Third Ward," a working-class neighborhood bordering the downtown business district and the heart of the machine's base. As public works commissioner during the 1880s, Fitzpatrick capitalized on the patronage opportunities the job provided by hiring his supporters on municipal projects, further strengthening his standing.[23] By early 1892, he was the machine's dominant personality and its unanimous choice as mayoral candidate, winning a narrow decision in the citywide elections, then graciously promising to safeguard prosperity and serve all classes equally. Although editors denounced the machine's candidate slate—announced one week before the election and predictably packed with scoundrels—Fitzpatrick received cautiously favorable coverage across the board.[24]

The honeymoon was short-lived. Troubling signs appeared soon after inauguration, triggered by the renewed tensions in the transportation industry. When corporate executives reneged on previously negotiated compromises, streetcar conductors struck again, prompting the business community to petition the mayor's office. During his tense meeting with a commercial delegation on the same day as the Rolling Fork shooting scrape, Fitzpatrick bluntly dismissed the businessmen who begged him to deputize them and crush the strikers.[25] His neutrality forced the streetcar companies to make significant concessions, triggering the summer organizing wave and damaging his reputation in elite circles. Leading up to the general strike, relations between the administration and the business community were borderline hostile, as the merchants pressured Fitzpatrick to suppress his own working-class supporters, or give them special policing authority to do the same—in other words, making demands that were beyond long shots.[26]

For the mayor and his business-minded opposition, the prevailing calm on Wednesday morning promised to shape their fortunes in completely opposing ways. So long as the general strike was peaceful, Fitzpatrick could boost his supporters by non-intervention, a worst-case scenario for merchants who had less to lose from a bloodbath. Desperate negotiations with the administration were going nowhere, even when they offered to pay the cost of mobilizing special police—not unreasonably, the mayor countered that emergency measures were quite unnecessary in a quiet city. Equally concerning, attempts to divide workers along race and class lines were no more effective. More than forty unions had joined the strike, with only a handful remaining on the sidelines. Weeks into the crisis, the walkouts were gaining momentum.[27]

Employers had one more card to play, but it was a good one—and it had just arrived on a special train from the capital. With the mayor unresponsive, they went above his head, calling on Governor Murphy J. Foster to mobilize Louisiana militiamen and promising $100,000 to defray the costs, along with enough citizen volunteers to crush the strike.[28] Six months removed from a bruising gubernatorial campaign, Foster recognized the dangers of choosing sides between the city's powerful commercial interests and white laborers who were loyal Democrats in statewide elections. Playing for time, the governor finally convinced Fitzpatrick to mobilize special police officers, but it was a fiasco. Discouraged by the administration's obvious disdain, only a handful of men showed up to be sworn—and most quickly deserted after realizing that authorities had no intention of actually deploying them.[29]

As the business week limped toward an end on Thursday morning, both sides faced a precarious situation. In practical terms, the general strike was an unprecedented success. For the first time in history, skilled and unskilled workers were cooperating across racial boundaries to cripple business in a major American city—and it was happening in the South, where unions had long struggled to make headway.[30] Porter and his fellow organizers had constructed a formidable coalition and strikers were staying disciplined, allowing the sympathetic machine administration to plausibly remain neutral. Yet the business community controlled the narrative. None of the city's four daily newspapers were covering the strike with any particular sympathy, although the tones ranged from restrained suspicion to Page Baker's venom. Despite a second night of peace, *Times-Democrat* readers awoke to stories completely at odds with the situation unfolding on the streets. Discovering a crisis "so grave that it would be almost impossible to exaggerate," many remembered the demoralizing wartime conquest and occupation as they read, "If New Orleans were surrounded by a hostile army, it would be preferable to what confronts us now."[31]

Narrative trumped reality in the end. Fitzpatrick held strong, but sensationalized reports of black troublemakers assaulting law-abiding white laborers raised pressure on public officials to end the strike. Rumors spread on Thursday morning that merchants were arming themselves and preparing to mobilize, the uncertainty heightened by comings and goings at the St. Charles Hotel, where the governor was hosting high-stakes negotiations in his luxurious suite. The strike leaders encouraged workers to stay the course, posting bulletins outside Three Brothers Saloon, but spirits plunged later that day when Foster released a proclamation shortly after meeting with the business delegates.[32] Condemning "the paralysis of industry, trade, and commerce," calling on "peaceable citizens" to avoid congregating in the streets, and vaguely promising to leverage his powers "for the protection of lives and property," his delicate phrasing barely concealed the ultimatum: an immediate resolution, or martial law. High-pressure negotiations stretched into the early morning hours, but with the writing on the wall, Porter and the other labor representatives had no real leverage without risking a massacre. The final settlement was essentially the same deal offered by merchants before the strike began: arbitration on wages and hours, no retaliation or discrimination against union members, but no formal recognition, much less a closed shop.[33]

As the news spread on Friday morning, merchants openly celebrated victory. In exchange for modest concessions to a limited group, they had defeated organized workers in principle and practice, discouraging future closed-shop strikes and securing a powerful weapon to combat the labor conspiracy threatening the city's long-term prosperity. For workers in

New Orleans, the outcome was somewhere between disheartening and crushing. They had staked everything on radical solidarity, accomplished something never before seen, and gained nothing in the bargain. Many blamed cowardly representatives for giving the game away too cheaply, but considering the gunpoint negotiations, the truth was more complicated. By focusing on process rather than outcome, some outside the city drew more hopeful conclusions. AFL leaders highlighted the interracial cooperation as an unprecedented success. "The white wage-workers of New Orleans would sacrifice their livelihood to defend and protect their fellow colored workers," celebrated President Samuel Gompers, failing to recognize that solidarity had gone both ways. "Never in the history of the world was there such an exhibition, with all the prejudices existing against the black man. To me, the movement was a very bright ray of hope for the future."[34]

By appearances, Mayor Fitzpatrick had also survived his first major crisis in a reasonably strong position by resisting pressure to betray his working-class base and staying on the sidelines long enough to allow a breakthrough in negotiations, even if the end result was underwhelming. Unlike the deadly clashes between Pinkerton detectives and Pennsylvania steelworkers during the summer's bloody Homestead Strike, serious labor troubles in New Orleans were peacefully settled and within days, business was booming again.[35] Addressing councilmen after the strike, Fitzpatrick compared the outcome under his leadership. "Although vast sums of money have necessarily been lost to us," he acknowledged, "we can rejoice that not one human life has been sacrificed."[36]

Celebrating bloodlessness as a leadership benchmark, the mayor badly underestimated the business community's feelings about losing "vast sums" and the long-term damage inflicted on the labor movement in New Orleans. Most ominously, by remaining faithful to working-class supporters in a losing battle, Fitzpatrick had destroyed any remaining possibility of compromise with the business community and made powerful enemies in the conservative press. Apologizing to readers for the "crude and maimed editions" published during the general strike, the outraged *Times-Democrat* editor symbolized the extreme deterioration, now demanding the removal of the same politician he had welcomed into office.[37] "Fitzpatrick should be impeached for his betrayal of the interests of the great city which he was sworn to conserve," Baker raged. "Why should the community allow him to remain?"[38]

* * * *

SHORTLY BEFORE NOON on September 14, 1894, many of the wealthiest men in New Orleans gathered outside the Civil District Courthouse, prepared to file a long-anticipated lawsuit on a day that symbolized liberation for the city's white residents. Marking the twentieth anniversary of the "Battle of Liberty Place," a bloody uprising by White League paramilitaries against the racially integrated police force established during Reconstruction, the meaningful date had been specifically chosen to launch another campaign against the forces of tyranny. Calling themselves the Citizens' Protective Association, the elite merchants who made up its executive committee had a simple purpose: to take revenge for the strike that had crippled the business community nearly two years earlier and punish the politician they deemed responsible for the crisis. They had compiled a staggering dossier of wrongdoings: "malfeasance, corruption, favoritism, oppression, and gross misconduct in office," among other sins. Now they were ready to land a haymaking counterblow against the Fitzpatrick administration, filing impeachment charges to force the mayor of New Orleans from office and bring the war to the machine. Praising their "zeal and courage" for unearthing the rottenness, the conservative press celebrated the filing as the beginning of the end. Just like the carpetbaggers driven from a liberated metropolis, John Fitzpatrick and his cronies would pay a heavy price for endorsing rule by race-mixing mob.[39]

The impeachment drama underscored the mayor's dramatic reversal of fortune since the general strike. The damage was partly self-inflicted, starting with a ridiculous controversy surrounding the construction of a new garbage disposal facility, which had been plagued by delays and cost overruns. The fiasco reeked of corruption. It significantly raised costs and interfered with pickup schedules, triggering a grand jury investigation and a damning report published in the spring. Meanwhile, trash mountains piled on street corners and spilled into the gutters, forcing residents to come up with creative solutions. "The garbage wagon hasn't visited the neighborhood and we're paying a negro to roll our garbage in a wheelbarrow for twenty-five cents per day," one white resident complained. "Isn't that an outrage?"[40]

While the stomach-churning stench of burning garbage hovered above New Orleans, the administration again fanned the flames of controversy toward the end of the business season. As wealthy residents prepared to vacation abroad in mid-May, machine councilmen quietly awarded a lucrative contract to construct a railroad to move goods along the riverfront wharves, signing a century-long lease at an unusually favorable price without opening the bidding to competing offers. The deal screamed corruption, but wealthy residents were even more outraged by the contractor's plan to run tracks through the historic Garden District neighborhood, which would reduce property values for some of the city's priciest residential real estate.[41] They responded by founding the Citizens' Protective Association to safeguard "our homes and private interests" and organizing protests targeting the guilty parties.[42] Facing pressure, railroad executives quickly withdrew the proposal, and councilmen repealed the franchise within two weeks, but it was too late to slow the backlash as it gathered momentum. More than five thousand residents staged a parade to celebrate the victory and vowed to continue the anti-corruption crusade. Editorials welcomed the protests as "AN UPRISING OF THE PEOPLE," framing the rich man's campaign as "a declaration of war and a brilliant promise for the future."[43]

The chance to purge New Orleans came sooner than expected. Although there was no evidence that Fitzpatrick was actually behind the controversial franchise, the problems facing his administration continued to escalate. Over the ensuing months, private investigators hired by the association uncovered massive corruption related to kickbacks and municipal contracts. Before summer's end, ten councilmen were facing charges stemming from multiple scandals. Looking on the bright side, the conservative press welcomed the admittedly "humiliating" exposures as necessary housecleaning, but Fitzpatrick refused to remove his indicted cronies.[44] Finally, on the twentieth anniversary of the white supremacist triumph, the scandal reached his doorstep. Using evidence gathered by the association's detectives, the district attorney filed impeachment charges on more than four dozen counts, each one so scandalous that everyone could see judgment day was coming. Thanks to its best citizens, New Orleans would become the first major American metropolis to forcibly remove a crooked mayor from office, transforming from a laggard into a trailblazer in the nationwide struggle for progressive city governance.[45]

While the obvious source behind the crises enveloping the administration was shameless fraudulency and the mayor's uncompromising loyalty to crooked machine operatives, structural forces also played a critical role in his deepening struggles. Although the business community was united and determined to defeat organized workers and their political backers, hard times provided the real opportunity to reverse union gains. After two decades of unreliable growth and painful economic downturns, there were signs of more trouble ahead during the early 1890s, but the recession that began only months after the New Orleans general strike was far worse than anticipated. Disappearing jobs revealed the disastrous consequences of workers failing to win a closed shop. As national unemployment rates reached double digits over eighteen brutal months, the Panic of 1893 reshaped labor markets, allowing employers in New Orleans to replace union members with desperate laborers streaming into town from the stricken countryside. Denouncing the unemployed as loafers, the conservative press welcomed the out-of-towners and downplayed the crisis.[46] Paradoxically, bankruptcy and stagnation empowered the business community, as wage cuts and mass firings passed with few signs of meaningful organized resistance. Less than two years after the general strike, the labor movement and the mayor blamed for its ascendancy were both spent forces, collapsing as dramatically as they once rose.

Marking the culmination of a crusade started by the conservative press and advanced by deep-pocketed citizens, Fitzpatrick's corruption trial began on the second anniversary of the general strike, perfectly on-the-nose symbolism for a politician whose rise and fall mirrored the fortunes of the workers who paved his path to victory. For the man whose fiery rants began the campaign, it should have been cause for celebration, but the *Times-Democrat* editor discussed another subject in the next morning's opinion piece, addressing late-breaking developments in a crisis that was dominating headlines and relegating Fitzpatrick's ordeal to third-page status. As the crooked mayor answered corruption charges in one New Orleans courtroom, lawyers for the West India & Pacific Steamship Company were hastily filing a federal injunction against leaders from the longshoremen's union in another one, after weeks of racially charged destruction on the levee.[47] Assessing the unstable situation, Baker once more pleaded with authorities to "punish those who have engaged in mob violence and suppress disturbances with whatever force may be necessary." His unexpected editorial raised the startling possibility that the conservative alliance had been, if anything, perhaps *too* successful in dividing workers. Fitzpatrick's supporters were going down with him, divided and conquered. But they were going down violently.[48]

* * * *

SOMETIME DURING THE autumn of 1894, twenty-eight-year-old Robert Charles packed his belongings and moved to New Orleans, leaving rural Mississippi behind for good. By the time reporters had reason to investigate the circumstances leading to his relocation, rumors were swirling that he was a notorious outlaw in his hometown, going by the alias "Curtis Robertson" and running an underground "blind tiger" saloon catering to like-minded desperadoes, but the truth was apparently less sensational. The black workingman had been maintaining a low profile since the unexpected trouble at the Rolling Fork railroad crossing, returning home and avoiding any further trouble, but hard times eventually caught up with him. Rather than fleeing from legal consequences, he came to the city for the same reason that thousands of black laborers made the same decision: survival.[49]

Moving to New Orleans from the countryside, Charles followed the migration patterns that were raising tensions in the city, where employers leveraged the flood of unskilled workers to slash wages and weaken unions. But ironically, the crisis unfolding during the 1894 business season centered on the one critical worksite that was relatively undisturbed during the general strike. Under the leadership of James Porter and others, dockworkers had pioneered interracial organizing in New Orleans during the 1880s, cooperating across race and class boundaries through the Cotton Men's Executive Council, a coordinating body for representatives from the various waterfront trades. Although segregated, union members collaborated to ensure equitable distribution of available work and collectively bargain with shipping companies. As workers in other ports suffered reversals, they secured wage increases and work limits. Practical solidarity was successful, but it was also fragile. Unresolved racial tensions and the controversial decision to admit some employers to the executive council led to a damaging schism and by the early 1890s, dockworkers were devolving into competing unions and squabbling factions, choosing to sit out the general strike in a short-sighted bid to preserve their own gains.[50]

As waterfront tensions worsened, it was skilled workers from among the most privileged classes who ignited an increasingly combustible situation. Cotton screwmen operated mechanical jackscrews to custom-pack 500-pound bales in oceangoing steamers; they were high-demand professionals who commanded prices commensurate with their expertise.[51] Shipping agents often complained that wages for the waterfront's highest-paid employees were "the backbone of all the excessive charges," but the screwmen's enviable bargaining position was deteriorating by the early 1890s. Companies running high-capacity vessels increasingly prized speed over precision, which gave stevedores the opportunity to stoke racial divisions, pitting segregated work gangs against each other in a race where second prize was being sacked.[52] Complicating the situation, white unions claimed the right to impose daily limits on black work gangs. Although they had previously not pressed the controversial issue, they began to aggressively enforce the cap as the recession deepened. Split between members who advocated cooperation and those who favored competition, black workers from the Screwmen's Benevolent Association divided into opposing camps. Then leaders from the breakaway organization offered to stow cotton for only thirty-five cents per bale, a 40 percent markdown from the customary price. White screwmen responded by threatening to boycott any line that employed black workers, and shippers unanimously agreed to respect the color line—with the sole exception of the West

India & Pacific Steamship Company, whose agent objected to giving workers a monopoly for any reason, even a racial one.[53]

Just after nine o'clock on Friday evening, October 26, 1894, the situation dramatically escalated following a two-week stalemate. Dozens of white men moved through the darkness on the levee between Seventh Street and Jackson Avenue, ducking behind mountains of cotton bales to conceal themselves. They had the whimsical appearance of Mardi Gras revelers, wearing masks, bandannas, fake beards, and other bizarre disguises, but they darted through the shadows with purpose. And they were armed. Approaching one of the West India & Pacific steamships moored along the levee, the raiders surprised a private watchman from Boylan's Detective Agency and scrambled aboard, easily overpowering the startled crew. They forced open the cargo hatches, took the jackscrews stored inside, and pitched them overboard, leaving a man behind to guard the captives as they moved on to the next vessel.[54] Over the next three hours, gangs boarded a half-dozen steamships owned by the company and repeated the choreographed vandalism, destroying equipment worth thousands of dollars before patrolmen finally stumbled across the scene and chased them away. There were no arrests—despite close encounters with the boarding parties, the hostages claimed they were unable to provide any leads. Nonetheless, everyone recognized the action as a declaration of war by white screwmen, who sabotaged tools used by black competitors while leaving valuable cargo untouched. The raid made the front page, but the company agent stubbornly refused to stop loading and demanded police protection.[55]

Sometime after two o'clock on Saturday afternoon, members of a six-man police squad were standing nearby as black screwmen packed bales into the ships targeted the night before, when angry white men began to gather nearby. As they realized that officers were doing nothing to defuse the situation, the startled dockworkers began to disperse, but it was too late. The mob descended on them, hurling paving stones, swinging heavy clubs, and firing pistols, stalking the waterfront for two hours as patrolmen stood down. Five men suffered gunshot wounds, including two white dockworkers suspected of participating in the violence. Several black screwmen who jumped overboard during the chaos were missing.[56]

Five days would pass before a stevedore discovered a bloated corpse in the water and notified the harbor police. His co-workers identified the body as a black foreman. James Gordon Taylor had drowned while escaping, leaving a wife and three children.[57] "Taylor was well liked by the colored people and was generally respected by white persons," reporters eulogized. "He was an industrious man and had a nice home."[58]

The bloody, premeditated offensive was a deathblow to waterfront solidarity, as white longshoremen unexpectedly followed screwmen by demanding the exclusion of black laborers. In sudden, desperate need of new allies, black dockworkers petitioned the business community, promising loyalty to any employer who stood by them. The appeals were framed around shared interests, but they were rooted in the grim recognition that patrolmen were implicated in the violence. Speaking with reporters on the day that Taylor's body was discovered, black screwmen complained that some white police officers had previously worked in the waterfront trades, while others were friends with dockworkers who shared blue-collar backgrounds with them. It was less that officers failed to anticipate the violence—they deliberately stood aside as white dockworkers they knew terrorized the competition. With little confidence that commanders would intervene without pressure from above, black workers appealed to the business community, concluding, "We can only rely on those who seek to establish New Orleans as a great port of entry."[59]

The crisis exposed underlying racial tensions in the machine's working-class coalition, unsuccessfully targeted by employers during the general strike. Business leaders denounced the violence and demanded a strong response, but Fitzpatrick downplayed the situation, unwilling to crack down on white supporters. As his corruption trial loomed, a political struggle precipitated by historic interracial solidarity in New Orleans was being overshadowed by its collapse. Two weeks of vandalism followed, climaxing in a suspicious fire—certainly arson—that destroyed thousands of cotton bales. On the same day that Fitzpatrick's defense began, lawyers hired by the West India & Pacific Steamship Company successfully petitioned for a federal injunction, which held the white unions responsible.[60] Court pressure momentarily stabilized the situation, but as the business season progressed, simmering tensions quickly led to another crisis. After a mid-December meeting, the Colored Longshoremen's Association announced unexpected rate cuts, which they justified by citing the violence. "They've driven us off without cause, although we've always been loyal to them," the former president explained, adding that hundreds of black union members were unemployed and starving. "We don't think it's right that we should have our men shot and killed on the levee like they were dogs. Taylor was a good man."[61]

Within days, the black longshoremen backed down and reinstated the customary rates, but as the winter passed in uneasy peace, the chance to break the labor stranglehold on the docks tempted the shipping companies. British diplomats reported an "opportune moment to draw the attention of our great ship owners carrying on a large trade with New Orleans," describing the union infighting and federal court rulings as a chance to win "the fight against the exorbitant and ruinous charges." But while they urged companies to take "concerted action," any frontline defense would require cooperation from the mayor's office—and as with police officers, his loyalties were dubious.[62]

In the end, the chance was too good to pass up. Executives from the Harrison Steamship Line made the first move in February, announcing the company's decision to hire non-union longshoremen at discounted rates. The move triggered a wave of abortive strikes, followed by a bidding war as the segregated unions slashed their rates to undercut the competition. By early March, loading prices had dropped by 40 percent and black longshoremen promised to maintain those rates, pledging to "stand firm to the firms that stood by us in time of trouble."[63] On Friday morning, March 9, 1895, shipping companies turned the screw on white unions when sixty-plus black screwmen from Galveston arrived in New Orleans, badly exacerbating a dangerously unstable situation. Reporters noted "the novel sight in a city where thousands of men are idle," but as the probability of violence approached certainty, the mayor refused to deploy police reinforcements. "New Orleans is free and open to all who come for lawful purposes," he told shipping agents. They could bring in scabs, but Fitzpatrick had no intention to protect them.[64]

Things deteriorated, immediately and predictably. Later the same evening, raiders easily overpowered watchmen and broke into the building where black screwmen employed by the Harrison Line stored their tools, repeating the property destruction that preceded the deadly October violence.[65] Despite the clear danger and growing pressure on the mayor's office, police squads were few and far between when dockworkers returned to the levee on Monday morning. Sometime around ten o'clock, white mobs stormed down Jackson Street and descended on the black screwmen working on the *Louisiana*, opening fire with pistols and rifles. When officers belatedly reached the scene, two men were suffering from gunshot wounds and the perpetrators were long gone. With no witnesses coming forward, detectives were unable to determine who participated in the broad daylight attacks.

Later that afternoon, would-be assassins opened fire on a black stevedore as he passed through the same neighborhood, barely missing him.[66] Dodging criticism that patrolmen openly sympathized with the shooters, police commanders complained, not implausibly, that the undersized force was stretched too thin to cover the miles-long levee.[67] Even more plausibly, press critics argued that Fitzpatrick was tacitly approving the violence by refusing to protect the obvious targets, black men, opportunistically hired by the Harrison Line to break the union. Laying the blame at the mayor's doorstep, they refused to recognize the more complicated reality: the business community had undermined interracial solidarity and was now paying the price. Mischaracterizing the general strike and disregarding the recent corporate brinksmanship, the loudest voice in the conservative press announced the grim prognosis: under bad leadership, the city was running in destructive circles. "We have come again to the same condition," Page Baker complained. "Unless the governor comes, as before, and prevents trouble, New Orleans will be at the mercy of a mob."[68]

* * * *

SHORTLY AFTER SEVEN o'clock on Tuesday morning, March 12, 1895, heavy fog shrouded the French Quarter wharves located directly across from Jackson Square, which were leased by the Harrison Steamship Line. With shipping companies and municipal authorities both refusing to back down, black dockworkers faced a gut-wrenching decision that morning: risk violence by showing up, or termination and starvation by staying home. Most had decided to take the chance, but every man there would quickly regret the decision. The longshoremen were gathering tools and tackle, preparing for a hard day aboard a three-thousand-ton steamship bound for Liverpool. Posted nearby, a six-man police squad waited to be relieved after an overnight watch. Struggling to see through morning fog that limited visibility to barely fifteen yards, officers spotted figures in the gloom, human forms massing. As the squad commander and three patrolmen investigated, there was an unmistakable explosion—gunfire.[69]

The eruption sent them scrambling. Accounts differed on where they headed. Although the on-duty corporal claimed he was confused by volleys coming from multiple directions, some witnesses testified that police officers sprinted to a nearby shed, where they hid until the gunfire stopped.[70] Surging through the French Quarter streets, hundreds of armed men descended on the wharves, encountering no resistance as they sprang the ambush. The physical coordination was striking. Attackers moved as an organized body that brought to mind experienced labor gangs rather than an "excited mob," seeming to confirm "a large and powerful organization conspiring against the peace of the city" rather than spontaneous brawling.[71] For the intended victims, it was chaos as they scrambled through the empty boxcars scattered along the levee, frantically running toward safety as bullets whistled and ricocheted. The attackers hunted with impunity, showing discipline as they chose targets. One gang spotted a petrified man hiding behind cotton bales and chased him for nearly a quarter mile, passing black union members working for another shipping company, who had been working in peace beside white longshoremen. According to reporters, "They were not interfered with in the slightest by the mob, who chased a negro from the French Market and shot him to death."[72]

Shortly after the gunfire ended, a patrol wagon brought reinforcements to the scene, where the officers who had taken cover when the shooting began gingerly made their way from safety. While searching a tarpaulin-roofed shed located near the tanks, patrolmen discovered the body of Henry James, about fifty years old, who lived across the river in Algiers.

After making his panicked dash along the levee, James had been cornered, crippled with a shot through the hip, and then executed with a round to the head.[73] Nearby, officers found the corpse of a second man, Morris Mitchell, who had been working for the Cromwell Steamship Company when he was run down and riddled with bullets.[74] Apart from them, it was uncertain how many others were killed. Many had jumped or fallen into the Mississippi River during the stampede. Some hid beneath the wharves or swam away, but with strong currents and so many recent arrivals, any number could have vanished without a trace.[75]

Gangs committed two more murders near Jackson Square that morning. Neither victim had anything to do with the labor troubles. During the headlong rush toward the wharves, mobs stormed past fifty-year-old Fred Lopez as he walked toward the French Quarter restaurant where he worked. Perhaps mistaking the Mexican national for a longshoreman, white men gunned him down. The victim staggered a few steps before collapsing on the banquette, where he quickly bled to death.[76] Later that day, Dr. Alfred J. Lopez identified his father's body at the morgue.[77]

After ten minutes and at least three murders, the rioters continued up the levee, where unwitting black and white laborers were preparing to weigh hogsheads in a shed across from the New Orleans Sugar Exchange. Warned of the approaching mob, Leonard Mallard grudgingly strolled away, complaining that he had a right to earn a living. As he prepared to board a passing train, someone pointed a Winchester rifle in his direction and fired. The round caught him above the right eye and smashed through his face.[78] Mallard was breathing when co-workers found him and called an ambulance, but with brain tissue spilling from his crushed skull, he was far beyond saving. "Mallard was a mulatto and possessed a good deal of intelligence," reporters wrote. "He was president of the Skilled Men's Protective Union, a married man, and had two children."[79]

In addition to the four confirmed dead, over a dozen black dockworkers were injured, along with a British sailor and two suspected attackers. Although the police officers posted at the scene had been unable to make a single arrest or identification, everyone knew who the killers were. Reporting one homicide on a standardized form, Sergeant Felix J. Conrad wrote down "rioters" on a line reserved for suspect names, adding "cotton screwmen" under occupation. No further information was available. "The smoke from the guns and fog was so thick that it was impossible to recognize any of the rioters," the sergeant reported, estimating "there must have been five or six hundred."[80]

Around the same time as the French Quarter ambush, police officers posted a few miles upriver had put up a more impressive fight against a second mob, which descended on the same West India & Pacific Steamship Company vessels already targeted for property destruction. The sequence started out the same way. Hundreds of armed men stormed the riverfront across from Jackson Avenue and opened fire on black longshoremen, but as they advanced, two squads—a pair of corporals and a dozen patrolmen—blocked the path. This time, the officers stood firm. After a tense showdown, the mob backed down. Reversing course, they fired aimlessly into the sky as they marched down the empty levee. Covering the only heartening story on an otherwise dismal morning, reporters fashioned a masculine fable. Its antagonists "worked themselves up to a high pitch of passion," but retreated upon facing resistance because "the prospect of getting a little of the medicine that they were administering to weak and unarmed men made them cringe."[81] Here was an elegant solution to a problem with profoundly structural roots: more guns, wielded by stronger men.[82]

In reality, the badly outnumbered squad turned back the mob through admirable bravery, but they made no arrests and were unable to disperse the angry men—thereby failing to stop a fifth killing. Shortly after the showdown, Sergeant Conrad learned there had been a shooting on the nearby levee. "I immediately proceeded to the scene, where I discovered a negro man in a dying condition, the bullet having entered his mouth and passed through the back of his head," he reported. "He was identified as Jules Payne, about forty-six years old, a cotton screwman."[83]

With five men confirmed dead and dozens more wounded by mobs now estimated in the thousands, police commanders finally decided to mobilize reinforcements. Patrolmen struggled to regain control as sporadic violence continued throughout the morning and into the afternoon. Yet even with chaos sweeping New Orleans, the mayor's office stonewalled. "There's nothing the matter that I can see," Fitzpatrick told baffled correspondents. "I've been all over the levee this morning. The men are working and everything is going on as usual."

"But do you think the police are equal to cope with the situation?"

"What situation?"

"The riot on the levee this morning."

"Oh, that's all over long ago," Fitzpatrick coyly replied. "This trouble has been brewing for a long time. At least the papers seem to give that impression."[84]

Outraged executives took matters into their own hands, convening a session attended by representatives from the city's leading commercial bodies—the New Orleans Board of Trade, Chamber of Commerce, Cotton Exchange, Louisiana Sugar & Rice Exchange, Clearinghouse Association, Young Men's Business League, and more. After a lengthy debate, they drafted a resolution calling on the president of the United States to mobilize federal troops, an extreme measure sure to cause a political firestorm in a place where conquest and occupation remained painfully fresh memories. Before the delegates could dispatch the message, a telegram arrived from Baton Rouge, reassuring businessmen that the governor was heading down, prepared to use emergency powers once again to stabilize the situation.

Shortly after eight o'clock that evening, Governor Foster steamed into town and made a beeline for the office building where business leaders were gathering. There he delivered an impassioned thirty-minute speech, punctuated throughout by resounding applause from his appreciative listeners. No lines were more crowd-pleasing than the governor's closing pitch, which explicitly—and justifiably—made good on a threat only gestured toward during the general strike's darkest hours. State militiamen would report to armories citywide before sunrise the next morning, ready to deploy if the trouble continued.[85] Momentarily satisfied, the business delegates drafted a public declaration. Promising to stay the course without bending to labor's demands, they stipulated that it was "not a question of wages or compensation, but whether the merchants of New Orleans shall conduct their own business in their own way." Staking the high ground by emphasizing principle rather than profits, they declared, "The commerce of this city shall be protected and every man who desires to perform honest labor shall be permitted to do so regardless of race, color, or previous condition."[86]

By sunrise on Wednesday morning, the business community and state authorities were on the same page. State militiamen were mobilized, circumventing machine politicians and police commanders. Everything was quiet along the levee—which was exactly the problem as the hours passed and traumatized black laborers refused to show up. Betrayed by fellow workers, they had little reason to trust employers who put them on the line to begin with. Unless there was a show of force, there was no chance they would make the same mistake again.[87] With the levee deserted and the press beginning to question his leadership, the governor redoubled his commitment to the business community later that afternoon, meeting with commercial leaders and finalizing plans to preemptively deploy militiamen. Speaking with reporters, Foster expressed confidence that the forces under his command were ready and able to protect black workers. There was certainly no need for federal troops.[88]

Before noon on Thursday morning, hundreds of uniformed militiamen began streaming from barracks across New Orleans, rifles propped against their shoulders. The part-time soldiers drew huge crowds, receiving a particularly warm reception as they marched by downtown office buildings and warehouses. "As they passed through the business section of the city, the boys were given many a hearty cheer to encourage them," observers noted.[89] But when they marched through the working-class neighborhoods of the Irish Channel, blocks from where Jules Payne was murdered in cold blood, the militiamen received an icy reception. Men shot them menacing glares and women jeered from the sidewalks. "You're not satisfied with taking the bread from our mouths," one shouted. "March away and shame go with you!"[90]

For nearly two weeks, black and white longshoremen loaded cargo under the watchful eyes of Louisiana militiamen, whose salaries were partially covered by contributions from the commercial exchanges. As the situation gradually stabilized, the consequences of the uprising began to manifest themselves, most significantly in the serious weakening of labor organization. Facing competition, the white screwmen's union accepted deep wage cuts and increased daily workloads, but they nonetheless faced pressure from cheaper alternatives. Before the business season ended, desperate screwmen agreed to work for companies who employed mixed union and non-union crews, along with black laborers, sweating alongside the same men they had terrorized only weeks before. Longshoremen faced even worse prospects. Remarking favorably on "peace and quiet on the city front since troops intervened," editors observed that "negroes have nearly monopolized the business of loading vessels," adding "white laborers have been driven from the levee almost entirely."[91] Describing the emerging status quo for New Orleans dockworkers, economic reporters were bluntly positive about the prospects for merchants and planters, concluding, "This complete surrender is expected to end the cotton handler troubles."[92]

The political consequences of the killings would take longer to materialize, but after the uprising, the relationship between the Fitzpatrick administration and the business community, antagonistic under the best of circumstances, reached new depths of hatred. Denunciations came from all quarters, but as always, the most passionate belonged to the hawkish editor perched in the *Times-Democrat* building, who surveyed three years of economic ruin under corrupt machine rule and a mayor who openly sympathized with hoodlums—now murderers—over the city's finest citizens. "In contempt of law, in contempt of duty, in contempt of his oath, he refuses to lift a finger to stop lawlessness and protect the lives of citizens," Baker protested. "Shall this man be permitted to disgrace the city and the people who have honored him?"[93]

The answer came quickly, although it was entirely unsatisfactory. Just two days after the deadly uprising and hours before militiamen retook the streets, the Fitzpatrick administration's downward spiral unexpectedly reversed course. After two months of painstaking deliberation, the judge in Fitzpatrick's corruption trial finally announced his decision. It took him three hours to read his ponderous, eighty-eight-page ruling—which cleared the mayor on every charge. The most scandalous charges lacked sufficient evidence, and while Fitzpatrick violated the municipal charter on technical counts relating to the railroad controversy, there was no smoking gun to prove that he did it on purpose. No reckoning, no removal, no justice. Baker rather predictably expressed horror at the "public calamity," but his competitors confessed to a grudging admiration for the "man of destiny" in the mayor's office, whose position had turned around so dramatically "at the very lowest point of his fortunes."[94] Some proposed a protest meeting, but the idea was rejected considering the potential for violent outbursts. Frustrated members of the Citizens' Protective Association gathered in a Garden District mansion and resolved to consult attorneys and appeal the decision, but there was little hope that it would lead anywhere.[95]

Others sensed vulnerability. Inside the cramped offices of the *Southwestern Christian Advocate*, correspondents from the South's most popular black newspaper had mostly avoided comment during the long-running crisis, choosing to run the church announcements, marriage notices, and moral instruction that were the bread and butter of the religious journal. But much better than white editors, they recognized the political damage that the perfect storm of troubles had caused the resilient boss whose prospects depended on New Orleans workers—all of them. During previous elections, machine candidates earned strong majorities among black laborers, who consistently supported their own economic interests, often despite objections voiced by conservative-leaning colored professionals and community leaders.[96] But after being abandoned by the administration during the bloody crisis, black supporters were reevaluating, dividing the machine base along racial lines and creating a prime opportunity for its opponents. In an editorial glossing over the newspaper's reform-minded sensibilities, *Advocate* staffers pitched a unified black vote. "Our sympathies are always with the laboring men," they reassured, "but when they discriminate against fellow laborers for the sole reason that they are colored, they put themselves beyond the pale of sympathy."[97]

Combined, black laborers and colored professionals represented one-fourth of the city's electorate, more than enough to swing elections, which made them strong potential allies for any opposition party. But without question, the business community would be responsible for leading the charge. After racking up expensive legal fees while pursuing a series of unsuccessful appeals, commercial elites from the Citizens' Protective Association ultimately dropped the ill-fated case and departed New

Orleans to relax in Gulf Coast resorts, Atlantic seaboard cities, and European vacation destinations in the unbearable summer months. But the customary exodus did nothing to slow the opposition's momentum. When the great commercial metropolis came roaring back to life at the beginning of another business season, reformers began laying the groundwork for a political organization—one strong enough to vanquish the machine and recapture New Orleans, once and for good.[98]

* * * *

HALF PAST SEVEN o'clock on Friday evening, November 8, 1895, thirty-eight-year-old Charles Janvier stood before an enthusiastic crowd numbering in the hundreds, the crowning moment of a reform crusade that was rapidly gaining momentum. Since the beginning of the business season, the young president of the Sun Mutual Insurance Company had been working diligently alongside fellow commercial leaders as they prepared a new platform to challenge the machine in citywide elections scheduled for the following spring. A few days before, selected recipients had received mysterious invitations to "a meeting of businessmen," signed by the richest men in New Orleans and making an urgent bid: "Action must be taken now."[99]

Packing multiple rooms in the Chamber of Commerce offices, audience members soon learned they were there to inaugurate the city's latest reform organization, the Citizens' League, based on progressive governing principles shared by similar groups across the country. The policy agenda would be hard-nosed pragmatism—merit-based civil service, more rigorous voter registration procedures, secret ballots, and a smaller city council—measures attacking the machine's political advantages by limiting patronage opportunities and reducing ballot access in the name of clean elections. They also focused on strengthening a police force that had failed so comprehensively, calling for hiring more officers and improving the criminal justice system to "speedily try persons accused of crimes" and punish the guilty. Reformers chose Janvier to head the executive committee, an elite group reflecting the organization's ideological orientation. Denouncing corruption and championing "an honest administration of affairs," they endorsed a high-minded vision of modern governance, promising to run the city based on "the same sound business principles as those of any other corporation."[100]

As both sides prepared for citywide elections in the spring, machine politicians struggled to sidestep the corruption and lawlessness associated with the Fitzpatrick administration. Seeking to capitalize on momentum and diminish the opposition's grassroots advantage, Citizens' League organizers established a downtown campaign headquarters and opened clubs in each of the city's seventeen wards, attempting to disprove the "silk stocking" label that dogged previous reform campaigns.[101] Yet they nominated one of their own for the mayor's office. A former attorney, businessman, and two-time president of the New Orleans Cotton Exchange, Walter C. Flower was returning from a premature retirement to save his beloved city, apparently recovered from recent health problems thanks to the "excellent climactic condition" of his country estate.[102] Flower's sterling résumé made him well-suited to run a business-minded administration, but less charitably, the first-time candidate amplified criticism that reformers valued pedigree more than governing experience.[103]

As the reform campaign steamed forward, rather unexpectedly, the machine was a ship without a captain, drifting toward the municipal elections with an incumbent mayor who refused to run for a second term. Fitzpatrick was vague about the reasoning behind his decision, although rumors suggested that outside pressure was coming from the highest levels of Louisiana politics, since city elections were held on the same day as the statewide contests. Normally there would be no concern in a state dominated by Democrats, but they were facing unexpected competition in the countryside, where black Republicans and white Populists were running cooperative "fusion" campaigns against candidates favored by wealthy planters, whose political dominance often put them at odds with poor farmers. With an unpredictable election ahead, Louisiana Democrats were pressuring the urban machine to endorse uncontroversial candidates, rightfully concerned that the lightning rod in the mayor's office would bring out a backlash vote that could also sweep them away. But others whispered that Fitzpatrick was stepping aside to avoid a humiliating loss.[104]

Arguably the biggest factor working against him was black voters, more specifically, the workers he had abandoned during the levee crisis.

Shortly before announcing his decision not to run again, Fitzpatrick had publicly tried to mend fences by warmly addressing black clergymen, but the result was less than promising.[105] As the campaigns began, a conversation between a Citizens' League organizer and an audience member attending a rally in the machine's Third Ward stronghold captured the problem. Flamboyantly proving that he was no "silk stocking" by hiking up his pants to reveal his cotton socks and flannel long johns, the organizer was midway through an energetic pitch when he spotted a black man in the crowd. Sensing an opening, he beckoned the man onto the stage, asking, "What's your business?"

"I'm a cotton screwman," came the response.

"What have the ringsters ever done for you?"

"They made me run for my life off the levee!"

"Well, that settles you, my friend," the organizer concluded. "They made you run then and they'll make you run again if they get a chance."[106]

With black laborers defecting in droves and the machine's prospects appearing more and more dubious, ward bosses delayed a decision before finally choosing a mayoral candidate only two weeks before the election, a first-term congressman with name recognition and nothing else going for him.[107] Fitzpatrick did everything he could to ensure victory despite his refusal to run again, especially because a loss would damage the machine's long-term prospects by eliminating the patronage used to reward—and ensure—loyalty. But with fifteen thousand voters designated "colored" by the registrar's office, many of them mourning friends and colleagues massacred on his watch, the mayor was losing the battle. The machine had sacrificed black voters, literally, by supporting white mobs. On the eve of the election, one speaker reminded his audience that "ring men were shooting Negroes on the levee."[108] Meanwhile, the president of the Colored Laboring Men's Alliance—a screwman who had been pistol-whipped by a white colleague during the violence—gave voice to feelings shared by fellow union members. "We're with the Citizens' League," he promised.[109]

As voters streamed to the polls on Tuesday morning, April 21, 1896, political observers recognized the profound evolution in the New Orleans electoral landscape during Fitzpatrick's four tumultuous years in office. Reformers anticipated a celebration on election night, but even the most optimistic among them were unprepared the scope of the victory. According to morning headlines, a "GLORIOUS UPRISING OF THE PEOPLE" ended in a "CITIZENS' LEAGUE LANDSLIDE." Boasting nearly 60 percent of the vote, Walter Flower had unsurprisingly carried the city's wealthy neighborhoods by impressive margins, but the mayor-elect had even turned the tide in the "Old Third," narrowly winning the mixed-race machine stronghold thanks to overwhelming support from its black residents. Completing the clean sweep, reformers won the down-ballot municipal races and earned a strong majority of statehouse seats from Orleans Parish. It was an undeniable mandate, enabled by a diverse coalition: business elites, the middle classes, and most significantly, a unified black community.[110]

Elsewhere in Louisiana, the results were less definitive. In the country parishes, nearly thirty thousand white voters had abandoned a Democratic Party dominated by wealthy planters, forming alliances with black sharecroppers to support Republicans and Populists across dozens of races. With the ballots counted, fusion candidates represented 40 percent of the state's new general assembly. Assuming cooperation from Citizens' League legislators, whose loyalties were uncertain, they had enough votes to block the Democratic majority—a sea change in Louisiana's one-party politics. Amid reports of violence and voter fraud, Governor Foster claimed a dubious victory in his reelection campaign, although his abysmal performance in New Orleans—where laborers embittered by his intervention during the recent troubles and reformers equally outraged by his close relationship with the machine—very nearly doomed his chances.[111] But despite these asterisks, those who had done everything they could to wrest power from the machine celebrated its demise. Basking in victory, the *Times-Democrat* editor reflected on his city's incredible leap forward and searched his expansive vocabulary to express his feelings. "It was a majestic and beautiful spectacle, this sudden and irresistible uprising against men who had come to imagine themselves masters," Page Baker rhapsodized. "New Orleans is among the municipalities which have risen up under the white banner and achieved a victory for honest government."[112]

Of course, the white banner was carried forward by black hands. Celebrating deliverance from slavery on the night of his freedom, the editor was far too excited to consider the electoral mechanics of the reform victory, which suggested that the city had been emancipated by saviors that complicated his white supremacist perspective on recent events. When the registrar's office released election returns from Orleans Parish, the numbers showed that 80 percent of ten thousand black voters supported the Citizens' League—precisely covering the margin of victory in the mayor's race. Running down the numbers, Baker eagerly pointed to the Citizens' League success in working-class neighborhoods as evidence that the machine's attempt to frame the election as "a fight of the laboring man against the capitalist was properly rebuked," but he failed to mention exactly *which* workingmen had been unmoved by those appeals. With the evidence staring him in the face, the South's leading editorialist could only manage what was a lukewarm gesture toward colorblind populism. "The more carefully the vote is examined and analyzed," he concluded, "the clearer it becomes that it was a victory for the whole people of New Orleans, not any class."[113]

The perspective was clearer inside the offices of the *Southwestern Christian Advocate*, where staffers celebrated election results that were extraordinarily promising for black residents, both in New Orleans and across the state. The outcome revealed divisions among Democrats and the possible strength of emerging interracial alliances, suggesting that old tropes were perhaps losing potency as Louisianans confronted hard times and disillusionment toward the one-party dominance that defined post-Reconstruction politics. Labeling white supremacist propaganda "the clever trick of second-rate politicians," editors concluded "the victory throughout the state" proved that the actual issue was "a good government for all people." Closer to home, the results decisively refuted the claims made by "certain Negro-hating journals." Endorsed by everyone from professionals to union men, the Citizens' League victory proved that black voters could be counted on to support good municipal governance. The election results put the black community in New Orleans on solid political ground, more advantageous than at any time in two decades, standing alongside businessmen and farmers in a common struggle for progress. Reflecting on lessons from the historic election, the editorial voice of the black community discerned a more hopeful future, where voters "given a fair and honorable opportunity" proved themselves among "the most reliable, loyal, and faithful citizens." For now, it was a wildly promising step forward. New Orleans was ready for a bright future.[114]

2

Visions

LESS THAN A MONTH AFTER THE CITIZENS' LEAGUE victory, Robert Charles asked a supervisor from the contracting firm where he worked for a recommendation. Approaching his thirtieth birthday, Charles had been in New Orleans for around eighteen months, but he had little to show for his time there—aside from the note, scrawled on a yellow time slip. It was short and standard, but it instantly became his most valuable possession, allowing him to negotiate an unpromising labor market with a white man's word to validate the claims he made about himself. During hard times, it could be the difference between starving and surviving. Despite a dozen relocations and roughly as many jobs, Charles would keep the recommendation for the next four years. By the time investigators discovered it in a dingy, one-room studio that had become a gruesome crime scene, the description was hard to square with someone who had become the greatest archvillain the city had ever seen: "To Whom It May Concern—This is to certify that R. Charles has been my employee for some time, and any person in need will find the bearer a good, honest, and reliable man."[1]

Able-bodied and hardworking, Charles was nonetheless strapped. He had relocated to New Orleans from rural Mississippi during the levee crisis, getting his bearings and earning a solid reputation. But he was restless and disillusioned, angered by the injustice around him and unsatisfied with his limited world. Dealing with the same gloomy prospects shared by thousands of unskilled black laborers, Charles had no unions to join and little reason to believe that elections would meaningfully change his circumstances—so he had already begun planning his escape.[2] A few weeks after he requested the recommendation, Charles received a second letter that he would keep for years, a certificate from the International Migration Society, which verified his contract with the controversial organization. As he looked for another job close to home, Charles was also chasing a glimmering dream, half a world away: Africa.[3]

Those prized possessions, the recommendation and the certificate, sketched a two-sided portrait of Charles and his outlook after eighteen months in New Orleans. Although the everyday demands of work defined his daily practice—finding it, doing it, keeping it—radical possibilities enlivened his perspective. They were never more exciting than during the spring of 1896, when the buzz around citywide elections in New Orleans paled in comparison to events happening elsewhere in the South. In early March, more than three hundred black emigrants boarded the *Laurada*, a ship chartered by the International Migration Society and scheduled to sail from Savannah to Monrovia, where passengers would build new lives for themselves in Liberia. An estimated ten thousand black onlookers cheered the departure, which created huge publicity for a movement that had been rapidly gathering momentum in recent years.[4] Like newspapers across the country, New Orleans dailies covered the voyage, reporting that the emigration society had "secured the cooperation of negro preachers" and exaggerating the "great numbers of negroes" across the region who were selling what little they owned and making plans to emigrate.[5]

Truthfully, the black community was far more ambivalent than white journalists understood. Always controversial but once favored by some abolitionists and slaveholders as a solution to antebellum social pressures, African emigration had since gained popularity among sharecroppers enduring repression, violence, and poverty in the post-Reconstruction South.[6] Entrepreneurs capitalized on their desperation, but some were more reputable than others.[7] Many black leaders condemned promoters as pipe dreamers and conmen, but agents were especially controversial in New Orleans, where the country's wealthiest black community rejected schemes that jeopardized the "equilibrium of peace" they had worked so hard to build.[8] Writing for a predominantly middle-class readership with no reason to consider such drastic measures, editors from the *Southwestern Christian Advocate* pointed to the "marvelous progress" made since emancipation. They argued that well-established social networks promised upward mobility to anyone with the ability to make good, concluding, "We don't believe in wholesale emigration to Africa."[9]

Among those who viewed hard work and respectability as the path to success, the Birmingham-based International Migration Society epitomized the problems associated with emigration schemes. Founded as a for-profit venture by white entrepreneurs, the company rapidly expanded by recruiting part-time agents, who received small commissions for signing up new members and a 5 percent share of open subscriptions. After paying a one-dollar start-up fee, subscribers would make regular payments toward the forty-dollar cost of passage and supplies. Founders advertised in black newspapers, aiming for those otherwise unable to afford the journey by claiming to have "reduced the cost of passage to almost nothing compared to what it would cost you by any other route."[10] Although the company's subscription-based structure and rock-bottom pricing did make the passage more affordable than alternatives—suspiciously so, according to critics—the model also prized growth at the expense of security and transparency. As agents fanned out across the South and recruited members in large numbers, virtually every transaction ended badly for buyers. Hustlers posed as salesmen and conned some prospective customers. Meanwhile, subscribers unable to continue the monthly payments were contractually obligated to surrender the balance of their accounts, losing everything they had already paid. Although the rule was loosely enforced, almost everyone abandoned the contracts eventually. Whether accidentally or by design, the society's business model usually milked a few dollars from hopeful subscribers before leaving them with nothing. One agent confessed, "Most of them lapsed after they made a few payments."[11]

While conservative voices in the black press criticized the International Migration Society as a "gigantic money-making scheme," most of its agents were drawn by the cause, not the commissions.[12] In May 1896, the society was gathering memberships in New Orleans thanks to forty-eight-year-old William Royal, the right choice to lead a collection of activists who spread the gospel of African emigration using existing grassroots networks that more frequently provided leads on jobs and cheap lodging. Royal drew on his contacts and his reputation as a traveling evangelist who also represented various mutual aid societies, passing out emigration circulars along with his own self-published pamphlets, which quoted militant Old Testament passages to make the case for a modern black exodus.[13] His ministry exemplified the resourcefulness and radicalism that drew struggling workers to the cause, including Robert Charles, who retained copies of Royal's circulars among his possessions. Drawn by the message, Charles would show uncommon devotion in the coming years, distributing the emigration literature to his co-workers, friends, and acquaintances and earning a reputation as a thoughtful and passionate advocate.[14]

Despite the grassroots enthusiasm, the International Migration Society was facing headwinds by the time Charles subscribed. Damaging reports from disillusioned emigrants were already surfacing by the time the *Laurada* reached Monrovia in the spring of 1896, where its arrival only compounded the logistical problems that had plagued two previous voyages. Though some emigrants chose to stay in West Africa, many others trickled home over the summer with harrowing stories. Leveling the worst possible charge, one returnee complained that he had been "taken out there on contract between the society and the Liberian government just as slaves were taken out of Africa," expressing remorse for accepting a fool's bargain. For those who opposed emigration from the beginning, these stories were parables. Describing how unsophisticated farmers were duped, abandoned, and returning home "sick and discouraged and most pitifully broken," they endorsed the conservative approach to racial progress as the only way forward: staying home, working hard, being respectable.[15]

Only months after Charles made a down payment on his radical new life in Liberia, the African emigration movement was quickly declining, as dreams of economic opportunity and social equality came up against the hard realities trapping black farmers and laborers in American poverty and exploitation. The society would continue operating for a few more years, but organizers were unable to raise money for a fourth voyage. Its founder later remembered a prolonged death spiral as "payments kept decreasing and finally dwindled" and the venture "gradually faded out of existence."[16] Like most other subscribers, Charles eventually stopped making payments and his account terminated, but evidently, there were no hard feelings on his end. Contact with emigration agents had sparked dreams that would define his remaining time in New Orleans, a desire to awaken his peers and escape a hostile society with them, chasing visions of freedom he could glimpse just beyond the dark horizon. And while the society's founder would deny knowing Charles to white reporters investigating his dangerous associate, he was lying. When civil rights activist Ida B. Wells contacted him following the shocking events that prompted the interrogation, the entrepreneur confessed to knowing the suddenly infamous man and described the nature of their relationship. For roughly five years, nearly his entire stay in New Orleans, Charles had "earnestly and faithfully" distributed the society's literature, "apparently motivated by his love of humanity and desire to be instrumental in building up a New Nationality in Africa." Even when the dream crumbled, Charles believed to the bitter end.[17]

Among his peers, the black workingman was a more ambiguous figure, a compelling emigration advocate whose radical ideas could easily attract dangerous attention from white authorities. Yet he moved easily through the worlds of unskilled laborers in New Orleans, joining social clubs and maintaining a wide network of co-workers and acquaintances, who respected Charles as someone who spoke with understated authority and carried himself with dignity. While those who warmed to his message did everything possible to remain underground after the events that made him notorious, Ida B. Wells would uncover glimpses of his outsized influence, corresponding with one man who agreed to share his memories—but only if he could remain anonymous. "Enclosed you will find one of the circulars which Charles possessed," he described. "Until our preachers preach this doctrine, we will always be slaves. If you can help to circulate this 'crazy' doctrine I'd be glad, for I shall never rest until I get to heaven on earth, in Liberia."[18]

Yet as Charles and his confidants in New Orleans chased dreams a world away, others in the black community were more hopeful about the prospects for racial progress closer to home. Delivering the critical votes that swung the municipal election to the Citizens' League, they had proven themselves as dependable allies to the city's powerful business community. Now in the aftermath of victory, the reform coalition was moving from strength to strength. Following through on campaign promises to purge corruption and modernize a commercial metropolis with unlimited potential, they were implementing an ambitious platform with stunning efficiency as New Orleans recovered from economic downturn and deadly labor violence. Storm clouds were gathering across the South, but for those who believed that formidable white friends and a rising tide were the only real way forward—a vision, not a mirage—the city seemed to be turning the page on its troubled history. Soon, it would become a place where there was no need for a "good, honest, and reliable" man like Robert Charles to look anywhere else for a chance to capitalize on his character and talents.

* * * *

ON THE AFTERNOON of May 7, 1897, the young president of the Citizens' League stood before a national conference of reformers, describing the heartening situation shortly after the one-year anniversary of the citywide elections. His speech was a bit grandiose, but Charles Janvier was in a bragging mood. Since the victory, Citizens' Leaguers in the state legislature had accomplished critical goals with astonishing speed, negotiating with Democrats in Baton Rouge to revise the New Orleans charter and change how business was done. They curbed patronage by creating an independent board to oversee city jobs and took on corruption by demanding open bidding on municipal contracts. After cleaning house in City Hall, reformers addressed election fraud by requiring voters to re-register on an annual basis and mandating secret ballots. As he evaluated the first year of clean governance, Janvier voiced optimism, but recognized the failures that had undone previous reform administrations. "We fully realize that much more remains to be done," he soberly concluded. "We haven't made the mistake of disbanding and clearing the field for the forces of evil, which never disband."[19]

Citizens' Leaguers were right to recognize the continuing threat posed by the defeated machine, especially because only a few days before his speech, an old enemy had resurfaced. "Captain" John Fitzpatrick had been keeping a low profile since the dreadful election, but he reappeared now at the grand opening of a mysterious clubhouse. To distance themselves from the discredited Crescent Democratic Club, bosses were rebranding the machine as the Choctaw Club of Louisiana, adopting a Native-inspired name as a tribute to New York's Tammany Hall and Chicago's Iroquois Club and choosing a nation that had "always been friends of the white man."[20] Fitzpatrick spoke vaguely about its purpose, calling for a "campaign of education" and describing the clubhouse as a place "where members could meet daily to discuss and listen."[21] Although he was too savvy to openly discuss strategy, the former mayor was already plotting a comeback for his new machine—and despite Janvier's optimism, reformers had already made a fatal mistake, giving him exactly what he needed to destroy them.

Ironically, the death blow had come as the Citizens' League achieved its signature policy victory, in a legislative session that opened the same day Charles received the recommendation from his former boss. As the governor signed the New Orleans charter reforms into law, he also signed a measure authorizing a referendum, endorsed by statewide Democrats and Citizens' Leaguers and scheduled to take place in January 1898. The referendum would ask voters to green-light a convention to revise the Louisiana constitution, although lawmakers only had one goal in mind: to disenfranchise black residents by any means necessary.[22] Speaking with the reporters who traveled from New Orleans to the state capitol in Baton Rouge as the referendum approached, the governor described the dangers posed by "illiterate and unworthy voters," bluntly explaining how the vote would return "the destiny of this great commonwealth to the hands of the white people who believe in honest government and honest elections."[23] Lining up to endorse the convention, New Orleans newspapers reflected the virtually unanimous opinion among white readers, including reformers, who embraced Reconstruction-era propaganda linking black voters to corruption and election fraud as they energetically campaigned to disenfranchise their own allies and dismantle a winning coalition.[24]

Signs of the coming disaster appeared only months after Janvier's optimistic speech, as both sides began to register voters during the summer of 1897. While the referendum outcome was a foregone conclusion, the real urgency came from choosing delegates to the convention, a chance for the Citizens' League to flex its political muscle and ensure that honorable men were entrusted with such an important job. But reformers soon discovered how outmatched they were by Fitzpatrick and his bosses, who leveraged the machine's organizing advantage and registered supporters far more effectively. The growing registration gap raised an unsettling possibility, gradually becoming closer to a likelihood. Although they had been booted from office, the ringleaders were pulling an end-around using the same election reforms Citizens' Leaguers had advocated. If they could dominate the Orleans Parish delegation, they would use parliamentary tricks and backroom deals to reshape the state constitution in ways that boosted the machine's political chances. Rather than delivering the city from black corruption, the convention would return New Orleans to its crooked working-class masters.

As the business season opened to heartening predictions that the economy was finally beginning to rebound, New Orleans reformers faced unexpectedly stormy political horizons, blundering toward a political disaster and struggling to close the registration gap. Compounding the problem, many wealthy residents had yet to return home from summers abroad, choosing to extend their customary vacations into the business season. The absences were highly unusual given how much rested on the early autumn months, but they spoke to the dire situation unfolding in the city, where a health panic was threatening to become an economic and electoral catastrophe. The conservative press sought to downplay concerns, admitting that "the scare has interfered with registration and some voters are out of town," yet underestimating the number as barely one in twenty.[25] But there was no hiding the reality. At precisely the wrong time, New Orleans was facing a menace older and more dangerous than dirty politics, one that threatened to overwhelm the reformers and undo all the good they had accomplished. The press denied it for as long as they could, but in the end, seven words were enough to evoke a century of nightmares for those old enough to remember the deadliest epidemics: "There is yellow fever in this city."[26]

＊ ＊ ＊ ＊

ON THURSDAY AFTERNOON, September 23, 1897, Mayor Walter Flower stood before reporters to announce the latest measures that his embattled administration was taking to battle an epidemic that was paralyzing New Orleans at the beginning of the business season. For nearly two weeks, yellow fever had been spreading. Officials had already confirmed more than one hundred cases, along with eleven deaths, a number that promised to rise dramatically. Surprised by the worst public health crisis in two decades and unwilling to spook business, the mayor's office had been painfully slow to respond, grudgingly agreeing to quarantines and other emergency measures after costly delays. But as the situation worsened, questions about where to treat poverty-stricken patients were vexing authorities. Doctors who feared spreading the highly contagious disease refused them admission to Charity Hospital, forcing officials to scramble to find an alternative. According to the conservative press, the choice was completely serendipitous. Considering his options, Mayor Flower spontaneously decided to repurpose a public school, "and someone proposed the Beauregard School," which met the requirements. It was roomy, bright, airy, and far enough away from surrounding homes.[27]

It was also political dynamite. Formerly an antebellum sugar plantation, Beauregard School had been remodeled and opened under the Fitzpatrick administration to serve children in the Third and Fourth Wards, working-class neighborhoods that made up his support base.[28] Despite assurances that proper sanitation would eliminate any long-term danger to students, the decision was bound to create a backlash—but the mayor's office badly underestimated the response. As the unwelcome news spread, angry residents descended on the campus, protesting that wealthy reformers were dumping yellow fever patients in a poor community they despised.

Someone pointedly asked, "Why don't they make a hospital out of schools up in the stylish neighborhoods?"

"It's because those places are too rich," another responded.[29]

Early in the evening, machine bosses appeared on the scene and promised to address matters with municipal officials the following morning, but the mood remained tense. "This is our school," someone declared. "Our children go there. If they get any fever cases into the building, it'll be when we're locked in jail—and it'll take a mighty strong force of policemen to take us there."[30]

Just before midnight, perhaps two hundred protesters remained on the scene, which was being guarded by a few patrolmen, stretched too thin for an effective cordon. Someone spotted an opening and made a move, creeping unseen onto the campus grounds with a five-gallon can of kerosene. They entered an outbuilding beside the main schoolhouse, spread the fuel in a kindergarten classroom, and struck a match.[31] One of the few black officers on the force was patrolling nearby when he heard a strange crackling noise and investigated. Running toward the source, Patrolman William Robinson discovered the blaze and raised the alarm. With the flames spreading toward the main schoolhouse, demonstrators rushed forward and offered to help—but it soon became clear that they had other intentions, distracting officers with silly questions and useless advice. When firefighters showed up and began dousing the inferno, unseen conspirators slashed the hoses to pieces. As the mob became more aggressive, badly outnumbered patrolmen sent a desperate message to downtown police headquarters, where operators forwarded the pleas for reinforcements to the highest-ranking officer in the city.[32]

The bad news reached Superintendent Dexter S. Gaster at his home, where he was recovering from the most challenging week during his seven trying years as head of the force. The fifty-three-year-old commander was used to harsh criticism. Reformers had been after him since the levee violence, but things had worsened in recent weeks. Scandals related to bribes and illegal gambling dens had come to a head, apparently in career-ending fashion. The day before, the mayor's office had announced that it would follow the recommendation made by police commissioners and demand his resignation. The conservative press strongly endorsed the de facto firing, describing the force under his leadership as "so hopelessly demoralized that it shows neither moral nor physical discipline." But the police superintendent had other ideas, refusing to step down.[33] With his career hanging by a thread, Gaster dressed and headed toward Beauregard School, where reinforcements had arrived to protect fire squads as they battled the blaze. By three o'clock in the morning, the protesters had dispersed and the flames were extinguished, allowing them to assess the damage. Several campus outbuildings were destroyed, but the schoolhouse was unscathed. No arrests had been made.[34] Before returning home, Gaster detailed men to secure the smoldering ruins, uncertain about how the latest excitement would affect his job status.[35]

Early the next morning, City Hall was a hub of activity. Groups huddled together to swap gossip, predicting how authorities would respond to the fiery protests. Flower opted for defiance. His decision stood— arsonists be damned, Beauregard School would be a yellow fever ward. "I am acting for the good of the people of New Orleans," he gravely affirmed. "The few may have to suffer for the many."[36]

After dismissing the Choctaw bosses who came to complain and notifying public health officials, the mayor consulted with his police chief and ordered him to mobilize officers to protect the campus. Gaster would remain in command, at least for now. But his department was not to be trusted, particularly when so many officers came from machine-friendly neighborhoods themselves. The police force would be the public face of law enforcement in the fever-stricken city, but the mayor was making contingency plans, meeting with President Charles Janvier of the Citizens' League behind closed doors. Journalists were cagey about what they discussed, saying the conversation was "supposed to have some reference to volunteer service in case of trouble," but the implication, too incendiary to announce explicitly, was obvious. Should less advantaged residents escalate the protests, the better classes were standing behind the reform administration, ready to mobilize if patrolmen failed to intervene.[37]

Special police officers ultimately proved unnecessary, but multiple crises battered the Flower administration over the next two months, undermining reformers as they implemented a controversial modernizing vision. Protected by reinforced police squads, Beauregard School served hundreds of patients before the deadly epidemic passed, but the fire dam-age reflected the combustible situation on the ground. As yellow fever spread in New Orleans, more than seven hundred public health officers enforced mandatory quarantines, planting red and yellow flags on af-fected homes and threatening to have violators arrested. Editors printed scathing pieces blaming miserable sanitary conditions in poor neighbor-hoods for the scourge, a long-standing tradition with little basis in real-ity. Meanwhile, businessmen weighed the personal and financial risks of evacuating during a make-or-break season. With much of the Gulf Coast quarantined, some local merchants were accused of mislabeling and smug-gling goods from banned ports, while others followed the trade restric-tions and faced crippling losses. And, of course, people died, in numbers not seen in a generation—from bleeding, shock, and catastrophic organ failure. By the time cool temperatures eradicated the mosquitoes that car-ried the virus, more than two thousand confirmed yellow fever cases killed nearly three hundred residents.[38]

With deaths heavily concentrated in working-class neighborhoods, businessmen who had extended their customary summer vacations fo-cused mostly on the economic losses, exacerbated by the city's dismal in-frastructure. Since the early 1890s, civic boosters had pushed officials to build cutting-edge sewerage and drainage systems to improve public health, but progress had been frustratingly slow. Early attempts to reclaim the mosquito-breeding wetlands surrounding New Orleans stalled when the dodgy corporation commissioned by the Fitzpatrick administration declared bankruptcy. Meanwhile, engineers drafted a comprehensive plan that called for paving streets, installing state-of-the-art pumps, and carv-ing out more than one hundred miles of canals, but for now, the most extensive—and expensive—improvement project in municipal history was a pipe dream.[39] Reflecting on "the paramount question of the day" after returning from evacuation, one anonymous businessman confirmed that New Orleans was "sadly deficient in many ways" compared with its Yankee rivals, desperately needing to modernize its antiquated infrastruc-ture in order to reach its commercial potential.[40]

While the devastating epidemic tarnished the city's reputation, stran-gled its trade, and exposed its creaky foundation, the police corruption

scandals continued to generate embarrassing headlines. After unsuccessfully demanding Superintendent Gaster's resignation, commissioners
formally charged him with permitting gambling dens to operate freely—a
charge one step below collusion—along with "general incompetency and
incapacity."[41] Facing public humiliation and a hearing sure to end with
his firing, Gaster finally agreed to step down, but things only worsened
from there. Amid rumors of squabbling and crooked backroom deals, police commissioners were unable to agree on a candidate to replace him,
which threatened to worsen the department's morale crisis as yellow fever ravaged the city. With no better option, Mayor Flower reversed course
and rejected the same resignation he demanded. "I am satisfied Chief Gaster will reform the police force," he limply excused. "His sin has been
too much leniency, which comes from a kindly nature."[42]

Truthfully, the endemic corruption within the police department
came from the same source as the city's infrastructure problems: one of
the most crushing municipal debt burdens anywhere in the country. As
stagnation followed economic devastation during the Civil War and Reconstruction, both machine and reform administrations responded to
severe budget deficits by slashing municipal services. By the early 1890s,
the police department's appropriation was down nearly 80 percent from
its previous highs, effectively crippling commanders.[43] With fewer than
two hundred patrolmen and a few dozen part-time "supernumeraries" policing two hundred square miles and nearly three hundred thousand
souls, New Orleans had the lowest officer-to-resident ratio of any major
American city.[44] Meanwhile, patrolmen who already earned 50 percent
less than comrades in comparably sized cities watched as real wages
steadily declined and payroll delays compelled them to sell unfilled wage
certificates to speculators for less than face value. Adding insult to injury,
overtime pay rates were slashed by nearly one-third under the Flower administration, reducing a critical source of supplementary income.[45] Cumulatively, the pressures contributed to a perpetual crisis. Reporting that
"the entire force is ill-paid and at times not paid," federal investigators
described a department that was "deficient in morale and totally inadequate in numbers," an opinion few officers would have contested.[46]

While abysmal salaries convinced many qualified candidates to avoid policing, those with more flexible ethics recognized the alternative revenue streams available to a man with a badge. Operating by design and out of desperation, many officers engaged in small-time hustles by shaking down gamblers, madams, and saloon keepers, padding their incomes and making a mockery of municipal ordinances. Although reformers blamed the department's corruption and discipline problems on poor leadership, others recognized the structural nature of the dilemma. Addressing city officials after the resignation debacle, police commissioners bluntly explained why it was so hard to find suitable candidates. "A policeman must be of good moral character, be able to read and write, be over five-feet-eight inches, courageous in the discharge of duty, sound in wind and limb, pay for two uniforms yearly, withstand abuse and above all things be honest," they described, before hitting the punchline: "For all these qualifications, he is paid fifty dollars a month, less than the day laborer on the streets."[47]

Although bribes provided some patrolmen with enough incentive to take an otherwise thankless job, others associated with law enforcement benefited even more substantially from the untenable situation. Founded by the city's former police chief and granted special privileges by numerous municipal ordinances, Boylan's Detective Agency boasted a two-hundred-man patrol strength—larger than the taxpayer-funded police force—and offered security options to residents and corporate executives who could afford its services.[48] It was an expensive solution, prompting one prominent businessman to complain that his was "the only city I know where people have to support a private police force larger than the public one." Here was an American metropolis, similar to its peers by the usual measures, but lacking even "ordinary protections" enjoyed by the others. "New Orleans has a reputation as a lawless city," he worried. "Is this a fair reputation to draw labor and capital? Why can't we issue more bonds? Why don't we wake up and get a move on? We are our own worst enemies."[49]

If the questions painted a depressing portrait of New Orleans as the twentieth century approached, the answers were an unintended indictment of the Citizens' League. Less than two years after the press celebrated

the beginning of a business-minded golden age, the reformers were struggling with the messy realities of municipal governance, entangled in losing battles against bad sanitation and corruption, and oblivious to
existential threats looming on the political horizon. As merchants gradually returned and tried to salvage another disastrous business season, the
reform movement had little to show for its best attempts to solve deep
structural problems with little more than unshakable self-confidence. The
future was slipping away, done in by epidemic disease, scandalous policing, and a lingering depression—unless there was a simple answer to all
the questions, one supreme reform from which all the others would flour-
ish, somehow. As the epidemic finally wound down, reformers urged
supporters to register for the constitutional referendum and elect delegates to represent an "enlightened, progressive, honest community." Baffled by the messy realities of governing, they were turning to a higher
principle. To save New Orleans, they would betray their black allies and
endorse white supremacy.[50]

* * * *

LONG BEFORE NOON on February 8, 1898, the galleries of Tulane
Hall overflowed with spectators, who had come early to witness history
being made. During the previous month's referendum, New Orleans voters had endorsed a constitutional convention by a nine-to-one margin, a
strong mandate that was echoed across Louisiana, where few black voters braved violence to oppose a preordained outcome.[51] Reformers had
strongly backed the convention, but realistically, the referendum was a
landslide victory for the Choctaw machine. Bolstered by an organizing
advantage, its candidates dominated the Orleans Parish delegation, giving urban bosses the largest voting bloc at the convention. But when dig-
nitaries packed the auditorium to open the proceedings, nobody seemed
to care about the particulars. After a blessing from a venerable Louisiana
clergyman best known for calling abolitionism "undeniably atheistic" and
blessing secession, the delegates were sworn and nominated a chairman,
whose name had been agreed upon in advance.[52] To bridge the divide between old-time veterans and ambitious climbers, both well represented
at the convention, Ernest B. Kruttschnitt was a savvy choice. For one, his

uncle had been the Confederacy's secretary of state, but the forty-five-year-old boasted his own credentials: head of the New Orleans School Board and the Democratic State Central Committee, among others—and a charter member of the Choctaw Club.[53] But there was no partisanship in his opening remarks, which described the convention as "a family meeting" among Democrats and promised, "We have no political antagonism here."[54]

White unity disappeared almost as soon as he closed his mouth, although the reasons had nothing to do with eliminating black voters. While delegates generally agreed on that principle, many shared little else in common. In the country parishes, wealthy cotton planters hoped to disenfranchise poor white farmers who undermined them. Reformers in New Orleans hoped to do the same to the machine's base, favoring heavy poll taxes and restrictive literacy tests to purge the naturalized European immigrants and other white undesirables who voted for the machine—obviously a non-starter for the Choctaw delegates.[55] Considering the competing agendas, the convention was probably always bound for controversy, but few predicted how bad things would become. Reflecting on his experiences, one Orleans Parish delegate would describe a three-month torrent of abuse, recalling, "A majority of newspapers all over the state lambasted the convention and the delegates from beginning to end."[56]

Among the many editors who condemned the convention, perhaps none began with more enthusiasm than the editor of the *Daily States*, the New Orleans–based daily that was the state's most uncompromising advocate for white supremacy. Approaching his sixtieth birthday, Henry J. Hearsey had spent three decades blaming black voters for everything wrong with Louisiana, a contribution that delegates recognized by unanimously choosing him to publish the convention's official record. "Major" Hearsey had begun his journalism career by founding a country weekly on the eve of secession, before rising through the ranks as a Confederate officer and earning his lifelong nickname. Embittered by his wartime experiences, the young publisher returned to the press corps on a mission, wielding his pen like an officer's saber to strike down his political enemies with every bloodthirsty editorial. Heading a small-town journal, Hearsey endorsed the assassination of Republican officials, which earned him statewide acclaim and a promotion to the big time. After a four-year tenure co-editing the New Orleans paper favored by Louisiana's ultraconservatives, the newsman founded his own *Daily States*, which started as a humble operation, but soon gained a following for its extremism. Although its circulation numbers lagged behind mainstream competitors, the publication had fans in high places. By the turn of the century, Hearsey was known for setting the hard-line agenda—an enviable position as the political winds shifted in his direction. "No Southern paper has a brighter future," declared one contemporary.[57]

Unsurprisingly, the editor was uncompromising on voting rights as the convention began. Whereas some delegates advocated more nuanced restrictions that would allow colored elites to participate, Hearsey called to disenfranchise all black voters regardless of qualifications; by his reasoning, education made them "not only dangerous voters, but extremely obnoxious citizens." But his position on "a class of men immeasurably more degraded and dangerous to society than the worst negroes of the community" was more controversial, particularly because "hoodlums," as Hearsey classed them, were white men.[58] Race made them especially dangerous by affording them undeserved social status, although his definition of who qualified as hoodlums was hazy—some combination of foreign-born, rough-mannered, hard-drinking, law-breaking, and other nasty characteristics. What really united them was that they voted for the machine when they had no business voting at all. To remedy perceived threats on both sides of the color line, the *Daily States* editor demanded total black disenfranchisement while also reducing *white* voters by 50 percent or more. He opposed grandfather clauses and literacy tests as too permissive, endorsing substantial property ownership as an "ideal qualification" better than any degree. "An educated man has no special qualification to govern and influence the destinies of his fellow men," he reasoned, "but the man who owns property has a decided stake in society."[59]

Although conservative editors statewide rallied to his position, the oligarchs' chorus would be badly disappointed, watching alarmed as the Choctaw delegates expertly positioned themselves as the dominant faction. When the convention released its first draft in March, the voting

restrictions were riddled with loopholes to protect the machine electorate. Registration could be completed in a candidate's native language,
while those with taxable property worth a few hundred dollars could by-
pass literacy requirements entirely. A grandfather clause covered native-
born Louisiana men who were illiterate *and* impoverished, while
naturalized immigrants who had resided in the state for only five years
received the same protections.[60] With those provisions, any notion that
the convention was a friendly conversation between right-minded Democrats instantly vanished. Louisiana's manhood was actually divided into
two dueling camps: "every corrupt politician, every hoodlum, and every
negro in the state," and "the property holders, the bankers, the merchants,
the farmers, the capitalists, and the professional classes," according to
Hearsey.[61] Thanks to the machine bosses, the dark side was winning. "We
expect nothing from New Orleans politicians," he seethed. "They will sacrifice the city and the whole state to secure the franchise for the riff-raff
and the hoodlum."[62]

After weeks of tense negotiations, the convention adopted the proposed revisions, including the generous qualifications for white voters
favored by the Choctaw delegates. In exchange, they accepted a token
one-dollar poll tax paid annually, although it would be delayed for two
years—meaning until *after* the next municipal election. Playing the advantage, the bosses pushed last-minute amendments to repeal civil service reforms and laws prohibiting booze sales on Sundays, before
ultimately abandoning them in the face of a strong backlash.[63] Still, it was
a demoralizing loss for the conservative opposition, which dreamed of a
convention to purify the vote and wound up hardly better than before.
As though sensing that his lifelong crusade was becoming a legacy of failure, the *Daily States* editor made a last-ditch attempt to salvage the debacle as the convention headed toward its disappointing conclusion.
Ignoring his own hysterical criticism throughout the process, Hearsey assessed its outcome as diplomatically as possible. Admitting the revised
constitution was "not without serious defects," he rhetorically questioned,
"Is it as bad as represented by its critics?"[64]

An ugly mood hung over the convention as delegates gathered to endorse the revised constitution, three months after the proceedings began

with jubilation. In his closing address, the chairman blamed hostile editors for the partisan bickering that defied his magnanimous opening. Emphasizing that the convention was authorized to pass the revisions without submitting them to a popular vote, he defiantly explained that "the people protected themselves against themselves" by giving the delegates "absolute and despotic power to adopt any constitution that we pleased." Dismissing the controversy over the many voting loopholes, he challenged, "What do I care whether the test we've created is more or less ridiculous? Doesn't it let the white man vote? Doesn't it stop the negro from voting? Isn't that why we came here?"[65]

Among press observers in New Orleans, the answers varied. With responses ranging from ambivalence to open hostility, each of the city's four dailies considered a convention that began with celebration and ended in confrontation. None was satisfied, especially with "large numbers of illiterate and shiftless whites" corrupting the electorate, but the constitution posed threats to the city's future with consequences beyond election results.[66] Just before the convention ended, Choctaw boss John Fitzpatrick had proposed a last-minute amendment to the constitution, authorizing New Orleans officials to issue $10 million in bonds to build a modern sewerage and drainage system. It should have been a welcome step toward funding critical infrastructure, but the devil was in the details. Based on his proposal, the money would be administered by an oversight board—one elected by registered voters.[67] Considering the former mayor's scandalous administration and the voters who would choose the overseers, critics reasonably concluded that bosses would mobilize the machine's base, pack the board with crooks, and transform the costliest improvement project in municipal history into a never-before-seen boondoggle.[68] Although the *Daily States* editor had joined with reformers to endorse a similar amendment when they believed that undesirable voters of *both* races would be disenfranchised, the disappointing convention now forced a retraction. The amendment flopped, leaving Hearsey to glumly justify his own role in its failure: "We confidently believed that the electorate would be purged, and the city's credit could be safely entrusted to the people left to control our elections. It has not been the case, so we've changed our minds."[69]

Scarcely three months after the opening of a convention that had begun as a celebration of unified white supremacy, its leading champion struggled to reconcile the culmination of his life's work with the uninspiring result and the related threats to civic progress in New Orleans, apparently unable to comprehend his own role in the proceedings. Shouting from the rooftops that "negro domination" was the greatest danger facing Louisiana for more than three decades, the old Confederate veteran had drowned out the partisanship and class warfare that complicated the convention. By disenfranchising black voters without pausing to consider the consequences, Hearsey and the reformers had given Choctaw bosses the keys to the city, a golden opportunity to return themselves to power by co-opting a supposedly noble cause. As things degenerated into a partisan scrap, the machine delegation carved out exceptions with nothing to fear from "silk stockings" and their schoolboy delusions. They had given white voters what they really wanted, delivering the state from make-believe corruption and fraud. Nothing else mattered. "We were pretty generally condemned by the newspapers, but we weren't condemned by the voters," one machine delegate explained. "We promised the people to put the negro out of politics. While the constitution wasn't perfect, it contained what we promised. And they were so satisfied that they elected us time and time again."[70]

* * * *

EARLY ON TUESDAY morning, June 6, 1899, commercial exchanges and banks across New Orleans were deserted, observing a rare holiday as qualified taxpayers voted to change the city's faulty stars. Yellow fever had come back during the previous business season, a comparatively mild epidemic that disrupted commerce and killed dozens. The second brush with disaster prompted authorities to act on the long-delayed sewerage and drainage system, putting together a revised version of Fitzpatrick's failed amendment scheme. Proposing a modest property tax increase to fund municipal bonds that would raise up to $16 million, the referendum also allowed voters to decide the proper means to choose a seven-man oversight board: reformers supported mayoral appointments, while the Choctaws naturally favored popular election. Neutralizing the machine's advantage, only affected taxpayers could vote, which limited the electorate to a comparatively privileged group—but for the first time in the city's history, eligible women could participate.[71] Declaring it "the most important municipal election ever held," the press unanimously supported the proposal. "The all-important issues are health and prosperity," editors contended, "a grand upward progress to greatness, wealth, and magnificence among the cities of the world."[72]

The next morning, front-page banners celebrated modernity's victory in New Orleans, although the *Daily Picayune* outdid the competition with a full-size cartoon picturing a woman riding a prancing stallion named "PROGRESS" over muddy streets and "STAGNATION," on toward "VICTORY."[73] As everyone predicted, the proposed increase won by a landslide, earning 95 percent approval from six thousand eligible taxpayers. Despite the nonpartisan outcome, the board question reflected more typical divisions, since the working-class wards favored elections and the average property values among those who supported appointments nearly doubled those who opposed them.[74] But notwithstanding the machine's efforts to force through elections and control the fund, mayoral appointments narrowly prevailed. It was a wildly successful outcome that promised to distinguish "a century of non-progressiveness from a future of great progress."[75]

The referendum should have been a watershed for the reform administration, which had made infrastructure a cornerstone of its platform and spectacularly fulfilled its promise. But as Citizens' Leaguers prepared for municipal elections scheduled for November 1899, they were struggling to survive a self-inflicted political crisis.[76] One major problem was the same weakness that had crippled previous movements—despite grand promises otherwise, reformers had failed to build a formidable grassroots organization.[77] Principally concerned with private business interests, part-time organizers were at a serious disadvantage compared to professional machine operatives who understood the ins and outs of municipal governance and the people whose votes they needed.[78] But even more profoundly, reformers were on the losing side of a straightforward numbers game: eight thousand black voters had supported the Citizens' League in the previous election, but after a disenfranchising convention reformers happily endorsed, fewer than fifteen hundred were now registered to vote in Orleans Parish, a 90 percent reduction outdone by even worse devastation statewide.[79]

As reformers struggled to make sense of the new electoral landscape, defections began. Eager to preserve their political careers, some enterprising Citizens' Leaguers reached out to prospective allies on the other side of the aisle—and found intriguing opportunities. Despite the Choctaw rebranding, John Fitzpatrick was as influential and controversial as ever before. Some bosses favored a clean slate and fresh candidates, viewing Fitzpatrick's scandalous reputation as unwanted baggage. In the Democratic primaries traditionally dominated by the machine, some loyalists handpicked by Fitzpatrick and his cronies faced challengers, ex-reformers promising to work for progress from within the organization. As he campaigned for a place on the machine's ticket in a wealthy Uptown neighborhood, one former Citizens' Leaguer received an unexpected endorsement. Only days after accepting the mayor's nomination to serve on the board overseeing the forthcoming improvement bonds, Charles Janvier endorsed his candidacy—and, shockingly, the Choctaw machine.[80]

Facing a harsh backlash, the former Citizens' League president tried to clarify why he would embrace the crooked politicians he once vowed to oppose with "sleepless vigilance," confessing that his about-face might seem hypocritical "to those not accustomed to looking beyond the surface of things."[81] But he could explain. Actually, responsible patronage could serve both political operatives and the public good, as long as bosses rewarded loyalists with lower-level positions and reserved the "high executive offices" for those with more sterling character and credentials.[82] In other words, the answer was a cleaner machine. While some reformers condemned the young executive's political opportunism, many others were open to pragmatic alliances, recognizing the Citizens' League as a lame-duck organization in a new political world. As more and more businessmen jumped from the sinking reform ship, the consequences rippled through the Choctaw machine, as Fitzpatrick and his bosses struggled to control primaries that were supposed to be coronations, not competitions. When the smoke cleared and the numbers were crunched, opposition forces had a clear majority of delegates, putting them in a strong position before the upcoming party convention.[83]

Yet as the delegates assembled at the Choctaw clubhouse for the long nights of wrangling that would determine the comprehensive list of candidates, there was absolutely no guarantee the backroom dealings would produce a clean slate. Anything could happen—and what usually *did* happen was powerful ward bosses getting whatever they wanted. Wheeling and dealing was a veteran's game and nobody was a better player than John Fitzpatrick, who still nursed aspirations of a return to the big office in City Hall, improbable though it seemed. The ex-mayor's shadow loomed over the Democratic convention in New Orleans and the rogues' gallery attracted to its possibilities: desperate office seekers, despotic bosses, sketchy corporate agents, and would-be councilmen waiting for the chance to redistribute power and wealth—after setting aside plenty for themselves, naturally.[84]

With ample reason for skepticism, battle-worn observers were prepared for business as usual, but when the dust cleared after three days of hard bartering, just about everybody was stunned by the outcome. The most notorious political figures were nowhere to be found, while some of the rumored favorites had been snubbed. Against the odds, the machine had produced a relatively clean slate. Disbelieving its own lackluster opposition, the conservative press confessed "the ticket contains more than the usual number of surprises."[85] And nothing was more surprising than the machine's choice for the top office. Unable to convince the necessary bosses that he could win again, Fitzpatrick had nearly succeeded in pushing his preferred candidate on the convention. But at the last second, there was a wrinkle. Another name surfaced, a dark horse. There was a wild scramble for delegates, but when a winner emerged, there was no doubting that Fitzpatrick's reign was finished. With improvements on the way, the reformers imploding, and everything hanging in the balance as New Orleans entered "the most important era in its history," the revamped Choctaw machine had somehow chosen a candidate above reproach, "a citizen of the highest character and standing in the business and social world." It was enough to make even the most jaded newsman believe that maybe dawn was actually coming.[86]

* * * *

LATE ON MONDAY evening, September 11, 1899, a white-haired gentleman, sporting an impeccable suit and an impressive walrus mustache, stepped from a distinctive mansion on Esplanade Avenue, the postcard-worthy boulevard marking the downriver border of the city's most famous neighborhood. If the French Quarter was among the most fashionable tourist destinations in America, the Pierre Soulé House exemplified the Old World ambience that made New Orleans a must-see for sophisticated visitors. Constructed by an antebellum politician, the property included gardens framed by ivy-wrapped magnolias, with a fountain leading to the main entrance of a residence notable for its "stately porticoes, broad galleries, and spacious surroundings," according to the guidebooks that sung its praises. For all its magnificence, fifty-seven-year-old homeowner Paul Capdevielle was the primary attraction for those fortunate enough to earn his invitation, an engaging host embodying the "culture and hospitality that made Old New Orleans distinctive."[87]

But on this evening, Capdevielle was uncharacteristically rushed. Climbing aboard a carriage waiting outside the property, the insurance executive headed downtown and entered the Grand Opera House, where the former mayor of New Orleans presided as chairman of the Democratic convention. The session had been scripted in advance over days of bruising debates, but as always, there were a few surprises in store. When the chairman opened by requesting nominations for mayoral candidates, a loud voice from the gallery shouted, "I nominate John Fitzpatrick!"[88]

As much as the Choctaw boss wished this was something more than just a spontaneous outburst, it was not the case. Fitzpatrick graciously declined the nomination and waited for the crowd to settle before repeating his call for nominees. Now on cue, a delegate from the Sixth Ward, which included the mansion on Esplanade Avenue, stood up to address the convention. He began by promising to nominate someone who could be unanimously approved. "A man whose ability is unquestioned, whose honor and integrity are so high, a Louisianan who has always lived here, who has been identified with every good movement for the city," he proclaimed, "Honorable Paul Capdevielle!"

"We're Americans in this country," someone hollered over the thunderous applause. "We don't want no Frenchman!"[89]

That was also unplanned. Another delegate seconded the nomination, launching into a prepared speech running down the candidate's credentials, but midway through, another man interrupted, "For him, a dollar a day suits the working man!"[90]

Reassuring the grumbling audience that Capdevielle was a generous employer despite ugly rumors to the contrary, the flustered delegate rushed through the rest of the nominee's bona fides: "As a young man, he served in the Confederate Army. He was an honorable member of the New Orleans bar for more than twenty-five years. He went into commercial life and by his intelligence and business-like methods, won the confidence and esteem of his fellow citizens."[91]

Rising to accept the nomination, Capdevielle attempted to resolve any lingering concerns. "I have always tried to do my duty as a man and as a citizen," he began. "If elected, I promise to do my duty to all classes, especially . . . the working class!"[92]

"A dollar a day!" the hecklers responded.[93]

The unexpectedly combative scene effectively demonstrated the nominee's strengths and weaknesses. Born at a time when tensions between American newcomers and established Francophone elites divided New Orleans into separate municipalities, the second-born son of a prosperous French merchant had been shaped by his city's tumultuous history. As a Confederate artilleryman captured during the Vicksburg campaign, Capdevielle had risked prosecution by violating a non-combat oath and rejoining his comrades after a prisoner exchange. He walked home from North Carolina when the war ended and graduated from Tulane Law School, building a thriving practice before switching to private business and compiling an all-around mediocre record. His public service was more impressive, including leadership positions in numerous progressive organizations and high-profile boards. Capdevielle was well established in elite social circles, enjoying an ideal pedigree and the genteel life that came with it.[94]

He was also a political novice. But although his nomination was as much chance as design, resulting from arm-twisting and posturing by competing ward bosses, the first-time candidate was a surprisingly inspired choice for a machine that was vulnerable to corruption charges. With his unimpeachable reputation and commitment to civic progress, Capdevielle was ethical and capable, but inexperienced enough that he was unlikely to challenge more established powerholders.[95] Even more advantageously, the nominee had formerly served as vice-president of the Citizens' League and chaired its election committee. Setting aside the awkward reality that he was working alongside old enemies to defeat his former colleagues, Capdevielle was an enticing choice for wavering reformers, and his surprise nomination drew positive reviews from the conservative press, even if some doubted his ability to overcome the scoundrels around him.[96]

Yet the same credentials that made him attractive to reformers made him suspicious to the workingmen who made up the machine base. Capdevielle had clashed with union leaders as a transportation executive, but he was even more controversial for a position he staked as president of the City Park Improvement Association, when he supposedly claimed that one dollar was adequate daily wages for the municipal workers under his supervision.[97] He strenuously denied the charges, but the convention heckling was bad enough that a few days after his nomination, Capdevielle invited labor organizers to examine the association's books to confirm that workers were treated fairly.[98] "The two gentlemen who made the investigation were perfectly satisfied that the charge was unfounded and disproved," he proclaimed, "and in the presence of Captain Fitzpatrick, shook hands with me and said, 'We're sorry that such a charge was ever made.'"[99]

Working overtime to cobble together a coalition of ambivalent reformers and equally apprehensive laborers, Choctaw bosses capitalized on the opposition's disorganization and demoralization. Belatedly attempting to broaden the base, reformers distanced themselves from the elitist reputation of the Citizens' League by ditching the name and rebranding as the Jackson Democratic Association, but the paint job did nothing to conceal the failing structure beneath. Although they re-nominated Mayor Flower for a second term, the relationship was unexpectedly awkward, since the incumbent had openly considered accepting the machine's nomination earlier in the election cycle.[100] Struggling to gather momentum, the Jacksonians announced the reform ticket with the usual fanfare, but "it was received with little cheering and apparently no enthusiasm" by those gathered at the association's clubhouse. Comparing the candidates on both sides, even pro-business observers conceded "no superiority in ability and quality" and predicted "the Jacksonian ticket has little chance of success, unless the corporations put up big money."[101]

There were no bailouts coming. Despite the customary speeches and spectacles, the dueling campaigns were drab and uninspiring, with both sides positioning themselves as the true champions of civic progress. Reformers claimed that costly improvement projects would become money grabs for unscrupulous bosses, which the machine effectively countered by pointing out the rampant corporate favoritism shown by the Flower administration.[102] With the reformers floundering, the biggest challenge facing the Choctaw bosses was keeping the machine's base in line behind the nominee. Capdevielle dealt with repeated charges relating to his union-busting history and the wage scandal on the stump, where the friendly fire was more dangerous than anything coming from the other side.[103] Union leaders grudgingly endorsed him, and Capdevielle tried to burnish his nonexistent credentials as champion of the downtrodden, creatively reframing his prestigious leadership position on the park commission as evidence. "The wealthy man may go to his villa and gasp through the summer," he explained, without mentioning his own luxury vacation home, "but the poor man must remain in the city while he earns a livelihood, relying on public parks to provide fresh air and recreation."[104]

The campaign succeeded despite Capdevielle's fumbling attempts rather than because of them, backed by a superior grassroots organization and insurmountable numbers game as the candidate bumbled toward the finish. Stung by the favoritism charges, failing to make inroads among white laborers, and unable to make up the difference by courting black voters, reformers were unable to stop the defections. Although one ex-reformer creatively suggested that backing the Choctaw bosses would convince them to "join the better class" by naming less corruptible candidates, the spin fooled nobody.[105] One machine boss explained the hypocrisy more candidly. "They didn't have a chance," he remembered, "and I have no doubt the leaders knew."[106]

As the city's whitest electorate since before Reconstruction went to the polls on Tuesday, November 7, 1899, most observers predicted a calm day and a landslide, although reformers had one cause for celebration.[107] According to the new election guidelines, registered voters had three minutes to select candidates in secrecy, marking the image of either a Jacksonian horseman or a Choctaw rooster to indicate straight-ticket voting.[108] There were a lot more cocks than riders. The machine's grassroots advantage was obvious from the beginning. Working from prepared rosters, poll watchers tabulated supporters as they appeared and passed the names along to ward bosses, who forwarded them to the Choctaw clubhouse. In the evening, designated precinct captains rounded up the absentees, ensuring that every loyal workingman had done his part to secure a victory that everyone knew was coming. The headlines were less effusive this time around, although the *Daily Picayune* ran an impressive front-page illustration featuring Capdevielle standing proudly in his Confederate uniform. Editors wrote the obituary for his old friends. "The opposition proved so weak that it was overwhelmingly defeated," they concluded matter-of-factly, "and it no longer has any reason for existing."[109]

If reform in New Orleans was dead, the cause was suicide. Despite the demoralizing circumstances, the winning margin was only six thousand votes—precisely the difference covered by the black vote during the previous campaign, when eight thousand men supported the Citizens' League and two thousand backed the machine. That outcome had been celebrated as vindication by the black press, but this time around, *Southwestern Christian Advocate* editors were mostly silent as reform self-destructed.[110] With comparatively few readers still eligible to participate, weeks passed before they commented on the election, and then only in passing. Favorably reviewing a recent article by Booker T. Washington, who urged black Americans to forge relationships with powerful white allies—what they had just attempted, with disastrous results—editors blamed demagogues who privileged whiteness over fitness. "Ignorant white men voted by the hundreds," they criticized, "whereas many Negroes who could read and write were prevented."[111]

Reformers had even more trouble comprehending the outcome, none more than the machine's staunchest enemy. The blue-blood *Times-Democrat* editor had backed the dying movement to the bitter end, breaking with the business manager of his own publication, who would serve as a city councilman under the incoming machine administration. Reflecting on the rebirth of a nemesis, Page Baker struggled to understand how such a white electorate could produce such a gloomy outcome. As he contemplated the abyss, there were no answers. "The cleanest administration in the recent history of New Orleans has been repudiated," he moped. "At a time when the city cannot afford the slightest risk, a great leap into the dark is about to be taken."[112]

* * * *

EXACTLY SIX MONTHS after the election, Superintendent Dexter Gaster stood outside City Hall with about twenty patrolmen, each wearing dress uniforms and white gloves to welcome the new mayor on his inauguration day. After barely surviving more gambling scandals in the spring, the perpetually embattled commander had particular reason to welcome the leadership change. His cash-strapped department had gone four years without an appropriations increase under the outgoing administration, which continued to demand the impossible from officers who already boasted some of the nation's highest arrest rates.[113] Gaster's final report to the lame-duck reform council had struck an exasperated note, emphasizing the unworkable challenge of covering so much ground with a force "entirely too small to adequately do the work." Now months after they received word that the department's budget was unchanged for another year, his men were there to control the crowds on hand—and hope that making a good impression on the new boss would bring change.[114]

Around noon, the mayor-elect made his way through rowdy well-wishers and into the council room, where the retiring president waited to address the convocation.[115] Touching on the unique challenge of governing

New Orleans, with its large black population "contributing little or nothing to the material welfare of this city in taxation," he generously acknowledged that the newcomers were "not expected to perform miracles."[116] And with those uninspiring words, the reformers adjourned and a clerk read a letter certifying the results in each of the city's seventeen wards—a clean sweep for the Choctaws. After being sworn, the councilmen began delegating roles, but the outcome was clearly predetermined. For each position, there was a single nominee confirmed by a unanimous vote.[117]

With the machine already humming along, the mayor of New Orleans delivered his inaugural address. Paul Capdevielle transcended his role as its nominal head, recapping success by previous administrations, praising the "great system of drainage" that was coming soon, and warning the councilmen against "granting privileges and franchises to grasping individuals and corporations."[118] Pledging to raise millions and construct the critical improvements, he spoke with executive authority, praising his reform predecessors, glossing race and class divisions, and pointing toward a prosperous future to be enjoyed by every citizen. His stirring performance and unifying words received universal acclaim, some from unexpected sources. Praising the speech, the man whose fiery editorials had dismantled the old machine reframed his opposition to its newest candidate. Saying that his newspaper "opposed the election of Mr. Capdevielle, but we never doubted his patriotism and integrity," Baker promised "earnest support in all his efforts to promote the general welfare."[119]

For all the optimism, there were also signs of dangerous, unresolved tensions on the streets. On the same day an olive branch appeared on the *Times-Democrat* editorial page, black laborers employed by the Edison Electric Company were completing a city contract to lay down conduits, working on the downtown project when white men began gathering in the area. They clustered around a nearby telegraph pole, where someone had posted a crude sign with a hand-painted message: "No White Labor Need Apply." Although nobody knew where it came from, the effect was chilling. "There was talk of getting shotguns, killing niggers, all that sort of thing," witnesses described. "Someone tore the sign from the telegraph pole and laid it on the paving stones, where it was even more conspicuous than before."[120]

Company executives denied putting up the sign, before a witness came forward and claimed he saw disgruntled former employees posting it early that morning. That afternoon, white workingmen descended on the mayor's office. They complained that companies were using cheaper black labor to underbid the competition on municipal contracts and denounced "this attempt to debauch and degrade white labor for a few cents."[121] Capdevielle warned them to avoid violence and threatened to deploy police if there were any more disturbances, but he also promised to investigate the situation. In a meeting with Edison leadership, the mayor reassured them that he had no intention to interfere with business, but he asked them to employ only white men until things calmed down. They agreed to pay the premium. When the labor men returned to his office, Capdevielle reported the good news, "clearing away the black cloud of trouble which had been brewing." The short-lived controversy symbolized the promising upside to warming relations between the mayor's office and the business community—and the worrying situation on the streets after nearly a decade of hard times and predatory hiring practices. With a respected corporate executive heading a forward-looking administration, a gentlemanly conversation was enough to resolve any tensions between labor and capital in New Orleans. For now.[122]

3

Eclipse

Before dawn on Monday morning, May 28, 1900, a crowd of thousands surrounded the new observatory at Tulane University, jockeying to catch a glimpse of the action. Inside the building, astronomy professors used the powerful telescope in its revolving dome to scan the eastern horizon, where shades of pink and gold brightened the edges of the low-slung clouds. As the scientists consulted in hushed tones, those outside waited anxiously for the prediction. Then cheers erupted, the low rumble of thunder as word began to spread and the audience responded. The clouds would burn away—they would have a perfect vantage when the sun disappeared.[1]

Celebrating good fortune after weeks of anticipation, the enthusiastic crowd spoke to the widespread fascination with the coming eclipse, bordering on obsession, particularly among those who considered themselves among the city's more educated classes. Reporters had been covering the advance preparations carefully, describing the modern instruments and techniques that would be used to document the phenomenon. Astronomers delivered lectures to packed auditoriums, using charts, diagrams, and maps to explain the mechanics behind the spectacle.[2] The public education was celebrated as the triumph of modernity, neutralizing the "unexplainable, uncontrollable forebodings of evil" aroused by the phenomena and replacing them with reasoned curiosity.[3] But despite the preparations, when the shadows faded around seven o'clock that morning, those gathered outside the observatory were caught by surprise.

Struggling to describe the change, a subtle dimness, slowly darkening, someone exclaimed, "The air doesn't look natural!"[4]

Others chuckled nervously. They were too self-conscious to express themselves openly, but everyone was feeling the same profound unease. "A change, sinister and disquieting, was creeping over things," observers explained. Umber smoke materialized, thickening as it billowed across the surface of the sun. Then suddenly the moon edged across the burning circle, steadily encroaching until only a shining arc remained. The planet Mercury—named for the Roman god of commerce who guided lost souls to the Underworld—appeared as a blazing point beside the dying sun.[5] A shrill whistle blast pierced through the murmurs, startling everyone in the crowd. "In the twinkling of an eye, the crescent disappeared, and a leaden-blue disk hung in the heavens, encircled by a brilliant fringe of silver with four luminous horns," awestruck reporters described. "It seemed to suggest nature's death."[6]

Ninety seconds passed, feeling like eternity. Then sunlight washed over the upturned faces, signaling the end's beginning. As the moon retreated, its silhouette teased onlookers with one more illusion, rich in symbolism: crescent-shaped projections flickering in the foliage and dancing along the ground, "the most graceful phenomenon ever witnessed in New Orleans."[7]

By some accounts, the accompanying human drama threatened to surpass the natural spectacle. As the sun darkened, correspondents scanned the spectators and scientists and reported their findings to readers eager to judge their fellow citizens. Astronomers earned glowing reviews, wielding barometers, spectroscopes, heliostats, and cameras with precision, but among the amateurs, performances were decidedly more uneven.[8] Some contemplated the sublime grandeur of the heavens with admirable stoicism. Others screamed uncontrollably. Streetcars converging on the downtown business district became stages for businessmen to demonstrate sober-minded appreciation for modern science, but even those high-stakes acts were spotty. Under an unearthly glow, breadwinners rushed the doors and windows and stared up with dumbfounded expressions, then grew sheepish and scrambled to regain composure when the eclipse ended. Describing how "many a temporary friendship" formed as men reassured one another and justified themselves, reporters wryly observed, "Nearly every person had something to say to relieve his feelings."[9]

Fortunately, journalists soon found more appropriate targets to lampoon, trolling the red-light district and describing the supposedly cartoonish reactions by black denizens, whose minstrelsy made the shaky responses by young businessmen pale in comparison. One woman allegedly tossed a shoe over her shoulder for six hours, hoping the "hoodoo chaser" would protect her from supernatural harm, but ultimately collapsing in exhaustion before the eclipse began. A few blocks away, a longshoreman smashed the front window of his own home and tried to smoke the shards over an oil lamp to fashion do-it-yourself sunglasses; they cracked under the heat's intensity, but the glass-faced clock that he threw at his wife's head when she dared to laugh worked perfectly. Meanwhile, drinkers poured from nearby saloons to stand in the streets, pledging abstinence and pleading to be saved as the sun disappeared. Even more sobering was the conversation between a patrolman and an "old darky," who was baffled by the darkness so soon after sunrise and remarked, "That's the shortest day that I've ever seen."

The officer stooped down and whispered, "Yeah, but this'll be the longest night you ever saw."

"Don't say that, don't say that!" came the frantic reply. "Here's a dollar, boss. Just fix it for me and no one else. Just fix it for me."

The cop took care of the situation for the bargain price, or so the punchline claimed. But although the fictionalized conversation was supposed to be humorous, reporters missed the poignancy of the exchange, particularly given the deteriorating social conditions faced by the butt of the joke. Symbolically, his nightmare—a darkness with no end—seemed to be falling on his community after emancipation's false dawn. Fully recognizing the significance of the eclipse in prophetic traditions, black congregations gathered to pray for God's deliverance as contemporary Israelites wandering in the wilderness. Of course, white observers misread the powerful scenes. "Around several of the negro churches were gathered large crowds of men, women, and children, who knew nothing of the real meaning, but that something terrible was about to take place,"

they described. "Loud and fervent prayers filled the morning air as the
light turned into darkness."[10]

As black congregations dispersed, contemplating the religious symbolism of the sun's death and resurrection, events happening eighty miles
upriver would send new shockwaves through a community already reeling from Jim Crow's advance.[11] Just outside the shadow path, the state
capitol in Baton Rouge had missed the most dramatic portions of the
eclipse, though the representatives convened there had no time for arm-
chair astronomy. Inside the antebellum neo-Gothic castle that drew unfavorable architectural comparisons to the next-door asylum—when fire
damaged "this little sham castle" in the 1880s, Mark Twain suggested dynamite rather than restoration—the first legislature seated under the
new state constitution had been in session for almost two weeks.[12] In elections held earlier that spring, Louisiana Democrats had leveraged black
disenfranchisement to reverse their previous losses, purging the opposition and claiming an overwhelming, although dubious, mandate.[13] The
new governor portrayed the landslide as the long-awaited triumph of
clean governance in his inaugural address, explaining that "committing
the commonwealth to its white citizens" would prevent corruption and
thereby "preserve the rights and liberties of both races."[14] He disingenu-
ously contended that voting restrictions had "done away with complaints
about fairness in our elections," comparing the relative peace of the un-
competitive campaign with the violence and fraudulence necessary to win
previous contests and concluding, "Elections under the new system have
been so just and fair that it has given unusual satisfaction."[15]

Among the unusually satisfied members of the statehouse was Harry D.
Wilson, a thirty-one-year-old freshman representative from just across
Lake Pontchartrain in "Bloody Tangipahoa Parish," which had earned
the nickname because of the nearly two dozen men who had been lynched
there since Reconstruction.[16] The grocer's son hailed from an unincor-
porated railroad crossing known as "Uncle Sam," overcoming his political inexperience thanks to his family name and party affiliation.[17] He had
already made a splash in Baton Rouge by introducing legislation to ban
cigarette sales to minors, but the ambitious politico had bigger plans.[18]
Just a few hours after the eclipse, Wilson stood before his colleagues and

introduced House Bill No. 82, "an act to promote the comfort of passengers by requiring all street railways to provide equal but separate accommodations for the white and colored races."[19]

Wilson's sponsorship would become a matter of controversy in the days to come, particularly because he came from a backwoods parish with no regular stagecoach service, much less a modern urban transportation system. Adding to the unflattering optics, proposed revisions would eventually restrict the measure to Louisiana cities with more than fifty thousand residents—that is, New Orleans.[20] From an uncharitable perspective, the proposal was the brainchild of a country bumpkin nursing an unhealthy grudge against the state's biggest city, though Wilson tried to defend his interest in segregation there. Speaking with reporters, he explained that his job with the Illinois Central Railroad frequently brought him to its southern terminus, where he witnessed the troubling deterioration of the racial hierarchies that defined social life in his neck of the woods. More significantly, Wilson explained that the legislation was really more about proving a point than solving an actual problem. "Separating the races is one advantage, but demonstrating the superiority of the white man is the greater thing," he told his interviewers, seeming amazed by their naiveté. "Don't you know? Don't you know that nothing shows it more conclusively than compelling negroes to ride in cars marked for their special use?"[21]

Inside the office of the *Southwestern Christian Advocate*, the editor who ran the Deep South's only surviving black-operated weekly understood exactly what the proposed measure represented.[22] As the youngest of fourteen children born to former slaves, forty-six-year-old Isaiah Scott had overcome incredible obstacles, testing the possibilities for an entrepreneurial black man in postwar Louisiana. After being ordained in Methodist Episcopal Church and earning his doctorate from New Orleans University, Scott was chosen as the first non-white president of a black seminary in East Texas, helping the struggling institution to survive the economic challenges of the early 1890s. Scott was rewarded for his stewardship, returning to New Orleans to serve as editor of the country's most popular black religious publication.[23] The weekly journal made considerable progress over his four-year term, adding subscribers and doubling in length while financial trouble forced its Catholic competitor to shut down. Strategically striving for balance in coverage and tone, Scott focused primarily on church matters and community announcements, advancing a modest progressive agenda on race. He advocated self-improvement and preached cooperation as opposed to agitation, earning favor among white church leaders, who saw the newspaper as a testament to Christianity's civilizing influence on a developing race. Criticizing the exuberance associated with black churches and citing Scott's journal as an "educational factor whose worth cannot be estimated," one explained, "What the Negro predominantly needs is not more 'glory in his soul,' but more workaday thrift and clear-eyed honesty, more salvation from squalor and fly-marked kitchen walls."[24]

Less than two weeks before Wilson introduced his segregation bill, church delegates had reelected Scott to another four-year editorial term by a nearly unanimous vote, but while the timing should have given him a strong platform to aggressively oppose the new Jim Crow legislation, his situation was more precarious than it appeared.[25] Although black journalists had spearheaded anti-segregation campaigns in New Orleans in the early 1890s, they paid a heavy price. Scott's predecessor had been defeated in a contentious reelection campaign after openly challenging white elders on the church's lukewarm racial advocacy. Learning from his example, Scott had been more conciliatory, gently pushing to elect a black bishop earlier that spring, but responding tactfully when his campaign ended in failure. Sidestepping the explosive implications of a vote that broke along the color line, he pointed to the limited positions and quality of the nominees as deciding factors, admitting "there are white brethren who did not see the necessity," before concluding, "We are fully convinced that our failure is more the result of his ambitions than his prejudices."[26]

As the frustrating outcome suggested, perhaps the most significant problem with his judicious approach was that so many white leaders were unresponsive to demands for racial justice in the 1890s, even those who served in a comparatively progressive denomination. Meanwhile, grassroots campaigns within the black community were also struggling to produce results. After his unceremonious ousting, Scott's predecessor had joined the Comité des Citoyens, founded by Creole elites to challenge a law that segregated passengers on Louisiana's interstate railroads. Although the alliance helped to bridge long-standing divides between the city's American and French-heritage black communities, the legal campaign reached the U.S. Supreme Court and culminated in the devastating *Plessy v. Ferguson* ruling, which effectively determined that segregation was constitutional.[27]

By the turn of the century, mild appeals to responsible white leadership and middle-class community-building were largely eclipsing more confrontational strategies, especially among the comparatively advantaged professionals who disproportionately made up the *Advocate* readership. Returning to New Orleans following reelection, Scott avoided public comment on the brewing streetcar controversy, but he made his office an unofficial organizing base for the opposition, which centered on a letter-writing campaign targeting the city's white mainstream newspapers.[28] Wisely sidestepping the race question, petitioners focused on the practical case against segregation. Writing from an expert perspective as a porter for the New Orleans City Railroad Company, thirty-one-year-old Jackson Kinchen comprehensively refuted the common pro-segregation argument that black riders were a unique problem, saying that white passengers were just as guilty of rudeness, sickness, and drunkenness aboard streetcars—and that conductors were perfectly happy to eject troublemakers in either case. "The separate car bill is not needed," he concluded. "It is unjust and would be a death blow to rapid transit in New Orleans."[29]

Others advanced equally compelling arguments by carefully tailoring the message to the sensibilities of white readers. Cleverly weaving together misty-eyed tropes and tough financial realities, Harold Griffin began by "appealing to the magnanimity of our former master and present employer for simple justice," explaining that he was reassured by the kindness and chivalry shown by white civic leaders. Those pleasantries aside, Griffin pressed his case in practical terms. "You have our gratitude, our love, our labor, and our money," he described, before explaining that "every dollar given to us goes back to you" through consumer purchases, and favorably comparing the black community's economic loyalty to

European immigrants who sent their wages home to family members overseas. Griffin separated civil rights from voting rights restrictions, which had been overwhelmingly supported by white residents. "After doing your pleasure in the matter of our political disenfranchisement, may we not respectfully appeal to your sense of justice," he concluded. "Kindly bear with us the twenty minutes we may be on the same car for expediency, economy, and other reasons better urged by the leading railroad and businessmen."[30]

Though carefully framed and delicately phrased, Griffin's reference to businessmen was a strategic nod to an uncomfortable reality for white residents. As readers streamed through the *Advocate* office and submitted letters, coverage in the city's mainstream dailies was revealing an unexpected outcome to Wilson's measure: while black residents were coming together in unified resistance, the segregation debate was dividing the white community along class lines rather than uniting them along racial ones. As he surveyed the situation, the *Advocate* editor could be satisfied that his plan was working brilliantly. "The streetcar companies of this city are said to be very much opposed to the measure, which will cause them a considerable loss," Scott observed. "There are hundreds of Negroes in this city who will not ride under any such circumstances, and they have already begun to organize. Who can blame them?"[31]

* * * *

ON THE EVENING of May 28, 1900, hours after the introduction of Harry Wilson's segregation measure, forty-five-year-old Andrew Van Kuren was guiding a horse-drawn wagon down Tchoupitoulas Street, carrying prisoners back to the lockup at downtown police headquarters. His unwilling passengers, two women and six men, were serving short-term sentences for petty offenses. They had been assigned to cleanup duties around the levee, a daily practice that reduced municipal expenses while supposedly teaching criminals the value of diligence. As he guided his team through a busy intersection, Van Kuren heard a piercing screech and turned—just in time to glimpse a streetcar barreling toward the wagon as the conductor slammed the brakes in a last-ditch attempt to avoid a collision. It was too late. With a heavy crunch, New Orleans City

Railroad Car No. 150 collided with the wagon, violently overturning the vehicle and pitching the unfortunate jailer and his passengers onto the ground.[32] Bystanders rushed to provide aid, but there was no need; a serious tragedy had been narrowly avoided. Van Kuren was taken to Charity Hospital as a precaution and his passengers were returned to prison, apparently unharmed. The wagon was lightly damaged. A few days after the crash, transportation executives received a brusque message from Van Kuren's boss, who explained that "reliable witnesses" had confirmed their conductor's fault in the crash. "I will have repairs made and bill your company for damage to the wagon," he advised.[33]

Retrospectively, the accident was an omen, foreshadowing a segregation controversy that would ensnare both politicians and transportation officials over the coming weeks. Less than a month into his four-year term of office, Mayor Paul Capdevielle had been basking in the afterglow of a widely acclaimed inaugural address and enjoying complimentary press coverage as he became acquainted with his duties: overseeing drainage projects started by the reformers, consulting with the city engineer's office on a Ferris wheel constructed by shady contractors, and briefing police commanders on complaints about beggars harassing Canal Street shoppers and gamblers disturbing Garden District residents with loud dice games. Yet the city's overburdened transportation system had been running with no more than the usual delays and there were no accidents before the jailer's brush with a runaway trolley. Segregated or otherwise, streetcars were not on the agenda—until the segregation bill arrived on his desk with a graceless thump.[34]

As word of the proposed legislation reached New Orleans, reactions among white residents were mixed, especially given its source. Over the coming weeks, supporters would argue that Wilson's perspective as a country representative provided him with unique clarity on urban race mixing. "No doubt Mr. Wilson visited our city, perhaps during Carnival, and witnessed gentle women and children standing up, while burly black men and women were seated," one local mused. "He'd taken too much ozone from the piney woods of Tangipahoa into his lungs to stand any insult to the white race, hence his bill to put the darky where he belongs—away from the Caucasian race."[35]

Meanwhile, opponents mocked the sponsor as a backwoods rube unable to cope with cosmopolitan urban realities. Questioning the sponsor's masculine authority and spiking his interpretation with the acid sarcasm favored by Southern humorists, one man scoffed, "That a country member of the legislature should have perhaps visited the city and felt a little uncomfortable seeing his wife or daughters seated comfortably by the side of some flashy negro cannot be regarded as unique," before adding that *real* New Orleanians "would never consent to defacing our beautiful cars with so much as a tin sign providing separation, especially with such congested conditions."[36]

Amid brewing controversy, representatives from the New Orleans & Carrollton Railroad Company traveled to Baton Rouge at the beginning of June, speaking for the city's transportation industry in meetings with the house committee on railroads. They complained that the proposal would create a financial mess and secured reassurances that they would be given the chance to testify before members reached a conclusion. But within two weeks, the politicians went rogue and endorsed the measure, provoking outrage from the executives. "The bill is a bad one," the company's vice-president complained to reporters. "It's been tried in this city before and found wanting."[37]

Representing one of the oldest streetcar companies in the nation, executives from the New Orleans & Carrollton Railroad had reason to expect that lawmakers would give them leeway on matters concerning an industry the company had pioneered. During the early 1830s, influential merchants had petitioned state officials to charter a streetcar line extending from the downtown business district to upriver plantations outside city limits, where a planned resort would serve wealthy pleasure-seekers—and boost the value of American-owned property at the expense of French rivals.[38] The charter established four-mile-per-hour speed limits and ordered the tracks to be removed at company expense if residents complained, but the concerns were unwarranted.[39] The mule-drawn streetcars were popular and profitable, dramatically reshaping transportation in New Orleans over the ensuing decades and rendering the early controversy retrospectively laughable.[40] "The charter is rather amusing in light of modern progress," one local historian observed at the turn of the century, noting that streetcar lines were now accessible virtually everywhere in the city.[41]

The 1890s were a decade of modernization and mergers for the trailblazing company, symbolizing trends sweeping across the industry. The city's oldest streetcar enterprise had led the conversion from a motley assortment of mule-drawn and steam-powered cars to a modern electric system, operating two hundred state-of-the-art streetcars along seventy miles of track while earning high praise from national observers.[42] Electrification and expansion reflected the importance of public transportation in New Orleans, a multi-million-dollar enterprise comprising more than two dozen lines and two hundred miles of railroad that carried passengers to and from the city's most iconic destinations.[43] Sightseers could ride the recently opened St. Charles Line from Canal Street to Audubon Park, a lush urban green space in a pricey Uptown neighborhood, while brave pedestrians could try to cross downtown when converging tracks snarled with rush-hour traffic and transformed the business district into a snake pit of squirming metal.[44]

Since the beginning, streetcars had changed the relationship between residents and urban space, but they also transformed social relationships. Originally founded to convey wealthy residents to exclusive upriver resorts, the expanding streetcar system helped to sharpen class divides over ensuing decades, allowing the rich to build homes farther away from the business and warehouse districts and distance themselves from the less desirable neighborhoods clustered around the city's industrial and manufacturing centers. Yet even as prosperous residents withdrew to fashionable suburbs, by necessity, streetcars were among the city's most egalitarian public spaces. The same vehicles that conveyed merchants from privileged enclaves also brought domestic servants and day laborers to employers scattered across New Orleans, expanding the geography of economic opportunity. And ride prices had plummeted since the earliest days, now starting at five cents rather than the original twenty-five, although the original system's opulence remained. As transportation companies competed for business, passengers enjoyed cars decked out with mahogany interiors, nickel appointments, and plush velvet seats. By the turn of the century, public transportation was both an economic necessity and a source of civic pride. "New Orleans has one of the best streetcar systems in the world," bragged corporate boosters. "The cars are handsome and comfortable, run easily, and preserve a steady schedule."[45]

Less comfortable was the question of segregation, which had been a problem since the beginning. Slaves were naturally forbidden from riding, but devising policies to govern free black passengers, some of whom boasted considerable wealth, proved more challenging. Facing protests, some antebellum companies ran designated "star cars," segregated vehicles painted with large black stars, but most refused them entirely.[46] The return of black riders and star cars during Reconstruction had renewed the controversy. Courtroom challenges to segregation unfolded amid unrest and resistance, as former slaves and free blacks mobilized in civil rights campaigns that pushed desegregation as a symbol of emancipation and equality. As the editors who founded the first black-operated daily newspaper in American history declared, "All these discriminations that had slavery at the bottom have become nonsense."[47]

The controversy became a crisis two years after the war ended, when a former slave forced his way onto a segregated vehicle and police arrested him for disturbing the peace, triggering mass protests.[48] As black demonstrators took to the streets, some threatened operators with clubs—one raised the stakes by tossing a conductor from his cab and leading officers on a wild chase through downtown.[49] "Threats have been made by colored persons that they intend to force themselves on cars reserved for white persons," a supervisor warned executives from the New Orleans & Carrollton Railroad Company, who favored continuing the star car system.[50] White residents responded by attacking black passengers, prompting federal commanders to finally intervene. Fearing open rebellion, they overrode transportation executives and ordered streetcar desegregation, ending the drama.[51]

As the process unfolded in relative peace over the following weeks, white journalists struggled to comprehend the meaning of the successful civil rights campaign. Some accepted complaints that the system had only enforced one-way segregation, since white passengers comfortably rode the star cars during rush-hour congestion—but most feared the campaign was cover for some radical conspiracy.[52] Meanwhile, the black press was less concerned. Observing that "white fellow citizens entered star cars as readily as any others" and managed to peacefully coexist when expediency demanded, they contended that the outrage was mostly just for show. "Few would complain today, were it not for the sake of showing their neighbors that they are 'good whites,'" they concluded. "In a few weeks, everyone will have forgotten a star car system ever existed."[53]

Time proved those predictions. By the turn of the century, transportation companies had enjoyed over three decades of peace and prosperity while running desegregated streetcars—until Wilson's unnecessary meddling. This time, executives strongly opposed re-segregating the system, especially because rider demographics and financial pressure in the cutthroat industry made it an expensive proposition. Careful not to challenge white supremacy in principle, they explained that competition "forced each company to its limits," which made it impractical to designate so many cars for black riders. It was comparatively easy for railroads to satisfy the "separate but equal" standard established by *Plessy v. Ferguson* by designating cars on a few long-distance trains, but doing the same on a streetcar fleet running every day from dawn to midnight would raise operating costs to unsustainable levels and worsen service for the riding majority. Unfortunately and ironically, legislation intended to prove "the superiority of the white man over the negro" would mean comfort for the latter while the former "would be crowded and inconvenienced in many directions."[54]

If cost and convenience were compelling concerns, transportation executives had even more significant reasons to oppose segregation. Rising costs triggered by the conversion to electricity beginning in the early 1890s had been driving smaller companies from the industry, sparking a wave of consolidation. Since January, the four survivors had been negotiating a merger to create a single corporation, although the deal was foundering due to the expenses associated with converting two hundred miles of track to a uniform gauge size.[55] Although establishing a transportation monopoly promised to ultimately raise profits, company executives recognized that segregation—and the added costs it would impose—was catching them at a particularly inopportune time. Further complicating an already tense situation, rumors were circulating that

New Orleans conductors and motormen were organizing another unionization push—and given past and present labor relations in the industry, both nationally and locally, that was an alarming possibility.[56] Streetcar companies were already notorious for abysmal working conditions and aggressive union-busting that drew serious attention from national union leaders. "Conditions among them were deplorable: long hours, little pay, irregular work, and practically no home life," AFL president Samuel Gompers remembered. "No organization received more thought and personal attention than the streetcar men."[57]

For businessmen in New Orleans, trouble in the transportation industry was particularly unwelcome because it brought back traumatic memories of the most significant labor crisis the city had ever seen. During the spring of 1892, successful strikes by conductors and motormen had contributed to an unprecedented organizing wave. Months before the general strike began, representatives from locals across the country had convened under the chairmanship of a New Orleans–based AFL organizer to form a national union.[58] Hosting the convention, Indianapolis workers were honored as Division No. 1—those from New Orleans were Division No. 2.[59] While the organization struggled to grow its national membership during hard times, Division No. 2 was a modest success, boasting almost two thousand members, but struggling to secure gains commensurate with its size.[60] When arbitration failed to produce an agreeable contract during the mid-1890s, union leaders appeared before state lawmakers to push for ten-hour workdays, but executives successfully defeated the legislation by convincing the division's former secretary to switch teams and oppose his comrades.[61] Betrayed and defeated, Division No. 2 collapsed because of bickering and infighting, a depressing sign of the times for workers in New Orleans, epitomizing the crippling reversals suffered by the labor movement once led by conductors.[62] Transportation insiders viewed its demise positively, claiming without evidence that organizing setbacks would actually "elevate the laboring classes" by transforming profits sacrificed during needless strikes into higher wages and "helping them see that the interests of employees and employers are mutual."[63]

Under the circumstances, rumors that conductors were making another union push were alarming enough for New Orleans businessmen, but during the summer of 1900, there was special reason to worry that streetcar workers could spark a dangerous chain reaction. Although union organizers in the transportation industry were slowly regaining the initiative, adding thousands of members and staging disruptive strikes across multiple states, few observers anticipated the violence that would erupt in the geographical heart of the industry.[64] St. Louis built more locomotives than any other American city, but running its transportation system was nearly as profitable.[65] During the late 1890s, its streetcar companies had merged to form the same kind of lucrative corporation that New Orleans counterparts were trying to establish, then used the monopoly to cut wages for conductors who earned about two dollars for each grueling twelve-hour shift.[66] As Louisiana lawmakers debated segregation during the spring of 1900, union organizers in Missouri formed a new division and demanded a better deal.[67] Officials from the St. Louis Transit Company adopted the same tactics employed by New Orleans executives before the general strike, pretending to negotiate in good faith, before refusing to rehire workers fired for organizing and punishing employees with sixteen-hour shifts that paid starvation wages. When frustrated conductors and motormen finally walked out in early May, company managers fired more than three thousand union members and hired strikebreakers to replace them. Strikers retaliated by sabotaging streetcars and forcibly shutting down the transportation system, which prompted executives to hire private guards and go on the offensive.[68] Masked assailants fired into union halls from rapidly moving streetcars, killing several protesters and wounding dozens more over three weeks of escalating violence.[69]

Two days after Wilson introduced his segregation measure, business leaders in St. Louis convened with authorities, who agreed to mobilize "1,000 able-bodied, law-abiding citizens" to suppress the supposed riots.[70] But things only worsened from there. Within two weeks, the deputized civilians opened fire under questionable circumstances, killing three strikers and an elderly man, struck by a stray round while standing in his yard.[71] Facing one-sided violence, union members popularized the "Song of the St. Louis Posse Comitatus," bitterly declaring the state-sanctioned militia to be a corporate death squad:

> *Then, when all this strike is o'er, those whose hands*
> *are red with gore*
> *Will exclaim while on our backs they fondly pat us,*
> *"Though you've shed your brother's blood, you for*
> *capital have stood,"*
> *As a member of the posse comitatus.*[72]

When the strike broke and conductors and motormen were forced back to work with nothing to show for the bloodshed, St. Louis residents considered the losses on both sides.[73] "The city has lost fourteen citizens killed, nearly two hundred wounded, a tremendous amount of business, and its good reputation," a local preacher observed. "The company's loss is estimated at $1,500,000. What has been gained?"[74]

As blood flowed six hundred miles upriver in St. Louis, the economic losses were particularly troubling to the Louisiana businessmen and policymakers who were debating the benefits and potential costs of segregation. While the price tag for purchasing new cars and painting them with black stars was burdensome, the sky-high costs of widespread violence were potentially disastrous. Even more disturbing, there were reasons to believe that New Orleans was primed for an eruption.[75] Unable to bargain collectively, its motormen and conductors were faring even worse than their counterparts in St. Louis, enduring fourteen-hour shifts for less than two dollars a day—lower wages than unskilled laborers earned.[76] Compounding the situation, performance evaluations were based on the most punitive system in the industry. Infractions ranged from wearing a rumpled uniform to falling more than ninety seconds behind schedule, determined by undercover agents and validated by managers without a hearing. Demerits based on this "reliable information obtained by officers of the company" were added to an employee's record, balanced monthly, and used to determine their eligibility for promotion to more desirable schedules.[77] While corporate observers praised the system as

"satisfactory to all concerned," unsurprisingly, national labor representatives disagreed. "Men are not promoted in accordance with their age
in the service of the company, but with the amount of 'merits' and 'demerits' they receive," organizers complained, adding that the system in-
centivized snitching and collaboration. In other words: "The biggest
sucker gets the best run."[78]

If the combustible situation in New Orleans recapitulated the corporate consolidation and abysmal conditions that were igniting streetcar employees in St. Louis, segregation was a flaming torch, threatening to
destroy the fragile peace. Part of the problem stemmed from the enforcement provisions of Wilson's measure, which required any conductor
who violated the law to pay a fifty-dollar fine or face thirty days in prison.[79]
But while allowing black riders in white cars could signify purposeful disregard for the law in Tangipahoa Parish, the situation was far more complicated on the other side of Lake Pontchartrain. One transportation
executive candidly described the problem. "Many bright mulattoes are
whiter than Spaniards and Italians," he complained. "There's nothing to
indicate they're negroes. Our conductors are intelligent men, but the
greatest ethnologist the world ever saw would be at a loss to classify passengers in this city."[80]

The practical dilemma of classifying passengers on the unreliable
basis of appearance would be compounded by humiliation and violent
reactions to misidentification, especially when few insults were as con-
temptuous as questioning a white person's racial heritage. Conductors
would be responsible for real-time determinations that could end in
fines, prison sentences, fistfights, or much worse, considering how fashionable it was for men in New Orleans to carry concealed weapons.
Imagining scenes as ironic as they were disturbing, editors considered
the racial and social disorder caused by segregation and warned, "Conductors will make serious blunders by assigning dark-complexioned
white people to the negro cars."[81] Adding insult to injury, others would
be forced to serve black passengers, which would emasculate white men
who already struggled to provide for their families and make the de-
merit system even more oppressive. Now underperforming conductors
would no longer simply be demoted to night shifts and undesirable runs.

According to the testimony of snitches and the machinations of vindictive managers, they would become white slaves to black masters in a world turned upside down. "Consider the motorman, compelled to halt by the dusky passenger waiting for him," one resident shuddered. "What about the conductor cut off from the society of his fellow white man for hours?"[82]

Recognizing the likelihood that racial provocation would push labor relations beyond the breaking point, transportation executives formed a united front against segregation. Speaking with reporters, the president of the New Orleans & Carrollton Railroad Company made the industry's case—delicately. "There are special cases which aggravate the riding public and make the people feel as though some legislation is necessary," he began, "but these instances are few and don't indicate the general demeanor of the negroes by any means." Acknowledging the racial concerns that motivated the proposed legislation, the businessman nonetheless warned against disrupting the status quo, saying that it would be "a great mistake to tamper with existing conditions," before closing with a figure of speech that had special resonance in a place where doctors bled patients and dosed poisons as misguided cures during yellow fever epidemics: "The public will find the remedy worse than the disease."[83]

Despite the controversy, transportation companies enjoyed strong backing from the business community in New Orleans, which understood how easily troubles in one industry could spiral into a citywide emergency. Beyond unhappy memories of the streetcar troubles leading up to the general strike, they could look to St. Louis, where violence and organized boycotts by national union leaders were taking an expensive toll—store closures, employee furloughs, and widespread property damage, among other hardships.[84] Where business led, the mainstream press followed. "The arguments in favor of the bill are social and sentimental, presented by the ladies," editors dubiously explained. "The arguments against are based on expediency and business." The right choice was unfortunate, but obvious. An unsophisticated politician from a country parish might sacrifice corporate profits in an unnecessary crusade, but New Orleans businessmen frowned on such hysterics. "We would gladly join the many ladies who have addressed us, but they must be put aside in the interest of men and business," they concluded. "There can be no separate cars for the races."[85]

As state senators prepared to debate the unexpectedly controversial measure in early July, the Capdevielle administration added its voice to the conversation, caving to pressure from editors and businessmen and calling on lawmakers to reject the measure.[86] At the state capitol in Baton Rouge, the spirited defense of local sovereignty—cities' rights—was making more and more sense to politicians, who fully recognized the challenge of reconciling rural sensibilities with the more cosmopolitan outlook from Louisiana's commercial metropolis, even before confronting the no-win proposition of streetcar segregation. Branding as a race traitor was a political death sentence, but as the disenfranchising convention demonstrated, New Orleans powerbrokers were powerful enough to influence state politics, including by punishing enemies. The final recommendation issued by the senate committee studying the measure—a five-to-four split in opposition—only underscored those challenges. Given the circumstances, the choice to do nothing and cede responsibility back to New Orleans was appealing. Editors there advised, "Leave well enough alone."[87]

With the end of the legislative session approaching, Louisiana senators accepted the suggestion and postponed a scheduled vote, supposedly to provide New Orleans authorities the chance to consider a local ordinance. The indefinite suspension was an elegant solution for state lawmakers, providing reasonable political cover while buying enough time for the session to expire. Logic notwithstanding, nobody wanted to go on the record as *opposing* segregation. Wilson's measure was spared the indignity of definitive rejection; lawmakers were spared uncomfortable conversations with constituents about why they chose corporate profits over white supremacy. Given the unexpected distastefulness of the situation, it was the closest thing possible to a win-win solution. Yet there was no doubt about what really happened. Political observers in New Orleans approvingly reported, "The streetcar bill was killed in the senate today."[88]

Few in the city mourned its passing, although some celebrated more than others. Preparing his forthcoming edition of the *Southwestern*

Christian Advocate, Isaiah Scott was particularly satisfied that his understated campaigning had paid such handsome dividends, achieving
locally what his predecessor had been unable to accomplish statewide in
the *Plessy* case. As he made sense of the lengthy controversy and drew
conclusions from the tortured public debate, Scott particularly savored
the dysfunctional relationship between segregation, sex across the color
line, and racial pseudoscience. Finding dark humor in dark times, he
chuckled over the attempts by his mainstream counterparts to differen-
tiate the "dark white people" from the "white colored people," which
produced more than enough bickering, but no consensus. "Whether
they are identical we are not prepared to say," he jokingly reckoned, "but
they cause the same embarrassment to those who would make the separation." Of course, there was a serious point to the wry observation: the
color line was purely imaginary, nowhere more than in New Orleans,
where private desires undermined the most strenuous attempts to enforce racial boundaries in public space. Historically, white men had
never discriminated so scrupulously when chasing sexual conquests,
sometimes consensually, but often through coercion and rape. Impossible to segregate, streetcars reflected the hypocrisy and moral failure of
the master class in microcosm. "Our city should be extremely liberal on
the color question," Scott dryly observed, "but to the contrary, we dare
say there is no city in the South more sensitive."

Couching his razor-sharp analysis in semi-good-natured jesting, the
editor of the South's leading black newspaper prodded the raw nerve exposed by the streetcar debate. Assuming a straightforward definition of
a maddeningly ambiguous category, one threatening the very foundation
of white supremacy—and doing it in the most racially bewildering city
anywhere in the country—Wilson's proposal underscored the dangerously inverse relationship between racial order and urban space. It was
an old problem, dating back to antebellum slavery and continuing under
sharecropping and pseudo-freedom. Planters had always needed New Orleans to transform produce into wealth, yet the conditions that allowed
them to dominate workers on a Tangipahoa Parish sugar plantation, for
example, were impossible to replicate in urban space, where residents
could hardly tell who belonged where, much less control them. Which

led to the second lesson, contained in a letter received from "one white gentleman," which refuted the case for segregation with a scenario no less disordered than a conductor forced to serve his supposed racial inferiors: investors stooping to employees whose salaries they paid. "There are colored persons of wealth in the city, some of whom have white people working for them," the anonymous writer observed. "I am certain they own stock in the street railroads. Where is the conductor who would attempt to bar *them* from riding in the white cars?"[89]

Both the question and the segregation controversy suggested an opportunity to build a renewed alliance based on shared economic interests, which might establish New Orleans as a racially liberal enclave, comparatively speaking, as attitudes toxified in Louisiana and across the nation. If businessmen had been treacherous political allies, they were saviors during the levee crisis. And now they seemed to be on the same side again, maybe for good. Yet there was also good reason to question whether the realignment had any meaningful legs—and strong evidence suggesting the opposite soon followed the victory on streetcars. As the debate in Baton Rouge slouched toward its anticlimax in late June, the New Orleans School Board met under the leadership of its president Ernest Kruttschnitt, the same attorney who presided over the disenfranchising convention. In a unanimous decision, members voted to eliminate public education beyond elementary school for black students. As the president explained, a fifth-grade education was more than enough preparation "for that sphere of labor and social position and occupation to which they are best suited and seem ordained by the proper fitness of things."[90] Compounding the damage, when the board reported the results from civil service exams, only four of the twenty-seven teachers who had applied for positions in the remaining black schools were deemed qualified. Scott bitterly observed, "Who is silly enough to believe that a board taking such unjust advantage of a needy people would accord a fair examination to those who may desire to teach?"[91]

For the black community, the implications were confounding. Following so close in succession, the streetcar victory and school closures pointed toward the double-edged sword of race and class that complicated resistance strategies.[92] If the former suggested an opening to work alongside white leaders and preserve civil rights by applying economic pressure, the latter revealed the profound limitations of that approach. Although colored stockholders could mobilize investments and working-class black passengers could pool five-cent fares to fight Jim Crow's advance, the profit motives that prompted white businessmen to oppose segregation also created the black underclass, one permanently fixed in "that sphere of labor and social position and occupation," emancipation notwithstanding. While its contradictions could be imperfectly leveraged to defend civil rights, capitalism necessarily conjured white supremacy to condone black exploitation, in slavery and now in freedom, ensnaring the many and now even threatening customary privileges enjoyed by colored elites who had long since escaped poverty.[93]

But as *Advocate* readers considered an uncertain landscape during a summer that had produced more questions than answers, the concerns raised by the education restrictions would be eclipsed by more imminent threats. Before the month ended, a sudden, unforeseen crisis would overshadow the school board's actions and seem to confirm the lessons drawn from the streetcar debate. With blood running in the streets and the community under fire, civil rights would be replaced by a more conservative goal—survival—and a simple strategy. "The colored man of New Orleans has learned a lesson he should not and surely will not soon forget," Scott would conclude. "He has learned that his only hope is to keep close to the best white citizens of our city."[94]

* * * *

A FEW DAYS after Louisiana senators tabled streetcar segregation, thirty-four-year-old Robert Charles gathered his things and moved into a cramped room in a run-down building, located near Morris Park in the heart of a working-class, majority-black neighborhood.[95] By then, Charles had been living in New Orleans for about six years, where the hand-to-mouth realities of his existence had become a grind of alternating drudgery and crisis as he chased unpredictable stints at menial jobs—laying cable and shoveling coal at the St. Charles Hotel, loading cargo on the Port Chalmette docks, working as a laborer for a local construction firm, and cleaning streets as an employee of the City of New Orleans—the jobs collectively known as "negro work." Charles had recently lost his position at the Pelican Sawmill Company's lumberyard, forcing him to scramble for new housing. He ultimately agreed to share a single room with a former co-worker who was dealing with the same challenges.[96]

With no security to show for those six backbreaking years, Charles was struggling to get by in a world far removed from the dreams of Africa that he continued to keep alive. But he was still deeply engaged with the more radical political currents of the day. Among the few possessions that he carried to the new accommodations were reading materials: pamphlets marked with his annotations, along with composition books filled with notes and completed writing exercises.[97] And he was putting his penmanship to good use, by reaching out to one of the most controversial public figures in America. One day after moving into the dingy studio, Charles mailed a registered package to the Atlanta headquarters of *Voice of Missions*, a four-page monthly that circulated widely among black readers in the South. The envelope contained funds raised by selling subscriptions and single copies, and it was addressed to the founder and editor of the inflammatory journal: Bishop Henry McNeal Turner of the African Methodist Episcopal Church.[98]

Born free in antebellum South Carolina, the bishop shared an early career path with his editorial counterpart in Louisiana, earning his preaching license from the M.E. Church as a precocious teen. But although Turner began preaching to enslaved congregations under the supervision of white ministers in the 1850s, his theological journey had taken him in radical directions.[99] His religious outlook was transformed after a trip to New Orleans just before secession, where he met the charismatic leader of St. James *African* Methodist Episcopal Church, who explained the origins of the denomination founded by black preachers denied access to the M.E. Church in the early 1800s.[100] After enlisting and serving as a chaplain in the Union Army, Turner had embraced radicalism as violence spread across the South during Reconstruction, using his role as editor of the A.M.E. Church's national journal to champion civil rights, black nationalism, and the possibilities of African emigration.[101] Serving as an honorary vice-president in the white-dominated American Colonization Society, he declared "no region so full of promise as the land of our ancestors," which needed only "the trained hand of civilization with capital and intelligent enterprise" to yield its abundance. Although his vision sometimes veered uncomfortably close to imperialism, it was primarily rooted in a pessimistic view of the prospects for black Americans fighting white supremacy at home. Turner declared, "Nothing less than nationality will bring prosperity and manhood to us as a people."[102]

Against the international backdrop of Europe's imperial Conquest of Africa and the domestic repression of Reconstruction and Redemption, Bishop Turner became the nation's leading voice for emigration, imagining black Americans as benevolent colonizers who could better themselves while developing a backward region. During the early 1890s, he embarked on the first of multiple journeys to West Africa and returned home with glowing reports on the economic and evangelizing opportunities he discovered. Flush with enthusiasm, Turner founded *Voice of Missions* to promote the A.M.E. Church's overseas missions, along with the broader cause of African emigration. Reprinting correspondence from black missionaries working in Liberia and Sierra Leone side by side with observational reports from clergymen, engineers, agriculturalists, and explorers, the publication detailed the boundless natural resources of the region, soliciting capitalists and skilled mechanics. "Africa doesn't need common laborers, but money and brains," one missionary explained, "educated men, black or white, with some capital behind them."[103]

Although emigration was controversial within the black community, it was Turner's unflinching condemnation of the violence and repression facing black Americans that made him so provocative. Writing near the turn of the century, the bishop summarized his position with a broad headline, "AMERICAN NEGRO," followed by characteristically unsparing subheadings:

HIS FREEDOM A FARCE

His Liberty a Lie,
Amalgamation the Jargon of Folly

Emigration the Historic Solution of
The Negro Problem—The United
States His Slaughter
Pen—No Race
Future Here.[104]

For condemning segregation and lynching while indicting both perpetrators and bystanders, *Voice of Missions* drew criticism from scandalized white Americans and more conservative black leaders, becoming one of the most notorious publications in the country. Leaning into the controversy, Turner denounced his detractors for mischaracterizing him as an incendiary and a demagogue without soft-pedaling his perspective. "I don't object to being a target because of my opinions," he explained. "It is well known to the nation that I see no manhood future in this country for my race."[105]

In the absence of alternatives, *Voice of Missions* was among the few newspapers to strongly endorse the white-operated International Migration Society during the mid-1890s, running the organization's advertisements and circulars, covering its voyages, publishing positive accounts from emigrants, and pushing back against criticism from the black press.[106] Even as enthusiasm waned and the company struggled with war-related service delays and economic headwinds, Turner continued to advocate African emigration, exploring alternative locations and operators while sharpening his denunciations of the repressive social conditions at home. By the turn of the century, his newspaper was a consistently radical counterpoint to more conservative religious publications like the *Southwestern Christian Advocate*, carrying a comparable blend of church news and moral instruction, promoting black nationalism, and challenging anyone who endorsed accommodation. As conditions worsened, Turner became more combative. "We've been denounced and ridiculed a thousand times by some mushroom pimps who know how to scribble a little for the press," he memorably ridiculed, "because we favor a moderate emigration to Africa as remedy for the lynching horrors that are exterminating the colored race."[107]

The newspaper's no-holds-barred style contributed to its popularity, but its affordable price—copies sold for a nickel—and uncompromising challenge to more conservative strategies made *Voice of Missions* accessible and relatable to struggling farmers and laborers. Meanwhile, a network of part-time distributors boosted its reach and ensured wide circulation across the South. Local agents received monthly bundles from Turner's Atlanta headquarters, earning a small sales commission as they hawked single editions and monthly subscriptions. Although the stipend was a modest source of supplemental income, agents were generally motivated by enthusiasm for the message more than financial concerns, distributing the journal along with other politically charged materials. Spreading black nationalism through working-class circles, they spoke to community members both inside and outside more formal organizing channels, contributing to surging undercurrents of grassroots radicalism.[108]

Robert Charles discovered *Voice of Missions* through his interest in African emigration, selling the publication on New Orleans job sites while maintaining steady correspondence with its Atlanta headquarters. Like other part-time agents, his affiliation was driven by his radical activism. As he visited with subscribers and talked up friends and co-workers, Charles also voluntarily circulated emigration literature, along with handbills denouncing segregation and lynching. Over time, he earned a reputation as a compelling advocate for racial equality and black nationalism, although his misrepresentation by a hostile press would force his admirers to defend him against charges of extremism. "His work for many years had been with Christian people, circulating emigration pamphlets and active as an agent for a mission publication," activist Ida B. Wells explained. "Men who knew him say that he was a law-abiding, industrious, peaceable man."[109]

Among more conservative members of the community, these descriptions, suggesting the coexistence of respectability and radicalism among some members of the lower classes, were the real concerns raised by black nationalism. Although colored elites had long dismissed African emigration as a get-rich-quick scheme that primarily ensnared the lazy and gullible, the possible spread of dangerous ideas among otherwise responsible workingmen was especially concerning. For the *Advocate* editor and his readers, the biggest problem with Turner's doctrine was less his trenchant critique of American race relations, but rather the practical implications of his radical conclusion. "Notwithstanding the many good things which may be said for the bishop, we are confident that he is doing more harm than good," Scott argued. "It's not likely that the worthless element of our people will pay attention to him, as they are doubtless too busy having a good time to care much for the bishop's wild schemes. But he is keeping unsettled the very class who, if let alone, would accomplish something for the good of the race."[110]

In other words, the problem was Robert Charles. When the *Advocate* editor published his critique, Charles had been self-educating and avoiding trouble for years, seemingly a man who might "accomplish something for the good of the race." Withstanding depression and personal setbacks, Charles had worked steadily throughout his time in New Orleans, earning high praise from the white supervisor who recommended him as "a good, honest, and reliable man."[111] His reputation among his peers was just as sturdy. Those who knew him described Charles as composed and distinguished, a workingman who spoke with authority and carried himself with dignity. "He was quiet and a peaceful man, very frank in speaking," a friend remembered. "Few could be found to equal him."[112]

By appearances, Charles should have modeled the upward mobility made possible by the doctrines espoused by the *Advocate* editor and others, choosing hard work and intellectual self-cultivation over dissipation. But he was foundering, trapped in a cycle of low wages and chronic underemployment that left scarcely enough to cover basic needs, much less provide a springboard toward a better life. Job insecurity had forced him to relocate frequently throughout his time in New Orleans, where he overpaid flophouse landlords with little hope of securing more stable lodging. Beyond the reading and writing materials that he brought to the one-room apartment, his possessions amounted to no more than necessities—cookware, tools, bedding, and clothes—all in poor condition. "His wearing apparel was little more than rags," reporters would describe, "and financially, he was evidently not in a flourishing condition. His room showed, in fact, that he was nothing more than a laborer."[113]

As a common drudge with uncommon reading habits, Charles seemed to validate Bishop Turner's grim perspective on race in America, defined by a history of oppression that denied "manhood future" to black men confined by a rigid caste system. No matter how hard they tried. Although his sharp mind and work ethic should have enabled a considerable rise, certainly above subsistence and perhaps even into the sizable class of colored professionals in New Orleans, Charles was barely getting by. The dissonance between his personal habits and his material reality—diligent study in a dingy room—pointed toward an unspeakable existence. While *Advocate* readers considered civil rights strategies in an increasingly hostile climate, they could scarcely afford to recognize the black laborers who were constrained by circumstance and design rather than by a lack of ambition or ability. Those doomed by race and capitalism.

Fortunately, there were also good reasons to question whether he really deserved more from life, at least for discerning social observers. For those who perceived a direct relationship between character and success, his new home—one of the uninsurable, fire-prone structures designated "negro tenements" by wary adjusters—was damning enough.[114] More generally, his surroundings showed that he was comfortable rubbing shoulders with sketchy characters. Although hardly the most scandalous neighborhood, the central city blocks above St. Charles Avenue were known as a rough area, one where residents frequently drew unwanted police attention. Stabbings were common and during the recent July Fourth celebrations, patrolmen made over a dozen arrests for gambling, drunkenness, disturbing the peace, and fighting.[115] Enforcing the law was all the more dangerous because so many working-class men carried pistols on them, defying an ordinance that banned concealed weapons— and Charles was no exception. He brought a big Colt revolver with him to the new place, along with his brother's Winchester rifle and a handheld mold for melting lead into bullets.[116]

There were other reasons to specifically downgrade Charles, whose habits would soon come under intensive scrutiny. Inside his room was a small bottle filled with cocaine, which was popular among the working classes, purchased in dime bags or diluted in red wine for fifteen cents a gallon.[117] But it was also increasingly controversial. Earlier in the spring, reporters had published a scathing exposé, which claimed an alarming rise in drug abuse and estimated that two thousand addicts were prowling the streets. Although they focused on the dangers posed by the uncontrollable "negro cocaine fiend," the drug often served a utilitarian purpose. For buyers coping with long hours and grueling work conditions, it was a cheap, reliable energy source. An anonymous saloon owner who sold cocaine illegally guessed that perhaps two-thirds of the domestic servants in his "fairly respectable neighborhood" were customers. "They come in and get dope in the morning before they go to work," he explained. "That's what keeps them up."[118]

Just as cocaine possession could signify either depravity or exhaustion depending on the observer's perspective, Charles was an ambiguous figure in a society with diminishing room for nuance, moving comfortably through the rough-hewn world of unskilled laborers while keeping his eyes fixed on one far more liberating. One week after moving into the one-room apartment, Charles reached out to an old acquaintance in Birmingham, keeping up a correspondence that he had maintained for more than four years. Although the International Migration Society had since folded due to bad publicity from canceled departures and disappointing outcomes to previous voyages, its former president continued to energetically promote emigration. Earlier that month, Daniel J. Flummer had chartered a new company, the Liberian Colonization Society. It shared the same purpose and subscription-based business model as his first venture—and the same questionable ethics, as the founder insisted that he was "in no way responsible for the contracts or debts of the old company."[119] Before launching the venture, Flummer was drumming up enthusiasm with a self-published manifesto titled *The Negro in Liberia*. His thirty-page pamphlet was mostly facts and fantasies about West Africa and the opportunities to be found there, but its foundation was a bleak outlook on race in America. "The oppression of the negro by the white man has reached a point where further endurance is almost unbearable," it began, referencing lynch mobs and Jim Crow laws, before turning to economic injustice. "He is denied the privilege of living decently like the white man and condemned for not doing so. Knowing his unequal chances under the law, his employer contrives to rob him."[120]

Speaking to desperate lives studiously ignored by white observers, the pamphlet drew little attention from outsiders, but it circulated widely through emigration networks. Charles was among its most dedicated readers, bringing copies from place to place as he moved and passing them along to friends and family members. Just after relocating to his latest slum, he reached out to his old acquaintance, requesting more. Charles had no way of knowing, but he was creating the only first-person record of his existence, his only words that would survive the firestorm that was coming. It was a short message, but it spoke to his devotion. Despite everything, he was still chasing the dream of a better world. And he wanted to share it with others:

> *Dear Sir—I received your last pamphlets and they are all given out. I want you to send me some more, and I enclose you the stamps. I think I will go over in Greenville, Miss., and give my people some pamphlets over there.*

Flummer would send the requested pamphlets to the enclosed address, but by the time they arrived, Charles was dead and New Orleans had been consumed by its deadliest violence in decades. As he struggled to make sense, the next month, the young businessman responded to a letter from civil rights activist Ida B. Wells, who requested more information about a shadowy figure who was being described in the white press as "the archfiend of the century." Reflecting on his relationship with Charles, the entrepreneur was bewildered as to the bloody circumstances that consumed his life—and the lives of those he killed. "He always appeared to be mild but earnest in his advocacy of emigration and to my knowledge never used any method that would appear unreasonable," Flummer swore. "If he ever violated the law before killing the policemen, I don't know."[121]

4

Specters

BEFORE SUNRISE ON JULY 23, 1900, NINETEEN-YEAR-old Leonard Pierce hopped out of bed with more energy than usual, ready to hit the streets and turn his luck around. Until recently, Pierce had been digging sewage ditches for the National Contracting Company, earning less than two dollars a day for backbreaking shifts in the scorching sun, but the work had dried up at the worst possible time. His mother and stepfather had recently separated, forcing him to find new accommodations. For an impoverished workingman living hand-to-mouth, losing a job and a bed in the same week could have been disastrous. Fortunately, a family friend had come to the rescue, thirty-four-year-old Robert Charles, a former co-worker who was also struggling to find a steady paycheck.[1] The men agreed to share expenses, renting a one-room apartment in a housing complex on Fourth Street, the heart of a working-class neighborhood packed with similarly cramped, fire-prone subdivisions.[2]

The roommates were an odd couple. The younger man was outgoing and eager to please, while the older man was brooding and morose, although he flashed with a fierce passion when discussing race and politics. A few nights before, Charles brought up African emigration, explaining his plans for a better life in Liberia and trying to convince his bewildered roommate to join him. The conversation ended badly. "I got him mad by saying that if I'd go there, those people would eat me up," Pierce remembered. "After that he didn't speak to me about Africa."[3]

Early on Monday morning, Pierce was more concerned with filling his own empty stomach. Putting on a rumpled shirt and worn trousers, he left the cramped room and began a familiar routine: wandering the streets, checking with recruiting offices, and swapping gossip with his network of friends and former co-workers, who relied on each other when misfortune inevitably forced them into similar circumstances. Despite his youth, Pierce could expertly navigate the fluid, word-of-mouth markets for day labor and short-term gigs, but everyone he spoke to related the same unpromising news. As the hours passed and the clouds towered overhead, building toward an afternoon thunderstorm, the day turned into another dreary lesson on the unfavorable economics of a mid-summer job search: all demand, no supply.[4] Dripping sweat as temperatures approached ninety degrees, Pierce knew that he was fighting an uphill battle against the seasonal rhythms of business in New Orleans, where the brutal summer heat drained the energy from men and markets. On the other hand, cooler autumn temperatures signaled the beginning of the bustling six-month period known as the "business season," when sugar and cotton steamed into town from so many plantations, followed by fat-pocketed planters ready to turn cash into good times. From that flood-tide of wealth, the smallest amounts trickled down to a man like Pierce, who spent the previous harvest chopping cane on a St. John Parish sugar plantation, along with other temporary farmhands. But now it was six weeks before grinding started—his only chance was to piece together shifts and make do until better times.[5]

Later that evening, Pierce returned home, disheartened by the unsuccessful search. Back in the room, he found his roommate hunched over a writing table, pen darting across the page. Charles was sharply dressed, wearing a clean white shirt, a black jacket, and dark striped trousers. A weathered slouch hat rounded out the ensemble. Looking the part of a shoestring dandy, he glanced up and nodded a greeting before returning to his composition. After a few minutes, he spoke up, saying they should meet up with his on-again, off-again girlfriend, who was returning from an excursion to Baton Rouge later that evening. Perking up, Pierce asked if there was anything in it for him. Charles said yes—his girlfriend had a roommate, an eligible bachelorette. With newfound energy, the teenager washed and dressed, this time putting on his best clothes. As they prepared to leave, both men tucked pistols into their waistbands—common accessories for workingmen in a rough-and-tumble town.[6]

It was shortly after ten o'clock by the time Charles and Pierce made it to the house on Dryades Street, only a few blocks from their own place, where their dates rented a room from an elderly white woman. As they reached the address, the gentleman callers waited outside the darkened house. They were hoping to avoid the landlady's attention, especially so late in the evening, but thirty minutes passed without any movement from inside. Pierce suggested they move along and Charles agreed. Black men caught loitering after dark could expect a rough time from patrolmen. They strolled away as naturally as possible, sitting on the porch steps of a nearby cottage. The sensible decision backfired spectacularly. "We had not been seated more than five minutes," Pierce remembered, "before the sergeant and two officers asked what we were doing there."[7]

Ironically, the suitors had committed a dangerous breach of racial etiquette through an abundance of caution, raising the suspicions of nosy neighbors. Chatting with her friends after an evening at church, an elderly black woman named Kate Clark watched suspiciously as the strangers neared the group, but it was where they stopped and sat down that really triggered alarm bells. "We noticed two men sitting on Mrs. Schwartz's steps and we thought it was suspicious," she explained. "The Schwartz folks are white and it looked peculiar to have two colored men sitting on their steps late at night."[8] The strange men seemed to be wary of the unwelcome stares. They shot glances toward the gawking women—maybe hostile. After a few minutes, Clark decided to do something. Gathering her friends, she herded them away to find the police.[9]

Commanding the Sixth Precinct night shift, Sergeant Jules Aucoin had been patrolling since before sundown when the women flagged him down. With more than three decades on the force, the sixty-six-year-old police veteran was one of the department's most experienced men, although he was far from its most reputable. His long disciplinary record was marred with the petty hustles that officers often used to pad their dismal salaries. Over the past decade alone, Aucoin had taken bribes for allowing illegal gambling and booze sales, extorted bar owners over expired liquor licenses, patronized brothels, and straight-up refused to participate in raids, while also facing charges for gross neglect and conduct unbecoming on multiple occasions.[10]

Despite his checkered record, the veteran sergeant had been particularly motivated in recent days. Unknown to him, Charles had moved into contested territory. Two weeks before he relocated, a resident hoping to "catch the eye of the proper authorities" had sent an anonymous tip to the *Times-Democrat* office, drawing attention to ugly scenes unfolding a few blocks from Charles's soon-to-be home. The complaint was a bombshell: black teenagers were swarming Morris Park and harassing white girls. The author explained that the neighborhood was "populated mostly by the middle and poorer classes," who were unable to summer outside New Orleans and came to the park to "enjoy the fresh air and cool breezes." Youngsters would play there in the evening, when predators descended. "I was told by eyewitnesses they insist on sitting close and lying on the grass, waiting for the maidens to pass near them," he explained. "They make it a point to abuse and insult them at every opportunity."[11]

Without corroborating, editors published the hearsay, along with multiple articles spicing up the sexual overtones. According to them, "young colored hoodlums" would strategically position themselves and "seize every opportunity to ejaculate questionable remarks" toward the girls, before subjecting anyone who tried to intervene to the same "objectionable ejaculations." The editors demanded a police response "to see that these abuses in the public parks are crushed," namely by making arrests with any force necessary.[12]

The editors had reason to expect action, particularly with officers under growing pressure to police racial boundaries in addition to preventing serious crimes. Arrest rates had risen dramatically in New Orleans in recent years, when patrolmen frequently doubled the numbers put up by their counterparts during Reconstruction, but the escalation was driven by changing enforcement patterns rather than spiking crime. Less than a fifth of arrests involved serious threats to public safety. By comparison, more than two-thirds were for ordinance violations and minor offenses, particularly drunkenness and disturbing the peace—and black residents were arrested at rates nearly doubling those of white offenders. As nuisance arrests became the basis for a broad campaign motivated by Jim Crow sensibilities, localized complaints transformed neighborhoods into hotspots where anyone fitting subjective descriptions—appearing suspicious, bold, shiftless, foul-mouthed, uneducated, conspicuous, objectionable, ill-mannered, and on and on—could be swept up in the displays of force that inevitably followed.[13] After demanding a crackdown, editors approvingly noted the enhanced surveillance in Morris Park and the surrounding neighborhood in follow-up stories, reassuring readers that police were "paying special attention to this section of the city."[14]

Under the circumstances, even an irresponsible officer like Jules Aucoin needed to step up his activity. Around three o'clock the previous morning, the sergeant had arrested eight residents—five women and three men, all black, mostly in their early twenties, their occupations listed as domestic servants and laborers—and charged them with "disturbing the peace and using obscene language," exactly the kind of strategic arrests that could send a message that police were watching the area.[15] Adding to the urgency, the Sixth Precinct had seen a string of high-profile burglaries. Unidentified suspects were targeting nearby Garden District mansions, abandoned by wealthy homeowners spending the summer months in more hospitable climates. Sitting adjacent to the rougher neighborhoods above St. Charles Avenue, the properties were inviting targets for professional criminals. Although there were no arrests or publicized leads, reporters made racially charged assumptions, warning, "New Orleans is now in the hands of an organized band of negro thieves."[16]

As the sergeant walked his beat late on Monday evening, both Morris Park and the recent burglaries mattered. Facing pressure to show force and operating under the assumption that black suspects were responsible for the unsolved break-ins, Aucoin took the meddlesome old women more seriously than his uninspiring service record suggested he would otherwise. He promised to investigate, then shooed the women away and blew three sharp blasts on his whistle.[17]

A few blocks away, Patrolman August Mora was walking the beat with his rookie partner when the piercing shriek cut through the nighttime calm. By his side, Supernumerary Joseph Cantrelle had been serving part-time for only three months, but he knew enough to recognize the call for backup.[18] When they found the sergeant nearby, Aucoin vaguely told them about "a report about two negroes sitting on some doorstep."[19] They headed toward the location and spotted two men sitting on the front stoop.[20] Before moving on the suspects, the officers spoke with the women who reported the disturbance, confirming the black men were strangers in the neighborhood. The officers sized them up as they approached. Both appeared strong enough to cause them trouble, especially the six-foot-plus suspect perched on the far side of the front stairs. Warily eying him, Aucoin told the younger patrolmen that if the situation went sideways, they should both jump the larger man. He would handle the smaller one a few steps below. Ready for action, the officers closed the distance and sprang the trap, catching them by surprise.[21]

Seated on the stoop, Charles and Pierce looked up, startled by the sudden appearance of police officers. Without giving the suspects time to gather themselves, Sergeant Aucoin began the interrogation, asking where they stayed.[22] After a short pause, the older man spoke. "We live here and we're waiting for some women folks of ours who went to Baton Rouge on an excursion," Charles replied, trying to smooth things over with a plausible blend of fact and fiction, unaware of what his interrogator already knew. "They have the keys to the house and we can't get in until they come."[23]

From the sergeant's perspective, the words rang with defiance. The cornered man seemed to be daring him to counter the claim. The suspect leaned forward and appeared to tense his body, preparing for action. Nearby, the patrolmen shifted in nervous anticipation, watching as their commander's lips tightened beneath his bushy goatee. "You're a goddamn liar," Aucoin finally sneered, reaching one hand toward his holster as the other shot out with surprising quickness, grabbing the younger suspect and dragging him to his feet with a sharp tug. He pressed the weapon against Pierce's head and growled, "Don't move, or I'll blow your brains out."[24]

Pierce froze. Panicked words tumbled from his mouth. "You don't need to shoot me, officer, I ain't done nothing to be shot," he pleaded. "I ain't gonna run."[25]

Charles made no such promises. He sprang from the steps in a wild lunge toward freedom, but the patrolmen grabbed him and held on. As he struggled to break away, the men stumbled into the muddy street and the action devolved into a bewildering tangle of thrashing bodies. Suddenly there was a startling explosion—a gunshot. The combatants instantly broke apart and three pistols barked at once. Charles stumbled to the ground, but quickly scrambled up and returned fire. One of the officers buckled. Staggering forward a few steps, Patrolman Mora collapsed onto the sidewalk and groaned, "I'm shot!"

More gunshots resounded, followed by silence. For a second, two remaining shooters stared one another down. Then the suspect turned around and sprinted away, running up the block and disappearing into the darkness.[26]

Less than a minute after the encounter began, three men had exchanged at least fifteen shots from point-blank range. The violence was sudden and confounding, so overwhelming that in the aftermath, participants who had been standing only feet away from each other told wildly diverging stories about what happened. Just months on the job, Supernumerary Joseph Cantrelle provided the most sensational narrative, a yarn ripped from the pages of dime store detective fiction. "I noticed Charles trying to get his hand up to his breast and trying to get a weapon of some kind," the rookie explained. "Edging up to him, suddenly I sprang forward and caught him. Instantly, Charles seemed possessed with superhuman strength."

Patrolman Mora jumped to his defense, but even the combined strength of two men was no match. "His frantic efforts were too much for us," Cantrelle continued. "Charles freed himself and reached the middle of the street with one bound. He stopped, straightened up, turned, drew a pistol, and fired."

The coolheaded rookie exchanged fire, hot and accurate, but the gunman once again demonstrated his freakish athleticism. "As Charles was shooting at us, he was sidestepping and bucking," Cantrelle claimed. "When he backed up on the sidewalk, he kept dodging; the man actually wriggled and writhed like a snake."

When his partner went down, the part-time officer was unfazed. Carefully drawing a bead on the acrobatic outlaw, he squeezed the trigger and waited for his well-aimed round to find its home. Nothing happened.

With a sickening feeling, Cantrelle realized that he was empty. "The situation was desperate and the only thing that saved me was that Charles also emptied his gun about this time," he gravely concluded. "I started to close, but he began to run, leaping like an antelope, and I lost sight of him in a few moments." Which was clearly understandable—if his story was to be believed.[27]

Recovering from gunshot wounds in a hospital bed, Patrolman Mora described a starkly different version of events. The veteran told reporters the altercation started when the sergeant grabbed the younger man, prompting Charles to spring up from the steps. "Cantrelle and I took hold of him," Mora remembered, "but he's a powerful man and he dragged us into the roadway. While we were struggling there, I pulled my billy and beat him over the head."

According to Mora's version of the story, Cantrelle panicked, drawing his revolver and firing a warning shot to frighten Charles into compliance. It was a rookie mistake. Harmless gunfire was certain to be misinterpreted by a suspect during a heated struggle, turning a simple tussle into something much more dangerous. "I'm almost certain that Cantrelle did what a number of inexperienced officers before him have done," Mora explained. "I think he fired the shot to intimidate him. As he did this, the negro hit me with an awful blow on the side of the head. I drew and the gunfight commenced, since Charles drew almost at the same time."[28]

Although they differed on key details, both patrolmen's accounts put their commanding officer in a bad position. According to them, Sergeant Aucoin had stood a few yards away from a desperate gunfight without once discharging his weapon. Attempting to account for his actions, Aucoin denied making the first move, telling investigators the altercation began when he accused the suspects of lying—and he claimed to have been a much more active participant than his subordinates acknowledged. "Both negroes jumped up and Mora and Cantrelle seized the large one, the man we afterwards found to be Robert Charles," he explained. "The other man, whom I subsequently arrested, immediately pulled his pistol and fired at me twice. I drew my pistol and returned fire."

Realizing that the account raised uncomfortable questions about his marksmanship, the sergeant expressed surprise that neither man had been wounded. "How we missed each other I can't understand," he confessed, before offering a possible explanation. "The flashes of our guns blinded us. There were fully eighteen or twenty shots fired. I shot twice, Pierce shot twice, Mora shot three times. All other shots were fired by Robert Charles."[29]

According to Aucoin's calculations, Charles had fired roughly a dozen rounds from a gun that carried only half as many, apparently without pausing to reload. Yet according to witness reports, the sergeant's behavior in the aftermath of the shootout was as questionable as his math. After the explosion of nearby gunfire, fifty-seven-year-old Michael Neader and his son had rushed to the scene, arriving moments after the shootout ended and discovering Aucoin, seemingly frozen in shock and still aiming his revolver at Pierce's head. Lifting the young suspect's jacket to pat him down, the father and son discovered a pistol tucked snugly in his waistband and confiscated the weapon.[30] Their testimony seemed to contradict the sergeant's claim that Pierce had drawn and fired the gun. When reporters pointed out the inconsistencies and pressed him about whether the young suspect actually participated in the shooting, Aucoin had an explanation. "I have charged him with shooting at me," he cagily responded. He claimed that just moments after attempting to murder him, Pierce tried to give up when his gun jammed. "He said that he would surrender and held out his gun to me," Aucoin explained. "I didn't know which end was pointed my way and I ordered him to put it into his waistband—which accounts for it being found there when he was searched."[31]

From custody, nineteen-year-old Leonard Pierce would also tell his story to reporters, saying that he was sitting on the porch steps when the officers approached. Charles twitched during the aggressive questioning and, virtually at the same moment, Sergeant Aucoin grabbed the younger man. Staring down the revolver barrel wavering inches from his face, Pierce watched his world collapse into the black hole. Terror warped time and dampened his senses. By confessing a human response to events too shocking to process, the youngest person on the scene perhaps most accurately captured the experience. "He acknowledges that the shooting started only a few feet away, but says he was too badly frightened to hear anything that anyone else was saying," reporters described. "All he could see was the big revolver pointed at his face."[32]

Shifting blame and struggling to piece together memories fragmented by panic and chaos, participants constructed their own narratives, bending them toward convenient fiction and obscuring the facts beneath impenetrable layers of subjectivity and self-protection. Yet as the smoke cleared just before midnight on a muggy July night in New Orleans, what began as a straightforward encounter had ended in shocking fashion. Patrolman Mora was sprawled on the sidewalk and writhing in agony. Bullets had sheared the tip from his finger and smashed into his right hip. Standing nearby, Aucoin was still holding his service revolver to Pierce's head, but Cantrelle and the gunman were gone.[33] After a few minutes, the rookie sheepishly returned alone, checking on his wounded comrade before heading toward a grocery a few blocks away.[34] Like officers stationed elsewhere, patrolmen in the Sixth Precinct carried keys to call boxes scattered across town, which theoretically allowed them to summon backup in an emergency. But poor maintenance and vandalism made the cutting-edge system mostly nonfunctional, and they more often used the phone at Julius Stendel's Drugstore, spending so much time there that locals nicknamed his pharmacy "the police station."[35] Cantrelle made the call and soon every man working the night shift was on the scene, where an ambulance took Mora to the hospital and a patrol wagon took Pierce to the station.[36]

Making his way back toward the scene, Cantrelle had no way to know that his failure to chase down the second suspect would catalyze one of the most transformative weeks in the history of New Orleans. Nor could he know that his actions, and those of his fellow officers, would come under intense scrutiny in the days to come. Speaking with detectives after the terrible events that followed, the rookie would struggle to convincingly justify his actions as the night spiraled from trauma to unthinkable tragedy. "I went as far up as Louisiana Avenue hunting for Charles," he explained. "Later when he was located at No. 2023 Fourth Street, I went up there with Corporal Perrier and was stationed at Fourth and Rampart. We heard the shooting, but until someone shot at us, I thought it was the police doing it all."[37]

* * * *

SHORTLY AFTER MIDNIGHT, there was an unexpected visitor at a charming cottage on Jackson Avenue, the new home of Captain John Day, commanding officer of the Sixth Precinct.[38] Strapping and rowdy, the handsome thirty-seven-year-old Day cut an imposing figure, his powerful physique matched only by his outsized reputation as "one of the best men on the force."[39] Over a decade or so on the job, the second-generation Irish immigrant had made a name for himself as a larger-than-life figure in New Orleans police circles, supplying crime reporters with a steady stream of sensational stories: exchanging gunfire with the infamous mobster Dennis Corcoran, apprehending the historically named villain Andrew "Stonewall" Jackson, busting up gambling dens in Chinatown, collaring a hot-tempered Italian who killed a fellow countryman in a dispute over annual Columbus Day festivities, and investigating rogue municipal workers for chopping down the prized live oaks fronting the mansions of wealthy Anglo-Saxon and French families.[40] As an up-and-comer on the force, Day had proven his regard for both man and commerce, saving lives during the devastating blaze that destroyed the famous St. Charles Hotel in the mid-1890s and helping to prevent the loss of valuable cotton bales during a steamboat fire.[41] All too uncommon among his comrades, dedication made Day a local hero, and when he was unanimously promoted to captain, the news made the front page.[42]

Day was sound asleep when the breathless messenger arrived, but snapped awake as he learned the grim word. Two black burglary suspects had ambushed his officers, seriously wounding a patrolman. One young suspect was in custody, but the other man was on the loose, armed and dangerous. Careful not to wake his eight-year-old daughter Cecilia, Day dressed quickly, reassuring his wife that everything would be fine. Married since the days when her husband worked as a cotton sampler for local firms, Mary had proudly watched as he transcended his working-class roots, transforming the family into a pillar of the community. Day had once served as president of the Policemen's Benevolent Association and was unusually active in the city's reform movements, rubbing shoulders with appreciative business leaders.[43] On a police force maligned for its infamous "don't care" approach toward enforcing the law, he was the very rare officer who was equally celebrated by beat cops and high society. And there was simply no better man for the task at hand.[44]

Day jumped into the covered patrol wagon waiting outside his home and directed the driver toward the Dryades Street crime scene, where his officers were already processing evidence.[45] He surveyed the situation, ordering the vehicle to bring Pierce back to the station, before turning his attention to a promising lead—blood droplets leading from the scene. The escaped suspect had been wounded. Feeling a familiar rush of adrenaline, Day followed the crimson smears upriver for more than a dozen blocks before he got bored and decided on a more direct approach: pumping the teenager at the Sixth Precinct lockup for information.[46]

Located just around the corner from the captain's cottage, the station on Rousseau Street stuck out like a sore thumb. Adorned with winged globes in the once-fashionable Egyptian Revival style, the sixty-year-old structure was badly dilapidated, its attached stable "condemned and liable to be blown down at any time by a strong gust of wind."[47] Although funds were authorized to fix the station's leaky roof and protect its valuable horses, prisoners were housed in "badly ventilated dungeons."[48] Stifling in the summer months, the lockup was even more hazardous in cold temperatures, when boilers designed for anthracite burned soft Pittsburgh coal to save money, causing the heating system to chronically malfunction.[49] Concerned about lawsuits when prisoners sleeping on concrete floors inevitably died, police commissioners had warned city officials, "The cells are damp, unhealthy, and foul-smelling," but nothing was done to improve the situation.[50]

Around two o'clock on Tuesday morning, Leonard Pierce was spending a sleepless night in the steamy cell block when Captain Day returned to the station, prepared to crank up the temperature even more by putting him through the "sweating process." Also known as the "third degree," both expressions were euphemisms for the controversial methods commonly used by officers to extract confessions, techniques ranging from sleep deprivation to savage beatings.[51] Progressive reformers condemned the "various modes of torture," mental and physical, used to "break the prisoner's will and undermine his sanity." But despite growing scrutiny, police brutality was both an open secret and an essential part of the criminal justice system: feared by prisoners, denied by practitioners, and enabled by court officers and crime reporters.[52] If they bothered to enquire, judges would be "assured that the criminal's battered and manhandled condition is because he resisted arrest or fought being locked up," while any journalist who questioned the cover-up would "never again get tips that are so valuable when one must have early and accurate stories."[53] New Orleans reporters enthusiastically supported both the sweating process and the unsparing men who mastered its violent techniques, and that included John Day. In one incident that made the newspapers, twenty-year-old Eugene Sullivan claimed that "he was punched in the face several times without any cause" when Day took him into custody. The young man had to be hospitalized with facial swelling so severe that he was unable to eat and drink, but reporters waved away the complaints, noting the captain's notorious strength and reasoning it was "strange that Sullivan's jaw wasn't broken if he was hit as hard as he claims."[54]

Now the captain's sights were on another young suspect, one charged with shooting at his men. Reporters wisely avoided details, but they described the outcome of the interrogation, saying Pierce "broke down and cried under the 'sweating' process, declaring that it was the first time he had ever been arrested in his life."[55] Between sobs, he told a story that was essentially the same as the one told by Patrolman Mora, describing a chance encounter that unexpectedly and explosively escalated. "When we were sitting on the step and the police came up to us and asked what we were doing there, I told them that we were waiting for women," he said. "Charles got up and started to run. The officer who got me put a pistol to my head and said that I shouldn't move, so I gave up—but Charles and the other officers began shooting."

Pressed on his relationship with the gunman, Pierce described his roommate as a casual friend and denied any conspiracy. "Charles wasn't working and I lost my job," he explained. "We wanted to get a room so the rent would be small. I knew he wanted Negroes to go to Africa, but he never told me to go against white people."[56]

Pierce gave a general location and a description of the place where they lived, warning that Charles also owned a rifle.[57] Although not entirely convinced, Day was satisfied that he had a good enough lead to make a move. He emerged from the room and triumphantly announced, "I know where I can get that nigger now."[58]

With his target fixed, the captain enlisted Aucoin and Cantrelle, both uninjured in the gunfight and hopefully eager to redeem themselves. Then he gathered the remaining men who were available. They were reliable. Corporals Honoré Perrier and Ernest Trenchard were veterans, as were Patrolmen Caspar Pincon and Peter Lamb. Each man had served roughly a decade on the force.[59] Before departing, Day asked his sergeant about the gunman. Aucoin responded that he was "a desperate man," advising that "it would be best to shoot him before he was given a chance to draw his pistol."[60] The rules of engagement erased the line between law enforcement and vigilante justice. Planning to shoot on sight under any circumstances, the squad was effectively a seven-man lynch mob. Boarding the patrol wagon, Day took the "big, murderous-looking" revolver confiscated from Pierce, a .38-caliber with considerably more stopping power than his service weapon. Double-fisting both guns, the captain bragged, "I'll have two now."[61]

It was shortly after three o'clock in the morning when they reached the neighborhood, a few blocks from the scene of the first showdown. Stopping outside a nearby home, Captain Day awakened the startled occupants and questioned them about "two strange negroes." They confirmed that Pierce was telling the truth. According to them, "two strange blacks had come there within the past week or so."[62] As he prepared to approach the targeted location, Day divided his squad, ordering three men—Aucoin, Trenchard, and Lamb—to follow him inside, while instructing the others to surround the building.[63] Alerted by the unusual flurry of activity, several civilians were on the scene, positioning themselves on nearby rooftops. Among them was twenty-nine-year-old Charles Merritt, a watchman who lived in the area and nursed aspirations of one day joining the force. As the squad prepared to move, Merritt nervously warned them to be careful. "Oh, pshaw," Day retorted, "I'll go and take that nigger myself."[64]

Pistol outstretched, the captain boldly led his squad toward the building, a clapboard structure in the middle of the block. Even in the darkness, the mustard-colored ruin made an ugly impression, looking "more likely a stable" to the reporters who soon toured the scene.[65] The property had no front entrance, but there was an unlocked wooden gate on the left side, which led to a foreboding alleyway, about fifty feet long. Bounded by the neighboring building, the wide passage was strewn with discarded household trash—tubs, trunks, and empty boxes. Wooden planks lined the ground, running between the gutter and steps leading to six doors, each providing entry to one-room apartments. A makeshift roof covered the length of the walkway, shading the passage during the day, but now transforming it into a darkened tunnel shielded from the streetlights outside.[66] "Even by daylight, the place wears an air of sinister mystery," reporters described with hindsight clarity, declaring it "an appropriate setting for a tragedy."[67]

The officers made their way to the gate and stepped into the passage. Sergeant Aucoin walked alongside Captain Day, carrying a bull's-eye lantern and training its thin beam down the dim alley. Trailing close behind, Corporal Trenchard held a wagon lantern. Neither lamp shed enough light for a proper view. Eyes straining, the officers knocked on the first of six doors, beginning with the apartment closest to the street and readying their weapons as they heard sounds of shuffling from inside. After a few moments, an elderly woman opened the door and identified herself as the landlady. Fanny Jackson told the gruff visitors that she lived on the property with her bedridden husband, but the officers seemed unconvinced. They pushed inside and began searching, demanding to know the whereabouts of the newest tenants. The fourth room, she said.[68]

Leaving the apartment, the four-man squad repeated the same procedure at the second residence. Fifty-nine-year-old Annie Cryder confirmed that men who matched the description had recently moved into the fourth room.[69] Sensing the climax approaching, the officers reentered the alleyway and edged forward again, more cautiously now, sidestepping debris and walking in pairs. As they neared the fourth room, Corporal Trenchard bellowed, "Open up there!"[70]

* * * *

ROBERT CHARLES WATCHED the officers from the shadows, peering through a cracked door as the police squad approached. Four hours had passed since he escaped the Dryades Street shooting, turning right at the nearest corner and then making a quick left to elude the officer who was half-heartedly coming after him. Two black men walking down Baronne Street at the same time later told detectives they encountered a suspicious figure moments after the gunfire stopped, misinterpreting his awkward stagger as drunkenness.[71] Charles had suffered a painful gunshot wound to his right thigh. He was leaving behind a mile-long blood trail as he hobbled to the corner of General Taylor Street before pausing to make a fateful decision, one that would transform him from a run-of-the-mill criminal into a man far more notorious: he turned around and doubled back to his room, choosing to face down whoever came for him.[72]

At least partially, the choice was made from sheer desperation. Charles had gunned down a patrolman, maybe killing him. The circumstances hardly mattered, and the likely consequences of being captured alive were too terrible to imagine. Those who committed racially charged crimes rarely survived long enough to make a courtroom appearance. Escape was unlikely, surrender was a grisly suicide. But even as his mind raced through equally hopeless scenarios, a deeper conviction took hold. Although the confrontation had been sudden and unexpected, it also felt like a predictable culmination. Hiding from paramilitaries as a child, reading daily about new racial horrors, endlessly searching for stable jobs, enduring the grinding poverty that prevented him from pursuing his dreams of Liberia—all manifestations of white supremacy, dogging his steps from birth, constraining him, gradually strangling him. Now its foot soldiers were finally closing the noose, coming to claim his life.

Facing death, Charles decided to return the favor in kind. He staggered through the darkness and safely made his way home. Once there, he moved through the apartment with purpose, bandaging his injured leg,

reloading his pistol, stuffing his pockets with cartridges, and finally taking down his brother's lever-action Winchester rifle. Then he waited until
he heard muffled voices outside. Snuffing his lantern, Charles stood in
the entryway and braced himself against the mantle. He cracked open
the door and peered into the dark passage, where shadowy figures were
midway down, maybe fifteen yards away. Unseen, Charles lowered the
barrel of his .38-caliber rifle, aiming at the burly man leading the squad
into ambush. He steadied his shaking hands, inhaled sharply and held
the breath. When they closed within five yards, he fired.[73]

* * * *

IN THE ALLEYWAY, Captain Day moved down the passage with
confidence. The head-on approach had never failed him before. He was
geared up for action, convinced that he would find the black bastard in
the fourth apartment and get revenge. Illumined from behind by the glow
of the wagon lantern, his silhouette was a perfect target when Charles
fired. Day saw the muzzle flash directly in front of him, but instantly, before his mind could register the significance of the blinding explosion, a
high-velocity round ripped through his broad chest and knocked him to
the ground. "I'm shot," he gasped. Lifting his head from the gutter and
summoning his remaining strength, Day turned toward his men and gave
them a final command. "Give it to him!"[74]

Ten feet ahead, the door flew open, crashing against the side of the
building. Charles stood on the threshold, leveling a rifle at the stunned
officers. "You white sons of bitches," he roared, "I'll give you all some!"[75]

Sergeant Aucoin finally sprang into action, firing wildly as the wood
framework around his target exploded in a shower of splinters. Charles
proved the better marksman. Shots blazed from his Winchester and a
.38-caliber round smashed through Patrolman Lamb's right eye socket
with sledgehammer force, shattering his skull and killing him instantly.[76]
Stunned by the ghastly spectacle, Corporal Trenchard froze momentarily,
then reflexively tried to return fire. Nothing happened. His gun was no
good. Poor maintenance caused its firing mechanism to malfunction, the
hammer stuck in a harmlessly half-cocked position.[77] Sitting ducks with
useless weapons, one empty, the other jammed, both surviving officers

scrambled backward and sheltered in the second apartment as Charles ducked into his room to reload. "I know I would have killed him if my gun hadn't gone bad on me," the corporal later swore.[78]

Both officers claimed they challenged the gunman despite the desperate situation. "I told him to go out into the yard where we could see him," Trenchard reported. "But he stayed in the doorway and then walked to the window, cussing us all the time."[79]

Surprised by the gunfire and the sudden reappearance of the officers, the room's third party remembered things differently.[80] "Those white men were scared," she told reporters. "I don't know which one was worse." As the terrified officers extinguished their lanterns and stared into the darkness, she predicted, less than comfortingly, "That man has a rifle and he's gonna kill y'all!"[81]

"I'll kill you white sons of bitches," Charles hollered, emboldened by the stunningly effective ambush.[82] Through the window, the surviving officers watched as he stepped into the passage and loomed over the fallen captain. "You son of a bitch," Charles exclaimed, surprised to find him breathing. "You ain't dead yet?"[83]

Day said nothing before the rifle barrel pressed against his nose and exploded. The gunpowder burned his face beyond recognition. Charles pumped three more bullets into the dead man's torso. "You sons of bitches," he raged toward the other room. "Come out here and I'll give you the same medicine."[84]

Glancing at the second victim, Charles decided not to waste any bullets. The patrolman's skull was sheared away, his brains splattered on the ground.[85] "My God, it's awful," Aucoin gasped. "It's awful."[86]

As the gruesome aftermath of the ambush unfolded, the officers stationed outside the kill zone responded to the sound of gunfire with stunning apathy. "At that time, I thought the nigger might run out and prepared to give it to him if he did," Patrolman Caspar Pincon told detectives. "After the first fusillade, the shooting stopped for a while." Thirty minutes passed with no word from inside. Growing uneasy, the patrolman finally approached the building and peered into the darkened alley. "I heard groans and thought they might have stayed in the building to wait for reinforcements," he explained.[87]

The hunch was true, although Pincon seemed to miss the obvious point that he and the others stationed outside the property *were* the reinforcements. Only ten yards from where Charles holed up, the two surviving officers were holding their position in the second room. Defending themselves from cowardice charges, they later claimed to have shouted for backup and pointed out the precarious situation. "We were helpless without ammunition or firearms," Aucoin argued.[88] Reporters suggested that his partner could have unloaded the jammed gun and given him the unused cartridges, since both officers were carrying department-mandated .32-caliber Colts.[89]

Two doors from the survivors, Charles was waiting for the furious climax when officers stormed into the alleyway. But as minutes passed, he slowly realized they were unwilling to make the first move—or any move—and decided to explore his options.[90] Following blood traces he left behind, investigators later determined Charles had clambered into the cramped space under the eaves, which ran the building's length. He crawled end to end, confirming there were no viable escape routes and returned to his room. Gingerly cracking the door and stepping into the darkened alleyway, Charles made his way to the rear of the property and pushed through a rotten fence, entering an abandoned two-story structure, but he discovered no better prospects for a getaway.[91]

After returning to his room again, Charles changed into a fresh shirt and considered his diminishing options, finally resolving to burst through the front gate with guns blazing.[92] There would be no chance of survival. Charles took his Colt revolver and Winchester rifle, along with a small pouch stuffed with ammunition. Then he reentered the passage, walking directly past the second apartment, where the surviving officers were positioned near the entrance. Not a sound. When reporters questioned them, both men swore to have seen nothing. "It's a puzzle to me how Charles got out of that room," Trenchard claimed.[93]

Charles approached the gate and scanned the street outside, stunned to realize that he had a clean shot at the only two police officers who were visible; they were standing sixty yards away and paying surprisingly little attention to the yellow structure. From a standing position, he aimed and fired, sending the round snapping between them—a narrow miss.[94]

Despite the ferocious gunfire and the long silence that followed, Patrolman Cantrelle and Corporal Perrier had been inexplicably stationary for more than two hours. Now they sprang into action. "The rifle shot whizzed by our heads," the corporal described. "Cantrelle dropped down and wheeled away from the corner so quickly that I thought he was shot."

Cantrelle was unharmed. For the second time that evening, the rookie burst through the door of Julius Stendel's Drugstore and frantically used the telephone to call for backup. Although the store was only three blocks away, an hour passed before he returned to the scene and reunited with his corporal, who had also taken flight at the sound of gunfire. Both officers would insist that they had been looking for phones. Neither returned to the ambush scene until after reinforcements arrived. Addressing the questionable timing of his belated decision to make the call, Perrier explained, "I didn't think of telephoning for assistance until the rifle shot came dangerously close to my head."[95]

Shortly after five o'clock on Tuesday morning, dozens of patrolmen and detectives were finally converging on the neighborhood. Sergeant Aucoin and Corporal Trenchard had spent more than two hours in hiding as Charles moved freely throughout the property, but the sound of reinforcements finally drew them outside. Still the ranking officer on scene, Aucoin sheepishly ordered patrolmen to establish a cordon, before directing detectives to scale the neighboring building and fire into the room. The bullets crashed through the door without a response. The officers inched toward the building and peered inside. There were no signs of life. That proved to be the remedy for reviving Aucoin's initiative. The sergeant grabbed an ax, stepped forward, and smashed down the door with two heavy blows. Officers piled through the doorway and into the dim room. One glance confirmed the inexplicable. Though cornered and outnumbered, Charles had made a clean getaway.[96]

* * * *

BEFORE DAWN ON Tuesday morning, police officers were combing the neighborhood around the Fourth Street murder scene, assisted by huge numbers of white civilians.[97] Wild rumors circulated that the fugitive was holed up somewhere nearby—*right there!*—sending them scrambling in seriocomic stampedes. "He's up in the garret," someone yelled, pointing to the window overlooking the street as men scattered to safety.[98] Determining that it was a false alarm, sheepish men reassembled around the building, only to rush toward a nearby outhouse when someone else shouted that Charles was in the sewage vault below. They tore up the floorboards and poured volleys into the noxious sludge, before dragging the outhouse from its foundation and predictably finding only human waste and paper scraps.[99]

As the search outside devolved into farce, detectives ransacked the suspect's shared room, searching for evidence and trying to establish a psychological profile. The space was unexceptional on first glance, the same as countless others inhabited by black laborers. There was a bedframe tucked in one corner of the room and shabby linens covering a worn mattress with a broken spring. An old trunk and some boxes containing personal things and clothes, little more than rags, stood by the foot of the bed. Pots and pans hung from the walls and a fireplace was evidently the primary heat source for cooking. Detectives found a bullet mold and metal tools for reloading cartridges above the mantelpiece, along with several battered leather holsters. On the whole, the possessions suggested there was nothing particularly special about the assassin, although they challenged early theories about his livelihood. If he was a professional criminal, he was a bad one.[100]

Despite the frustrating lack of physical evidence, the search provided some promising glimpses that he was a dangerous man. Searching the shabby clothes found scattered across the room, detectives found a small vial filled with cocaine in the pocket of some pants, pointing toward a disturbing connection to the drug epidemic "among the lower classes of negroes," which reporters had recently been promoting. Although the drug was more frequently used as an energy source among the city's working classes, its presence at the crime scene provided a possible motive, allowing reporters to proactively associate Charles with a sinister subculture. "His associates were the riffraff of the negro community," they concluded, based solely on a trace amount of cocaine that may not have belonged to him. "He made his home in the nooks where the unwashed masses abound, rarely seen on the streets except under the influence."[101]

Drugs aside, the fugitive's reading habits were perhaps even more alarming, shedding considerable light on his troubled mind. Neatly bound stacks of *Voice of Missions* revealed that Charles both consumed and sold the inflammatory publication. Leafing through editions, reporters were scandalized by what they read. "The editorials are anarchistic in the extreme and urge the negro that the sooner he realizes that he is as good as the white man, the better it will be for him," they shuddered, dubbing *Voice of Missions* the journal preferred by "haters of the white race." Articles promoting emigration, handbills denouncing lynching, and pamphlets advocating armed self-defense confirmed the ideological profile. Charles was a dangerous extremist who embraced radical notions like racial equality. The investigation also showed that he was actively writing. Considering his reading interests, even the mundane penmanship exercises in composition books were damning evidence. "Textbooks filled with handwriting showed that he burned the midnight oil," they described, "improving himself intellectually so that he might conquer the hated white race."[102]

Black observers, of course, would reach much different conclusions about Charles, although weeks would pass before contradictory opinions surfaced. After investigating the case and soliciting information from his acquaintances, civil rights activist Ida B. Wells would argue that Charles was the victim of character assassination by white journalists, who portrayed a nemesis to fit the horrible nature of his supposed crimes. "The reporters of the New Orleans papers, who were in the best position to trace the record of this man's life, made every possible effort to prove that he was a villain," she explained. "Because they failed to find any evidence that Charles was a lawbreaker and desperado, his accusers gave full license to their imagination and distorted the facts in every way possible to prove criminality, which the records absolutely refuse to show."[103]

While mainstream reporters imaginatively reframed the fugitive's reading and writing as evidence of conspiracy, Wells characterized them as what they actually were—attempts to resolve the most pressing dilemma of his time and place. "Robert Charles was not an educated man," she explained. "He was a student who faithfully investigated all phases of oppression from which his race has suffered."[104]

After consulting with his acquaintances, Wells convincingly argued that mainstream depictions of a dangerous fanatic were entirely fabricated. Considering the "law-abiding" and "peaceable" man described by those who actually knew him, she concluded. "So he lived and so he would have died had he not raised his hand to unprovoked assault and unlawful arrest on that fateful Monday night."[105]

Early on Tuesday morning, contradictory evidence hardly mattered in the immediate aftermath of a shocking double cop killing. But even as white reporters fanned out across the city and chased leads in the most sensational crime story in living memory, their interviews with the assassin's neighbors and acquaintances uncovered ambiguous glimpses of a more complicated figure. Speaking with reporters, forty-year-old Hyman Levy confessed that he was impressed by Charles, who was a frequent customer at his Poydras Street clothing shop. "He was a stylish negro," Levy explained, determining that he was "above the average darky in intelligence." While the sharply dressed scholar had guarded his privacy, the white salesman was surprised by the charges against him. "The negro was a puzzle to me," Levy confessed. "But he seemed so honest and upright that it hardly seemed possible to me that anything was wrong."[106]

The elderly occupants of the apartment complex where Charles ambushed the officers reported similarly positive descriptions. Although the mysterious tenant consciously maintained his distance, he nonetheless projected authority. "There was an air of elegance about Charles," they explained. Despite these characterizations verging on admiration from diverse parties, press observers had no interest in presenting a balanced portrayal under the circumstances, even if few witnesses were cooperating. Trying to make sense of his motives, reporters struggled to find anyone willing to say anything bad about him. "Although he was known to scores of negroes in New Orleans, curiously little can be learned of his habits," they confessed, before concluding, "He was known as a quiet, rather surly fellow who had little to say and generally performed his tasks in morose silence, but managed to convey the impression of being a man of more than ordinary intelligence."[107]

Confronted with evidence that Charles was an engaged student of race and politics, reporters eventually crafted a headline that unintentionally spoke more to their own tortured efforts to make sense of him: "MAKING OF A MONSTER." Supposedly, Charles began his career as the sort of "Zip Coon" character popularized by antebellum minstrel shows, putting on an aristocratic façade to conceal his true motives. They drummed up evidence that Charles was a charlatan who championed black nationalism to advance his personal ambitions and bragged that he "didn't have to do no more mudslinging" and could "live like a gentleman" thanks to the commissions he made in the emigration scheme, although they admitted to uncertainty regarding "exactly how he received his remuneration" and made no attempt to square his alleged windfall with his dismal living conditions. According to the half-baked theory, Charles gradually became a victim of his own fraud. Studying the propaganda to better mislead his marks, he started to actually believe the outrageous claims made by pamphlets, which were "cunningly designed to stir up discontent among the Africans." Then the real danger manifested. "Charles developed into a fanatic and neglected business to indulge in wild tirades," they surmised. "Money became a secondary consideration."[108]

While reporters struggled to reshape the narrative as the facts emerged, detectives were struggling to make sense of a crime that was shocking even by the standards of a notoriously lawless city. New Orleans had always been a dangerous place for its peace officers, but the previous decade was the deadliest in the department's history. A dozen officers had been killed in the line of duty, most of them in similar circumstances: caught alone in explosively escalating confrontations, either outnumbered or overpowered by known criminals, often in booze-fueled brawls. Charles was an unusual cop killer by comparison, particularly because case files revealed that he had no record in New Orleans. Coupled with his premeditation and the crime's disturbing political overtones, the ambush slayings were completely incompatible with the unassuming workingman described by his co-workers and acquaintances. Searching for a smoking gun, detectives kept on digging—and soon discovered a witness who could shed light on the suspect's twisted mind.[109]

Suffering through the "sweating process" at the Sixth Precinct police station, Leonard Pierce had given officers a name: Virginia Banks, his roommate's girlfriend and the supposed reason for the fateful rendezvous. Before noon on Tuesday, detectives had tracked down the mystery woman, searching her apartment and bringing her downtown to police headquarters. As she waited to be questioned, the twenty-six-year-old New Orleans native favorably impressed reporters, who scrutinized the "young, brown-skinned woman" and concluded she had "more than average intelligence." Editors allowed readers to make their own judgments by running her picture on the third page, showing a neatly dressed subject gazing pensively beyond the camera's eye.[110] Surrounded by hostile investigators, Banks soon put her sharp mind to good use, claiming she had slept through the shooting and only learned of the tragedy that morning. Banks described a one-sided relationship with Charles, which had begun three years earlier with a chance meeting at a social club. Although she was uninterested, she soon found herself in his sights. The unwanted suitor was low-key dangerous, keeping a pistol in a holster fastened around his waist at all times. When she asked why, Charles vaguely copped to serious crimes in Vicksburg, saying that "he wanted to get even with the white people and start a race war as soon as any policeman attempted to arrest him."[111]

Scanning the room, Banks saw that she was making a good impression and continued the story, her lover becoming more dastardly with every passing episode. She told detectives that Charles had abused her many times, once trying to strangle her and toss her body into a murky canal, only stopping when a passing tugboat spooked him and saved her life. More recently, he had taken her to Morris Park and forced her into the surrounding trees, stripping her naked and beating her savagely. When she tried to escape by train earlier in the month, Charles suddenly appeared in the passenger cabin. He reached into his pocket and produced a roll of bills, then a revolver that he menacingly placed beside him, threatening to wreck the train and kill its passengers. He forced her to return to the city and kept her hostage for three days, then dragged her into the streets, beating her and threatening her life again. She escaped narrowly and had been living in fear ever since, certain that Charles would return to finish the job. "I was afraid to have him arrested," she pleaded. "He was waiting to kill me when he shot Officer Mora."[112]

As with the participants in the confrontation outside her window, Banks produced a narrative in which fact and fiction were impossible to disentangle. Even accounting for some exaggerations, the portrait of Robert Charles as a raging psychopath was dubious, especially given his absence from police records. Yet parts of her story rang truthfully—he *had* been in trouble near Vicksburg, getting into an unexpected shooting scrape when he accompanied his brother to retrieve stolen property. Charles angrily denouncing white supremacy was certain, while abuse was absolutely possible despite his clean record. As a black woman, Banks knew that such crimes were a non-priority for officers in New Orleans, but they could easily put her in danger if her abuser learned that she had gone to police. And there were even reasons to believe that her explanation of his presence outside her home—a planned ambush—was credible. The roommates were apparently waiting outside her place for more than thirty minutes when they were stopped by officers, suggesting that Banks was not expecting midnight visitors. And while it was not especially uncommon, both men were armed. There were definitely some rough edges, but was it possible that Charles was a closer friend than Pierce admitted, that an impressionable teenager had willingly followed his mentor on a revenge mission against a woman who resisted his authority?

It was, although the other witness accounts called that characterization into question, as did his behavior on Monday evening—dressing up and bringing along a roommate seemed more befitting a hopeful boyfriend than a deranged one. But if there were reasons to believe or question her story, it was brilliantly tailored to satisfy her interrogators and save a woman who understood her dangerous proximity to a black man charged with unimaginable crimes. Banks confirmed what detectives already believed and gave reporters irresistibly scandalous details. According to her version, Charles was a villain with a mysterious history, a radical who stripped young women naked and threatened spectacular mass murders. Surrounded by skeptical white men predisposed to doubting her innocence but convinced of her partner's vicious nature, Banks turned the situation to her advantage. By giving them what they really wanted, she gave herself what she desperately needed—a new identity as a helpless woman in the hands of a sadistic fiend, the kind who could slip from the headlines and back into the shadows with so many of her sisters.

Armed with a motive as monstrous as the assassin's crimes, reporters were up and running with the description as Tuesday's newspapers reached the streets. Published before news of the double homicide spread, the morning editions were only bare outlines, flippantly reporting on the Dryades Street shooting by relating how "two blacks, who are desperate men and will no doubt be proven burglars, made it interesting and dangerous for three bluecoats."[113] But as news of the shocking double cop killing spread, the narrative soon changed. Informed by the story told by Banks and the evidence found in the assassin's room, the mainstream dailies had to strike a tricky balance. Although the specter of extremism would sell more than a few copies, portraying New Orleans under siege by black revolutionaries could lead to trouble and paralyze business, particularly with Charles on the loose and other conspirators unnamed. Editors cobbled together a consensus that was both alarming and reassuring. They determined that Charles was planning to assassinate Banks when the officers confronted him, but that his vicious nature and radical ideas ultimately inspired his fierce resistance, concluding, "The negro was just downright wicked and hunted for trouble."[114]

While press observers were actively creating the villain demanded by white readers, perhaps the biggest threat to the emerging narrative was not the man on the run, but rather the one in Charity Hospital, recovering from his wounds. Though sketched in crude stereotypes, Patrolman Mora's witness statement was unintentionally nuanced, capturing the perspectives of each participant and laying out the most plausible sequence of events. Officers had responded to a complaint and surprised two men who likely expected nothing more than a night on the town, acting with the aggression customary when confronting unknown black suspects. When one attempted to break away, a rookie's mistake dramatically escalated a harmless tussle and created a life-and-death situation. Although he escaped during the ensuing chaos, the wounded suspect had been left with a bleak choice: surrendering to face a gruesome death, or going out fighting. Traced to its logical conclusion, Mora's story pointed to the disturbing likelihood that structures intended to protect racial and social order in New Orleans had caused the tragedy. On a typical Monday evening, contingencies aligned during a routine confrontation between police officers and black suspects—the kind that happened countless times in any given month—leading to an unusual but logical outcome. Reconstructing the sequence from a hospital bed with surprising clarity, Mora almost seemed to grasp the problem, but ultimately failed to comprehend the chilling implications of his own near-death experience. "I was lying here, thinking of all the trouble a trifling negro has caused," he mused. "Do you know, there are plenty of negro thieves in New Orleans capable of causing just as much trouble?"[115]

Rather than questioning the heavy-handed tactics that escalated a run-of-the-mill stop, reporters chose to go in the opposite direction. Compared with the assassin, police officers had put up a dismal performance, raising serious questions about the competence of the guardians charged with defending the city from its "negro thieves." But if the spectacle of white men being so easily outgunned was alarming, press observers were not entirely without options. The stain could be lifted, at least partially, by praising the martyrs and reframing the narrative surrounding their deaths, beginning with the Tuesday afternoon editions and continuing in the days that followed. Rather than carelessly rushing to his death, largely driven to his doom by a misguided sense of racial superiority, John Day was an example to his fellow officers. Honoring a man who "was greatly admired by his superiors, as well as his subordinates," contemporaries remembered, "The brave captain was always in the vanguard when danger was expected."[116]

Yet even as correspondents prepared eulogies for the slain hero, the desire to celebrate the captain's virtues intermingled with an equally powerful compulsion to witness the terrible destructive power that had brought him down. Around seven o'clock on Tuesday morning, a grocery wagon arrived outside the yellow house on Fourth Street to collect his muscular corpse and bring it to the Orleans Parish Coroner's Office, where police officers were struggling to control the crowd of hundreds that gathered on the sidewalk and streets outside the morgue. As the wagon approached, onlookers jockeyed with one another to witness the macabre spectacle as the body passed. For those unable to catch a firsthand glimpse, correspondents reprinted the coroner's report in full and annotated the proceedings, describing Day's "terribly powder-burned" remains, and the gruesome trauma to his comrade. "The wound was a horrible one, almost as bad as a shot from a shell," they observed, before graphically detailing the damage caused by a high-velocity round. "The skull was completely shattered and the brain torn into rags."[117]

To those willing to confront death's savage face, the damage inflicted on Captain Day demanded a forceful response, yet his courageous end underscored the deficiencies plaguing the police. As civilians descended on the crime scene and the morgue, attention fixated on the surviving officers, who had abjectly failed to embody the captain's idealized masculinity and served as his photo negative. Lambasting the survivors as "wretchedly poor shots" who were found "hiding under the wings of two old negro women," editors condemned the men who allowed Day's murderer to escape unpunished.[118] Under a damning headline, "DEFECTIVE POLICE PISTOLS," they reported unfavorably on Trenchard's malfunctioning weapon and questioned the decision to arm officers with .32-caliber revolvers "conceded by experts to be entirely too small for police service and not used in any of the larger cities."[119] Perhaps sensing that his own inability to stop Charles might be questioned, Patrolman Mora eagerly distinguished himself from the disgraced corporal and reinforced those concerns. "My gun worked perfectly, but in my opinion, .32-caliber is too small a weapon," he said in self-exoneration. "I gave the nigger a fair fight and I feel sure that I hit him. Of course, a man can't do much with a little gun."[120]

Assigning blame and addressing the miserable state of policing in New Orleans was imperative, but with Charles and his co-conspirators in the wind, the more pressing concern was whether officers were up to the job—and if anyone doubted the stakes, the angriest white supremacist in New Orleans was ready to remind them. Publishing his regular *Daily States* editorial, Confederate veteran Henry Hearsey reflected on the crime and gave voice to rage. As it so often did in his estimation, the problem came down to emancipation, America's original sin. The misguided experiment in black freedom had been disastrous, so much so that Hearsey perceived a direct line between Reconstruction's street battles and the Fourth Street cop killings. Despite every opportunity, black residents were naturally unable to succeed, which enflamed the "native race hatred of the negro," men like Robert Charles. With law enforcement officers so clearly bested, Hearsey feared that it would "give the worst negroes a contempt for the police and encourage them to bolder crimes." The danger was much worse than previously understood. "Under the dark mass of humanity that surrounds us, all appears peaceful," he warned, "but we know not what hellish dreams are arising underneath, what schemes of hate or arson, murder and rape, are being hatched in the depths."

Within hours of the Fourth Street ambush, efforts to reimagine and reframe the narrative had begun, transforming a confrontation shaped by a series of harrowing contingencies into something far more menacing. Through wild leaps of racial logic and historical revisionism, the white supremacist mouthpiece refashioned a chance encounter on darkened streets into evidence of a bloody racial apocalypse generations in the making, "a servile uprising," in Hearsey's words, formerly hidden in the dark confines of black hearts and minds, but now blossoming into deadly violence that only promised to worsen. Driven only by race hatred, Charles had fired the first shots in a modern slave rebellion. For seasoned readers, there was nothing especially subtle about the piece. With patrolmen outgunned and outmanned, it was demanding a painfully costly measure that had proven necessary, time and time again, since emancipation. White men needed to restore order and retake the streets. The editor was calling out the mob.[121]

5

Flambeaux

By late Tuesday morning on July 24, 1900, scorching summer temperatures were already pushing beyond ninety degrees, but passions were burning much hotter as the sun beat down on the Fourth Street murder scene. Drawn by incendiary rumors that something terrible had taken place in the vicinity, huge crowds were descending on the working-class neighborhood, where black residents soon appreciated the dangerous volatility. Agitated white men swarmed into the area by the hundreds, milling in the streets and surrounding the ugly yellow building at the center of the action, where detectives were combing through the room shared by the suspects. Patrolmen had belatedly established a cordon to encircle the long-escaped assassin, but they showed less concern about protecting the crime scene, which quickly became public property as rubberneckers and souvenir hunters descended. They piled into the bloodstained alleyway and jostled one another as they waited impatiently to enter the room, then pushed inside and loudly condemned the villain behind the tragedy as they tore through his few remaining possessions.

As the details filtered back to those outside, morbid curiosity transformed into rage. Civilians armed with clubs, axes, and guns began to arrive in numbers, swearing vengeance. Blurring the blue line, many had been summoned by patrolmen, who were canvassing the neighborhood and enlisting white men to join the search. Most were temporarily satisfied to assist police officers, but frustrations mounted as it became more and more obvious that Charles had escaped. With the assassin nowhere to be found, some began searching for alternative targets. Burning his lair to the ground was the runaway favorite. Would-be arsonists made hasty preparations, but patrolmen were alerted to the danger and intervened with help from "the more cool and level-headed citizens," who pointed out the bedridden old women inside the building and made a convincing enough case against roasting them alive.[1]

Darting through the crowds, reporters dismissed murderous white rage as understandable emotion stirred by the tragedy. Yet when they saw black residents clustering on corners, warily eying the hot-tempered men they worked and lived alongside, the reporters spotted telltale signs—gestures, expressions, inflections, mannerisms—which absolutely confirmed some unknown conspiracy. Here was alarming evidence that black residents viewed Robert Charles not simply as a sympathetic figure, but also as a revolutionary. "Some of the bolder negroes began to swagger about as if proud of what had taken place," they described. "Some of them even became rash enough to boast of 'a few game niggers' being able to clean out the whole police force."[2] These were outlandish accusations. Surrounded by white men, heavily armed and hysterical, black residents were said to be brazenly sympathizing with the assassin. But the false narratives validated white paranoia and justified vicious scenes unfolding in the neighborhood, as disorderly search parties devolved into dangerous gangs, roaming the streets and striking with impunity. "A few blacks talked too much and were punched and rapped with clubs," reporters flippantly described, "and finally hurried to jail."[3]

The reality was more chilling. Patrolmen who had mobilized the vigilantes watched passively as they hunted, intervening at the last second to arrest the black victims and hustle them to Julius Stendel's Drugstore, where a patrol wagon picked them up and brought them to the Sixth Precinct lockup.[4] Outside the store, white gangs continued to abuse the shaken prisoners while rowdy onlookers cheered from banquettes and balconies, a strangely festive atmosphere more appropriate to a particularly raucous parade than a police response. But the wild energy served its purpose. The patrolmen and mobs were operating in tandem to retake the streets and drive black residents behind closed doors, transforming the mixed-race neighborhood surrounding the crime scene into an occupation zone. It was a preemptive strike on imagined revolutionaries and a terror campaign against prospective sympathizers. Reporters praised the officers for preventing "negro lynching bees" and approvingly described how "terror-stricken" black residents disappeared following the brutal displays of force.[5]

Among the prisoners inside the dilapidated station on Rousseau Street, it was impossible to distinguish between those attacked by civilians and those brutalized by the police. Nursing a battered face and badly swollen arm, twenty-four-year-old John Burns recounted his story to reporters. "I was just standing there when the cops jumped me," he complained. "They charged me with disturbing the peace and resisting."[6]

Throughout the morning, race-based arrest patterns defined the boundaries of acceptable behavior outside the Fourth Street crime scene. While dangerous white mobs roamed the neighborhood and attacked pedestrians randomly, black men were arrested for disturbing the peace.[7] Most were simply in the wrong place at the wrong time, often taken into custody while going about their regular business. Twenty-year-old Dan Hatter was caught up while making his usual morning rounds and delivering produce to grocery stores. "I haven't done a thing to be arrested," he worried. "If I lose my job, it'll be a shame."[8]

Twenty-one-year-old Edward McCarthy was exceptional among the detainees, a white Navy veteran working aboard a New York–based cargo ship that had completed the coastal trip to New Orleans. McCarthy was enjoying his furlough when he investigated the disturbances—and revealed himself to be dangerously moderate on race.[9] "He was standing at the corner when a man came along and said that all the negroes should be lynched," one witness remembered. "McCarthy argued it wasn't right that *all* of them should be lynched."[10]

The modest suggestion went down like a lead balloon. "Get a rope and let's lynch the nigger-loving bastard," someone shouted. The mob grabbed McCarthy, but before they could fashion a noose, patrolmen rescued the oblivious Yankee and charged him with loitering and disturbing the peace.[11] In court the next morning, the judge would give the defendant a chance to take back his inflammatory statements, asking him, "Do you consider a negro as good as a white man?"

"In body and soul, yes," McCarthy responded.

For standing by his principles, the young sailor was convicted of disturbing the peace.

Unable to pay the twenty-five-dollar fine, McCarthy received a thirty-day sentence, although according to savvy observers, he had been fortunate to avoid a self-imposed death sentence.[12] "As it was, he was pretty roughly handled," they concluded.[13]

McCarthy was in good shape compared to thirty-year-old George Meyers, who was also among those suffering in the station's holding cells. The black laborer had been arrested by two officers a few blocks from his home, but the patrol wagon was gone when they arrived at the drugstore. As the officers headed toward St. Charles Avenue to commandeer a vehicle, Corporal Trenchard sprinted up to them, wild-eyed and waving his gun. Overeager to demonstrate his authority, Trenchard had been challenging his rumored cowardice by energetically harassing black pedestrians all morning. Now as he joined the trio, the corporal seemed to be completely unhinged, jabbing the prisoner with his pistol at every step, so violently that white onlookers were convinced Meyers was the assassin. "Kill him! Lynch him!" they screamed.[14]

The arresting officers put the prisoner in an empty ice wagon and assigned a part-time supernumerary with less than two years on the force to protect him.[15] The decision was nearly deadly. Slowed down by a reluctant mule and delayed when a gang stormed aboard and assaulted Meyers, the short trip took over thirty minutes, but the situation only worsened when they reached the Rousseau Street station, where hundreds were gathered to welcome the wagons transporting black prisoners. White men punched, kicked, and tore the prisoner's flesh as his overmatched escort struggled to drag him inside. After taking a brutal five-minute beating, Meyers finally crawled through the doors, begging those inside to save him. Officers denied him medical attention and booked him for fighting and disturbing the peace before dragging him to the cells. According to reporters, "He was semi-conscious and bleeding profusely, the clothes were ripped from his back and his face was unrecognizable."[16]

Although the rookie patrolman emerged to raucous applause, the mood outside the station was darkening quickly. As word spread that one of the suspects from the Dryades Street shooting was being held inside, the conversation soon turned to storming the facility, overpowering the guards, and slaughtering the black prisoners inside. Confronted with the growing likelihood of a massacre, officers finally drew the line and decided to relocate the second most hated man in New Orleans to the high-security parish prison, which required a dangerous crosstown ride in the back of the patrol wagon. Leonard Pierce was understandably petrified, observing the mistreated captives around him and recognizing that law enforcement officers often cooperated with lynch mobs to stage choreographed kidnappings. Patrolmen forced him into the wagon, someone gave a signal, and the driver whipped his team as the officers held the crowd at bay—barely. Although he survived the downtown journey, Pierce faced a daunting court battle and the strong possibility that his end would be the same: a noose, this one legal, despite mounting evidence of his innocence. Scheduled to be arraigned on grave charges the following morning, he would remain behind the iron gates and brick walls of the South's most formidable building, protected from white residents who were growing more volatile as the manhunt for his deadly roommate intensified.[17]

* * * *

AROUND NOON ON Tuesday, Virginia Banks was at the center of the storm, nervously waiting at police headquarters as leads poured in from across New Orleans. She was relieved that detectives seemed to believe her story, but that changed when they told her she needed to identify Robert Charles, who had just been captured. With rumors swirling that the assassin once worked at Port Chalmette, an eager supervisor had spent the morning tracking down a former employee and passed along information about his whereabouts. Officers located the suspicious black man—surnamed Charles and said to resemble his description—shoveling coal at the American Sugar Refinery. They took him into custody and drove him downtown, where Banks would make the identification. As the door swung open and detectives paraded the miserable man into the room, she glanced up—and instantly realized they had the wrong man. Someone asked if she knew him. There was an excruciating pause, threatening to raise fresh questions about her story. Was she petrified that her abuser was still in the wind? Was she weighing the gut-wrenching choice between implicating the wrong man and sending police back in search of the person she loved? Whatever the cause behind the ambiguous silence, her composure concealed its true meaning. Seconds passed. Banks finally shook her head. Not him.[18]

Nearly doomed by his unfortunate surname, Aleck Charles escaped with his freedom, but he was hardly the only innocent black man threatened by what was quickly becoming the largest manhunt in the city's history. With every detective in the department assigned to the case—and seemingly every white man in New Orleans chiming in with supposedly valuable information gleaned from God knows where—police headquarters buzzed with activity all morning and afternoon. Some leads were more promising than others. Bursting into the building, an excited young man exclaimed that he had just encountered Charles, wearing a black hat and leaning menacingly against a lamppost only blocks away. Just as the white youth passed by, the assassin had suddenly lunged at him and shoved a gun to his head, growling that he had already killed two white men and was ready to do a few more. The witness somehow escaped to tell the tale, but when patrolmen rushed to the scene, the improbably theatrical villain was nowhere to be found.[19]

Deluged with false leads, police commanders took comprehensive measures, laying a dragnet that disrupted the rhythms of mid-week business. Fittingly, the waterfront served as the focal point of the search. If the Mississippi River had long been the city's commercial lifeblood, the muddy artery was also the greatest contributor to its perpetual crime problem. Carrying goods that had been shipped southward and from across the Gulf of Mexico to the prosperous hub, the river also provided mobility and comparative anonymity for passengers, some more savory than others. Shady characters—desperadoes, gamblers, and escaped slaves—came and went freely, making a mockery of the law.[20] Fearful that Charles might hitch a ride on one of the steamboats bobbing along the levee, commanders moved to shut down a promising escape route, with unpromising results.[21]

As patrolmen chased phantoms on the levee, others scanned the wilderness stretching between the city limits and Lake Pontchartrain, a

soupy tangle of cypress groves and heavy vegetation once feared as a breeding ground for deadly miasmas and a refuge for self-liberated slaves. The
notorious "backswamp" was enjoying a resurgence in the public imagination, as local authors capitalized on a thriving market for antebellum
mythmaking.[22] Transporting readers back to a time when slavery was
"one of the pillars of our prosperity and progress," one historian described
how the devilish labyrinth had undermined the "benevolence and patri-
archal affection" between master and property.[23] Lurking on the fringes
of civilization, fugitives stole provisions under cover of darkness before
retreating into the wasteland. They undermined the slave regime and
made fools of New Orleans police officers who needed no help in that
regard, a "worthless pack of knaves" and "contemptible body" whose reputations had scarcely improved since the antebellum period.[24]

Nobody had treated the force more contemptuously than Bras-Coupé,
the most infamous black villain in the city's history. Three decades before emancipation, the one-armed fugitive had made a home in the backswamp, defying slave patrols, bloodhounds, and skilled trackers with
superhuman ease. The uncatchable slave had become a local obsession,
dominating white men's conversations in workshops, markets, and commercial exchanges and following them home, where his name was "pronounced in hushed and subdued tones to frighten children." And adults.
When he was finally murdered for reward money by a treacherous accomplice, white residents paraded through Jackson Square in droves to view
his decomposing and badly mangled body, which had allegedly suffered
postmortem mutilation at the hands of police officers. Authorities buried him in an unmarked grave in the potter's field, smartly recognizing
the potential for even worse abuse.[25]

As patrolmen searched for Robert Charles in swamps that evoked antebellum terrors, municipal authorities confronted the growing likelihood that familiar criticisms would resurface. For decades, successive
administrations had been charged with fostering a permissive culture
toward crime. Whenever there was a high-profile outrage, feckless patrolmen and corruptible politicians inevitably shared the blame. Despite the
usual campaign promises and partisan blame games, progress was maddeningly elusive. The department's shoestring budget and consistently

poor record made it a political liability whenever public attention turned its way, no matter who was in charge. And now Charles was rapidly becoming a painful reminder that systems designed to protect white residents from "the negro's savage nature" were as vulnerable as they had been during the days of Bras-Coupé. In any case, the escalating crisis was a worst-case scenario for a three-month-old machine administration on a shaky political foundation, threatening to crush its ambitions beneath the weight of history. Everything rested on finding and neutralizing the assassin. Quickly.[26]

Farther beyond the city limits, white men also responded to past and present terrors as the explosive news spread to nearby communities. For generations, planters in the outlying parishes had viewed New Orleans ambivalently, profiting from its insatiable appetite for sugar and cotton, while fearing its notorious dens of vice and crime would send dangerous exports their way. Slave patrols had secured the countryside during the antebellum period, but emancipation unleashed new violence, as white supremacist paramilitaries waged a bloody insurgency across Louisiana.[27] Untold hundreds of black men were murdered during Reconstruction, while nearly three hundred more had been killed by statewide lynch mobs since its fall—almost triple the number who had been legally executed over the same period. Nobody had been convicted related to the unlawful killings.[28]

Even by the brutal standards of the emerging Jim Crow South, the region surrounding New Orleans had been particularly dangerous ground in recent years. Eleven black men and an interracial couple had been lynched in neighboring Jefferson Parish in the 1890s, making it the nation's second deadliest site of mob violence during the decade.[29] A newcomer to the parish captured the contagious bloodthirstiness, saying her neighbors had "a great antipathy toward the nigger in general" and were "daily shooting and lynching them without apparent cause," before confessing that she had begun to feel the same urges.[30] Among the dead was James Hawkins, who mysteriously vanished from the Gretna jail cell where he was being held for slapping a white police officer's nephew, allegedly as revenge for his father's killing. Reporters had pieced together the events leading to his death by the time his bloated corpse was recovered from the Mississippi River several days after the kidnapping, weighted down and so badly mutilated that it sickened the crowds that came to enjoy the spectacle. Masked vigilantes had encountered no resistance when they stormed the prison and strangled the victim before dumping his body.[31] Speaking with frightened black refugees who relocated to New Orleans in the aftermath, reporters were told that such disappearances from police custody were common in the parish, authorities "often putting a negro in jail and evidently losing the key, as he is never heard from again."[32] As the search for Charles expanded, journalists confidently predicted another lynching if he was foolish enough to be captured in Jefferson Parish.[33]

The same danger extended to any black man who raised suspicions while passing through the killing fields outside New Orleans, particularly because nobody could actually describe the fugitive with any certainty. Searches were already underway when the first vague description appeared in the Tuesday afternoon edition of the *Daily States*, but the accompanying composite sketch looked nothing like the hand-drawn images soon circulating in the morning dailies, supposedly based on family photographs taken from the ambush scene. Robert Charles would continue to change appearance as the search continued. He was "very black," unless he was a "brown skinned negro," or rather a light-colored "mulatto." The assassin preferred a clean shave—actually, it was a "long black moustache," either neatly clipped or drooping over the corners of his mouth. He was five nine, although he sometimes stood six foot two. He was thirty-seven years old and entering middle age, yet he could also be described as a younger man around thirty.[34] Without a meaningful description, searchers adopted the same vague criteria that caused police to stop Charles in the first place: any thinly articulated suspicion that could be attached to any unknown black man who passed within shooting distance. Fifteen miles upriver from New Orleans, a station agent noticed two dark-skinned men hitching a ride on a freight train and arrested them on suspicion that one was Charles, although the evidence was dubious. The "Cuban-colored negro" was missing the fugitive's mustache, but his upper lip was "said to have the appearance of being freshly shaven." Protesting that they were brothers heading to the St. James Parish sawmills, both men were locked up until authorities could send someone to clear things up.[35]

Across the river from New Orleans, search parties were even more aggressive. Bands of armed men lined the railroad tracks running through downtown Gretna, stopping trains to search for "suspicious-looking negroes."[36] After a frustrating afternoon, things picked up in the evening, when searchers spotted a black man resting on a coupling between two boxcars and dragged him from the perch. Assuming that he was about to witness a lynching, a second black man made a break for safety as the train slowed down, bounding toward the locomotive and zigzagging as gunmen simultaneously fired a wild fusillade. As he leaped through the cab and then onto the sidewalk in desperation, the fleeing man was wrestled to the ground. Someone stepped forward and fired toward his writhing body from point-blank range, but he wriggled free after a mad scramble and managed to escape, apparently unscathed. Authorities pried the captured hitchhiker from the mob and took him into custody. A close examination revealed that he looked nothing like Charles, but deputies decided to keep him locked up for his own safety.[37] It was a wise decision. Before sunrise, the gunmen finally hit a black man hitching a train home—after closely examining thirty-year-old William Rollins, they concluded he was the wrong man and sent him to be treated for gunshots to the hip and buttocks.[38]

The near-fatal encounters in Jefferson Parish showed how vigilantes were using the crisis as cover for otherwise controversial acts of violence that strategically enforced white dominance. New Orleans editors had condemned the lynching epidemic for damaging the city's reputation, particularly because too many killings had been indefensible, among them the murders of Lottie and Patrick Morris, an interracial couple whose twelve-year-old son identified a policeman in the mob who shot his parents to death and decapitated them.[39] Under normal circumstances, only the most naive or cynical observers would defend random attacks on black migrants in the countryside, but the Charles manhunt legitimized a terror campaign targeting a labor force whose mobility made them both economically valuable and socially dangerous. With a black radical assassin on the loose, even the vaguest suspicions were an unassailable defense—and the same editors who condemned the Jefferson Parish lynch mobs promoted violence that drew its potency from its wantonness. "Every suspicious negro was stopped and questioned," they promised. The random attacks were a clear message. Because *any* black man could be "mistaken" for Charles, *every* black man should prove themselves non-threatening. In case the lessons from a bloody decade had been forgotten, this was white supremacy as it was: arbitrary, deadly, self-justifying. Behave accordingly.[40]

Back in New Orleans, white gangs were sending the same message. Patrolmen were standing down as troublemakers roamed the streets in bands, threatening to murder anyone foolish enough to challenge them. Nobody dared. Some frightened black residents bunkered down inside their homes. Others fled to calmer quarters, sheltering with friends and family. Meanwhile, nearby business owners nervously watched the chaos and decided to close shop, choosing to lose sales rather than risking property destruction. With afternoon temperatures surging, the crowds gradually thinned and a strange calm descended on the normally lively community, where shuttered windows and empty streets evoked a ghost town.[41]

The peace was only temporary. After finishing their shifts and refueling, workingmen descended on the murder scene as the sun dipped below the horizon, with full bellies and rekindled appetites for violence. The crowds slowly gathered shape and purpose. Glimmering streetlights transformed the streets around the yellow house into disturbing phantasmagorias, "weird and exciting," as men brimming with nervous energy stalked back and forth under a dimly flickering orange glow, "shadowy and ghostlike" in the haze. A few dozen patrolmen had been assigned to control the nighttime crowds, but they were quickly outnumbered by twenty to one.[42] The strange atmosphere and intense emotions set the stage for extraordinary scenes. As weary patrolmen half-heartedly confronted bloody-minded civilians who viewed themselves as allies rather than adversaries, a remarkable dialogue unfolded, revealing the ambiguous and contested nature of their dueling roles: what did law and order really mean?

Officers reassured the growing mob that authorities would hold Charles accountable, calling on them to support the investigation by staying calm.

Demonstrators countered by pointing out the common cause they shared, complaining "it was very tough that niggers could come and shoot down two policemen and the police must guard the niggers from the people who wanted to avenge them," according to reporters who witnessed the scene. When the police and court system failed, they argued, the black community should be held responsible, collectively. Police officers reassured the crowd that they understood its noble intentions, saying "if they knew where the nigger was, they would let them go ahead," but the possible destruction caused by mass retribution was too risky. The mob was too righteous to disperse, but also too dangerous to unleash.[43]

With neither the police nor the mob willing to delegitimize the other side, a cagey game of cat-and-mouse played out during a surreal night in the restless city. Some ambitious spokesman would stand on a street corner and launch a tirade against black criminals, drawing a crowd and rousing them to action. When the feverish mood seemed close to reaching critical mass, patrolmen would rush to the spot and break up the gathering. After a short lull, some group would assemble a safe distance away, beginning the cycle again. As the hours passed, a rotating cast of oddball Napoleons took the stage: a comically short-statured merchant from a leading financial house and a peg-legged veteran wearing a soiled and rumpled Confederate uniform and brandishing a double-barreled shotgun, among others. Inevitably, they made a mess of things. As the succession of speakers stammered, stumbled, and repeated themselves, fluffing their lines, the mostly unarmed audience members shot each other sidelong glances, unsure if they should overlook the obvious incompetence and play along, but never managing to get past the silliness before patrolmen spoiled the party. The mood grew darker as the spectacle edged toward burlesque, wavering somewhere between deadly seriousness and slapstick farce. "There was the spirit of fight in the crowd, although in some respects it was ludicrous," reporters confessed, describing the odd cocktail of mockery and simmering race hatred. "The laughter mingled with a deeper undertone, which meant trouble if there was a start made."[44]

No spark came. For all the combustible material, none of the outmatched speakers could seize the moment and bring the crowd to mobbing. As the hours passed, the restless energy gradually ebbed and when rumors began spreading just after midnight that Charles had been cornered somewhere in the suburbs, commanders sensed the moment was right to peacefully disperse the gathering. Unwilling to force a confrontation, the disappointed rioters melted away into the darkness. An uneasy calm returned to the crime scene. Patrolmen stood around on the surrounding street corners, discussing the deadly ambush and their own role in breaking up the mob. Among the few black residents who remained in the neighborhood, the bravest peered through cracked doors and covered windows, careful not to draw attention from the officers who were barely protecting them.[45]

Although the scenes around the Fourth Street crime scene had been comparatively subdued, elsewhere in New Orleans there had been more dangerous confrontations. Several blocks from where the mobs were pleading with officers to allow them to take revenge, two black men had been attacked with bricks and stones before they managed to escape. Others had been chased down and assaulted nearby, but perhaps the most ominous scenes had been at Lee Circle, located on the edge of downtown, where a crowd of "angry and excited men" gathered and began a march down St. Charles Avenue. They made it a dozen blocks before a councilman showed up and managed to talk them down.[46]

It was not the only close encounter between a politician and a violent mob. Around one o'clock in the morning, demonstrators retreating from the crime scene spotted a black pedestrian and chased him to the front of a home on Jackson Avenue, where another councilman, William Mehle, had been preparing for bed after a long day. With the new mayor traveling for business and pleasure, the ambitious machine operative was temporarily serving in his place. Mehle had visited the Fourth Street crime scene to address the angry crowds earlier that afternoon. Speaking with reporters, he had expressed confidence that the situation would remain calm—a prediction that now seemed disastrously misguided as he investigated the disturbance and discovered his neighbors attempting to murder an innocent man on his doorstep.[47] For the second time in twelve hours, the acting mayor talked down an angry mob. The attackers gave up the chase, promising to reassemble the following night for a real hunting party as they finally headed home. For the time being, the crisis had passed.[48]

* * * *

ON WEDNESDAY MORNING, July 25, 1900, New Orleans residents woke up to oppressive humidity and ominous clouds. Things had settled down momentarily, but as the sun rose and the workday began, white and black workingmen watched one another with more suspicion than usual. Segregated groups clustered on job sites citywide, swapping rumors, debating the likelihood of violence, and discussing how it might affect them, as victims or as perpetrators. The mood was especially volatile around the watering holes favored by white laborers, where the only topics of discussion were the recent murders and what to do about them. Everyone agreed that the problem was much bigger than a single assassin. Most believed that conspirators were hiding the fugitive and that the black community was celebrating his crimes, suspicions that were quickly becoming consensus wisdom. The prospects for collective accountability were sky-high and rising.[49]

Wednesday's first chance for real trouble was the arraignment of Leonard Pierce, which was scheduled to take place around midday in a courtroom located in the same complex as the prison.[50] Five deputies posted outside his cell led the prisoner to the hearing chambers, where patrolmen were stationed as reinforcements—but there were surprisingly few witnesses in the gallery and the proceedings went smoothly, aside from one minor plot twist. Prosecutors were planning to charge Pierce with attempting to shoot Sergeant Aucoin, but after consulting with the magistrate, they additionally charged him as an accessory to Patrolman Mora's wounding. After a perfunctory hearing, the judge remanded the prisoner without bond and deputies returned him to his cell, where Pierce continued to protest his innocence.[51] "I'm telling you the truth," he pleaded. "Charles never told me to go against the white people."[52]

Several hours after the hearing, the presiding judge departed his chambers and made the short journey from the downtown justice complex to an unassuming cottage on Jackson Avenue, where one of the year's most significant public events was underway. Politicians, business leaders, and other prominent citizens gathered at the Day family home before the captain's funeral service, passing through the parlor and pausing before the open casket to pay respects to a fallen hero.[53] The benevolent association had taken charge of arrangements for the former union head, while police headquarters was responsible for the most elaborate garland: a three-foot wreathe, constructed from purple flowers and emblazoned with a solemn declaration, "Answered the Last Roll Call."[54] Surrounded by sympathetic friends, his widow sat to the side, heartbroken. "They say that he's a hero," she sobbed. "What poor consolation now that he's gone."

Around four o'clock in the afternoon, a priest administered last rites and pallbearers bore John Day's body into the gloom outside, where a massive crowd was mostly failing to maintain a respectful silence. Headed by sixty officers in dress uniform, the grim procession marched on toward St. Michael's Church, where bells tolled and somber organs announced the cortège. Candles shed mellow light over the mourners in the sanctuary, while thousands gathered in the streets outside, straining to hear the eulogy. Father Michael Coughlan began by praising the "noble, brave, and generous captain," saluting "a man who loved to do his duty," to his city, country, and God, to his parents, wife, and child. Then his sermon turned ominous, his voice taking on a menacing timbre as he pivoted into more dangerous territory. Coughlan praised the police and defended them against public criticism, then addressed the most divisive events in the city's recent history: the assassination of Chief David Hennessy and the bloody retribution that followed, which made New Orleans infamous during the early 1890s. When nine cases against the alleged killers ended without convictions, jurors were accused of corruption and cowardice. Nearly a decade after those events, Coughlan warned the mourners against repeating the mistake, darkly concluding, "I trust the assassin will be found and brought to justice."[55]

Among those attending the funeral, Superintendent Dexter Gaster was listening to the sermon with special attention, recognizing the priest's faith statement for what it was: a warning. Should civil authorities fail to respond decisively enough, mobs would take matters into their own hands—precisely as they had done when jurors denied them justice in the

Hennessy case. Ambushed on his doorstep and shredded by shotgun blasts, the dying Hennessy had supposedly unmasked his killers with a single word: "Dagoes."[56] With everyone convinced that the beloved chief was murdered by the Mafia for daring to oppose its criminal agenda, then detective Gaster had been given "the power to conduct investigations according to his own theories and plans," which included arresting more than two hundred Sicilian immigrants with little or no evidence.[57] The dragnet had earned him a big promotion to head the police force, but when the shaky cases crumbled in the courtroom, a lynch mob headed by leading reform politicians and businessmen finished what he started, storming the prison where the defendants were being held and killing eleven captives, including some who had just been acquitted. As carnage unfolded in the predominantly black neighborhood bordering Congo Square, an elderly resident supposedly exclaimed, "Thank God it wasn't a Negro who killed him."[58]

Now her words had become a prophesy. After a decade of worsening race relations, New Orleans was once again on the verge of chaos, the dread hanging over the city becoming more palpable as the afternoon shadows lengthened and clouds gathered overhead. When the service concluded, pallbearers loaded John Day's corpse into a hearse and the wagon headed toward the family plot in St. Louis Cemetery No. 1, located only a block from where he had been killed. As mourners streamed from St. Michael's Church with God's blessing to restore order by any means, Superintendent Gaster understood more than anyone that he was racing the clock to stop a second massacre. Detectives were combing through too many leads, as sergeants canvassed the black community, pressuring informants and threatening doctors who may have treated the fugitive. Captains were reassigning patrolmen and supernumeraries to watch railroad depots and search the countless ships docked along the miles-long levee. Special detachments were detailed to the suburbs, where reports were flying thick and fast that the fugitive was spotted, cornered, and captured—here, there, nowhere. But despite an unprecedented manhunt for an unprecedented menace, Robert Charles was a free man. And New Orleans was out of time.

* * * *

SIGNS OF TROUBLE appeared shortly before sunset at a predictable location. A grassy acre centrally located on St. Charles Avenue near the downtown business district, Lee Circle was a traditional site of demonstrations, unruly or otherwise. Bordered by a busy roundabout, it had been known by another name until Redemption, when municipal authorities commissioned an enclosed monument to celebrate the victory over tyranny.[59] While a severe financial crisis delayed the ambitious proposal, the opening ceremony was a stunning triumph. Thousands gathered on George Washington's birthday, among them Jefferson Davis, an army of Confederate veterans, and Robert E. Lee's daughters, celebrating as their father's larger-than-life bronze was revealed. Perched on a marble column towering above his misty-eyed former soldiers, the weary general looked northward, reminding white residents, according to local lore, to never turn their backs on a Yankee.[60]

Around seven o'clock on Wednesday evening, another massive crowd gathered beneath General Lee's contemplative gaze, renewing the promise to defend New Orleans against its enemies: "Kill the niggers! Shoot them down!"[61]

Responses came from the shadows. "Hang 'em! String 'em up!"

As the energy gathered, prospective mob leaders announced themselves and made impromptu speeches. The results were far more promising this time. When someone tried to caution the crowd, unappreciative listeners picked him up and pitched him over a fence. This was no place for peacemakers. White men had been waiting for catharsis for nearly two days. Now it was finally at hand. Those who had witnessed the debacle on Tuesday night could sense the difference, an oppressive, sinister atmosphere. It was a serious tonal change over the previous twenty-four hours. No more grandstanding, no more farce. "Oratory was applauded, but only one brand seemed suitable," they explained. "And that was the violent type."[62]

Perhaps nobody on the police force was better prepared to handle the situation than Sergeant Gabriel Porteous, but as the forty-seven-year-old watched the scene with growing concern, he knew that his badly outnumbered squad was no match for a determined mob.[63] Formerly a boss teamster who switched careers shortly before the general strike, Porteous had quickly demonstrated a genuine talent for dealing with unruly crowds, honed by years supervising rowdy drivers. Matching his impressive physique with a commanding presence, the sergeant had earned good conduct commendations during the annual mayhem of Mardi Gras more than once. But it was his reputation for treating men fairly across race and class divides that won him admirers in diverse circles. With over a decade of policing experience, Porteous was the rare commander who earned both respect and affection from his men.[64] "Gabe was one of the most popular officers on the force," observers vouched. "He knew how to manage a crowd."[65]

The past few days had been particularly tough for the highly regarded veteran, who had personal connections to the families affected by the tragedy. That afternoon, Porteous had been a pallbearer for John Day, his longtime friend.[66] Further complicating things, his brother-in-law was being charged with cowardice for his actions during the ambush: his younger sister Katie had been married to Ernest Trenchard for fourteen years.[67] But despite the heavy emotional burden, the sergeant was maintaining his professionalism, earning strong reviews for effectively handling the rowdy mob at the Fourth Street crime scene the previous evening, coolly appealing to more reasonable men and eventually convincing them to return home.[68]

By comparison, the situation at Lee Circle was already becoming more dangerous and the sergeant's persuasion was going nowhere.[69] The violence started gradually, simmering frustration building toward bloodthirsty rage. Growing restless, opportunists struck out in groups, making good on aggressive boasts by attacking black pedestrians who unwittingly strayed too close.[70] Although patrolmen made half-hearted attempts to chase them down, the first successful forays only emboldened the wandering bands. Men ran beside passing streetcars, pounding the trolleys with sticks and barking at the petrified black riders. Finally, someone suggested that the mob should march on the crime scene. Shortly after nine o'clock on Wednesday evening, fully two hours after they began assembling at Lee Circle, white men began marching up St. Charles Avenue. Eager to avoid repeating Tuesday night's toothless scenes, self-appointed field marshals shadowed the mass, prodding it into formation. Spanning the wide boulevard, the torchlight procession took on a more menacing appearance, surging more than a mile upriver along the boulevard, before making a sharp right turn and passing within a block of the Fourth Street murder scene. Anticipating trouble, police commanders had deployed additional patrolmen to protect the neighborhood, but they showed no interest in disrupting the marchers, who finally stopped when they reached Morris Park, a block from the cemetery where John Day was buried.

Despite the scattered attacks around Lee Circle that evening, there had been no serious bloodshed. Now speakers rose to address the men once more, urging them to defend women and children from predators, namely by murdering any black person they came across. As the scenes edged toward mayhem, one young speaker attempted a last-second intervention. Just twenty-two years old, St. Clair Adams was already known in the right social circles for the right reasons. The president of his Tulane Law School graduating class was an accomplished orator who had campaigned for the machine during the previous election cycle, when he earned a reputation as "one of the most entertaining speakers in the ranks."[71] With chaos threatening, Adams tried to use his talents to talk down the crowd, starting with a predictable applause line by proudly declaring he "had grown up in the city and stood up for the Caucasian race."[72] The crowd roared its approval, but the mood turned when Adams argued the assassin was the only black man who should be lynched. "That's not what we want," they replied. "We don't want you! Let's get the niggers. Kill any we find!"[73]

Sensing an opening, thirty-nine-year-old Samuel Cowen took his chance. Standing on a soapbox to address the crowd, he announced himself as the mayor of a nearby town and said that he had come to New Orleans to assist its white residents. His audience seemed unmoved, but the politician had another trick up his sleeve, waving his arms to demand attention. "I've killed a nigger before," he proclaimed, "and in revenge of the wrong done to you and yours, I'm willing to kill a nigger again. The only way you can teach these niggers a lesson is to lynch a few of them. That's the only thing to do—kill them, string them up, lynch them."[74]

The crowd perked up. This was the speech they wanted. "On to the parish prison," he cheered. "Let's lynch Pierce!"[75]

The mob surged forward. Dividing into two main bodies and following parallel routes along Franklin and Rampart Streets, they headed toward the downtown business district and the prison complex where Leonard Pierce awaited his fate. Both groups searched for victims as they marched. The second party drew first blood. Employed as a porter by the Mutual Life Insurance Company, forty-two-year-old Thomas Sanders was the only black passenger riding in a passing streetcar when the mob forced it to stop. Attackers beat him with sticks and rocks, gashing his scalp and knocking him unconscious before a bullet shattered his kneecap and a Bowie knife plunged into his side. Convinced that he was dead, the mob moved on, but not before someone grabbed his watch. Horrified witnesses carried Sanders to his home and called a physician, who pronounced the patient's condition dire. After thirty minutes, an ambulance arrived and brought the gravely wounded man to Charity Hospital, where he slowly recovered from life-threatening injuries.[76]

Minutes after the first attack, the Rampart Street mob found a second victim. Alexander Ruffin had arrived in town after a twenty-six-hour shift as a Pullman porter on a Chicago-based passenger train. He was planning to visit his ailing son when he boarded a streetcar near the station. "I saw a lot of white folks shouting to 'get the niggers,'" Ruffin remembered. "Two or three men jumped on the car and started after me. One of them hit me over the head and they started shooting at me. I jumped out and ran, though I'd done nothing wrong."[77] Ruffin managed to escape death when white bystanders rescued him, but he carried an unwelcome souvenir from his fateful trip south for the rest of his life. "Two bullets were in his body," his attorneys would advise city officials. "One was removed, but the other cannot be. The injuries were very severe and he almost lost his life."[78]

After seriously wounding two victims, the Rampart Street rioters sought out weapons, focusing on the pawnshops clustered on the outskirts of downtown. Spotting firearms in the windows of Jake's Place, a local brokerage, the mob smashed the windows and forced its way inside. Some rioters armed themselves, but others bypassed the guns and focused on the store's jewelry and valuables. Alerted to the looting, storeowner Jacob Fink showed up and tried to convince them otherwise, but the intervention ended badly. Someone punched Fink in the mouth, sending him crashing to the ground with two broken teeth.[79] Reporters echoed the anti-Semitism of many readers, approvingly describing, "As the hooting crowd went along, the Jews who keep these places hastily put up their shutters."[80]

Looting was a mixed blessing for the Rampart Street mob. Although heavily armed, the undisciplined men trained gunfire on unintended victims, including fellow rioters and white bystanders. Meanwhile, the procession had squandered momentum, losing its cohesiveness and purpose. Some participants returned home to count the spoils. Others wandered aimlessly and searched for targets of opportunity. But the most dedicated churned forward toward Orleans Parish Prison, followed by swarms of curious onlookers. The reorganizing mob announced its approach with random gunfire as it bore down on the prison complex where police commanders had concentrated their strength. They had allowed the mob to rampage with comparatively little resistance, choosing to establish a strong defensive perimeter around the lockup, where Leonard Pierce was among the many black prisoners inside. It was a high-risk gamble with the potential to end disastrously. If officers were unable—or unwilling—to hold the line, for the second time in less than a decade, New Orleans would see the deadliest mass lynching in American history.[81]

* * * *

BACK IN HIS office, Superintendent Gaster had been fielding reports of chaos across New Orleans, but despite rumors that hundreds, maybe thousands, were marching on the Fourth Street murder scene, the chief had been remarkably lackadaisical about protecting black residents. Gaster sent a few reserve officers to the area, but continued to concentrate on defending Orleans Parish Prison, holding back more than one-third of the department's total force—about one hundred men—to protect a complex that also encompassed police headquarters. The defenders were strengthened by the arrival of Sergeant Porteous and his thirty men, who had doubled back after failing to prevent the mob forming at Lee Circle. They reached the prison as word arrived that hordes of armed men were heading downtown. Speaking with reporters who gathered to witness the showdown, Gaster put on a brave face, promising, "They can be repulsed by the men we have."[82]

Unfortunately, the chief had a spotty record with these sorts of predictions. Earlier in the afternoon, mourners at St. Michael's Church had been reminded of the mob that brushed aside deputies, stormed the Old Parish Prison, and lynched eleven Sicilian inmates. Although the warden had requested backup from police headquarters, there was an inexplicable delay before Gaster deployed reinforcements, which reached the scene too late to stop the carnage. The performance did nothing to harm his reputation in New Orleans, where editors praised the murders as community justice in response to a corrupted system.[83] But federal officials condemned both the "deplorable massacre" and its handling by local authorities, particularly after grand jurors refused to charge the perpetrators, saying the mob represented "the entire people of the parish and city" when it stormed the prison and slaughtered the victims.[84]

Confronted with scathing criticism and damage to the city's reputation, authorities responded with symbolic reform, moving forward plans to replace the six-decades-old prison described as "physically and morally abominable" by a visiting clergyman.[85] Within months, they opened bidding to construct a cutting-edge criminal justice facility that would double as a bold campaign to rebrand lawless New Orleans.[86] From the beginning, the ambitious project was a fiasco, but after lengthy delays and costly overruns, it finally opened and the controversy was mostly forgotten.[87] Sprawled across a city block in the heart of downtown, the Romanesque stronghold was intended to demonstrate "the march of improvement in New Orleans" since its moment of international disgrace. Home to the police headquarters, the new parish prison, the coroner's office and morgue, courtrooms, judges' chambers, and jury deliberation rooms in one centralized location, the complex was a justice assembly line, "so conveniently arranged" that a defendant could be "tried, convicted, sentenced, and executed without leaving the building."[88]

Architects had taken precautions to ensure that only lawful killings would take place in the new facility. The contained design also discouraged outside interference, since the imposing appearance was more than a façade—it provided absolute security. Snipers covered the streets from strategically positioned watchtowers and fifty-foot brick walls guarded the prison, which was only accessible through a stone archway protected by heavy iron gates. Long corridors and locked doors maximized interior visibility and created deadly choke points. Should unauthorized visitors breach the defenses and make it inside the building, they would regret succeeding.[89]

Just after ten o'clock on Wednesday evening, hundreds, maybe thousands, bore down on Orleans Parish Prison, ready to test the defenses that forward-thinking citizens were relying on for rehabilitation. They had weathered bruising controversy and authorized breathtaking sums, but no matter how formidable, defenses were only as dependable as those who manned them. On first glance, the scene outside the prison was promising. Electric lights brightened the streets outside, where scores of club-wielding patrolmen surrounded the facility, watched by riflemen posted in the watchtowers and upper floors.[90] Behind the gates, the defenses were just as formidable. Lights illuminated the main passageway the attackers would need to pass through, but the interior was otherwise darkened. Deputies were stationed behind heavy steel doors, armed with double-barrel shotguns loaded with deadly buckshot. They were ordered to hold the prison at all costs.[91]

As police commanders prepared to withstand the coming storm, the inmates confined inside the complex were realizing that something was very wrong. Rumors had been swirling about the frightened teenager being guarded by deputies, but the flurry of activity confirmed that something high stakes was about to happen. Administrators had contingency plans to save Pierce by hustling him to safety through secret tunnels if the defenses failed, but any mob was unlikely to start or end with him. When deputies evacuated the cells facing outside streets, the prisoners realized that an attack was coming. Some begged to be spared, while others seemed paralyzed by dread. A strange calm descended as the life-and-death moment approached.[92]

Scouts rushed to the prison and raised the alarm. Then the mob announced its advance in a steadily rising crescendo, a low rumble and strange crackling, transforming into thunderous roars punctuated by unmistakable sharp reports—revolver fire. The sentries shouted a warning from above. Suddenly the storm broke. Determined men surged through the downtown streets, gathering momentum as they descended on the prison. But the fierce wave ebbed prematurely as it came upon the blue line ringing the stronghold. Purpose gave way to confusion. This was no token resistance.

Although they outnumbered and outgunned the officers defending the prison, the mob once more hesitated to use force against the men they were supposed to be avenging. Milling in the neutral ground, they would push forward and probe the police line, searching for signs it would give way. Thirty minutes passed, but they found none. Squad commanders barked orders and patrolmen lashed out with clubs whenever the confused mob ventured too close. Frustrated men began peeling away from the stalemate to chase passing streetcars. As the offensive forays sputtered, police reinforcements arrived from the Fourth Street crime scene, decisively tipping the balance toward the defenders. Captains sensed the shifting momentum and ordered their men to advance. The crowd wavered momentarily as the cordon marched forward. Civilians eyed one another hesitantly, but with no mutual determination to make a stand, they shuffled backward, then began a full-scale withdrawal, scattering in a dozen or more directions.[93]

Against the odds, authorities had successfully prevented bloodshed at Orleans Parish Prison, mostly because the avengers were unwilling to directly confront officers unwilling to play along. But despite the spirited defense, the potential for violence was high. Commanders had allowed the mob to dematerialize on its own terms. Disappointed, but unbroken, the attackers began to regroup. Switching tactics, they looked for softer targets—and settled on the perfect hunting ground. Only blocks away, black dancehalls were packed with customers, day laborers and domestic servants, unwinding and dangerously oblivious. As the reanimated mob approached, it began to move with purpose again. "Let's go for the niggers," someone hollered. "We'll get a nigger down there!"[94]

* * * *

SHORTLY AFTER TEN o'clock on Wednesday evening, Big 25's was unusually crowded, packed with dancers swaying, shuffling, and trying to shake away the mid-week tensions. The club sat at the heart of working-class culture for black New Orleans, anchoring a rowdy neighborhood on the edge of downtown. It offered an intoxicating blend of strong drinks and ragtime standards, along with brash sounds announcing the birth of something original and daring. Jazz was a revolution, a whirlwind— and unbelievably, fifteen-year-old "Big Eye" Louis Nelson was in the eye of the storm. Among the musicians featuring on the club's famous stage, he was the youngest performer and newest member of Charley Payton's band, having recently earned a coveted invitation to join the freewheeling musicians whose wildly creative styles were calling the new artform into existence. Flanked by Buddy Bolden, the teenager was playing bass, soaking in the atmosphere, and doing his best to keep up with the trumpet player known as "the blowingest man ever lived since Gabriel."[95]

For the young musician, the opportunity to join a famous band was welcome for more than creative reasons, or even for the eye-opening experience. Musicians playing in established groups could earn steady wages from rotating gigs in New Orleans dancehalls, something that comparatively few black workers in any occupation could rely upon. Nelson's own father was a butcher by trade, but business had been slow and the family was living in poverty. Although his parents had quickly grown wise to his suddenly nocturnal lifestyle and had reason to object to his participation in a notoriously rowdy nightclub scene, they reached an unspoken understanding. He would make desperately needed contributions to the family finances—and they would avoid questioning where the money came from.

On this Wednesday evening, both Nelson men were earning money for the family, the father by driving his meat wagon through the French Quarter near Big 25's, where his fifteen-year-old son commanded the stage with some of the most brilliant musicians of his generation. As the siege unfolded outside the downtown prison, word reached the club that something big was happening only blocks away, but early reports were ambiguous. Partway through the performance by Charley Payton's band, a woman raised the alarm about the chaos unfolding nearby and suggested that they call it an evening. Payton assured her that nothing would happen and stomped out the beat for the next song, signaling the others to begin. Straddling his bass and perched on the farthest end of the bandstand, the youngest musician watched the exchange with rising dread and faced a wrenching choice. Sacrificing wages and risking his spot in the rotation over rumors was a bad play, but everybody knew that violence was a real possibility. Bowing to peer pressure, Nelson moved his fingers over the strings and struck the tune. It was a decision that haunted him for the rest of his life. "We kept playing," he remembered, "Lord, I've wished many times I'd gone home to warn my people."[96]

At police headquarters, Superintendent Gaster was discussing the continuing prison defense with his subordinates when a messenger frantically burst into his office, breathlessly warning that armed men were heading toward the black dancehalls. "God, that place must be packed with darkies," Gaster exclaimed, turning to one of his detectives. "Get down there and scatter them!"[97]

The curious decision to dispatch a single man to warn so many endangered civilians epitomized the questionable choices that would be made throughout the remainder of a long, bloody night in New Orleans, where police maintained a defensive perimeter around the prison as mobs ran the streets. It was a strangely toothless response, but authorities were prioritizing a symbolically rich victory over black lives. The prison complex marked the community's advance over the previous decade, the progressive energy that made it a safely profitable bet for outside capitalists. Its defense was worth an army—and it got one. The dancers would have to make do with one detective.

Less than eight hundred yards from headquarters, the crowd was blissfully dancing when Gaster's messenger burst into the club, reaching it just moments ahead of the rampaging mob. Wading through the sea of bodies, he grabbed the manager by the shoulders. "Clear this place," he shouted. "There's a mob coming, hunting niggers!"

Jumping on a table, the man shouted, "Run for your lives, there's a mob on the way to kill you!"[98]

On stage, fifteen-year-old Louis Nelson barely comprehended what was happening. There was a disturbance in the club, followed almost immediately by the sound of gunshots coming from outside. They were close. Sitting on the edge of the bandstand and cradling a heavy bass, Nelson had no time to react before the stampede began. "All them boys flung themselves on me," he remembered. "The bass was bust to kindling and I sailed clear across the back of the room, so many of them hit me so hard."[99]

Nelson managed to scrabble out a window and into an alleyway, where Bolden and another musician joined him, but it was already jammed with frightened people and they decided to escape onto Basin Street by cutting through the high-class brothel run by Josie Arlington. When they knocked on the back entrance, the madam answered, screamed, and slammed the door in their faces. The musicians improvised, climbing a fence and making a mad dash to a friend's house, where they counted the damage: scratches and missing clothes, but thankfully nothing more serious.[100]

Nelson had been fortunate, or so it seemed. For others, the nightmare was only beginning. Moments after the scramble, the mob swept through the neighborhood. As the hunt spilled into Storyville, the infamous red-light district bordering the dancehalls, the drama veered toward a violent burlesque. Leaning from balconies, prostitutes encouraged the champions who had come to protect them from black predators, parodying the justification favored by lynching advocates across the South.[101] "White women were out on their stoops, shouting to the crowd to go on and kill negroes for them," reporters described. "Their shrill voices could be heard above the hoarse and guttural tones of the men."[102]

Tucked away from the most luxurious bordellos on side streets and between run-down speakeasies, the "cribs" where black women entertained clients for rates starting at a dime were less receptive. "The colored women pulled their doors shut and put on every fastening," observers described, casually adding that a few were clawed and punched before managing to protect themselves.[103]

Surrounded by brothels and disappointed by the absence of targets, the boisterous white men finally gave up any semblance of discipline. Small gangs splintered from the main group, shambling through the French Quarter and streaming downtown, shouting threats and aimlessly shooting into the darkened sky. The disorganization gave rise to confrontations, strange and dangerous. Trailing behind the mob as it marched on Storyville, twenty-year-old Wallace Sabatier heard someone bellow, "There's a fucking coon!" Bullets zipped over his head and Sabatier realized that he was the black man in question. He ducked under a nearby streetlight to make himself more visible.[104] Quick thinking saved his life. Once the target was illuminated, the trigger-happy marksmen realized their mistake. The shooters moved on, untroubled, followed by one lucky white man, who straggled behind, careful to maintain a safe distance.[105]

Over more than three hours of chaos, the mayhem had not been deadly—but that was about to change. August Thomas was working the night shift for the New Orleans City Railroad Company when gangs roaming near the French Quarter spotted him riding a trolley. "Here's a negro," someone hollered. They clambered aboard and forced the motorman to stop, decoupling the train in the process and plunging the interior into darkness. Shrieking riders dove away as bullets showered the cabin, but when the lights flicked back on, Thomas was gone.[106] Concealed by the shadows, he darted across the semi-darkened street and seemed poised to escape—until he passed under a streetlight and gave the shooters a second chance.

Revolvers cracked. Thomas stumbled, then recovered his balance and started running again. But the split-second lapse was enough. Attackers surged forward and surrounded the semi-crouched man, knocking him down with heavy blows and stomping him into the mud. A vicious kick slammed him into the gutter and his face slipped beneath the brackish sludge.

"Pull him out, don't let him drown!"

Strong hands dragged the sputtering, half-conscious man back into the circle, where the brutal assault became more methodical. The attackers smashed Thomas in the face with clubs and paving stones, pausing to strike matches and holding them up to his eyes. When there were signs of life after a half-dozen rounds, someone exclaimed disbelievingly, "He ain't dead!"

Another man pushed his way to the center of the crowd. He drew a pistol, pressed it to the victim's stomach, and fired. The bullet traveled upward into his lungs. Thomas drowned in his own blood. Death was an unmeant mercy.[107]

The body was taken to the morgue, where the coroner examined it and documented his findings on a standard form, scrawling "Unknown" where a name should have gone.[108] The next afternoon, an estimated four thousand curiosity seekers would view the "hideously bruised and mangled" corpse in a ghoulish parade, but nobody could identify the man and authorities buried him in the potter's field before his family could step forward to claim his remains.[109] Belatedly, white reporters would add a few details to prove the victim's innocence. "Thomas was said to be an honest and industrious negro," they eulogized. "It is reported that he owned a property."[110]

After the ghastly murder of August Thomas, the bloodletting continued for three more hours as small bands roamed the streets, attacking unsuspecting targets and proving far more dangerous than the huge crowds. Patients streamed into Charity Hospital, where doctors were treating a gruesome array of injuries: fractures, contusions, slashings, stabbings, and gunshots, bodies torn and battered by metal, wood, and bone. Eleven-year-old Joseph Lewis was the youngest casualty—he was standing on St. Charles Avenue when adults surrounded him and smashed him on the head with baseball bats.[111] Esther Fields was attacked outside her home, the washerwoman suffering heavy bruising and a gashed forehead.[112] Going on the record, victims described shock and awe, unexpected violence shattering their evening routines with no warning. Responding to a disturbance outside the market where he worked as a night watchman, George Morris spotted a familiar face in the crowd, a white man who gruffly warned, "You'd better go home—they're after your kind."

Recovering after being slashed across the back and brained with a club, Morris wryly reflected, "I didn't know what he meant, but I found out soon."[113]

As casualties flooded into Charity Hospital, word of another vicious attack reached police headquarters. Sometime around midnight, Louis Taylor had been manning his soda water stand in the famous French Market, a century-old riverfront institution described by contemporary travel guides as "the most uniquely picturesque sight in the city."[114] On this unusual evening, the twenty-six-year-old man saw an armed group gunning for him and bolted out the back of the building—straight into the arms of a second rampaging gang.[115] Patrolmen took several minutes to reach the scene, where they found the victim lying on the ground. After shooting him multiple times, the gangs had savagely beaten him before leaving him for dead. Taylor was still breathing, somehow. Officers half-heartedly shooed away the crowd without bothering to make any arrests, although some civilians bragged openly to reporters. "The nigger was at the soda water stand and we started shooting at him," one said. "He put his hands up and ran. We shot until he fell."

Taylor was taken to the hospital, where he would cling to life for another twenty-four hours, but in the end his injuries were too severe. A bullet had tunneled through his stomach, tearing open his intestines and infecting his abdominal wounds with his own waste.[116] Poisoned from inside, Taylor died early on Friday morning, less than two days after being ambushed at his workplace.[117]

Despite the brutal murders, patrolmen continued to stand down as rampaging French Quarter mobs continued to seek and find victims. Just after two o'clock on Thursday morning, seventy-five-year-old Baptiste Philo was heading toward the scene of the deadly French Market attack as he prepared to begin his backbreaking predawn shift hauling boxes between wagons and butcher stands. A white gang stumbled across him, easily knocking the defenseless elderly man to the ground. Someone stepped forward and shot him, but when the gunman stooped down, he was disappointed. "Oh, he's an old negro," he observed. "I'm sorry I shot him."[118]

Suddenly ashamed, the attackers wandered away and Philo staggered a half-mile to the nearest police station, where officers called an ambulance. Struggling to cope with the mass casualties, doctors at Charity Hospital had established a triage system, but when Philo arrived, medical students quickly decided that he was a low priority. Midway through his eighth decade, the old man had survived slavery, Reconstruction, and Redemption, promising and heartbreaking transformations, but one glance was enough for trained eyes to determine his prognosis. This was where his story ended.[119]

Within thirty minutes, officers from the same station responded to another attack in the French Quarter and found a middle-aged man sprawled in an intersection. His skull was crushed. Witnesses said that he was dragged from his meat wagon by unknown assailants. The comatose driver was taken to Charity Hospital, but nothing could be done to save him.[120] Nobody recognized the dying man—until just after sunrise, when his son reached the ward. Back home after a close brush with death at Big 25's, fifteen-year-old Louis Nelson learned that his dad had not returned from his overnight rounds. Someone directed him to Charity Hospital, where mob victims were recovering. "It was full of folks all crippled and shot up," Nelson described. "The sisters told me that a man had been brought there in very bad condition and died around sun-up. It was my daddy. They snatched him off his meat wagon and killed him."[121]

As a traumatized young man identified his father's corpse, authorities were confronting the grim consequences of a disastrous night in New Orleans. Two dead, two dying. Dozens wounded, including women, children, and a few white men, both perpetrators and bystanders struck by reckless gunfire. When reporters checked the prison, they discovered cells packed with black men facing minor charges—but none of those responsible for the carnage. Countless white men had participated in the bloodletting. None were arrested. "No attempt was made to take any members of the mob into custody," they explained. "Several policemen expressed themselves as being in favor of shooting the negroes."[122]

According to the fifteen-year-old who narrowly escaped death and discovered his father's body among the victims, many cops had done more than sympathize. "They claim the police was trying to stop the mob," Nelson bitterly remembered, "but fact was, the police were worse than the others."[123]

6

Revelations

EARLY ON THURSDAY MORNING, JULY 26, 1900, BLACK
New Orleans woke to a nightmare. Although most of the attackers had
returned home, scattered bands roamed the downtown streets, hunting
for more victims. Police were nowhere to be seen. Just before sunrise,
mob remnants began to reassemble outside the New Orleans and Western Terminal, hoping to ambush workers heading to Port Chalmette,
but the depot was deserted. The longshoremen had been warned—mostly.
Then an opportunity. Black men turned onto Canal Street and headed
toward the station, but they spotted the welcome party just in time,
dashing for safety as bullets whistled overhead. Drinking had given the
gunmen courage, but fortunately it did nothing to improve their
marksmanship.[1]

With police officers nowhere to be found, the random attacks continued all morning long. Twenty-year-old newlywed Chester Columbus was
heading downtown to work as a porter in the *Times-Democrat* photo-
engraving department when a gang suddenly charged. Columbus tore in
the opposite direction, but more white men responded to the commotion
and blocked his escape route. Thinking quickly, he ducked into a nearby
grocery store and the shopkeeper locked the doors, saving his life.
Rather than directly summoning officers, Columbus smartly called his
employers, who persuaded commanders to dispatch patrolmen to rescue
and escort him to the same building where reporters were actively down-
playing the dismal police response. The young man made it to work unharmed, in the process demonstrating a necessary survival strategy for

black residents in New Orleans: cultivating powerful white patrons in a city where the cops responded to some calls and ignored others.[2]

As the sun climbed, the mobs grew bolder and more organized. Shortly before noon, the morning's biggest crowd assembled directly across from City Hall in Lafayette Square, waving pistols and attacking two black pedestrians who wandered too close as patrolmen watched and did nothing to intervene.[3] Blocks away, a few dozen bricklayers were renovating a building at the Jesuit College when they attracted the wrong attention. White men swarmed the campus and surrounded them. As things escalated, the workers took shelter in the chapel and outbuildings, where the priests tried to protect them. But with no help coming, the terrified builders faced a growing likelihood: massacre. Panicked, some men prepared to leap from the upper floors, choosing a mercifully quick death over slow torture by a lynch mob. The priests broke the stalemate, putting themselves on the line by forming a human shield and shepherding the targeted men to the rectory, where they remained secure. Disregarding the patrolman who was passively watching the scene, the fathers decided to keep the workers there rather than chance sending them home—the officer's inaction during the showdown had done nothing to inspire confidence that he would protect the laborers.[4] Shocked by the nonchalant response to the attempted massacre of his employees, a senior partner in the construction firm contracted by the mayor's alma mater expressed his outrage to reporters, who described citywide clashes "where negroes were driven from work by crowds of white hoodlums" and compiled them under an ominous headline: "LABOR INTIMIDATED."[5]

Among the workingmen targeted by mobs, word of the danger was spreading quickly, but incompletely. Unaware, two longshoremen stumbled into an ambush that morning on the levee at the foot of Jackson Avenue, only two blocks from the cottage where mourners paid respects to Captain Day the previous afternoon. They were cornered and beaten by howling gangs, scarcely able to process what was happening before the violence escalated. Some attackers drew knives, stabbing and slashing until the blood-soaked men stopped moving. Before moving on, the mob tossed the bodies in an empty boxcar along the levee. Hours passed before a watchman from Boylan's Detective Agency responded to the

disturbance, heard groaning, and discovered the victims, barely breathing, but somehow clinging to life.[6] Despite a grave prognosis, surgeons
at Charity Hospital were able to stabilize sixty-year-old Charles Washington, who had survived slavery and would recover from his ghastly
wounds.[7] His companion was less fortunate. The following morning, editors reported on his desperate condition as part of their list of daily casualties: "Nathan Brown, negro, stabbed in the throat, breast, and face.
Reported to be dying."[8]

The attack cast a long shadow over the levee, where chants and songs,
mingling with jokes, insults, and cock-and-bull stories, typically energized
the workday. But on this unusual Thursday morning, the scattered black
deckhands loading and unloading steamboats worked in tense silence.
Reporters surveyed the gloomy scene and found an improbable silver lining, concluding that "better work was done more quickly than usual" by
workers determined to "make themselves as inconspicuous as possible."
Unlike the deckhands who lived aboard the steamboats where they
worked, the longshoremen who resided locally and regularly serviced
oceangoing ships were even less noticeable. Most chose to stay home.
Those who showed up eyed their co-workers suspiciously—white union
leaders were actively warning the rank and file not to cause any trouble,
but there was no telling how many laborers had joined the previous night's
blood spilling before showing up to work alongside the survivors. The
longshoremen managed to coexist peacefully, but the turnout was crippling. As dangerously undermanned crews struggled to handle the heavy
cargo, many among them decided to abandon ship. By late morning,
supervisors agreed to dismiss the remainder and an eerie silence descended
on the usually boisterous docks.[9]

Elsewhere in New Orleans, the profit-sapping consequences of the
chaos were equally obvious. With thousands of endangered black workingmen behind closed doors, business was paralyzed—everywhere. Construction sites were abandoned, the skeletal frames of unfinished
buildings providing the grim backdrop for boisterous gangs patrolling
deserted blocks.[10] Empty wagons sat on half-finished streets: the teamsters had been beaten during the morning rounds and the pavers returned
home after being attacked at the municipal asphalt works.[11] The down-

town business district normally teemed with low-sided drays carrying goods from dock to storage and back again. Now it was desolate. Several black drivers had already been jumped and the others decided against risking death for wages averaging less than two dollars a day.[12] Rather than sending them home and losing the day's work entirely, merchants reassigned them to stores and warehouses, which reporters praised as "showing both wisdom and humanity."[13] But despite the brave spin, the situation everywhere was dire. Listing commercial houses whose fortunes were synonymous with prosperity in New Orleans, editors counted out-of-commission wagons and numbered them alongside the wounded and dead. Human or monetary, the casualties all pointed toward one conclusion. Wednesday night's seemingly mindless violence had actually been the opening shots of something far more concerning: a bloody campaign against black workers, one which promised to destroy everything businessmen had worked so hard to accomplish.[14]

Aboard streetcars descending on the downtown business district for the morning rush and on the marble floors of the commercial exchanges, the usual conversations about commodity prices and financial outlooks were replaced by heated debates. Although merchants expressed moral outrage to the press observers wandering through the buzzing conference rooms, they seemed more focused on the economic consequences than the humanitarian ones.[15] Going on the record, the chairman of Louisiana's railroad commission managed to fold both concerns into the same conversation. "That quiet, peaceable colored men and women—our house servants, if you please—should be wantonly shot and killed simply because they have black skin is an unspeakable outrage," he condemned, before pivoting. "Of course, the trouble may affect the value of state and city securities and jeopardize the public improvement bonds. To what extent I don't know, but there's no denying."[16]

For the business community, the emergency came at an especially precarious time. Notices had begun appearing in newspapers early in July, opening the months-long bidding process for the municipal improvement bonds that would fund the sewerage and drainage projects that would modernize the city's infrastructure. One-fifth of the winning bid would be made available for immediate use, but there was a catch. The overall value of the bond issue depended on public confidence. If bullish buyers agreed to 3 percent annual interest rates, up to $16 million would be issued to fund the critical improvements. But if investors pushed 4 percent instead, the issue would drop to $12 million, reducing the funding by one-fourth and forcing painful compromises. With chaos on New Orleans streets precisely as capitalists across the country evaluated its prospects, the city stood to lose millions in both short-term liquidity and long-term interest payments if the bankers decided that it was a risky gamble.[17] Considering the bad timing, not to mention the corruption scandals, economic downturns, fever epidemics, and other hardships, so many false dawns and golden ages, snatched away just when they seemed in the grasp, the injustice was unbearable. "Hardly any city has its burden of sorrows more than ours," one businessman complained. "Scarcely over one calamity, there's another forced upon us."[18]

Elites nervously waited for news to arrive from the nation's investment banking centers, where the performance of existing bonds would suggest attitudes toward the new issue among likely bidders. Although they wanted to believe that the financial consequences of the crisis would be limited, news from Wall Street confirmed a worst-case scenario. State and local bonds were sharply dropping as investors moved capital to more stable instruments. For the first time, the emergency had a price tag—and it was a big one. The killings were disturbing, deplorable really, while the campaign against black workers was more concerning. But the plunging bonds were undeniably disastrous. This was nothing less than a full-scale assault on their ledger books and "a body blow to the credit of the city," with consequences too maddening to contemplate. As the business community woke up to the crisis, a question remained: Were authorities in New Orleans willing and able to join with them and reclaim the city?

The answer was uncertain. Less than three months in office, Mayor Paul Capdevielle had been hard to reach in recent days. Retreating to his country estate, the former insurance executive had missed a scheduled public appearance, reigniting concerns about his health. Aides reassured reporters that he was "simply worn out," nothing more serious, but more than a week had gone by without an update.[19] Apparently recovering from the mysterious affliction, Capdevielle was still resting when he received word that his city was in chaos and financial markets were revolting. He sprang into action. Returning aboard an early train, the mayor scoured the morning newspapers as he prepared to face down the first crisis of his administration. And it was a major one. Capdevielle was back in his office by nine o'clock on Thursday morning, where he addressed the reporters clustered outside. "It's simply horrible," he agreed, before promising to do whatever it took to stabilize the situation. "I'm going to take harsh measures today."[20]

The first step was demanding action from his police force. Capdevielle scrawled a communiqué to commanders demanding that patrolmen begin making arrests, before taking additional steps.[21] Reporters who covered the violence would be interrogated to secure the names of the mob's ringleaders, while troublemakers were to be held without bond. Saloons would be closed until the crisis ended. Yet rounding up bad guys and sobering up everyone else were only half-measures, particularly when the police department was unmotivated and badly overstretched under the best circumstances. The mayor's biggest problem was not enough boots on the ground. Fortunately, there was a ready-made solution, an ultra-risky move that could reverse the political fortunes of his unexpectedly beleaguered administration.[22] By noon, Capdevielle was prepared to issue his first public statement on the emergency, crafted with one audience especially in mind. "I, Paul Capdevielle, Mayor of the City of New Orleans, do hereby call for the services of 500 citizens, to assist the authorities in maintaining the peace and good order of this city," he declared, instructing citizen volunteers to come directly to his office to be sworn. "I hereby proclaim that no recurrence of the lawless disturbances will be tolerated and assure the people, regardless of color, that they shall have protection in life, liberty, and property."[23]

There it was—the solution favored by the business community during the general strike and the levee violence in the 1890s, yet denied to them by Capdevielle's machine predecessors. Deputizing civilians was a dangerous escalation, one that could easily lead to much worse bloodshed, but it was certainly the best chance to restore order and reassure investors reconsidering a multi-million-dollar gamble on the city's future. But success also depended on who answered the mayor's call—and to make sure his proclamation reached the intended audience, Capdevielle ordered it posted outside the New Orleans Board of Trade, targeted advertising for those he hoped to mobilize. When municipal workers reached the downtown building to post the mayor's proclamation, they discovered that businessmen had already beaten them to the punch. On the board outside, they found "the notice of the meeting already called at the Cotton Exchange." It seemed that private citizens were already planning to take matters into their own hands. And given the bloody consequences the last time businessmen struck back when the system failed them, there was a good chance that Capdevielle was already too late to prevent even worse bloodshed.[24]

* * * *

FROM HIS SPACIOUS office on the fourth floor of the New Orleans Cotton Exchange, a breathtaking Second Empire structure in the heart of downtown, thirty-seven-year-old John M. Parker had spent much of Thursday morning planning the private sector's counterattack on the gangs roving beneath his windows.[25] Despite his young age, the chairman was the natural choice to spearhead the campaign, particularly when cotton prices were probably the best single measure of the city's economic health. Nonetheless, he understood the importance of coordination. After consulting with members, Parker dispatched a short message to his counterparts at the other mercantile exchanges, calling for an early afternoon meeting in the director's room of the Cotton Exchange, where the business community would plot its own course for restoring peace, stabilizing bond markets, and limiting the damage already done to the city's reputation. Conjuring unwelcome memories from the early 1890s, the decision was a desperate one, bound to have serious political consequences. But these were truly desperate times. With no word from City Hall, the Cotton Exchange and its green president would coordinate the business community's response. Let the chips fall where they may.[26]

Given his own controversial background, Parker might have seemed a strange choice to suppress a mob. As a younger man, the chairman's name had appeared beneath a carefully worded notice that appeared in the city's most popular daily, announcing a mass meeting "to take steps to remedy the failure of justice in the Hennessy case." Sixty others had signed, including leading businessmen and social elites.[27] Whether through misplaced confidence that such trustworthy gentlemen would "not permit any excited appeals to the worst passions" or outright complicity, editors had advertised a mob's plan to storm the parish prison and massacre the Sicilian captives.[28] Parker had been among the primary organizers, an association he wore as a badge of honor that boosted his reputation and prospects. Before his thirtieth birthday, he became the youngest president in the Board of Trade's history, taking the first step in a splendid political career that would eventually culminate with his election as governor of Louisiana. His stunning rise following the shocking murders came as no surprise to those who understood the lynching conspiracy. Although it was framed as a spontaneous uprising against the Mafia, the killings were executed by established businessmen, striking back against immigrants whose growing economic and political influence was threatening the status quo.[29] Calling the conspirators "my own personal friends," an up-and-coming attorney whose father presided over the farcical grand jury investigation explained, "Every exchange and commercial body in New Orleans endorsed what had been done. It was conceived by gentlemen and carried out by gentlemen."[30]

For men like Chairman John Parker of the New Orleans Cotton Exchange, the real question was not the legitimacy of vigilantism, but rather whose order it served. Whereas the Sicilian coup was "conceived by gentlemen and carried out by gentlemen," a masterstroke hardly diminished by the controversy that followed, what might have been dismissed as drunken hooliganism on Wednesday night was morphing into something more closely resembling class warfare by proxy. As white workingmen used the cop killings as a pretense to terrorize black competitors, they were challenging the employers who pitted them against each other in the first place—which made the mobbing far more dangerous than any menace posed by Robert Charles and his co-conspirators, especially given the low probability that anything revolutionary was actually planned in the black community. From his vantage behind the most powerful desk in New Orleans, one purchased in blood, this was nothing less than laborers rising up against the proper order of things—a communist rebellion.

There was no choice but to meet the challenge in the field. As Parker prepared to meet with his elite peers and plan a course toward restoring order, there was nothing incongruous about businessmen cracking down on mobs claiming to avenge the police martyrs. The response had nothing to do with suppressing "race rioters" and everything to do with reasserting class privilege. It would be a messy but necessary showdown between violent white collectives, workers and employers, both justified in a bewildering ideological labyrinth riddled with contradictions, now written in blood on the streets of New Orleans.

Fortunately, the businessmen would not be alone. Returning from his mysterious exile and assuming command, the former insurance executive in the mayor's office fully grasped the concerns driving commercial leaders toward action, along with the precariousness of his own position. After all, the old machine had been derailed by its toxic relationship with the business community. Paul Capdevielle had no intention of suffering the same fate, especially when he counted many of those summoned to the director's room at the Cotton Exchange among his closest friends. Acting immediately after reassuming control, the mayor arrived in the nick of time, barely managing to preempt the private gathering before it could spiral into something more dangerous to his administration. Shortly after his proclamation appeared outside the Board of Trade, selected business leaders received personal requests, redirecting them to the mayor's office to coordinate with municipal authorities. For a community with reason to be wary of the newly empowered machine, it was a welcome sign.[31]

The meeting in the mayor's office was even more encouraging. A comprehensive response leveraging both public and private resources quickly took shape. State militiamen would be mobilized for possible intervention, but deputized private citizens were charged with supporting police and immediately asserting the business community's authority. The delegation approved the mayor's plan to deploy special police officers, but advised tripling the force to fifteen hundred men—more than seven times the police department's patrol strength. And they were also prepared to underwrite the expansion, pledging guns and money, furnished by an executive committee established during the levee violence in the mid-

1890s. Composed of commercial elites, it had been maintained precisely for this purpose: the moment when class warfare met a mayor willing to mobilize a business-minded militia. Now members offered a private armory and significant cash reserves, ready to turn the tide and transform a worst-case scenario into something more profitable. Capdevielle eagerly agreed to the mobilization and accepted the weapons and funds, before consulting with "leading business and professional men" to find the right man to lead the special police force. "The choice was universally applauded," reporters described, citing the commander's impeccable reputation. "His courage, coolness, and determination are conceded by everybody and it was generally agreed that a better man could not have been named."[32]

For more than his temperament and experience, thirty-nine-year-old Elmer E. Wood was a politically savvy choice to strengthen the collaboration between public and private actors. Supervising his father's coal empire and maintaining a lucrative side business selling military hardware to the federal government, Colonel Wood was a Spanish War veteran who had commanded the 2nd Louisiana Regiment and overseen the U.S. Army's Havana garrison during the Cuban occupation.[33] Fashioning himself as an officer and a gentleman, Wood had recently begun working on his unpublished wartime memoirs, a ponderous slog—heavy on camp life and light on action—suggesting his decidedly conservative sensibilities. Favorably comparing his own departure for Cuba with imagined scenes of Confederate soldiers leaving New Orleans, the Pennsylvania native was impressed by the crowd's enthusiasm, although considerably less satisfied with his own men. "From the armories, this mob marched through the streets," he remembered. "We reached camp as a heterogeneous mass of our cosmopolitan population, almost every nationality but Indians and negroes and every costume the civilized world can witness."[34]

Although he managed to whip his motley crew into shape, Wood encountered troubling problems over the course of the campaign, particularly as he struggled to reconcile military and civilian hierarchies. Explaining that his volunteer regiment included "a large number of young men from the best and most aristocratic families in New Orleans," he recalled how many revolted against the "inferior station" occupied by army privates, the rough egalitarianism among the lowest ranks seeming "to their sense of education, perhaps the gravest injustice." These were hard lessons for young men who associated domestic service with black women, but military regulation and tradition prevented exemptions from duty on the basis of breeding and social status. "This subjected many of our best soldiers to unfortunate hardships and labors that were both distasteful and perhaps, in a sense, degrading," Wood sympathized, referencing the mayor's own neighborhood to illustrate the absurdity. "I have seen wealthy Esplanade Avenue residents chopping wood and cleaning latrines."[35]

Sensitive to the particular challenges of mobilizing the better classes for sometimes disagreeable service, the second-born son of an established businessman was a particularly inspired choice to lead a citizen militia drawn almost exclusively from elite circles.[36] By early Thursday afternoon, the mayor's petition was quickly circulating, supported by the executive committee and commercial exchanges, spreading through the same networks that regularly carried rumors of fluctuating commodity prices. Reporting on the response, press observers gushed over the enthusiasm "coming from the best citizens," merchants, lawyers, doctors, bankers, clerks, skilled mechanics, and "upper class representatives," all descending on the downtown business district to be sworn as special police officers.[37] By those accounts, the process of commissioning special police officers ran as smoothly as a well-oiled machine. Throughout the afternoon, civilians streamed through the mayor's parlor to be sworn into service by his secretary. Approvingly watching the spectacle, Capdevielle was especially pleased with the demographic composition of his force. "The special police were quite representative of the commercial community and the response delighted him," reporters noted, publishing extensive rosters to prove the claims. "Most were young men, seeming to come from the wholesale and retail stores."[38]

On the streets around City Hall, prevailing tensions were soon replaced by a festive atmosphere, more Mardi Gras than martial law, as co-workers from leading mercantile firms and members of the most prestigious social clubs showed up together to be sworn. As the men formed up and began parading through the surrounding streets, massive crowds lined the banquettes, cheering the whimsical scenes with equal parts sarcasm and enthusiasm, an eerie reprise of Wednesday evening's oddly combined revelry and rioting. After the swearing ceremonies, the deputized officers were dispatched to the armory of the Continental Guards, a distinguished militia organization with origins dating to the antebellum period, when the primary security threat was rebellious slaves in the sugar parishes surrounding New Orleans. Now called to protect the city from a different menace, they were divided into squads, given weapons, and fashioned with white silk ribbons inscribed with a simple designation: "Special Police."[39] Outside, photographers snapped pictures of young professionals sporting bowties, suit jackets, and straw hats, brandishing rifles and posing with stern expressions.[40]

By late Thursday afternoon, the delayed response to the bloody uprising was finally rounding into shape. In the armory, special police commanders huddled to discuss strategy as squad members lounged nearby, preparing to patrol the restless streets from dusk to dawn. Coffee and food supplies were on hand to replenish the men as they returned, as were doctors, ready to "perform any services that might be required."[41] According to some, the businessmen made a formidable impression. Everywhere reporters looked, purpose and efficiency seemed to be the orders of the evening, animating everything from the tactical preparations to the eating arrangements—squads departed headquarters and marched on nearby restaurants "as rapidly as possible," according to the accounts they published.[42] The dinner bills were pricey, including the St. Charles Hotel and other top-shelf establishments, but restaurateurs were hardly the only beneficiaries. Even as private citizens coordinated with the mayor's office to restore peace and reestablish leadership, a parallel campaign, enlisting corporate bodies, gathered steam to address the logistical challenges associated with staging a military-style operation. When city officials began reaching out to corporate stakeholders to secure necessary resources, as with the response from businessmen, the difference between civic duty and personal gain was tough to discern.[43]

At the offices of the New Orleans City Railroad Company, corporate executives had reason for concern regarding the continuing violence, especially because streetcars had been specifically targeted by roving mobs. Black passengers were attacked and savagely beaten on the major lines, but the city's largest transportation company had suffered the worst damage: trolley windows shattered by clubs and gunshots, one motorman slightly wounded by a stray round, and a black trackman chased from a downtown streetcar and murdered in cold blood.[44] That morning, the company's ticket agent had urged black passengers to temporarily avoid the service, but with no authority to ban them and with so many workers needing the day's wages, more violence was nearly certain. Meanwhile, transportation executives descended on the mayor's office to promise their services, designating trains to transport patrolmen and special police to hotspots. This was a desperate attempt to protect corporate property and share prices, but reporters praised executives for their civic-minded generosity, saying they "came to the assistance of the mayor nobly."[45]

By comparison, stagecoach companies were uncooperative, refusing to provide horses and wagons for hazardous service despite reassurances that the city would cover any damages.[46] The agent for American Express explained that his teams were working twelve-hour shifts and too exhausted for additional overnight duty.[47] His counterpart at Wells Fargo had a more creative excuse. The agent explained that his only available horse was recovering from sickness, adding that five more horses had recently been reshod and were suffering from tetanus—all of them, simultaneously—while others would be working. "I very much regret to be in this condition," he apologized, "as I realize the situation."[48] Confronting a disappointing string of rejections, the mayor clarified his proposed terms by ordering special police officers to commandeer as many teams as they needed during the ongoing emergency—whereupon the horses miraculously healed themselves, much to the delight of the reporters who covered the story.[49]

Shaming uncooperative companies and cheering the property seizure, the press underscored the complex interplay between coercion and private sector cooperation during the mobilization, but the case of wholesaler A. Baldwin & Company showed how pressure could also work to corporate advantage. Dating to the antebellum period, the mercantile firm was a major player in the local and regional economies, with more than one hundred employees and traveling salesmen who covered ground from Florida to Mexico. "Mr. Baldwin is one of the best-known men in the city," boosters described, "interested in very many local concerns."[50] Before inheriting the family business, Albert Jr.'s concerns had once included crime fighting. After signing his name to the Sicilian massacre announcement alongside John Parker and others, the young merchant had distributed Winchester rifles to the execution squads that stormed the Old Parish Prison—Baldwin & Company guns were among those used to murder the eleven victims. Perhaps trading on his familiarity with logistics and lynch mobs, Baldwin had shown considerably more foresight than police commanders on Wednesday evening, posting white employees and night watchmen to defend his warehouse from possible looting until a police squad arrived to reinforce his private militia.[51]

As special police squads mobilized on Thursday afternoon, Baldwin epitomized the business community's about-face on lynch mobs, quickly contracting with city officials to arm special police officers with 500 pistols, 480 rifles, and 5,000 rounds. Whether motivated by civic duty, concerns about the rowdy crowds milling outside his warehouse, or the example made of a competitor whose gun store was shuttered for "selling ammunition to people of the lower class," Baldwin enthusiastically pushed his wares on the special police commander who came to pick up the guns. But when the officer questioned the need for so many guns, the businessman waved away his concerns. "I suggested to Mr. Baldwin that I didn't think we would require that many," Colonel Wood's second-in-command reported, "but he advised that an arrangement had been made." Days later when he attempted to return some unused weapons, an ulterior motive for the merchant's insistence emerged. Baldwin refused to accept them. All sales were final—sorry, no refunds.[52]

If the confusion and borderline profiteering suggested perhaps something less than a considered response from city leaders and civic-minded corporations, no doubts surfaced in the narrative that was rapidly coalescing. By Thursday evening, public and private resources were marshaled to suppress ongoing violence in the streets. Chastened by the mayor's office, police commanders were demanding that patrolmen step up and make arrests—there would be no repeating the previous night's performance.

Designated streetcars were ready to bring officers to hotspots, where respectable citizens with reliable pedigrees would help disperse crowds and arrest troublemakers. The strategy was simple: hundreds of guns on the streets, wielded by men determined to restore social order on unilateral terms favored by the business community. While the effectiveness of the coordinated response was uncertain as darkness fell on New Orleans, the conservative press had newfound optimism, inspired by the leading men in a depressing saga poised for a promising turn. Describing the "business-like preparations," reporters concluded, "Coming from the united commercial bodies, this hearty action did much to relieve the early gloom."[53]

These were comforting words, bringing to mind coolheaded merchants rallying to restore unstable markets—that is to say, the unvarnished reality of the situation. Hopefully it would be enough, but as editors pushed a positive angle on an otherwise grim story, they confronted another daunting challenge: accounting for the horrors that had taken place in the previous twenty-four hours, along with an emergency response that divided the white community by class rather than uniting it in the search for a dastardly black assassin. As merchants prepared to deploy, politicians and business leaders faced tough unanswered questions with consequences to be determined. Without some very creative accounting for exactly why mobs had been able to shut down the city, the new administration would be delegitimized in its infancy, bond markets would be poisoned, and the city's reputation would suffer a damaging, perhaps irrecoverable, blow. In other words, the battle of New Orleans would be lost already.

* * * *

AS CORRESPONDENTS FANNED out across New Orleans to cover the business community's counteroffensive and respond to ongoing citywide disturbances on Thursday evening, editors on Camp Street were busy polishing stories whose slants now seemed a foregone conclusion. It was a job complicated by the reality that publishing an accurate narrative was completely out of the question. With shaken readers mostly counting themselves among the better classes mobilizing to save the city, they could hardly write about how racially charged, profit-driven hiring practiced by white employers had contributed to the explosive conditions triggered by a chance meeting between a black workingman and aggressive officers. Nor could they question the sluggish response by municipal authorities during the slow-motion buildup to catastrophe, the obvious police complicity, and certainly not their own culpability for printing racist propaganda, which undeniably pushed the public mood toward violence as it teetered on the razor's edge. Confronting a crisis that had been substantially worsened by their own sensationalism, editors took a daring approach: collective amnesia.

The work of making sense of the spiraling tragedy had started on Tuesday afternoon, when *Daily States* newsboys selling the "Leading Evening Paper of the South" circulated the first full-length account of the Fourth Street murders.[54] It was soon joined by others. Based on these accounts, tensions were escalating for thirty-six hours before deadly mob violence erupted. But after tense standoffs between police officers and mobs on Tuesday evening, only the city's least popular, Republican-leaning daily had taken a proactive stance rejecting bloodshed, warning that it would compound the challenges already facing the city.[55]

It was overshadowed by its more-popular competition, Democrat-friendly newspapers whose positions ranged from comparatively moderate to essentially genocidal. Running the oldest and most popular daily, *Daily Picayune* editors followed tradition by tacking toward the middle, linking the ambush to the decade-long pattern of deadly violence against police officers and highlighting the need for new tough-on-crime policies without explicitly addressing the race angle.[56]

Heading the second-ranked daily, editor Page Baker was more provocative, citing the Morris Park controversy and blaming the "large number of worthless and dangerous negroes that have made New Orleans their refuge." Confessing that he had received numerous letters from "worthy colored men" denouncing the assassin and protesting against punishing the community for one individual's crimes, the editor questioned why they had allowed Charles to freely distribute anti-white propaganda, but settled for threatening rather than endorsing mob violence. Complaining that black residents "do nothing to help the community punish outlaws of their own race," he warned that they needed to cooperate with police to suppress "all the dangerous and suspicious negroes," or suffer the consequences.[57] Of course, in sending this strong message, Baker was ignoring his own newspaper's coverage. The same edition that published his editorial also reported on the black leaders who visited police headquarters within hours of the ambush, fully recognizing the risk to vulnerable residents.[58] Speaking with Baker's correspondents, one black attorney denounced "the murderous action of that black-hearted negro" and emphasized that Charles was an outsider who "did not belong to this community." Others actively debunked the complicity myth, promising that law-abiding black residents were outraged by the crimes and would fully cooperate with authorities.[59]

But during the run-up to violence, nobody in the conservative press had been interested in exonerating the black community—and if there were any doubts, readers only needed to turn to the *Daily States*, owned and operated by a Confederate veteran whose uncompromising white supremacist vision placed him on the ideological margins of polite society. Henry Hearsey had been predictably outrageous, all but cheering on the mob. Yet his musings on labor questions were perhaps even more controversial, holding white employers partially responsible for the race problem and claiming "the prosperity of Southern cities, New Orleans particularly, would be greatly enhanced if the negroes were relegated to plantations where they belong and white men employed in their places."

The problem: his argument was so obviously baseless, since virtually every white man with a payroll and ledger books proved it wrong on a daily basis. Nevertheless, the editor argued that employers overvalued black laborers, who were seen as "more effective and more reliable," rightfully so when desperation forced so many to accept brutal conditions and starvation wages. But economic and social desirability were profoundly at odds, Hearsey contended, particularly in urban space, where "the younger generation of blacks" was especially unruly, surveillance was a challenge, and criminals were protected by civilian sympathizers— assuming there was any real distinction between the lawbreakers and the black working classes to begin with. Now the cop killings had revealed the deadly consequences.[60] "Let this be a lesson preached to employers giving preference to negroes on the levee and elsewhere," Hearsey lectured, "over honest and able-bodied white men."[61]

As was so often the case, the *Daily States* editor was alone in his outrageous stance. Yet as he denounced profit-chasing employers for sacrificing the common good, glimpsing the common thread between class struggle and racial violence—even through the distorting prisms of white supremacy and black criminality—the most provocative voice in the New Orleans press corps was closer to the heart of the matter than his more restrained colleagues. Only weeks afterward, some would reluctantly acknowledge the disturbances as "bread riots" staged by white laborers "crowded from work they formerly fed and clothed themselves with." But as the crisis unfolded in real time, mainstream editors steadily refused to acknowledge this reality, even as the uprising forced them to confront an uncomfortable truth: the city's prosperity rested on the backs of laborers, black and white, forging a fragile truce every day as they were forced into a loser's bargain, pitted against one another in a race to the bottom of the wage scale.[62]

Waking up to the deadly consequences on Thursday morning, *Daily Picayune* editors dealt with an ugly truth by denying it categorically. Downgrading the crisis under a definitive headline, "NO RACE WAR," they dismissed the bloodthirsty predictions coming from many quarters that the overnight violence was the beginning of the end. They conveniently glossed over recent history, concluding that "the great body of white people and the masses of negroes" were fundamentally opposed to such a confrontation. This was the first stage of damage control, but although New Orleans could scarcely afford a white uprising that was quickly becoming more costly than the levee crisis during the mid-1890s, interracial labor solidarity was similarly unprofitable. Preserving the status quo required a careful balance, threading the needle's eye between union and explosive antagonism. Getting it back started with denying the relationship between labor tensions and violence targeting black men where they worked. Suddenly keen to emphasize how both races peacefully coexisted on job sites across the South, editors claimed a black man could "work as may please him, not even dominated by trade union organizations," perversely reframing the destruction of organized labor as evidence of freedom. With both sides getting such a good deal, they equated the assassin and the mob and concluded that it would be a shame to let a few bad actors spoil things. "There are bad negroes, just as there are bad whites," they argued, "but these lawless demonstrations can do irreparable damage to this city and the perpetrators must be crushed without mercy."[63]

Published as Thursday morning's lead editorial, the piece was part of a conservative press campaign to reframe the uprising in three steps: deny labor tensions, blame rogue actors on both sides of the color line, and demand a crackdown. An unwieldy front-page headline, "NEGROES HUNTED ALL NIGHT BY MOBS MADE OUT OF BOYS," reinforced the story by dismissing the participants, an improbable assemblage "composed almost entirely of boys under twenty-one years old." These were hardly "able-bodied white men" hard done by heartless employers— they were kids driven by a vaguely understood desire for vengeance and their own selfish motives. As reporters concluded, "They were hoodlums, given free rein."[64]

It was a compelling story, only weakened by the fact that it was so demonstrably untrue. As patrolmen finally began making arrests, the prisoners taken into custody were a far cry from the drunks, thugs, drifters, and juvenile delinquents blamed by newspapers. Accused of crimes ranging from disturbing the peace to brutal homicides, they were laborers, blacksmiths, longshoremen, boilermakers, and mechanics, a diverse collection of blue-collar tradesmen who more closely resembled a snapshot of the city's working classes.[65] They also revealed the combination of race hate, grievance, drunkenness, and opportunism that motivated them, along with the mental gymnastics required to blame outcasts. Named among the mob leaders, Joseph Roses promised that "a dozen witnesses" could verify that he was on duty as a watchman, suggesting that reporters were falsely accusing a man with a notorious criminal history.[66] More unexpected was the case of forty-six-year-old fireman George Blanque, who would eventually be convicted of disturbing the peace for drunkenly shooting at a black pedestrian near the Company No. 2 engine house on Thursday afternoon. Facing administrative charges before the Board of Fire Commissioners, the fireman readily confessed to his murderous actions, acknowledging that he "fired at the darky."[67] Concluding that Blanque was among the "men that the mayor was endeavoring to suppress with the aid of the citizen police," the board unceremoniously canned him. The difference between a fireman and a "hoodlum fireman" was apparently impossible to spot until he pulled out a pistol and started shooting.[68]

If those in custody challenged the press narrative, so did postmortem analysis of the overnight violence. Although editors portrayed the mob as spontaneous and haphazard, its movements suggested otherwise. Workers assembled at Lee Circle, a politically charged locus for demonstrations and a monument to white supremacy, then marched in formation by the Garden District mansions on famous St. Charles Avenue. They passed the sacred ground where the officers were martyred, then continued to Morris Park, which they reclaimed in response to the recent controversy. After pausing to honor the dead, they advanced on Orleans Parish Prison, mimicking the coup executed by elites a decade before. Black passengers in nearby streetcars were opportune targets, but also a way to show outrage over the failed segregation push, shut down that month by resistance from the companies whose customers they attacked and property they vandalized. When they were turned aside at the prison gates, the remaining demonstrators moved toward the next best hunting ground, Storyville and its surrounding dancehalls, where black laborers entertained themselves off the clock and rich white men enjoyed sexual license in luxurious brothels where prices started well beyond a workingman's daily wages. Rampaging through the notorious neighborhood and cheered on as champions by cheap white prostitutes, they returned the favor by attacking the black women who sold competing services from run-down cribs, before the demonstrations finally devolved into a boozed-fueled massacre leaving four black men dead—each one killed while earning a living. These were not rioters following a random course. This was a bloody statement by protesters moving with purpose at every step, a challenge by workingmen who had turned away from black comrades after the general strike and were now demanding that employers share the profits of white supremacy.[69]

Doing so, they forced a stunning reversal from the man who had done more to destroy interracial solidarity in New Orleans than anyone else.

During the streetcar controversy, the *Times-Democrat* editor reassured readers that his newspaper was "a strong supporter of white supremacy," before siding with executives against segregation.[70] But that was three weeks ago. Now confronting an economic crisis brought on by its rowdiest defenders, the editor reversed course. "The grand idea of white supremacy has become the stalking horse of anarchy," his Thursday morning editorial declared. From his pro-business perspective, the greater threat to prosperity was no longer the black menace—it was a red scare as dangerous as anything seen during the general strike. It seemed interracial labor solidarity and race war were Janus-faced sides of the same coin: united or divided, workers were trying to strong-arm employers. "Negro rule was not shattered to place the reins in the hands of the white disciples of the Commune," Baker warned. "Every industrious and law-abiding negro must be protected."[71]

Surveying the damage on Thursday evening, the editor understood how critical it was to assign blame for the crisis. The obvious choice was the administration he had campaigned against only months before. But given the promising early returns from a mayor who seemed eager to support the business community, Baker trained his guns elsewhere: on a broken police department and its enablers, the commissioners charged with discipline and promotion. How else to explain why a black radical and a few white outcasts had been able to plunge a great city into anarchy? The cowardice and dereliction on the force were plain as day, while the board was packed with appointees from previous administrations who "time and again allowed offenders to go free or pay trifling fines." That policy was "disastrous, in a double sense," demonstrated by a demoralized force standing down as empowered criminals ran the streets. By one reading, the pro-reform editor was paving for the next round of partisanship and targeting another machine administration. But his framing actually made space for coalition-building. Mayor Capdevielle had already taken a first step in the right direction by unleashing "the right-minded masses" to suppress the mob—Baker's editorial pointed the way forward after the deputized citizens did the job. Police corruption and indiscipline were existential threats to prosperity. The two-month-old administration should not be held responsible for its present state, but it would need to embrace overdue reforms to affirm its pro-business agenda. "We must economize our strength if we are to hold a place in the procession of modern progress," Baker concluded. "A great commercial city cannot live without absolute guarantees for the safety of labor and capital."[72]

Taking shape as businessmen prepared to retake New Orleans on Thursday evening, the consensus press narrative was based on whiplash repositioning, stunning hypocrisy, and willful blindness. It was also instantly gaining momentum across the political spectrum, from Henry Hearsey's *Daily States*, which unfavorably compared the police department to "an old discarded foot rag," to the black preachers who damned the "lawless element of both negroes and whites" and pleaded with authorities to "use the strong arm of the law with equal justice for all."[73] From this perspective, a dangerous, unforeseeable crisis had been caused by bad actors, but municipal authorities were responding aggressively, using methods favored by the business community. Police officers and administrators would be held responsible, while the mayor's office would be absolved—so long as it continued to make the right moves. With merchants coordinating strategy and hundreds of well-heeled young men preparing to clash with low-born hoodlums, the uprising was, just maybe, producing a welcome revolution in municipal affairs.[74] It was a story so promising that former political enemies were on the same team. John Parker had once served on the Citizens' League campaign committee, leading the crusade to destroy the old machine. But speaking with reporters, he expressed "absolute confidence" in the mayor's leadership and blasted those responsible for allowing the situation to get so bad. "The cowardice and striking inefficiency of the police force are a slur on the good name of New Orleans, and these men are unfit to wear the uniform," the young businessman complained, forcefully expressing opinions shared by his influential peers. "Thugs and hoodlums have been allowed to flaunt their misdeeds in public for two days—and not a single arrest!"[75]

With the police force in shambles, for the time being, it was up to the better classes to rescue the city. By Thursday evening, two dozen squads were sworn, equipped, and deployed under volunteer captains who also doubled as business leaders: executives, bankers, lawyers, brokers, and more. Reporters were following close behind, ready to write the next chapter in a narrative that was certain to inspire. Although deputizing civilians to serve as peace officers was a dicey strategy, the press ran with a different story, a heroic tale, recording exploits by young men drawn from the finest social circles. Some adventures were admittedly more thrilling than others. Posted to defend Orleans Parish Prison, members of the Pickwick Club soon realized there would be no repeating the previous night's showdown and arranged to have refreshments sent from their clubhouse. Other special police squads were a bit more active, patrolling the streets and breaking up crowds that looked threatening.[76]

Perhaps unsurprisingly, reporters attributed the evening's finest performance to the most prestigious social organization in New Orleans. "With a limited membership of bankers, professional men, leading officials, and merchants," according to guidebooks, the six-decade-old Boston Club—named for the card game, *not* the viper's nest of abolitionists—typically offered more genteel recreation to members. But they nonetheless made short work of a boisterous downtown mob that gathered shortly before sundown.[77] Confronting the "open-neck collar type," the genus unsuited to even serve them drinks, the young clubmen supposedly dispersed the hoodlums with no trouble. Courage was contagious, starting at the top and eventually working its way down to some patrolmen, who had been watching from a safe distance. After witnessing the scene, the officers perked up and "got really saucy with the crowd and called them dirty rats," an embarrassingly pale imitation of the upper-crust resolve they had just watched.[78]

As described by reporters, the confrontations in the heart of the business district were Social Darwinian fables, reinforcing hard-learned lessons from the crisis. Whereas the police were unable to bear the burdens of manhood, unable to neutralize the black assassin or turn aside white hoodlums, the finest private citizens were mastering the situation within hours as patrolmen watched enviously and hurled insults from the sidelines. Enabled by weakness, the worst had risen up, but they were now being suppressed by a better class. "The hoodlum does not like to look at a Winchester in the hands of a gentleman," reporters explained. "They are not afraid of the police, but when they see a strong, intelligent face behind a gun barrel, they edge away."[79]

Reinforcing this critical lesson, reporters described scenes from outside Baldwin's warehouse that afternoon, where the young clubmen entered to jeers from crude specimens gathering to gawk at the spectacle. But when they emerged "carrying weapons, death-dealing ones," the crowd silenced. These clerks were special police officers. Journalists recreated the scene as a montage, all idealized masculinity and looming violence, "blue-barreled weapons" almost as impressive as the "determined faces" behind them.[80] The phallic images were so compelling that the dialogue was only figurative. "'Those fellows sure will shoot,' remarked a young hoodlum who was loitering as a group of grey-haired businessmen marched through the door quietly.'"

"'You bet your life,' his companion agreed, and they slunk away."[81]

Raging in the imaginations of reporters, though not quite so intensely on the streets outside press offices, the real-time stories told about the ongoing struggle for social dominance were shaped by competing demands of race and class. For a business community responding primarily to an economic crisis, favorable press coverage served a critical purpose, reframing a counterrevolution to preserve capital's access to cheap black labor as a defense of *all* laborers. Obscuring the race-baiting opportunism that made possible such a wildly inequitable wealth distribution and refocusing on vaguely defined property rights and generalized prosperity enjoyed by the law-abiding classes—the only class that mattered—a fiasco might transform into triumph. But only so long as events on the ground cooperated reasonably. Although the clubmen turned away the ruffians on Canal Street before sundown, as darkness fell on restless streets and special police steeled themselves for nerve-wracking overnight shifts, the prospects for a peaceful night in New Orleans were anything but certain.

* * * *

FIFTEEN MINUTES AFTER midnight on Friday morning, Douglas and Hannah Mabry were sleeping in the second room of a shotgun-style cottage, located near the corner of Rousseau and St. Mary Streets, less than three hundred yards from the Sixth Precinct police station.[82]

The residence was home to three generations of New Orleans natives, shared by the couple's son and his wife, who had been married less than three years and had two young daughters.[83] The six occupants were sleeping when there was a sudden clamor outside, rousing twenty-four-year-old Harry Mabry, who shuffled to the front window and peered into the darkness. Several dozen white men were gathered outside. Heavily armed and apparently intoxicated, they shouted for the residents to send out three brothers who sometimes stayed with the family. When he received no response from inside the home, one of the besiegers stepped forward and doused the porch with coal oil. Then he struck a match and tossed it onto the flammable liquid. As orange flames danced across the steps, some rushed forward, tearing the shutters from the large glass windows and firing wild volleys into the residence, while others knocked down the front door and tried to force their way inside. After several minutes of chaos, the pandemonium subsided.[84]

As the mob melted away through back alleys and abandoned lots, Douglas Mabry gingerly made his way through the shattered home, bleeding from a severe gash on his foot caused by the broken glass. Taking stock of the damage, Mabry observed that his son had disappeared and his daughter-in-law was bleeding from her mouth—someone had punched her in the face, knocking out a tooth. His granddaughters were terror-stricken, but unharmed. Then he heard moans coming from the back of the house. Following the sounds of distress to the source, Mabry found his wife of three decades, curled up on the floor and groaning in agony. She had been running toward the backyard when a round struck her just below the right shoulder blade. Blood was filling her ruptured lung and she was struggling to breathe.[85]

Posted within earshot of the crime scene, members of Special Police Squad No. 1 had been resting and socializing at the Sixth Precinct police station when they heard the gunshots. Rushing toward the scene, they faced the wrath of white residents.[86] "Nigger lovers," came the shouts.[87] Reaching the cottage as the mob remnants scattered onto darkened side streets, the special police officers managed to make one arrest before entering the home and finding the Mabry family hiding inside. Among the squad members was a physician, who examined Hannah's wound and "said that it was caused by a .38-caliber bullet and that it was a very dangerous one."[88] Squad members summoned an ambulance and spread out to canvass the predominantly white neighborhood, where they received a cold reception. Hostile witnesses denied knowing the perpetrators, whose familiarity with the Mabry family raised suspicions that they lived nearby. After a useless search, officers escorted the shell-shocked Douglas Mabry to the Sixth Precinct stationhouse, where he struggled to comprehend the sudden, unimaginable suffering. "He could not realize why his little family had been so murderously attacked," sympathized reporters, "and he was inconsolable when his wife was driven off in the ambulance, piteously moaning in her pain."[89]

As the ambulance reached Charity Hospital, where surgeons worked desperately to save Hannah Mabry's life, the mayor was three blocks away, finalizing his Friday morning press release. Addressing reporters outside his office during the day, Capdevielle had boldly declared his purpose. "I'm here to stay until I have the situation met and conquered," he swore, bringing to mind a general before a battle, or maybe tough business negotiations. "I'm going to take this thing by the throat and refuse to let go until my terms are met."[90]

Now with special police officers flooding the streets, by one o'clock Friday morning, he was prepared to declare victory. Detailing the decision to mobilize special police officers and his pride that the proclamation had met with "an instant response from the best classes," Capdevielle confidently pronounced, "I feel that we have the situation well in hand."[91]

As the mayor worked on his press release, surgeons were struggling to repair the damage caused by the bullet that had torn through Hannah Mabry's right lung. They were losing the race as blood continued to flood her chest cavity. Two hours after Capdevielle declared peace on the streets, as reporters finished confidence-inspiring stories and the mayor prepared for bed, Mabry expired. Later that morning, medical examiners would complete a state-issued death certificate, standardized documentation for an unusually tragic end: "Be it remembered, that on this day, Hannah Mabry, colored, native of Louisiana, aged fifty-two years, departed this life at the Charity Hospital in this city. Cause of Death, Gun Shot Wd. Of Thorax, Int. Hemorrhage."[92]

Hannah's death was a problem for editors. It was too shocking to ignore, but it threatened to undermine the mayor's rose-colored perspective on the situation, a view they were desperate to promote. So they settled for cognitive dissonance. Reporting both stories on the front page, the *Daily States* placed optimism and outrage side by side, relying on readers to somehow square the difference. Under a reassuring headline, "PEACE AND ORDER REIGN," one story praised city officials and business leaders for suppressing the uprising. "While there may have been instances where negroes were troubled by hoodlums," it assured, "no serious difficulties have occurred."[93] Inches away, another headline reported one of those unserious instances: "A FOUL MURDER." Illustrations showed before-and-after images depicting the humble Mabry home transformed into a bullet-riddled crime scene. That story began: "By far the dastardliest outrage committed by the murderous bands of hoodlums who took charge of the city until Mayor Capdevielle, with the better elements, mastered the situation, occurred this morning at a cottage tenanted by negroes. It was a fitting climax to the carnival of crime . . ."[94]

Between sundown and sunrise, the city's finest citizens had recaptured the streets from mindless juvenile rioters and an innocent woman had been murdered in her home, mutually exclusive narratives advanced by dueling front-page headlines: New Orleans as it was and New Orleans as its business community needed it to be. For respectable white residents, conflicting stories might coexist so long as bond purchasers expected peace and the murders were confined to certain demographics. But as the sun rose on Friday morning, closing out the most disastrous business week in anyone's memory, circumstances on the ground were playing rough with the press narrative, despite the handful of white men arrested on Thursday for disturbing the peace and public intoxication.[95] Just after sunrise, another gang randomly attacked a black man who was job hunting downtown, knocking him through a glass display window near Hyman Levy's clothing store.[96] Meanwhile, black longshoremen desperate enough to risk their lives worked under armed guard, and rumors circulated that white lynch mobs and black revolutionaries were mobilizing across the city, ready to bring on the race war that editors were strenuously denying.[97]

But if reassuring stories had done little to stabilize the perspective from the streets, they could shape perceptions among residents—and those observing from a distance. Inside the commercial exchanges, businessmen were spending another nervous morning, waiting on news from the nation's investment banking capital. More than any front-page crime story, the financial scoreboard would determine the success or failure of the special police mobilization. When the news finally arrived, this time it sparked widespread celebration. "Yesterday, under the influence of unfortunate local disturbances then existing, state bonds declined from 108½ to 107¾," business reporters explained, "but the complete restoration of tranquility in the city has been followed by perfectly reestablished confidence in state and city securities, thanks to the masterful handling of the trouble and prompt suppression of peace disturbances by Mayor Capdevielle." Publicly traded companies showed equal resilience: street railways and slaughterhouses were both identified as particularly strong performers.[98]

The welcome financial news gave editors a desirable narrative arc through which to frame the city's recent trauma: crime, crisis, counteroffensive, calm, and confidence restored. The only missing piece was closure, since the third day searching for the assassin had been as frustrating as the others. On Thursday afternoon, more than a dozen officers had responded to reports that Charles was holed up in a downtown apartment building, but they found nothing when they surrounded and searched the place, arresting an unrelated black man for carrying a concealed weapon.[99] Later that evening, word arrived from neighboring St. Bernard Parish that the fugitive was in custody on a local plantation. Reporters excitedly rushed to the scene to secure the scoop, but they discovered nothing more than muddy fields for their troubles.[100] With bond markets surging, *Daily States* editors preparing the newspaper's Friday afternoon edition declared victory over white hoodlums who had momentarily seized the spotlight and refocused readers on unfinished business: the whereabouts of the black villain who caused all the trouble. On the front page, they asked the question that was thankfully beginning to dominate the story once more: "WHERE IS CHARLES?"[101]

7

Crucible

SHORTLY BEFORE THREE O'CLOCK ON FRIDAY AFTER-noon, July 27, 1900, an intriguing memo reached the Second Precinct stationhouse on the corner of Terpsichore and Chippewa Streets, where Sergeant Gabriel Porteous was preparing for another tense evening. The police veteran had been tested to his limits by the week's events. After he earned praise for preventing bloodshed on Tuesday evening, Porteous was a pallbearer at his murdered comrade's funeral the following afternoon, even as rumors swirled that his cowardly brother-in-law allowed the cop killer to escape. Later that evening, Porteous was unable to stop the mob that formed at Lee Circle and marched down St. Charles Avenue, which divided the precinct between its Garden District mansions and the working-class neighborhoods where officers were a more common presence. Given his personal stake in the frustrating search, Porteous was primed for action when the message arrived suggesting that Robert Charles was supposedly hiding somewhere in the overcrowded quarter bounded by railroad depots, lumberyards, and cotton presses.[1]

The information was sketchy, but it came from a promising source. The previous day, a black laborer named Fred Clark had given police a potential lead. On its face, the tip was no better than countless others that had poured into headquarters and sent officers scrambling on pointless searches, but Clark was a known snitch with a reputation as a "good negro" among detectives, someone who regularly supplied them with reliable information.[2] According to Clark's sources, Charles had a half-brother named Silas Jackson residing somewhere nearby. Word on the street was that his wife, Martha Jackson, knew something about the assassin's whereabouts. It was thin, so much that police commanders waited over twelve hours to pass it along to the Second Precinct stationhouse. But despite the growing consensus that Charles had somehow fled New Orleans, the lead ultimately reached a sergeant who was particularly motivated. Porteous decided to investigate. Reporters would portray a dramatic scene, claiming the sergeant was handpicked for a life-threatening mission. Just as his murdered friend had done, Gabe Porteous responded with manly stoicism. "I know that it'll be dangerous to get the negro, but that's what I'm paid to do," he declared. "It's my duty to go—and I am going to do my duty."[3]

The truth was a bit less stirring. When the message arrived on Friday afternoon, the stationhouse was almost deserted. Most of the patrolmen had returned home for early dinners, anticipating another long night to start the weekend. Others were walking beats, but Porteous was at the station, supported by one of the department's most experienced officers. Corporal John Lally had begun his law enforcement career as a doorman in the suburbs, working his way through department ranks over more than two decades and earning a reputation as a brave and dependable man.[4] With time to kill before sundown, both officers decided to investigate the late-breaking lead. They instructed the station's clerk to send any returning patrolmen toward the neighborhood to reinforce them. According to reporters who interviewed police commanders, the decision to go it alone suggested that neither assigned much value to the tip. "Porteous was very careful," they noted, "and while his bravery was never questioned, he didn't believe in taking unnecessary risks."[5]

The officers picked up reinforcements at the railroad terminal, where two patrolmen were stationed to watch the promising escape route. With only cross streets and the vaguely described woman named Martha to go on, the makeshift four-man squad headed toward the general location and began questioning pedestrians, who pointed them to the corner of Saratoga and Erato Streets, where a small cottage adjoined a bustling fruit stand. Steeling themselves to face unknown dangers, they instead confronted Martha Williams, an elderly woman crippled with rheumatism, who had been ironing clothes when the unexpected visitors showed up on her doorstep. The officers were stern, telling her about the troubling information they had received and demanding to search the house. They brusquely pushed inside and rummaged through every closet and cupboard, even checking the unfinished space beneath the eaves. "They went through every place in the house," she complained, "and then the big man asked if I knew Si or Martha Jackson."[6]

Williams directed the officers to a green apartment complex about a block away, then watched as the confused squad paused outside the wrong house once again, where a woman pointed them toward the right building. "The officers went into Martha Jackson's house and a few minutes afterwards, I heard a shot and then several others," she remembered. "I knew they had found the man."[7]

The apartment where Martha Williams had pointed the squad was located near the end of Saratoga Street, a few houses from the three-way intersection with Clio Street, which served as the downriver boundary that separated the residential neighborhood from adjacent sawmills and lumberyards. The property formed a deep rectangle—the shorter side facing the street—and it was shared by two buildings, one on the street and the other separated by a small courtyard. Both were covered in weather-beaten clapboard and painted the same pale green shade. Positioned directly against the banquette, the primary building was a two-story duplex with both sides divided into top and bottom two-room apartments, four separate living spaces in total. Covered alleyways ran along both sides of the structure and provided access to the courtyard, which was divided by a low, vine-covered fence. Beyond the open space, an outbuilding occupied the rear of the property. It was smaller than the main structure and also divided in the middle, forming two separate apartments, each made up of single rooms on the top and bottom floors, the ceilings so low that it was more accurately described as a one-and-a-half-story structure.[8]

Living arrangements in the apartment complex reflected the integration of the city's working-class neighborhoods and the ingenuity of its poorest residents, who often blurred the color line while navigating the pricey realities of New Orleans rental markets. Working as a machinist, thirty-five-year-old John Joyce owned the uptown side of the main building and lived there with his wife and two young daughters.[9] The white family's next-door neighbors were a black married couple, Silas and Martha Jackson, who rented from a white man and lived on one side of the rear building with their two young daughters.[10] For the previous decade, Silas Jackson had been something like a business partner to his landlord, subleasing rooms in the remaining three apartments to friends and family members who needed accommodations, an arrangement that made sense to both sides. The landlord received a guaranteed income from the property, while the entrepreneurial Jackson family patriarch rented the rooms at a small markup, charging an informal broker's fee in exchange for his services. It was a side business made possible by his day job as a mechanic for the railroad company, which connected him to the world of mobile black laborers, who were easy marks for swindlers who promised cut-rate deals on housing. Jackson provided a trustworthy option to an extended network of family members, acquaintances, and referrals.[11] Seven tenants currently shared the rental spaces. Silas Jackson, his family, and his cousin Burke lived in the rear building. Six people shared four rooms on the downtown side of the main building. Two older couples—Annie Gant and Albert Jackson, along with Boss and Imogene Nixon—lived on the lower floors, while Silas Jackson's brother and cousin, Charles and Isaac, occupied the upstairs rooms.[12]

While the Jackson and Joyce clans had peacefully coexisted for years, shocking events would soon divide them into camps that corresponded to the color lines they blurred: innocent and guilty. Although the white residents would be presumed blameless, the connection between Silas Jackson and Robert Charles was unexpectedly tough to unravel. They were originally reported to be half-brothers, but the men shared no family ties, blood or otherwise. Like the snitch's original information, which had sent officers after a crippled old woman, the actual connection had been garbled in translation. Silas Jackson did have a brother named Charles who lived on the property, but he had nothing to do with the case. More significantly, his wife was the mysterious Martha, a Mississippi native from the same county as the fugitive, hence the connection. Although the tip was wrong on critical details, it gave police enough to retrace the rumor to its promising source, the complex where an old friend of Robert Charles lived with her husband and a brother-in-law with a dangerous name. After a few detours, they finally reached the Jackson family's doorstep.

Shortly after three o'clock on Friday afternoon, Silas Jackson returned home from work early, preparing for an out-of-town job. Ten other people—five residents and five visitors—were on the property. Inside the main building, Imogene Nixon was playing cards with George Ford, a family friend who was visiting from Texas, both waiting for her husband to return from his own job. Jackson greeted them and made his way to the rear building to clean up and eat dinner with his wife, but after thirty minutes, he heard a commotion outside—some muffled conversation, Nixon's voice calling out to him, and crunching footsteps. From the second-story window, he saw two police officers approaching the back property. Feeling a surge of dread in his stomach, Jackson descended the stairs to greet the unwanted visitors.[13]

By the time officers finally arrived, they were starting to suspect that the unpromising tip might be leading them in the right direction, toward the suspect's hiding place. Residents had confirmed that a man named Charles, related to Silas Jackson, lived on the premises. And yes, a woman named Martha. The coincidence was striking. Outside the property, Sergeant Porteous ordered his second-in-command, Corporal Lally, to follow him into the passageway, leaving the two patrolmen to guard the street in case the suspect was actually there and attempted to run. They knocked at the main building and spoke with a black woman inside, who directed them to the smaller duplex at the back of the property.[14]

The officers crossed the narrow courtyard and reached the rear building, where Silas Jackson greeted them nervously. Without exchanging pleasantries, the men gruffly demanded entry, before shoving inside and scanning the downstairs room. Sunlight streamed through a small window, somewhat brightening the cramped space—twelve by eighteen feet, according to later reports. On first glance, nothing appeared out of the ordinary. The room was tidy and furnished. An armoire and sewing machine stood to the left of the entrance, while a square bedframe sat awkwardly in the middle of the room, leaving barely enough space to access the staircase that wrapped around the back wall. Behind a door and tucked under the steps, there was a narrow storage space.[15]

Momentarily satisfied, Sergeant Porteous turned his attention to the nervous subject in front of him, demanding to know the whereabouts of his half-brother, the fugitive known as Robert Charles. Seeming bewildered, Silas admitted that his brother Charles was staying in the main building, but his last name was Jackson and he had nothing to do with any murders. Now less certain, the officers suggested that his name was Robert Charles Jackson, but Silas insisted. They were wrong.[16] Frustrated and flustered, Porteous threatened to arrest him for obstruction, but the man responded that he had nothing to hide and welcomed the chance to clear his name. "I told them I wasn't afraid to go to jail because I hadn't done nothing," Jackson recalled. "They said that I didn't want to go, but I told them I did and wouldn't give them any trouble."[17]

Flummoxed by Jackson's convincing performance, Sergeant Porteous decided to place him under arrest and bring him to the station for questioning, then paused to evaluate the situation. The apartment was stifling. As his adrenaline ebbed, the veteran officer seemed to notice the ninety-degree heat for the first time. The department's summer coats were made from lighter flannel, but the high-buttoned jacket and long pants were uncomfortable on a sweltering July afternoon.[18] Then he spotted a water bucket and dipper by the staircase. Porteous said he was thirsty and began to make his way across the room, unaware that the closet door had been cracked open since he entered the room. Concealed in the darkness, a Winchester barrel rose up.[19]

There was a booming report, followed by the deafening roar of five shots fired in rapid succession. Jets of flame erupted from the closet as Robert Charles furiously worked the rifle's lever action. Porteous doubled over instantly as the first shot hammered him in the abdomen, punching through his liver and kidney. Before he could respond, two more bullets slammed into his right thigh, sending him to the ground. He was flat on his stomach when a fourth shot ripped into his side, piercing his heart and lungs, killing him instantly.[20]

Looking away when the deadly barrage began, Lally had only seconds to process the sudden explosions, but managed to spin toward the closet door and reach for his weapon. Before he could draw, Charles shot him through the stomach, the bullet passing through his intestines and tearing apart his colon. Blood gushed from the hideous wound as the corporal crashed to the ground, falling almost on top of his partner's dead body.[21]

The closet door burst open and Robert Charles bolted from hiding, sprinting up the stairs with his Winchester rifle and Colt pistol, his pockets stuffed with shells. From the second-story bedroom, he could hear groans coming from downstairs and realized that his only viable escape was blocked. He grabbed a shovel and smashed the flimsy plasterboard that divided the rear building into separate apartments, creating a hole large enough to pass through. Despite the new escape route, Charles remained in the rear building. From windows on both sides of the upstairs rooms, he had clear shots at the courtyard and the houses facing the opposite street, fields of fire that commanded both entrances and much of the surrounding neighborhood. Shielding the windows using curtains, shades, and shutters, Charles positioned himself near the staircase. Then he watched and waited.[22]

Beneath the sniper's nest, Silas Jackson wandered around the open space, handcuffed and badly shaken, but unharmed. Stunned by what happened, Jackson had stared at the fallen officers for a few moments, barely reacting as the gunman burst from hiding. Finally the truth seemed to dawn on him. "Oh Lord," Jackson shouted. He wheeled around and ran from the room, before stopping in the courtyard, stumped again. Aimlessly wandering between the buildings, over and over again, he cried, "Oh Lord! Oh Lord!"[23]

As the traumatized man paced the courtyard, others on the property responded to the explosion of gunfire. At home entertaining with her visiting mother and sister, Margaret Joyce scooped up her two daughters and ran to a neighbor's house, where they waited for police reinforcements to arrive. Martha Jackson did the same, grabbing her infant daughter and running to safety, but she was arrested by the police officers she encountered. It was a fate shared by the other black residents and visitors. While the white homeowners were treated as victims from the beginning, they were accused of conspiracy from the earliest moments of the investigation, even though nearly everyone could make a plausible case for innocence.[24]

Suspicion would extend beyond the property line, as black neighbors faced potentially serious consequences for being near the scene and responding logically to the sudden violence. One door down, twenty-nine-year-old John Willis was known to friends and neighbors for his anxious disposition, but his nerves had been taxed to the breaking point in recent days. On Friday afternoon, the construction worker was unwinding at home when he heard the sounds that he had been dreading since the crisis began. "I was in my house when I heard shots and thought that the white folks were killing us again," Willis explained. "I made up my mind to run and went out the back way."[25]

The decision backfired. Willis bolted out the door and hurdled a fence separating his home from the murder scene, drawing attention from white onlookers who mistook him for the gunman. "There he goes," someone shouted. "There he goes over the fence!"[26]

Startled by the eruption of gunfire, the two patrolmen stationed on the street outside the complex responded to the commotion. "We ran and saw a negro climbing over the fence," they explained. "We grabbed him and turned him over to some other officers who had come up."[27]

One block from the Saratoga Street apartment complex, Patrolman Peter Finney was napping at his nearby home when his sister roused him, saying there was gunfire nearby. He rushed to the scene and encountered two fellow officers, who had returned to the station and been sent as backup. They entered the property through the passageway and spotted Silas Jackson in the courtyard, taking him into custody before approaching the rear building. When they peered through a broken window, they saw the fallen officers, sprawled on the bloody floor of the downstairs room.[28] Porteous was clearly dead, but the corporal was gasping and turned to the patrolmen who entered the room. "I'm fatally wounded," Lally groaned. "I'd like to see a priest. Go and get one quick."[29]

By now, curious bystanders were descending on the neighborhood, drawn by gunfire and fast-spreading rumors about the source of the disturbance. There was nobody to establish a cordon and the boldest civilians were piling into the courtyard, including a young man who shared a strange connection to the escaped assassin.[30] Nineteen-year-old Albert Brumfield was among the Southern News Company's best salesmen, a "bright and intelligent boy" who sold refreshments to passengers aboard the trains that crisscrossed the countryside.[31] Several weeks before, Brumfield was arrested in Copiah County—the birthplace of Charles—charged with illegally selling liquor as his train passed through the dry county.[32] Brumfield had been confined to the company's office on Rampart Street since posting bond, where he spotted a patrolman and a priest and decided to follow them back to the scene.[33] He was standing there along with a dozen or more men when a police officer stepped outside, demanding silence as the father administered last rites to the dying man. With the death toll rising and the fugitive apparently in the wind—again—the onlookers were growing more and more restless, angrily questioning, "Where is he?"[34]

At that moment, the answer came in thundering booms. The sound was unmistakable. "I knew that a Winchester rifle had been fired," a witness remembered. "I looked up quickly and saw the arms of a negro thrust out of the window."[35]

The onlookers scattered, but agonized shrieks revealed that damage had been done. One round had pierced Brumfield's stomach, burrowing through his intestines and lodging against the back of his pelvic bone.[36] Crashing to the ground, paralyzed, the teenager screamed, "Oh, God!" Alone in the courtyard, he dragged himself up a few steps, then turned toward the shooter above him and pleaded. "For God's sake, don't shoot!"

Charles fired again. The round slammed through Brumfield's torso, destroying his heart and killing him instantly. Inside the rear building, the priest and three armed police officers were frozen. The low ceiling creaked as Charles paced above them, but none made any move to climb the stairs and confront him. Remembering an ordeal that would continue for more than thirty minutes, a witness described the helpless feeling in words rich with unintended meaning. "The negro had only fired four shots," he remembered, "and he was the master of the situation."[37]

* * * *

BARELY SIX HUNDRED yards from the scene of the ambush, the mayor of New Orleans was maintaining his string of extremely poorly timed absences on Friday afternoon, relaxing in the Turkish baths at the

St. Charles Hotel, which ranked "among the finest in the country" according to those who knew these things.[38] Although the fugitive was in the wind and the mood on the streets remained tense, Paul Capdevielle was soaking away his troubles when calls from police headquarters interrupted his downtime and forced him back to the office. There he prepared new emergency measures with support from administrators, business leaders, and special police commanders. Capdevielle ordered citizens to remain home and charged police to enforce the curfew. He mobilized Gatling guns commanded by Louisiana militiamen and authorized the machine gunners to open fire if necessary—only after giving unruly mobs a five-minute warning. Then he sent an urgent message to the armory directing every available man to the scene of the shooting.[39]

Special police officers were way ahead of him. At the makeshift headquarters, a few dozen men had been relaxing and socializing before the overnight shifts began. Despite the partially successful deployment the previous evening, the mood was subdued. For three days, the unavenged police deaths had poisoned the atmosphere, an unanswered challenge hanging over the white citizenry. But that was about to change. As word of the ambush reached them, Colonel Wood and his commanders sprang into action—so quickly that there was no time to validate credentials—handing out guns to anyone who presented themselves. "I didn't feel that it was a time when red tape should be insisted upon," his second-in-command explained, retrospectively admitting his mistake. "Many of those men never came back and their arms got into the hands of others."[40]

The promiscuous weapons distribution symbolized the breakdown of barriers between special police and lynch mobs. Authorities understood the imperative—despite the mayor's orders, the showdown with Charles belonged to the entire white community—but as enraged gunmen descended on the majority-black neighborhood, there were uncomfortable parallels to Wednesday night's disorderly mobs. Newspaper stories that appeared the next morning would make critical distinctions, explaining that "businessmen, professional men, and men high in both commercial and social circles composed the vast majority of those who hurried to the scene," as well-bred women "stood in their doorways with blanched cheeks, but the same determined light in their eyes that was reflected from every man."[41] Published on Friday afternoon as the events were actually unfolding, the *Daily States* special edition more accurately captured the chaos with its real-time headline: "BLOODY RIOT UP TOWN."[42]

Terrible scenes elsewhere in New Orleans further undermined the press narrative. As vigilantes rushed toward the shooting, gangs roaming near the French Market struck again. Joseph Scott was walking along the levee and carrying a dinner pail when white men spotted and chased him into the courtyard of a Gallatin Street warehouse. He scrambled upstairs and vaulted from a second-story balcony, crashing onto the banquette and springing to his feet as bullets snapped around him. Scott raised his hands in a last-ditch surrender and begged to be taken alive, but it was hopeless. There was a volley and he crumpled to the ground.[43] Some time passed before police arrived to reclaim his body. Scott was shot multiple times, stabbed postmortem, and stripped of his few possessions.[44] With nobody around who could positively identify the victim, reporters wrote his eulogy from what they could gather at a glance: "The murdered negro was copper colored, about five-feet-eleven-inches, thirty-five years of age, and dressed in blue overalls."[45]

As mob scenes played out across town, the situation on Saratoga Street was quickly heading in the same direction. Scores of armed men had the complex surrounded, but although the shocking execution of Albert Brumfield had cleared the courtyard, three uninjured police officers and a civilian were still trapped downstairs in the rear building, along with the priest and Corporal Lally, who was on the brink of death.[46] Meanwhile, Charles was upstairs, preventing the men below from escaping. Soon they were alerted to another potentially deadly scenario, when rounds began showering the house from outside, bullets penetrating the thin siding as "the lead began to hit the house like so much rain."[47] Gunmen scrambled onto neighboring rooftops and angled for position on the streets outside the property, firing with no pretense of discipline. Incoming rounds ripped through both stories of the rear building from every direction, a barrage so hot that buckets of water had to be brought to cool overheating rifle barrels.[48] For the officers and civilians trapped downstairs, the white men surrounding the building posed a more serious threat than the black man presumed to be upstairs.[49]

Among the most recognizable faces outside the property was a long-time machine boss whose printing shop had cornered the market on municipal publishing contracts, which included annual police reports. Recognizing the hazard—and perhaps sensing an opportunity—he ordered special police officers to cover him and enlisted a young reporter to join the relief mission. They burst from the alleyway and sprinted to the rear building, dragging the dying corporal to the street outside. The distraction bought time for the trapped civilians and officers to scramble to safety. Now strengthened by reinforcements, the two-man rescue party returned to reclaim the bodies of Gabriel Porteous and Albert Brumfield.[50] Although the politician supposedly downplayed his bravery, reporters upscaled the scene to biblical proportions, describing the silence and collective "prayer for the salvation of their souls" as the crowd watched the rescuers going to their deaths, before "the great delight when the two fearless men came out of the alley bearing the bodies shook the very ground."[51]

As the downstairs room cleared, more than thirty minutes after the ambush had been sprung, Robert Charles was finally alone in the rear building. Peering through shutters and curtains, he assessed a bleak situation. Hundreds of armed men surrounded the property, joined by thousands of civilians. The position was inescapable. Scattered rounds fired from windows and rooftops were becoming a dangerous nuisance, regularly punching through the structure's thin walls and buzzing the room. There were even more immediate concerns. Less than ten yards away, the upper windows of the main building exposed his position to accurate gunfire. Pushed back against nearby property lines, sheds behind the parallel houses fronting Rampart Street provided similar advantages to attackers within easy range. But despite these multiple dangers, the defensive position had its advantages, particularly a commanding view of the courtyard and alleyways leading to the street outside, which prevented attackers from easily storming the rear building without risking heavy casualties. On balance, the chokepoints partially diminished the lopsided odds and offered a skilled rifleman the possibility of extending the siege, but nothing more promising.[52]

Surrounded, outgunned, and facing certain death, Charles played a nerve-shredding cat-and-mouse game to perfection. Excruciating minutes passed as bullets hummed over and through his sanctuary, with no signs of movement from within. Frustrated gunmen jockeyed to find cleaner shots from positions around the property, exposing themselves to return fire. None came. Suddenly the curtains rustled and the shutters creaked, drawing a wild fusillade. In a flash, a rifle barrel darted from another window and unseen hands smoothly worked the Winchester's action to unleash a withering barrage—three rounds, five rounds, terribly accurate. Then the shadow disappeared as the scorching response chewed the wood siding to pieces.[53]

With his extraordinary composure and physical courage, Charles posed a dangerous challenge to his attackers, but also to the reporters struggling to make sense of the unbelievable spectacle from a safe distance. From the Dryades Street shootout to the Fourth Street murders, they had attributed his success to raw savagery rather than tactical brilliance, essentially the same ferocity shown by the ravishers, brutes, desperadoes, and other racialized villains they covered regularly. The gunman on Saratoga Street was harder to put in those familiar categories. He was cerebral and technical, showing coolheaded prowess in a highest-stakes performance witnessed by thousands. Charles was making his opponents—including special police officers from the finest stock in New Orleans—seem uncomfortably impotent by comparison. White observers conceded the undeniable. "With desperation and the determination to take as many with him as possible, Charles fought with deadly strategy," they acknowledged. "He worked the weapon with incredible rapidity, his wonderful marksmanship never failed him, and when he missed, it was only by the narrowest margin."[54]

As the minutes passed, the other side paid a heavy price. Among those surrounding the property was forty-five-year-old Andrew Van Kuren, who guarded petty offenders at the minimum-security police lockup downtown. He was unarmed, helping to reload weapons and watching the gunfight from the ground-floor kitchen of a nearby home, cheering on the shooters. "Whoop it up!" he hollered. "Kill that son of a bitch!"

As Van Kuren bounced around the room, someone warned him to be careful. "I'm the real thing," he scoffed. "I ain't afraid of no nigger on earth!"

Suddenly, there was movement in a second-floor window in the rear building, prompting a hot barrage from the attackers. It was another ruse. Using a metal rod, Charles had pushed open the shutters from a safe distance as fire ripped through the window. Van Kuren chose this moment to get a better view, stepping from the kitchen and onto the back stoop. The jailer was straining to see when a rifle barrel rose up behind a broken pane, concealed by curtains. The gun bucked and Van Kuren collapsed, his fingers desperately grabbing his throat as he bled to death on the stairs.[55]

Van Kuren's senseless death underscored the frustrations shared by white men across New Orleans as the afternoon shadows lengthened. Despite a searing enfilade sustained for more than ninety minutes by a hundred guns or more, strategic bursts coming from a single man were proving far more dangerous, including to fifty-six-year-old Howell Batte, an insurance salesman who was desperately wounded by a bullet that passed through both lungs—it would take him three days to die.[56] By late afternoon, perhaps twenty men had been struck by rounds piercing arms, shoulders, legs, abdomens—and more sensitive regions. Among the injuries, reporters documented a "perforating gunshot wound of right forearm and scrotum," sustained by a notable local businessman and "inflicted by Charles."[57]

By concluding definitively that his wince-inducing wound had been inflicted by the coolheaded assassin in the rear building as opposed to the countless gunmen firing wildly in his general direction, reporters cosigned one unappealing narrative to avoid a perhaps even more embarrassing truth—the city's leading players, panicking and unmanning themselves. Fighting on the winning side of hundreds-against-one odds, the variously skilled shooters participated in a spectacle that was as much public performance as honest-to-God gun battle. Simulating bravery mattered more than shooting prowess. The dangers, real and exaggerated; thunder and smoke, obscuring good and poor marksmanship; the many hangers-on with no weapons, hovering around the shooters and jabbering advice, as confident as it was useless; the mad energy, the freewheeling burlesque; and the audacious villain in the rear building, doing the impossible and holding back an army—it was chaos as mythmaking,

manly incompetence redeemed by volume alone. When the shooting finally ended, witnesses counted an estimated five thousand holes pock-
marking the rear building.[58] Just as the patrolmen needed Charles to be
something more than a desperate subject with a gun, special police needed
him to operate with superhuman speed and precision. He needed to be
everywhere, endangering every man. "A bullet would sing from a front
window down into the little yard; another would whistle over to the side,"
reporters described. "These replies would come from all four windows in-
discriminately, showing that he was keeping a close watch in every
direction."[59]

Less than a mile away from the shooting, editors in the Camp Street
press offices were racing in real time to shape the undesirable scenes into
a vaguely plausible narrative, but passions soon threatened to draw them
into the action. Unable to reach the working-class neighborhood where
gunshots resounded, huge numbers of white men began converging to
receive word straight from the source, milling in the muddy street and
standing transfixed before the bulletin boards outside the *Times-Democrat*
building, which served as a low-tech ticker for breaking news. Starting
with hazy reports about a shooting, staffers were posting regular updates,
but as the bare facts appeared long before editorialists could attach sooth-
ing explanations, the mood darkened considerably. Nervously eying the
potentially combustible and soon thousands-strong crowds gathering outside their windows, reporters described a "throbbing, ominous sound,
like a severe storm approach" when they posted confirmation that two
more police officers were dead. Subsequent updates did nothing to calm
the mob. As the scoreboard continued to reflect a one-sided rout of the
home team, the situation was deteriorating quickly. Little more than two
hours into the siege, New Orleans was back on the brink of anarchy—
and authorities were getting desperate.[60]

Over at the mayor's office, the strategy sessions were veering toward
absurdity. The fire chief suggested dynamiting the rear building, insist-
ing that his men were skilled enough to avoid, say, blowing up the neighborhood. State militia officers countered that Gatling guns were the
better option, but Mayor Capdevielle was no more enthusiastic about
spraying the general area with automatic weapons fire, especially with

thousands of civilians packing as close to the property as they could.[61] Gradually the conversation turned to a more plausible option, but one that was nearly as risky. Properly executed, setting a controlled fire could smoke out Charles and end the siege. But there were good arguments to be made against such a reckless course. The city had twice burned to the ground during its colonial period and in the century since, its residents had reconstructed hotels, theaters, and entire blocks on countless occasions following devastating blazes.[62] With its tightly packed wooden buildings and top ranking among major American cities in per capita fire insurance claims, New Orleans could make a strong case for being the most flammable metropolis in the nation. Considering the ultra-risky strategy, officials initially rejected the plan to torch a wooden structure in a dense residential neighborhood.[63] But as casualties mounted and the accurate gunfire coming from the ramshackle building on Saratoga Street showed no signs of slowing down, those calculations shifted. Fear and faulty reasoning provided enough cover to reach an incendiary conclusion: "Charles had to be smoked from his hiding place."[64]

* * * *

IT WAS SHORTLY after five o'clock on Friday evening when the men outside the Saratoga Street apartment complex finalized preparations to smoke out the assassin. Shooters were positioned on both floors of the main structure by now, overlooking the courtyard separating it from the rear building. At a signal, they provided covering fire while a squad of firemen darted across the open space and entered the rear building, a safe passage that perhaps called into question the need for arson in the first place. Dragging an old mattress from the ambush site to the first-floor room on the uptown side, they slashed the sleeping pad open with shears and removed the horsehair bedding, soaking it in kerosene and piling the clumps at the bottom of the staircase. Then someone struck a match and set the endgame in motion. Acrid wisps climbed toward the upper rooms where the supernatural assassin had singlehandedly frustrated a mob for two hours. "The smoke curled up the stairs, while the fire smoldered," observers described, emphasizing the choreographed precision as men tended the blaze with water buckets. "Then it broke into a flame."[65]

Cool deliberations notwithstanding, someone had miscalculated. Flames caught some drapes near the foot of the stairs, spreading rapidly throughout the structure as the squad hastily retreated to the main building.[66] Five minutes passed. Smoke billowed from the stronghold, but once again, Charles remained preternaturally calm. When the air became unbreathable, he descended the stairway to escape the deadly carbon monoxide filling the upstairs rooms. Moving around the ground floor of the burning structure, he surveyed the hopeless situation, careful not to expose himself to the shooters outside. For the special police officers who caught glimpses of the assassin from across the courtyard, Charles truly seemed like the demon they imagined him to be, unaffected by the searing heat and untouched by buzzing swarms of bullets. Eyes strained and nerves shredded as the stalemate dragged on and on. Then it ended, in a blur of violence so fierce and sudden that nobody could definitively say exactly what happened.[67]

From across the courtyard in the Joyce family dining room, twenty-two-year-old Charles A. Noiret watched anxiously as fire engulfed the rear building. Despite his young age, the Tulane medical student had already played an active role as a member of Special Police Squad No. 1, which had responded to Hannah Mabry's murder scene the previous evening. Now he was in a far more dangerous position, watching the sniper's perch from a downstairs window only ten yards away from the burning structure.[68] Armed civilians and police officers were also camped out in the Joyce home, covering the fire squad's approach and retreat from the rear building as a daring *Times-Democrat* reporter took notes. As the first gray wisps curled over the rear building, Charles fired once into the dining room, striking a special police officer standing next to the young medical student and prompting a wild burst of gunfire in response. The others scrambled to help the victim—and to remove themselves from the line of fire—leaving Noiret alone in the room momentarily.[69]

Charles had fired the round as he struggled to breathe through the smoke, trying to buy a few more seconds—but the bullet would sow confusion and confound his killers. What followed would become a source of controversy rather than closure, with three different men claiming starring roles. It would prompt investigations, public campaigns, contentious arbitration, and ultimately, an official decision that left nagging doubts about what *really* happened.[70] With his final act of courage, Robert Charles obscured his death from white men's certainty and forced witnesses to the climax to explain why they disagreed on how his story ended. "It all happened so quickly," someone explained, charitably, "and the small room was so crowded and filled with smoke."[71]

Noiret's version was eventually upheld through arbitration, although critical details would change over the coming months.[72] He took a position by the door after barely avoiding the incoming round, then saw movement in the rear building, directly across from him. Charles appeared in the doorway and stepped onto the stoop, maybe thirty feet away, blood-soaked and clutching the deadly Winchester rifle. Noiret shouted, "Here he comes!"[73]

Charles sprinted toward the main building, shooting once from the hip and barely missing Noiret's head as he rapidly closed the distance between them. He was across the courtyard and nearly in the doorway when the young man returned fire, a desperate shot at powder-burn range. "He was barely three feet from me," Noiret remembered. "I didn't stop to aim."[74]

The round struck Charles in the upper chest and he stumbled, churning forward, crossing the downstairs threshold, crashing against the dining room table, and finally collapsing to the ground. For a half-second he stared upward with a bewildered look on his face, before turning onto his side. Standing over him, the horrified young man believed that Charles was poised to spin around and begin shooting again. Noiret fired a sharp burst from point-blank range, maybe three rounds. And then Charles was dead. Stunned by the terrifying sequence, an overwhelming eruption of motion and sound, Noiret could scarcely comprehend the frenzy that followed the killing. "This all happened instantly," he explained. "The next I knew the room was filled with a crowd of excited men."[75]

Special police officers and civilians, all respectable white men, clambered over one another to get their hands on the body. Shrieks filled the crowded room. "No living witness could accurately describe the panorama," a reporter confessed. "The howls and curses were terrible."[76]

On the streets outside, the news spread like a contagion. "They've got him! They've killed him!"[77]

Suddenly men burst triumphantly from the main building, dragging a grisly prize behind them.[78] Men surged forward, stumbling and falling amid the chaos, then rising up to fire revolvers and rifles into the body, while others stomped its head into the sludge. Among them was Ernest Trenchard, who showed considerably more courage now that Charles was finished. Bursting through the crowd, the disgraced corporal pressed a double-barrel shotgun against the corpse and discharged both loads, incongruously questioning, "Now who says I'm a coward?"[79]

Men scrambled for cans of kerosene, but before the mob could roast the body, police officers pushed their way through the crowd. They were attempting to take charge when a young man shouldered forward and jumped on its face, crushing the skull and leaving only a portion of the forehead in its rightful place. Reporters identified him as twenty-eight-year-old William Porteous, whose brother Gabe had been the first to die that afternoon. They played down the savagery. "He was crazed with grief and evidently scarcely knew what he was doing," they explained, "only that he was consumed with the raging desire to wreak the most terrible possible vengeance."[80]

Cursing the assassin, the officers tossed the corpse onto the floor of a patrol wagon and began to push through the crowd. "The murderer's body fell in such a position that the hideously mutilated head—kicked, stomped, and crushed—hung over the end," reporters described. "As the patrol wagon rushed through the rough street, the gory, mud-smeared head swayed and swung and jerked in a sickening fashion, dark blood dripping onto the steps and spattering the wagon."[81]

Patrolmen brought the unrecognizable remains downtown, leaving those at the scene with a bitter aftertaste. Nothing had gone to script, including the final act, especially when "death had come too swiftly for the fiend who had slain brave men."[82] Some decided to narrow the score. Patrolmen were rounding up random black residents who lived in the neighborhood, bringing them downtown to police headquarters for questioning. Among those arrested were two men who lived in an adjoining building, one of whom had been disguised as a woman when he was captured. As officers hustled the second man through the angry mob, unfounded rumors spread that he belonged to the Jackson family—and was therefore responsible for everything that happened. Men crowded around, lashing the prisoner as the escorting officers struggled to pull him through the mob. Someone drew a pistol and darted forward. He pressed the barrel directly against the captive's neck and shot him through the spine.[83] The man collapsed, dying almost instantly as the bloodthirsty mob erupted in cheers. As with the unidentified man killed near the French Market earlier in the afternoon, the body was taken to the morgue, where it would receive a hostile reception.[84]

For almost two hours on Friday afternoon, hundreds of men had been assembling outside police headquarters, the third site of mass mobilization in New Orleans. Anxiously watching the flurry of ambulances and patrol wagons rushing through the complex gates, drawn by galloping teams of horses, they were distressed by what they saw. If the departures revealed the scale of the emergency unfolding less than a mile away and suggested a strong police response, the returning vehicles told a more disturbing story. The first wagon to return carried Silas Jackson and John Willis, but soon the assassin's victims were brought through the gates. Witnessing the quick succession of corpses, one disturbed witness asked, "Are they killing nothing but white men?"

Desperate to even the score, one bystander pleaded with officers, "Give us guns and we'll get some niggers!"

Suddenly, a patrol wagon careened around the corner, carrying police officers armed with Winchester rifles. One of the patrolmen shouted, "We've got him, the black brute! It's Robert Charles!"[85]

The crowd surrounded the wagon and tried to desecrate the already unrecognizable corpse a second time, but officers pushed through and reached the iron gates guarding the building. Authorities ignored the volatile situation outside to usher friends and acquaintances through the dead house doors, supposedly to view the slain officers and pay their respects. Many seemed to have ulterior motives. They momentarily paused beside the white corpses to offer perfunctory words before rushing to the far end of the room, where a dark-skinned body lay on a stone slab. Witnesses gawked at what had once been Robert Charles, now disfigured beyond recognition. Mashed and swollen, his head was a "thick black disc," its features "so distorted that they bore no resemblance to what they had been in life."[86] An autopsy reported the full extent of the damage: "Thirty-four bullet holes in trunk and three large openings, undoubtedly due to volleys. Right forearm and wrist broken; skull fractured or shattered and almost beat to a pulp. Seven wounds about the legs: four in the right and three in the left. One wound of penis."

Contributing a mysterious piece to the investigation, the autopsy also revealed a partially healed gunshot wound to his upper right thigh, wrapped in green medical gauze and dressed with petroleum jelly: someone with medical experience had treated Charles for the wound he suffered during the Dryades Street gun battle.[87]

At the Saratoga Street crime scene, detectives were also pushing the investigation forward, combing through the main building and the assassin's den, which firemen had saved from total destruction. They were not alone. Patrolmen stationed outside were doing nothing to prevent the masses from entering the property. Men climbed the back fence and scrambled through the alleyways, pouring into the courtyard and pushing into the buildings. Bystanders opened trunks and strewed the contents on the ground, somewhere between souvenir hunters and thieves as they took whatever they pleased from both the Jackson and Joyce homes.[88] The competing searches uncovered some unexpected witnesses. Since the beginning of the ambush, Annie Gant had been hiding in her downstairs bedroom, farthest away from the courtyard. Loud knocking on the back door of the main building drew her from hiding. Putting on her bravest face, she answered the door and invited the men to search her room. "Come in," she said. "But white folks, for God's sake don't kill me, I don't know nothing about the man."

Speaking with reporters later that evening, Gant explained, "One of the white gentlemen said to me, 'You better get out of here, you damned old fool,' and I ran out and didn't take time to get my shoes." The elderly woman clearly feared retribution. "I can't say no more," she told interviewers. "The white folks will shoot me if I do."[89]

Even stranger was the case of George Ford, who had been playing cards before the trouble began. Souvenir hunters searching an upstairs room of the main building spotted a boot sticking out from beneath the bed. When they tore the mattress from the bed, they found the frightened man hiding underneath, pretending to be dead. Ford was alive, but he barely survived discovery.[90] According to one eyewitness, "Those present advised shooting him to make sure he was dead."[91]

Strangely enough, white paranoia saved his life. Believing that he knew valuable information about a vast conspiracy, patrolmen intervened to prevent his execution, taking steps to ensure the prisoner's safe transportation to police headquarters, where Ford promised to tell them everything he knew. "Through him," reporters gravely noted, "what is now considered an organized gang of desperate negroes may be run down."[92]

Despite the chaos engulfing the crime scene, detectives nonetheless managed to piece together some clues about the assassin's connection to the residents of the apartment complex. Solid evidence suggested that Charles had been hiding in the rear building for several days, likely arriving shortly after escaping the Fourth Street murder scene. In the closet where he sprung the ambush, investigators found lead scraps, a charcoal furnace, and a melting ladle. On the ground nearby there were several pieces of hollow steel pipe, with openings roughly the same diameter as a .38-caliber rifle. Charles had apparently been spending his spare time making bullets.[93]

Given the evidence, detectives who interviewed Martha Jackson on Friday evening had reason to be skeptical of her story. The frightened Mississippi native admitted that she had known Robert Charles for several years, first encountering him when he was promoting African emigration. She claimed that Charles had showed up on her doorstep early that same morning, brandishing his rifle menacingly and demanding entry. Jackson told investigators that she was upstairs when the officers entered the rear building. Borrowing from the same playbook as Virginia Banks, the sharp-minded woman who had painted a chilling portrait of her on-again, off-again boyfriend, Jackson said that she had cooperated with his demands for lack of a better option. "I knew he was a desperate man," she begged, "but I was afraid to give him away for fear he would kill me."[94]

While his wife pleaded with police investigators, Silas Jackson strenuously protested his innocence to reporters. Unable to claim physical intimidation, the workingman chose a different gendered defense, claiming that his wife had been hiding the fugitive in their home while he was away working. "My wife must have secreted him there and kept the secret from me," he pleaded. "I don't know how long Charles could have been in my house."[95]

Among the black men arrested during the disturbances, Silas Jackson's neighbor in a nearby cell was the most agitated. John Willis had been arrested at gunpoint as he fled the scene, but his psychological condition had deteriorated in the hours since. "Willis was insane with fright," reporters described. "He groveled at the feet of his questioners, tears streaming down his face." Unable to extract a coherent statement and increasingly uncertain regarding the prisoner's guilt, they uncomfortably concluded, "Willis prayed to be saved and sobbed over and over again that he was innocent."[96]

By twilight on Friday evening, New Orleans was once again under martial law. State militia had been mobilized earlier that afternoon, while hundreds of additional special police officers had been sworn, adding to a force of deputized civilians swelling into the thousands. Despite fast-moving rumors that black residents inspired by Charles were plotting a rebellion, they were nowhere to be seen, hiding behind closed doors and hoping to survive. With few targets to be found, the troublemakers were mostly subdued, huddling together on downtown corners and boasting about what they would do if given the chance.[97] The peace lasted until shortly before midnight, when special police officers heard gunfire near Morris Park and moved to investigate. Discovering nothing, they were returning to their posts when they saw flames erupting from a three-story building only a few blocks from the murder scene. Named for a black real estate magnate who had been a lifelong advocate of integrated public education, the Thomy Lafon School had recently opened and served hundreds of black students as a rare symbol of post-Reconstruction progress. Now the building represented something far more disturbing.[98] A large white crowd gathered to watch towering flames consume the structure, leaving only scorched bricks and charred timbers by the early morning.[99]

Coming a few weeks after the school board decided to eliminate post-elementary public education for black students, the burning of the community's finest institution was an undeniable message, but white observers sought other meanings in the flames. Some claimed that while the schoolhouse burned, a huge explosion confirmed suspicions that black residents were using it as an ammunition dump. Others explained that the fire was a funeral pyre for the murdered Gabe Porteous, whose home was nearby. But most were satisfied to blame the anonymous hoodlums who had already caused so much trouble. None was arrested.[100]

Early the next morning, Ernest Kruttschnitt and another school board member were going to examine the ruined building when they heard a commotion and stumbled across a white gang mercilessly attacking a black pedestrian. The administrators intervened and managed to drag the victim to safety. They poured water over his head to revive him, before sending him on his way. Presumably without pausing to consider the big picture, the Choctaw politician who had chaired the disenfranchising convention and the vote to eliminate public education for black adolescents continued on toward the burned-out schoolhouse to assess the damage caused by unaccountable hoodlums.[101]

* * * *

BEFORE SUNRISE ON Saturday morning, the sheriff and a few deputies marched Leonard Pierce down the dim corridors of Orleans Parish Prison, through the special police officers forming a cordon around the courthouse. Despite assurances from his captors, Pierce was sure that he was being taken to his death. But rather than stopping in the courtyard, where gallows would be erected to carry out executions, the party entered the coroner's office and continued into the morgue, where three unidentified corpses rested on stone slabs. Each body showed signs of serious trauma—and all of them were dark-skinned. Pointing toward the corpses, the sheriff ordered him to tell the truth. Looking at the first body, Pierce stared and said nothing, but slowly shook his head. He repeated the same process at the second table, before making his way over to the final corpse, illuminated by an electric bulb overhead.[102] Twelve hours had done nothing to improve the body's appearance: head crushed, face badly mutilated, the features indiscernible.[103] Staring intently, Pierce hesitated. "It looks like him," he finally stammered. One of the deputies grabbed a light and held it up to where the dead man's face once was. After a few seconds, Pierce spoke. "Yes, that's Robert Charles."[104]

Later that morning, Silas and Martha Jackson completed the same process, along with several white men who had known the assassin. Repeated again and again, the procedure was done for more than bureaucratic necessity—it was also a critical security measure. Despite the bloody finale, conspiracy theorists were claiming that the black man killed in the Joyce family dining room was someone else. Speaking with reporters, the mayor promised that the whispers had no basis in truth. "Everything and everybody associated with the man tends to prove this," Capdevielle explained. "His expert manipulation of deadly weapons, his size, teeth, and clothes, the character of literature taken from the body, and the identification by those who knew the negro as the outlaw."[105]

Although confirming the death of Robert Charles was a necessary step toward stability, destroying his lingering spectral presence, his representation of threats posed by every able-bodied black man in New Orleans, would be more challenging. Although the mainstream press covered the fiery climax extensively, focusing primarily on the heroism displayed by the white men that brought its antagonist down, the accompanying opinion pieces were strangely understated. Editors recognized the continuing volatility and avoided the inflammatory coverage that had contributed so much to the crisis, looking to defuse the tensions they had fueled earlier in the week. They neutralized fears of a black conspiracy, declaring Charles the "most desperate and dangerous negro ever known in Louisiana" and reassuring "there is not another negro in the state who can perform such acts."[106] Looking to the bigger picture, they painted the crisis as a moral struggle, praised municipal authorities for taking such decisive action, and congratulated the better classes on the community's remarkable forbearance. They sidestepped the racial violence with equivalency, explaining that society had "resolved into its elements, the vicious and lawless of both races standing against the right-thinking and right-acting classes."[107]

Of course, it remained to be seen if white New Orleans would cooperate with the reassuring narrative. By Saturday afternoon, authorities were receiving alarming reports from all quarters, many from business owners concerned about threats to corporate property. Five years removed from the levee uprising, but painfully aware that machine politicians scorned pleas for protection during the lead-up to that violence, the shipping agent for the West India & Pacific Steamship Company warned the mayor's office that he had "reliable information" that lynch mobs were planning to attack black dockworkers gathering for payday. Requesting armed guards to protect the employees, he added, "For your information, there are 6,000 bales of cotton and other valuable property on our wharf which will be in jeopardy should any trouble arise."[108]

Fortunately, those fears were baseless. Twenty-four hours after the siege ended, the reports were proving more smoke than fire as the situation on the ground rapidly stabilized. Taking a cautious approach, the mayor requested that all businesses close by sundown and extended the barroom closure through the weekend, but with special police officers patrolling the streets, black residents sheltering behind closed doors, and the villain dead, authorities were satisfied that order was finally restored.[109] Aside from a few scattered disturbances, New Orleans was calm on Saturday evening—apart from press row, where editors worked on front-page stories emphasizing the return to regular operations after five days of trauma. Any remaining danger had vanished with the death of Robert Charles, they argued, although they recognized that not everything was back to normal. "A stranger visiting this city yesterday could not have imagined this was the largest negro community in the country," they reflected. "There was distress by housewives at the absence of cooks and servants, and the commercial community felt the absence of laborers."[110]

For municipal authorities, what remained was to permanently remove the assassin's unwelcome presence. A few hours before dawn on Sunday morning, a workhouse wagon clattered through the desolate streets and pulled up outside Orleans Parish Prison, where the driver guided his team through the gates. He paused outside the morgue, where stone-faced police officers and state militiamen watched over a rotting corpse. Officials had planned to preserve the body for a few more days, but with no refrigeration, high summer temperatures had sped decomposition to intolerable levels.[111] Four black prisoners were charged with preparing the corpse. Under the glow of lanterns, the captives worked mechanically, their movements casting shadows that danced eerily across the dead house walls. They placed the body in an unadorned pine coffin and screwed the lid into place, before the wagon departed the prison, moving slowly for a few blocks. When the driver was satisfied that his dangerous cargo had aroused no suspicions, he whipped his team to a canter and reached his destination in fifteen minutes.[112]

Sprawled across five acres outside town, Holt Cemetery had been established on the grounds of an antebellum plantation.[113] As the least fashionable resting place in a city where the honored dead were laid in marble mausoleums, the potter's field was among the only cemeteries where bodies were buried underground—although the dead resisted the practice. Wooden boards were supposed to designate individual and common graves, but sun-bleached bone fragments and tattered cloth were strewn across the overgrown grass. And when strong winds blew across the ground on humid summer afternoons, the stench was unbearable.[114] As the wagon bearing Robert Charles arrived outside the cemetery, attendants were standing beside an open grave. Somewhere nearby, the mob's unidentified victims had been buried in the same potter's field the previous day. Officials assumed that the black men were migrants from the rural parishes, but there was no way to be certain and no guarantee that loved ones would ever learn their fates.[115] Working silently, the gravediggers were wise enough to keep any reflections private—after all, black lives seemed particularly cheap in recent days. They smoothed the last shovels of dirt over the unmarked site, before returning home to clean up in time for church.[116]

As parishioners gathered for Sunday morning services, a strange atmosphere hung over the churches and cathedrals of New Orleans, where attendance was notably strong. Priests and pastors made scarce mention of the events that had transpired since last week's sermons, venturing nothing more controversial than condemnations of the slain assassin and prayers for his victims. On the record, the reverend of the city's oldest Protestant church told reporters that the crisis demonstrated the need for a larger and more effective police force, saying the problem was "simply a business proposition." But clergymen otherwise avoided uncomfortable topics, explaining the crisis "was all over and that it had taught its lesson," without specifying exactly what that lesson had been. From the pews, it was easy to imagine that the whirlwind events had been nothing more than a feverish nightmare, ugly days when God's face had turned away from New Orleans, only for the city to be redeemed by its brave citizens.[117]

All that remained was to move forward. Later that afternoon, the mayor released his final proclamation—suspending emergency measures, promising a rigorous investigation, and declaring the conclusion of the crisis. "Peace and order have been reestablished," Capdevielle proclaimed, "and the good people of the town may come and go freely, resume their usual occupations, open their places of business, and carry on the peaceable affairs of life."[118] As he demobilized the special police force and freed the deputized businessmen to return to work on Monday, the mayor announced one last measure: a commemorative badge, to be distributed to citizens who had been sworn as officers. More than a simple memento, the badge represented both past service and future commitments. As the mayor explained, it granted the bearers the right to take up arms if called upon by authorities. It effectively created a private army at his fingertips, "a body of citizens to aid him in times of great stress and emergency." The badge symbolized the remarkable sea change that had taken place during the most remarkable business week in anyone's memory—and suggested its long-term consequences. Emergency measures were no longer necessary, but collaboration between public and private elites would be extended indefinitely. Armed businessmen would be waiting in the shadows, ready to move against threats to life, property, and commerce.[119]

8

Redemption

On Tuesday evening, the last day in July, coun-
cilmen from the city's seventeen wards convened for the first time since
the violent clashes that rocked New Orleans. Less than three months
after the inaugural celebrations, the mood was grim, but the politicians
were there to affirm an uplifting narrative that had been gathering momentum from the early stages of the crisis. It was a spirited session,
marked by parliamentary wrangling and rowdy exchanges, but ultimately,
decorum prevailed and the proceedings ended in good spirits. Councilmen unanimously passed a resolution celebrating the mayor's "courageous and public-spirited action" during the crisis, a compliment Paul
Capdevielle magnanimously returned, saying no public servants in America better understood "the highest requirements of good citizenship."[1]

The self-congratulatory spectacle was predictable, yet over the following days, those sentiments would be echoed in less expected places. With
blood running in the streets, editors had understandably supported the
administration—but as peace returned, it was increasingly clear that a
more fundamental change had taken place. Among the most influential
opinion makers anywhere in the South, editor Page Baker of the *Times-
Democrat* had spearheaded the destruction of the old machine during the
mid-1890s and strongly endorsed reformers in the recent citywide elections, but now he sang a different tune, celebrating the authorities as "men
who knew their duty and were entirely ready to perform," before offering the ultimate compliment by declaring them rightful successors to "the
heroic men who restored the shaken fabric of white supremacy during the

dark days of Reconstruction."[2] Likewise, the business community unanimously supported the machine administration from the top down. Looking to resilient bond markets, directors from the New Orleans Board of Trade published a resolution celebrating leadership "calculated to confirm public confidence," serious praise coming from men whose fortunes lived and died on that maddeningly elusive currency.[3]

The reason behind the confidence was obvious. Breaking from the old machine's intransigence, the mayor had mobilized special police officers, proving that merchants and property holders—white elites whose material interests compelled them to value stability above everything—would have reliable allies in city government and a determinative role in setting its agenda. Consulting with business leaders and deputizing the better classes to retake the streets had limited the economic damage, absolving his administration of its abject failure to prevent the bloodshed. Between white fortunes and black lives, the former determined the administration's political viability. And it had passed the test with flying colors. Although Capdevielle had done no better than his predecessor in protecting his city's most vulnerable residents, his cooperation and decisiveness contrasted favorably with John Fitzpatrick's stubbornness during the levee uprising, confirming the machine's newfound willingness to collaborate with business on terms of its own choosing. By sharing—or ceding—leadership in the crisis, paradoxically, the Choctaw administration was strengthened in the aftermath. For some observers, the emerging alliance suggested the hand of higher powers. "Your action is a splendid vindication of those who stood by you in our municipal election," one progressive-minded citizen praised, "and a providential rebuke to your opponents."[4]

The same validation applied to private citizens who had answered his call and been sworn into service. As the narrative emphasizing the starring role played by special police officers in rescuing New Orleans from lawless mobs became dogma, the ambitious young men who had borne the burdens of white manhood anticipated rising status in the community. They had earned admission to the same prestigious club whose members, Confederate veterans and White League paramilitaries, were heavily represented among the older generation of elites. As municipal authorities published duty rosters and prepared to distribute the medals honoring special police service—gold for the officers, silver for the rank-and-file—letters flooded the mayor's office, written by those whose names were missing.[5] Some had fallen through the cracks, while others claimed they had served without being officially sworn. Many wrote on letter-heads from notable firms, trying to lend weight to their claims. But they all wanted the same thing. "I would very much appreciate a medal, assuring you of my services any time New Orleans needs me," one magnanimously wrote.[6] Another twenty-five-year-old clerk concluded, with unintended pathos, "Hoping not to be forgotten."[7]

For those who could not serve, honoring the fallen police officers provided a second chance to publicly distinguish themselves. Even as debates about personal cowardice and structural reform intensified, campaigns to support the bereaved families gave private citizens the chance to memorialize the faithful martyrs—and to build on the pro-policing consensus without diving into controversy. While they railed about the dysfunctional police leadership and demoralized force, editors carefully noted that "not a syllable can be lisped against the bravery and splendid courage of the officers who were ruthlessly done to death while nobly performing their duty." Their sacrifice was "an example which the community will take to heart and profit from," but with the fallen breadwinners unable to provide for their broken families, it was also a challenge to those who remained. Editors responded, promising, "The widows and orphans of the gallant dead shall be cared for by the men, women, and children of New Orleans."[8]

To boost the campaign, reporters visited the homes of the courageous martyrs, describing the scenes of domestic tranquility destroyed and detailing the financial pressures confronted by dependents "still as crushed by overwhelming sorrows as the day when they were told that the head of their household was no more."[9] Four women and eleven children stared down poverty, especially when annual death benefits only amounted to three months' salary.[10] Philanthropy would ease those burdens, but it also served as a powerful restorative for businessmen whose fortunes had been threatened by the crisis, confirming their status as the patriarchs of the community. As donations poured into multiple funds established by public and private interests, newspapers published the receipts, allowing readers to judge the wealth and benevolence of fellow citizens. Among the more generous contributors, Cotton Exchange president John M. Parker offered fifty dollars, one month's salary for a patrolman. On the questionable side, President Charles Janvier of the Sun Life Insurance Company made an eyebrow-raising donation of only ten dollars—and refused to pay the insurance policy on Albert Brumfield, the teenager gunned down at the beginning of the siege.[11] Whereas leading citizens were recognized individually by name and position, contributions from workingmen were mostly published under the names of their employers—for example, "Employees, A. Baldwin & Company," who pledged thirty dollars—rehabilitating businesses that had played dubious roles during the crisis.[12] Yet editors also endorsed a white communalism that rose above class, promising to credit all contributors and naming a few one-dollar donations from students and laborers alongside the much larger sums pledged by social elites.[13] As money poured into the mayor's office, donors received the same response from his secretary:

I acknowledge receipt of your donation of _____ as a contribution to the fund for the widows and orphans of the police officers whose lives were lost in the discharge of their duty. The mayor desires to assure you of his appreciation of your charitable action.

Filling the blank were sums ranging from one to five hundred dollars, but regardless of size, the typewritten message was always the same.[14]

Making space for both hierarchy and egalitarianism, editors and politicians endorsed an orderly white community, but despite high-minded statements about honoring the martyrs and providing for the families, public recognition was a primary motivation for most donors. As with young men overlooked during the medal distribution, appeals from contributors whose names had not appeared in newspapers flooded the mayor's office as the campaign progressed. Writing for businessmen whose reputations alone could underwrite risky transactions, the secretary of the New Orleans Board of Trade was among those who double-checked with officials about missing names—although the desire for recognition also included those without much face to lose.[15] After waiting a few days, a machine councilman and underworld boss jokingly nicknamed the "Mayor of Storyville" penciled a handwritten note asking about his twenty-five-dollar donation and requesting recognition.[16] Within hours, Tom Anderson would be added to the donor lists being published every afternoon, ensuring the city's vice king would be recognized alongside its gentlemen elites.[17]

Over the ensuing weeks, every white man in New Orleans performed benevolence—publicly, of course—as the city hosted an endless array of benefits: sporting demonstrations, excursions, concerts, and plays. Leading firms appeared in program advertisements and wealthy families purchased luxury boxes for spectacles honoring the dead—and sometimes the living. Responding to a request from the mayor's office, managers provided the newly opened Crescent Theatre without charge and bought the best seats in the house, gifting them to Paul Capdevielle and his police chief as a show of gratitude.[18] Less scrupulous operators twisted the same idea by mailing tickets to politicians—along with the attending bills, challenging them to deny such a self-evidently worthy cause. Saying the mayor had already made a personal contribution to the police fund, his secretary turned down the chance to win a silver-plated liquor set and returned unsolicited raffle tickets; another official claimed "unlimited calls from other sources" while rebuffing a purchase made in his name.[19]

Ultimately, the scams did nothing to diminish the successful campaign. As it wound down, the mayor summoned a select group of journalists and executives to his office to finalize distribution plans.[20] More than $15,000 would be distributed proportionally, according to family size. Although editors had already written extensively about how the fund reflected the community's generosity, they also acknowledged that it served another purpose. While the longer and more controversial work of police reform in New Orleans remained to be done, the distribution was a critical first step toward redemption. The adoration of the martyrs would be the rallying point for the most ambitious pro-policing movement in municipal history, pointing the way forward for a department viewed as a source of corruption rather than civic pride. By providing for the bereaved families, businessmen and leading citizens proved themselves as champions of those who served the community and its interests with courage and integrity. As editors explained, the money was "assurance to other faithful and brave officers that the people will not allow their families to suffer when their supporters and protectors are lost while serving the city." It was a down payment on future sacrifice, a high-stakes bid to secure loyalty from a demoralized force that had sided with the mob when prosperity was under fire.[21]

* * * *

AS WHITE RESIDENTS in New Orleans attended weekend benefits on Saturday evening, eight days after fires raged through the rear building near downtown, twenty-nine-year-old John Willis suffered in Orleans Parish Prison, facing a bleak future. The bricklayer was one of ten black defendants facing charges for allegedly conspiring with the assassin, but among them, his guilt—and his mental state—were particularly dubious.[22] Arrested as he fled from his home adjacent to the Saratoga Street crime scene, Willis had been pleading his innocence ever since, saying that he was running away from the mobs descending on his neighborhood. As he languished, the prisoner's moods had become unstable, swinging wildly between eerie detachment and uncontrollable tears. Fasting and praying, he begged for divine intervention. But no answers came from above—and something finally broke inside him.[23]

Just after seven o'clock on Saturday evening, Willis secured a handkerchief around a metal loop that anchored the hammock in his prison cell and waited until deputies passed by. He slipped the ligature around his neck and sat on the ground. Then he leaned forward, strangling himself with his own body weight until he lost consciousness. Thirty minutes passed before guards found him, slumped over and unmoving, but faintly breathing. Deputies called an ambulance, but by the time help arrived, Willis was dead.[24] Reporters were unsure what to make of the suicide. Some argued that because "instances of negroes taking their own lives are very rare," his desperate act was "indication that he had a hand in the assassination of the officers and feared the penalty."[25] Others raised doubts and suggested an alternative explanation. Discerning subtle clues from his complexion, self-declared race experts discovered hidden depths of feeling. Noting that "Willis was lighter in color than the others arrested for the Saratoga Street tragedy," reporters explained. "It was said by someone versed in negro crime that very seldom was a full-blooded African guilty of suicide, while there were many cases of mulattos and those with more Caucasian blood taking their lives."[26]

Regardless, as the sun rose on Sunday morning, John Willis was the last thing on the minds of white residents, who were obsessing over more sinister events unfolding more than one thousand miles away. One week before, on the same evening that Charles had been killed, twenty-five-year-old Lillian Jewett had organized a meeting for the Boston Anti-Lynching League, raising funds for the mob victims and their families in New Orleans. It was a spirited gathering. According to local reporters, speakers denounced the systematic civil rights violations harming black Americans and discussed organized legal opposition. One participant recognized a white businessman from New Orleans and threatened to eject him, but the crowd had calmed down before Jewett took the podium to make her own moderate proposals, saying telegrams would be sent to anti-lynching organizations across the South, where similar protests were expected. "The white man has not yet come forward, but he will," she promised. "Justice is on our side."[27]

Word of the meeting took several days to reach New Orleans, but when it arrived, newspapers described a far more disturbing scene, portraying the peaceful gathering as the strategy session for a bloody revolution. Rather than a few anti-lynching meetings, Jewett had supposedly promised an army, "150,000 men ready on the Congo River to come to this country, fight for us, and annihilate the whites." According to reporters, collections from the meeting were not for suffering black families, but rather to support the invasion force, which would soon march on New Orleans to lead a black rebellion—at least according to editors there, who treated the outlandish conspiracy with deadly seriousness in the coming days. Mainstream newspapers covered the response from the Green Turtle Club, an obscure society whose vice-president was a New Orleans patrolman, which supposedly placed a bounty on the "Joan of Arc of the negroes" and made plans to ship a coffin northward as a warning.[28] For several weeks, journalists in both cities reported on the supposedly escalating situation, as attorneys traveled south from Boston to investigate the assassination plot and received a predictably chilly reception. Of course, the fuss amounted to nothing: the Congolese army never arrived and the activist's representatives returned to New England, rightfully convinced that no grand jury in Louisiana would charge the assassination plotters, assuming such a plan ever actually existed.

For editors in New Orleans, the outrage was soon forgotten, but not until it had served its critical purpose. Cynically exploiting the same charitable fundraising they scrupulously covered and praised when honoring the slain police officers, they denied black residents the same chance to mourn their dead and comfort the survivors, while forcing community leaders to denounce conspiracy theories in the aftermath of a massacre. Appearing only hours after an innocent man, John Willis, killed himself in a prison cell, a full-page spread in the Sunday morning *Times-Democrat* co-opted black voices under a banner headline: "NEW ORLEANS NEGROES WANT NO OUTSIDE HELP."[29] Introducing a quote compilation from colored elites, who unanimously condemned Jewett's supposed conspiracy and pledged to cooperate with local officials, editors advanced a conciliatory narrative. They explained that the "representative and right-thinking colored citizens have allied themselves with law and order and urged the negroes to aid the authorities in bringing the culprits to justice."[30] Over a dozen professors, lawyers, doctors, preachers, and bureaucrats had gone on the record—the most recognizable black leaders in New Orleans—denouncing criminality, black nationalism, and meddlesome Yankee activists. The president of the city's most prestigious black college, founded during Reconstruction, highlighted a "great need for the better and more intelligent negroes to draw the line sharply between themselves and the low and vicious classes of their own race."[31] Meanwhile, five pastors from leading black churches described the toxic effects that white anti-lynching activists would have on already unstable minds. "Such people encourage men of the Robert Charles type to commit violence and bring disgrace upon the race," they complained. "If these people would take the trouble to familiarize themselves with the race problem in the South, they would find that the cases of oppression are mainly from disciplining the lawless ones."[32]

The statements were part of a campaign endorsed by elected officials, business elites, and the conservative press. It was a coordinated response, enlisting leaders of both races to come together as uneasy allies, endorse a consensus narrative, and enforce order in their respective communities. Explaining that "the very worst element of the whites" was responsible for the mob violence, prominent black attorney J. Madison Vance contended that "the very best white people of New Orleans, those who have material interests at stake, who possess education and wealth," intervened to stop the bloodshed.[33] Now he promised reciprocity, saying that preachers across the city were damning Charles from the pulpit and censuring "pamphlets meant to enflame the worst passions against white people."[34] Community leaders were also planning an anti-crime organization to cooperate with police and expose perpetrators hiding among them. Equating the criminals lurking on both sides of the color line, Vance promised cooperation from "every negro in the city who works for a living or attends church on Sunday" and constructively concluded, "The white population is no more responsible for the actions of white hoodlums than the negro race is responsible for the actions of hoodlums like Charles."[35]

The pressure to denounce bad actors within the black community encompassed not only criminals, but also those who espoused dangerous ideologies. Sensational exposés denouncing emigration literature as a source of violent radicalism were part of the same campaign. Quoting selectively and focusing especially on Bishop Henry M. Turner's writings, editors denounced them as "beyond all comparison the most inflammatory documents in this region," worse than the most outrageous abolitionist propaganda from the antebellum period. They waved away claims "so self-evidently false that they would excite derision in any intelligent person," then quoted passages that described the everyday indignities and horrors suffered by black Americans in the Jim Crow South as supposed evidence.[36] Loudly playing out in the New Orleans press, the propaganda campaign prompted a response from city officials and police commanders. When he spoke with reporters, the mayor promised an aggressive, if constitutionally dubious, response, saying that appropriate steps would be taken to punish those who distributed the offending literature.[37] Police commanders assured reporters that detectives were investigating, explaining that "those selling the circulars will be arrested and prosecuted" as soon as the city attorney gave the go-ahead.[38]

The most popular black newspaper in the South amplified the mainstream campaign against criminals and radicals, deepening the divide in a community already fractured along class lines. For more than four years, Isaiah Scott had used his position editing the *Southwestern Christian Advocate* to stress respectability, urging his middle-class readership to educate and uplift the less fortunate. But those strategies had to be reconsidered after mass violence. "The better class should seek to save others *if possible*," he clarified, "but we should be just enough to condemn their wrongdoing and leave them to perish in their folly." Rather than risking guilt by association, the respectable black community should redouble its self-policing and cooperation to secure mutually beneficial alliances. Recent history suggested just how unreliable the strategy was, but perhaps in the darkness of the most recent crisis there was hope, the path toward a more secure future. "When businessmen found that the mob assaulting and killing innocent Negroes had affected the standing of the city and state in the stock market in the North, they put a stop to the violence," he observed. "The colored man has learned that his only hope is to keep close to the best white citizens, who recognize his worth as a laborer and a well-behaved citizen and will stand by him in his time of need. Let us hope that the entire city—and for that matter the entire country—may profit from these lessons."[39]

On both sides of the color line, New Orleans editors rewrote the Robert Charles crisis, fashioning a morality play that asked readers to choose between diametrically opposing sides. Black and white, the city's better classes were united against radicals, criminals, hoodlums, and desperadoes to stabilize and secure New Orleans on its progressive march toward a prosperous future. But if the alliance disproportionately benefited those in a position to capitalize, some cases threatened its very foundation—none more than the unfortunate John Willis, whose innocence was not enough to save him. The distinction between the criminal and better classes was nonsense. Willis was the living and dead reflection—selling his labor cheaply, living in the wrong neighborhood, running from gun-fire, suffering false arrest, and vainly pleading with reporters who were writing a conspiracy, not an exoneration. But for the alliance to survive, the line was a necessary fiction. While mob rule had no place in the world being fashioned from the crisis, the physical and psychic violence neces-sary to maintain order would be mostly relegated to dark corners, to Or-leans Parish Prison, the state-of-the-art injustice system marking the city's progress. For its most vulnerable residents, honoring the imaginary di-vide was critical precisely because the "lower and criminal classes" were so easily collapsed into a single group. Here was respectability politics re-duced to its foundational violence: "If you desire the best white man to stand by you and your family, you must identify yourself with the best people." And pray to God they identified themselves with you.[40]

While an innocent man's suicide was an acceptable cost of progress, a false positive within a false system to distinguish black criminals from respectable citizens, negotiating the equally troublesome distinction be-tween white hoodlums and outraged workingmen was maybe even more dangerous, particularly in a world built on racial supremacy. Charles was dead, his co-conspirators arrested, and black leaders were showing new-found enthusiasm for eradicating criminals in their community. But al-though municipal authorities were saying the right things about enforcing the law fairly on both sides of the color line, it remained to be seen if those commitments to protecting black residents would amount to anything. Accepting a compromise that saw them denounce criminals, real and imagined, while moving away from racial solidarity across class lines, black leaders demanded equal justice under law. "Now that every Negro who lived in the houses where the murderer was found has been arrested," they questioned, "what are the authorities going to do about those who murdered the old colored lady in her bed, burned the schoolhouse, and committed offenses during the carnival of crime in this city?"[41]

* * * *

ON TUESDAY MORNING, August 7, 1900, sheriff's deputies and police officers crowded the courtroom where the remaining defendants in the Robert Charles conspiracy were to be arraigned. They scanned the gallery for troublemakers, but the room was hushed as the nine accused men and women entered the courtroom. Surrounded by armed guards, they moved like sleepwalkers, eyes darting as though anticipating the moment when a lynch mob would storm the proceedings and drag them away to their deaths. They were still reeling from the weekend suicide, although reporters attributed the sullen demeanors to ignorance. With no attorney yet appointed to represent them, the prisoners sat alone behind a table. They listened quietly as the presiding judge read the charges against them. When asked to enter pleas, every man and woman quietly responded, "Not guilty."[42]

The arraignment ended anticlimactically. As expected, the prisoners were remanded without bail and deputies escorted them from the courtroom and returned them to the cells, but elsewhere in the court building, more controversial proceedings were unfolding. Grand jurors were busy questioning the witnesses against Mike Foley and George Flanagan, white laborers arrested for the home invasion slaying of fifty-two-year-old Hannah Mabry.[43] The victim's son, Harry Mabry, had identified the construction workers as members of the mob that stormed the family cottage, but he would soon join his mother's accused killers in prison after missing a preliminary hearing. Supposedly trying to prevent witness intimidation, police arrested Mabry and brought him downtown, locking up the petrified man alongside his mother's alleged killers until the trial began. For daring to identify them and rightfully fearing the consequences, Harry Mabry would spend three months in prison.[44]

Other white laborers were also facing homicide charges for the mob killings. Six had been arrested for chasing August Thomas from a streetcar and brutally executing him, while another was charged with murdering Joseph Scott as he walked down the levee. Reporters closely followed the proceedings for both white and black defendants, frequently publishing updates on both groups in the same columns to prove that grand jurors were "determined that the hoodlums who participated in the mob that terrorized New Orleans shall be punished."[45] Then again, "New Orleans" had not been terrorized so much as its black community, where many viewed the indictments as a welcome sign, but remained skeptical the prosecutions would end in convictions. Acknowledging how much evidence there was against the defendants, but how little it really mattered, they explained, "It remains to be seen whether they will be punished by the courts, which are prepared to prove anything they wish."[46]

As the cases against the white defendants moved forward, the campaign to eliminate the dangerous outlaws supposedly embedded within the black community proceeded far more decisively. Police commanders were understandably eager to prove themselves following a series of questionable displays, but these efforts were bolstered by the enthusiastic response coming from private citizens. As dark rumors of black conspiracies swirled, white residents eyed their neighbors suspiciously and reported possible threats to the mayor's office, which forwarded the concerns to police headquarters. The tips were sketchy, based on little more than speculation and profiling. But that did nothing to diminish the heavy-handed crackdown that followed, which focused on spaces that raised suspicions during the crisis. "From information that comes to us, No. 1312 Toulouse, between Franklin and Treme, is nothing more than a harbor for disreputable and dangerous negroes," the mayor's secretary informed police commanders, mischaracterizing a self-defense strategy as suspicious. "Our information is that during the recent troubles, 12 or 16 negro men were in this house. When this house is full of negroes, will you please raid the place and bring charges against them?"[47]

Long viewed as fountainheads of criminality, saloons favored by black laborers were also singled out for police action. "Complaints have been made about the saloon at Amelia and Tchoupitoulas, which is frequented by the lower class of negroes," administrators complained. "As you will remember, this neighborhood was the seat of considerable trouble. A few arrests might prove beneficial."[48]

As suggested by the scattershot targets, the informal surveillance network uncovered nothing more than minor nuisances, but heightened responsiveness from municipal authorities gave white private citizens the opportunity to police black residents in ways rarely seen since emancipation.[49] Many participated enthusiastically, focusing on sources of suspicion and frustration in their neighborhoods and transforming the city's everyday racial integration into an intelligence windfall. "A crowd of dis-

reputable negroes congregates daily at the corner of Marais and Baga-
telle, in front of a 'bar-room' located there," one woman complained. "It
is very embarrassing for ladies and children to pass, as they gamble on
the sidewalk and use the vilest language imaginable."[50]

Without bothering to investigate, the mayor's office forwarded the information to police headquarters and ordered, "Please attend to these
individuals and put a few in jail."[51]

In other cases, authorities responded to white suspicions with stake-
outs. Citing reports from a wealthy lumber salesman, the mayor's secretary contacted police headquarters, ordering, "With reference to the
complaint of Mr. Charles McDowell as to disorderly negro occupants in
rear of tenement house at 1032 St. Charles Street, please have strict surveillance of these premises continued."[52]

Carried away by rumor and enthusiasm, private citizens even offered
to serve directly as undercover agents. Responding to erroneous reports
that a "secret vigilance committee" was being formed, one salesman vol-
unteered his services as a covert operative, saying he had served as a special police officer and portraying himself as uniquely positioned to
infiltrate the black underworld. "My business brings me in daily contact
with all classes of negroes," he explained, then cautiously added, "As I am
well known by many negroes, it would not be well for me if my name
should be made known."[53]

Clarifying, the mayor's office explained that special police officers
might be mobilized in the future, but no shadow organization was being planned, while objecting to the salesman's use of a euphemism more
commonly associated with lynch mobs. "A 'vigilance committee' is an
extralegal body," officials explained. "The special police were called under
law."[54]

As white paranoia subsided and the surveillance failed to expose any
actual conspiracies, enthusiasm for the campaign began to decline. Authorities and businessmen in New Orleans were eager to distance the city
from events that had drawn widespread criticism, adding to its unruly
reputation. The crisis had been front-page news across the country, and
outside the South, the press had mostly condemned elected officials for
once again failing to prevent mass violence. Editors and corporate

boosters in New Orleans were customarily defensive, blaming Republicans for opportunistically using the violence in the ongoing presidential campaign, but it was a weak defense and the charges stung. While bond markets had stabilized, the business community had reason for concern about the long-term consequences of the city's damaged reputation, particularly with the bidding to fund the sewerage project open—then quite unexpectedly, they finally caught a break.[55]

Roughly two thousand nautical miles away, New York had been regarded as a sister city during the antebellum period, although the relationship had soured during the ultra-partisan wartime years and the aftermath. Editors there had been highly critical during the Charles crisis, but an eerily familiar mood descended on the city when a black suspect wielding a razor blade mortally wounded an NYPD patrolman. As word of the officer's death spread, hundreds of white men gathered outside his home, angrily demanding revenge. The mob rampaged through Hell's Kitchen, attacking pedestrians as unmoving police officers watched the chaos unfold from the sidelines. Black residents defended themselves by throwing bricks and paving stones from the upper floors of tenement buildings, barely preventing a massacre. The ugly scenes forced editors in New York to retract their earlier criticism, as they conceded, "It was a scene on very much the same order as took place in New Orleans."[56]

For white residents in Louisiana, the disturbance was the closest thing to vindication, proving that there was nothing peculiar about the Southern metropolis. However unwelcome, the mutual troubles and their own city's unique demographics presented an opportunity to educate their misguided Yankee counterparts on how challenging it was to enforce racial order in urban space. Although it was only one-tenth the size, New Orleans had the larger black community, constituting nearly one-third of the population when New York's population numbered in the low single digits. The associated challenges bred hard-won expertise, which they were quite eager to pass on across the South-North boundary that had done so much to shape the diverging destinies of the former sisters. Sharing race knowledge, mainstream editors in New Orleans simultaneously exonerated their own city. "The negro question is not changed by going a few hundred miles north or south," they explained.

"The trouble is that criminal class of negroes who have settled in our larger cities and are a source of constant danger and crime."[57]

They spoke of an old problem with new confidence, now certain that modern policing and criminal justice reforms would make possible the breakthroughs promised in the coming century. Once more emphasizing the need for enforcement on both sides of the color line, they provocatively questioned which city would prove better at protecting "innocent negroes from mob violence by the rougher and lower classes." But despite all the posturing about harsh consequences and evenhandedness, disheartening signs were already manifesting. Recognizing the real possibility that New York's mobs had been at least partially inspired by the violence in New Orleans, editors telegraphed the mayor's office in Louisiana, questioning the possible connection. "Do you think the negro riots in New York last night are the outgrowth of the intense anti-negro feeling growing from the race riots in your city?" they asked. "What course would you suggest in handling this problem?"[58]

Scrawled in his own handwriting and relayed by telegram, the mayor's response was as stunning as it was unequivocal. "There were no race riots in this city," Capdevielle boldly claimed. "Since you ask what course I would suggest for New York to pursue, I would say go to your mayor, give him your support, and he will do what is right."[59]

* * * *

BEFORE EIGHT O'CLOCK on a sweltering mid-August evening, police commissioners in New Orleans gathered for the most important meeting in the board's checkered history. Although it was the officers accused of cowardice who were scheduled to defend themselves, the hearing had become a de facto referendum on the machine administration's seriousness about reforming public safety. Notwithstanding the public-private campaign to absolve the mayor's office, blame was spreading widely after the catastrophic failure to protect lives and property during the crisis. Some of the gravest charges centered on the administrative body, packed with political appointees responsible for resolving disciplinary matters. The controversy threatened to reignite long-standing complaints about patronage and corruption. Two long-serving commissioners had already stepped down, but rumor among those who packed the hearing chambers was that others would soon follow—perhaps even the entire board. Observers recognized the sky-high stakes, openly acknowledging, "The police board was as much on trial as the individuals against whom the charges were made."

As the hearing opened, the surviving commissioners wisely sidestepped the dangerous leadership questions looming over the proceedings, postponing resignation discussions and diverting attention to more dramatic affairs. There were ominous murmurs when they called Sergeant Jules Aucoin for trial and the defendant failed to materialize, but someone produced a doctor's note, which cited "nervous prostration" to explain his absence. His partner took the chance to request that his own trial be suspended, but commissioners waved away Trenchard's petition and the corporal put on a brave face, declaring, "Gentlemen, I'll go to trial."[60]

What followed was more made-for-press spectacle than sober-minded inquiry. Jointly tried with three others charged with cowardice relating to the Fourth Street ambush, Trenchard mounted a spirited defense, vigorously cross-examining the dozen-plus witnesses, black and white, who took the stand. On both sides, the questions bordered on absurd, centered mostly on reputation, perception, and questionable deduction rather than actual eyewitness evidence: whether audibly squeaky shoes indicated a panicked retreat as opposed to a calculated withdrawal; if being known to exaggerate also made someone a likely coward; and so forth. In the end, none of it mattered very much. When the testimony concluded, commissioners withdrew for deliberations and returned nearly as quickly, the chairman pronouncing, "Officers, you've all been dismissed from the force."[61]

Coinciding with the campaign to provide for the families of the police martyrs, the trials and seemingly predetermined verdicts were a direct response to white paranoia and its political consequences. Robert Charles had targeted no civilians, aside from those who put themselves in harm's way. Yet the threat posed by his co-conspirators—unproven and unseen—to say nothing about run-of-the-mill black criminals emboldened by the dismal police display, made purging and strengthening a force that had been unable to neutralize a lone gunman about far more than

overdue reform: it was life and death. Editors applauded the decisive response from commissioners, arguing that a speedy conclusion was more
humane for the accused men and critical when the charges threatened
to jeopardize the department's morale at such a precarious time. Besides,
there was no reason to delay a foregone conclusion. "No other judgement
was possible," they concluded.[62]

For the Capdevielle administration, sacrificing a pair of long-serving
commissioners and a few widely condemned police officers was a way to
show resolve without risking controversy, but serious questions remained
whether that would be enough. The police board had faced harsh criticism during the crisis. Editors denounced "its notoriously bad methods
of administration, its failure to hold the police to accountability for non-
performance of duty, its glaring favoritism, and its inability to discern
the inevitable consequences of its actions," unanimously concluding that
law enforcement in New Orleans was rotten "at its very foundation."[63]
Although its alliance with the business community had directed outrage
toward the new administration's predecessors as opposed to its own fail-
ings, the possibility remained that inadequate police reforms would poison the relationship before it could solidify. When an Orleans Parish
grand jury published its report on the uprising toward the end of the
month, the findings confirmed that sweeping reforms were desperately
needed. Grand jurors condemned the departmental command structure
and endorsed a reorganization "from the police board down to the hum-
blest patrolman," before reaching a damning conclusion that supported
the claims made by black eyewitnesses. "After a very serious and thorough
investigation, embracing testimony from some 200 witnesses," they determined, "we find that the police, with a few exceptions, were undoubtedly in sympathy with the mob."[64]

Yet what remained to be seen was not simply if the new administration had the desire to pursue sweeping reforms, but also whether it had
the necessary resources, particularly given the long-standing financial obstacles that made the New Orleans Police Department one of the nation's most poorly funded and undermanned forces. For those who
favored structural change, almost immediately, there were worrying
signs that business community leaders were sizing up the price tag and

reassessing what reforms were *really* needed. Arguing that demands to dismiss commissioners and reorganize the force were being made without due consideration, one Board of Trade member suggested a modest increase to the department's patrol strength, which could "give the commissioners a chance to prove their competency."[65] Doing so, he gave voice to an emerging consensus on the structural problems facing beleaguered officers, who needed an attitude change more than anything else. Editors commented favorably when the police board announced its two new members, both well-known businessmen selected by the mayor's office, expressing optimism about the department's newfound direction. "With the experience gained, especially during the late troubles," they explained, "it will be possible to bring the New Orleans police to a high standard of excellence."[66]

Evident in the trials of the accused officers, the new understanding was unmistakable. Just as hoodlums were responsible for the uprising, bad apples were to blame for the dubious police response, a few officers too cowardly to confront the ugly characters prowling the streets of New Orleans. Responding to the public mood, the reconstituted police board was unusually active in the short term, continuing the pattern of personalized accountability by showing unprecedented enthusiasm for discipline. Eighteen officers would be dismissed from the force before the year ended, surpassing the previous record for annual terminations; misconduct fines reached the highest rates since the board's reorganization at the beginning of the previous decade.[67] At the same time, councilmen showed considerably less eagerness to address the department's budget crunch. Requests for emergency funding to hire part-time officers went unanswered, and nearly two years after the crisis, the department's budget was unchanged, although the full-time strength of the force had been increased—by six officers. The machine and its allies were shifting responsibility onto overburdened patrolmen, who were expected to police more aggressively, or suffer the consequences.[68]

Emphasizing discipline rather than enacting more substantive changes, policymakers focused on another area where patrolmen had come up short during the shootouts: lethality.[69] One month after the gunfights, commissioners determined "it was necessary for the members of the force

to be more proficient in the use of weapons" and authorized construction on the first dedicated shooting range in the department's history.[70]
Meanwhile, a private rifle club offered free access to its facilities.[71] No less
significant were questions regarding which guns the men would be carrying. Just two years before, new regulations had standardized weapons
across the force, requiring officers to carry .32-caliber pistols.[72] Amid
widespread criticism that patrolmen lacked the stopping power necessary
to police New Orleans, the board organized a special committee and
hosted a salesman from Colt's Firearms Company for a presentation, ultimately ordering a department-wide upgrade to the latest .41-caliber
model—even more powerful than the .38-caliber pistols that were being
phased in by many urban departments across the country.[73] Doubling
down on the military-style approach toward public safety, police commanders ordered bimonthly drills at precincts citywide, overseen by
captains. "A policeman should be a soldier," editors concluded.[74]

Cumulatively, the changes were far less significant than the comprehensive reforms recommended by the grand jury investigation. But they
were nonetheless profound, both symbolically and pragmatically, reflecting the most consequential philosophical evolution in departmental history. Arming police had been controversial since the antebellum period,
a debate pitting racial paranoia against concerns over questionable competence, endemic corruption, and the high proportion of foreign-born
officers. But paired with the newfound emphasis on discipline, the more
aggressive stance earned positive reviews from a press corps that had long
made the force and its enablers a dependable punching bag. Approaching the first anniversary of the crisis, the conservative press acknowledged
past criticism as well-deserved, but praised "the present course of the
board" and predicted that the double emphasis on militarized discipline
and more rigorous enforcement would "give us a splendid force," so long
as commissioners stayed the course.[75]

Of course, the dangerous consequences of the downward pressure on
patrolmen were obvious from the very beginning. Only hours after the
telegram from New York reached the New Orleans mayor's office, two
patrolmen were making their rounds, just a few blocks from the apartment complex where Robert Charles met his death, when they spotted a

young black man standing on a nearby corner and moved to challenge him. The reasoning behind the confrontation was hazy. Some reports suggested that officers were specifically looking for nineteen-year-old Aaron "Moon" Harris, who was notorious as a "bad negro" despite his youth, but others claimed that he was unknown to officers, who spotted him "lurking" and tried to arrest him for being "dangerous and suspicious." The sequence that followed was equally uncertain. Some described the patrolmen edging closer before Harris spotted them, triggering a wild chase; others presented a more dramatic version of events, saying the suspect drew a gun and began shooting as they approached, prompting them to return fire.[76]

Nobody was harmed despite the supposed exchange from close range, although the suspect escaped. Identifying him as the infamous "Moon," the patrolmen contacted police headquarters and within minutes, officers flooded the neighborhood and surrounded his mother's home, where they found Harris in one of the downstairs bedrooms and took him and another young man into custody. Outside the property, they were confronted by angry white men, who surrounded the prisoners and threatened to lynch them. Patrolmen fought their way through the fray and brought the suspects downtown. As with the circumstances surrounding the shooting, there were conflicting reports on whether police recovered a weapon, but it hardly mattered. Following so soon after the crisis, the ambiguous circumstances surrounding a showdown between jumpy officers and a black man with a nasty reputation were eagerly refashioned into something more readily comprehensible, particularly when reporters interviewed white residents. "Harris is an impudent, bad, and dangerous negro," they explained, before directly tying the episode to demographics and recent events. "The negro population outnumbers the whites in that neighborhood and the ladies and children are in constant dread, especially since the killing of the police officers by Robert Charles."[77]

Convicted and sentenced to five years, in the end, Harris would more than justify the association, serving his time, returning to the streets, and becoming one of the most notorious scoundrels in New Orleans.[78] Reflecting on his early career and describing the infamous bad men who prowled the city's early-twentieth-century underworld, jazz musician Jelly Roll Morton would describe Harris as "no doubt the most heartless man I've ever seen," rumored to have eleven murders on his scorecard and so fearsome that he inspired a song, explaining, among other things, why he managed to walk the streets with impunity:

All the policemen on the beat, had old Aaron to fear,
You could always tell,
When Aaron Harris was near.[79]

Evading death in a controversial showdown with police officers only two weeks after Charles met his bloody end, Harris embodied the cop killer's complicated legacy in more ways than one. He symbolized the heightened dangers facing black men in New Orleans, along with the potent and continuing threat they posed to the conservative alliance and its policing regime, one rough-and-tumble escapade at a time—real-world, legendary, or both. Reputed to employ a hoodoo woman for protection, Harris would remain a larger-than-life menace for more than a decade before he finally met a fitting end, gunned down in self-defense when he attacked a "stool pigeon" who allegedly gave him up to police. Booming in red-light-district dancehalls, his ballad unapologetically celebrated an antihero whose transgressive masculinity unnerved the foot soldiers of a repressive order and enlivened the soundtrack of a resistance campaign without end, playing out nightly on the streets of New Orleans.[80]

There was another song that appeared around the same time that officers confronted Harris, although its words and melody would be lost to history, too dangerous for even the boldest musicians to perform. Jelly Roll would remember it as "the story of the man who was maybe even more dangerous than Aaron," a mild-mannered character who sold papers and ultimately "tore up the entire city of New Orleans" after his own encounter with police. Saying that he was living only a few blocks from Charles at the time, four decades removed, the musician described the details as he recalled them. Some were embellished, others were strikingly accurate, from the shootout on Dryades Street to the precise layout of the Saratoga Street complex where the assassin was finally brought down.

More than anything, Jelly Roll remembered the man at the center of things, imbuing him with the same mythical qualities that astonished those who witnessed his handiwork firsthand. "Every time he raised his rifle and got a policeman in his sights, there'd be another one dead," Jelly Roll reflected. "It was never learned how many police were killed. Some said thirty-two. Some said eighteen."[81]

Decades after the events unfolded, Jelly Roll's recollections provided a faint glimpse of a story lost to history, a grassroots countermobilization that paralleled the police campaign, away from the probing eyes of reporters and public officials, a flourishing conversation as the black working classes in New Orleans made sense of those spectacularly combustible days. The memories also revealed the devastating consequences of the crackdown, which purged the historical record of those powerfully countervailing voices, those who secretly celebrated Charles and his superhuman assault on white supremacy, who imagined themselves perhaps one day following in his footsteps. Even if it was imaginable, it was mostly unsayable and certainly unsingable. "They had a song out on Charles, but it was squashed very easily by the police department," the jazzman described, choosing that safely anonymous pronoun, the third-person plural, despite the four-decade gap. "Not only the department, but by any of the surrounding people that ever heard the song, due to the fact that it was a trouble breeder. . . . I used to know the song, but I found it was best for me to forget it and that I did, in order to go along with the world on the peaceful side."[82]

While the crackdown effectively suppressed most visible support for Charles within the black community, there would be a brazen coda to his resistance song. A month after he passed along the information that eventually led authorities to the fugitive's hiding place, twenty-three-year-old Fred Clark was sitting on the porch of his Rampart Street home when a neighbor approached. The relationship between the longtime acquaintances had grown tense in recent weeks. Just shy of his thirtieth birthday, Lewis Forstall served drinks at a barroom favored by black laborers, where he was heard denouncing the younger man as a snitch and threatening revenge. On this Sunday evening, Clark glanced up and saw his accuser striding toward him purposefully. Forstall reached into his pocket and drew a pistol, then aimed and tried to fire, but the hammer snapped harmlessly—bad cartridge. Clark jumped up. Before he could move, Forstall pulled the trigger again. This time a gunshot pierced the calm evening. Clark instantly crumpled to the ground, blood pouring from a gaping neck wound. Satisfied that his mission was accomplished, the assassin waited patiently as his neighbor bled to death, then surrendered to police when they belatedly reached the scene. Investigating the unusual homicide, officers both recorded and failed to comprehend the motive. While they recognized the murderer gunned down the victim "for being on friendly terms with the police," they concluded that his killing was "apparently without any cause or provocation," as though unable to grasp that collaboration was a capital offense in some circles.[83]

Although white editors were usually eager to splash sensational black crime dramas across the front page, they buried the snitch's death—and its alarming ties to Charles—on the seventh page, beside advertisements for men's shoes and headache pills. Some crimes were too concerning to magnify. With mainstream observers turning away, the final lesson fell to Ida B. Wells, the black activist who was hated across the nation for fearlessly telling the truth about life, death, and lynching in America.[84] "The white people of this country may charge that he was a desperado," she concluded, "but to the people of his own race, Robert Charles will always be regarded as the hero of New Orleans."[85]

* * * *

THE BUSINESS SEASON was underway by the time George Flanagan and Mike Foley answered charges for the murder of Hannah Mabry, three months after she was murdered in her own home. Jury selection was unusually challenging for the notorious case, but when the trial finally opened, things went badly for the prosecution. On the witness stand, neighbors, patrolmen, and special police officers provided no help. They described a chaotic mob scene, but none could name the shooters. The victim's daughter-in-law was more forthcoming, as Nancy Mabry identified one of the defendants who fired directly into the home, but reporters were skeptical despite her certainty.[86] Her husband fared even worse. After spending three months in prison, Harry Mabry created a sensation.

Taking the stand with visible reluctance, Mabry recanted everything, claiming to have lost his mind after his mother's death and saying he could no longer identify her killers. Although the stunning turnaround was highly suspicious, the district attorney immediately abandoned the trial and the former star witness was taken into custody on perjury charges. "Thus ended the first of the celebrated riot cases," reporters concluded, "and judging from appearances, the state will find it just as difficult to convict any of the other accused."[87]

Court observers were right to note the decreasing probability of convictions related to the murders, but there were a few telling episodes as the cases slumped through the system. After he pled guilty to perjury, Harry Mabry eventually related the circumstances leading to his recantation. While being held as a state's witness in Orleans Parish Prison, he received a hand-scrawled warning that his wife and baby daughter would be murdered if he testified against his mother's killers, delivered with the knowledge, likely complicity, of the deputies who guarded his cell. His only perjury was the panic-stricken denial that ended the trial.[88] Despite his ordeal, Mabry would serve eight months in Angola Penitentiary, the only person convicted on charges relating to his mother's homicide.[89] One by one, the district attorney dropped the remaining cases against the defendants charged with murdering black victims. There was none of the editorial fanfare that followed the indictments. White residents had prematurely congratulated themselves on a colorblind justice campaign, before conveniently forgetting to follow the story to its disillusioning conclusion. Aside from a few convictions for public drunkenness, disturbing the peace, and other minor charges, the grand crusade against "white hoodlums" amounted to nothing.[90]

Perhaps more unexpected was the outcome of the cases against the alleged Charles co-conspirators. They produced only a single manslaughter conviction against Silas Jackson, a verdict so dubious that it was immediately overturned, whereupon the state abandoned the prosecution entirely, along with the other remaining cases. They were mostly paper-thin and it was virtually impossible to prove who knew what about the fugitive's presence on the property. Nevertheless, the outcome was a striking admission that there was nothing left to be gained by prosecuting those tangentially connected with the tragedy, especially because innocence was very rarely enough to exonerate black defendants charged with notorious crimes. The abandoned cases were then perhaps the most compelling evidence that from the white perspective, the police crackdown on the black community was producing the desired outcome. With disciplined police officers patrolling dangerous neighborhoods and black leaders assisting them, there was no continuing need for show trials, snarling editorials, and dark warnings—the old methods that had proven so explosive over the past four decades.[91]

Those who favored symbolism could look to the passing of the Old South's editorial champion to confirm the sea change. One day before Halloween, the *Daily States* announced the death of the newspaper's founder Henry Hearsey, telling readers the Confederate veteran had died unexpectedly after six weeks of declining health.[92] The fire-breathing newsman had been a lightning rod for his uncompromising perspective on race relations, which sometimes veered uncomfortably close to genocidal. In death, both private citizens and public officials remembered Hearsey as a Southern gentleman and progress-minded booster for his adopted hometown.[93] Addressing the major's widow, passing along condolences to his colleagues, and ultimately honoring a request to serve as a pallbearer at his funeral, Mayor Capdevielle mourned the community losing "a brave and public-spirited citizen."[94] Press corps members marked his passing with tributes to his literary talents and his attacks on "corrupt politicians during Reconstruction," which made him a key figure in "restoring good government to the state."[95]

For all the misty-eyed eulogies, there was an underlying sense that white supremacy's bloodthirsty advocate had served his purpose. In recent years, the venomous tongue that once pushed him to the bleeding edge of Louisiana politics now made him an ambiguous figure: too righteous to ignore, but too outrageous to actually sanction. The summer crisis had been his one final chance to rain fire and brimstone, to call out the white mob in a heady climate that gave his pronouncements about "the negro problem and its final solution" the gravity of end-times prophecy.[96] But as the business season once more enlivened a great commercial metropolis, now protected by its conservative alliance and aggressive police force, his apocalyptic visions were diminished, along with the visionary. The emerging order would thrive despite the men whose righteous violence he voiced, those unable to adapt hard-line ideologies forged by secession, total warfare, and occupation to the socioeconomic realities of a brighter dawn: the twentieth century. Mourning "one of the most remarkable personalities from the newspaper field of the South," his fellow editors remembered an old veteran who had probably outlived his prime, "an original, as they are seldom found these days."[97]

Two days after Hearsey's passing, the governor of Louisiana, its two U.S. senators, the mayor of New Orleans, and other luminaries enlisted as honorary pallbearers escorted the esteemed publisher's body into the Army of Tennessee tumulus in Metairie Cemetery, where the same clergyman who delivered the opening benediction at Louisiana's disenfranchising convention gave Major Henry Hearsey a fittingly grandiose farewell. Placing him among those "the Lord endowed with great intellectual power and penetrating wisdom," Reverend Benjamin M. Palmer reassured that while the editor's passing might seem to threaten the social order he had contributed so much to securing, his legacy would endure. "The worker may be removed, but the power of his influence remains," he pronounced. "A strong life once lived does not end in death— its influence goes down into the generation that follows."[98]

Funeral-goers missed the eulogy's more sinister implications. Indeed, it was a noteworthy testament to Hearsey's unimpeachable reputation that virtually every commercial powerhouse in New Orleans had joined the politicians to honor him—on a weekday afternoon, at the start of the business season—particularly given the extraordinary events unfolding on the ground. Scarcely two months after the crisis, the alarming predictions about possible economic consequences were a distant memory. Predictions had suggested a good harvest after frustrating years of recession and agricultural stagnation. But as cotton bales steamed along waterways and railroad tracks, the snow-capped mountains piling up on the levee revealed something much more: an unprecedented bumper crop.[99] On the same day that Hearsey's former rivals covered his funeral service, they published a special notice describing the most remarkable month in the city's economic history. "New Orleans has broken all its commercial

records, sending and receiving more cotton than ever before and showing how great a port it has become," they bragged, publishing the numbers to prove the sensational claim.[100]

Of course, "New Orleans" was not breaking anything. Black and white
dockworkers were, thousands of them, working at a backbreaking pace.
It had not been without some drama. Earlier that month, union members from the Colored Laboring Men's Alliance had gone on strike after
a wage dispute, but soon discovered that shipping companies were newly
equipped to force down payroll despite the insatiable labor demand.[101]
After threatening to replace the strikers with Italian immigrants, agents
leveraged the campaign to suppress black criminals, complaining that
lawless agitators were responsible for the trouble and pinning the blame
on "a few idle and worthless persons, who prevent others from working."[102] They successfully called on black leaders to denounce the troublemakers and urged police commanders to do something. Raids on black
saloons quickly followed, applauded by editors as more evidence that the
department's leadership was taking its new mandate seriously. The strike
broke within days and the most exhilarating business season ever seen in
New Orleans roared forward, memories of the summer crisis fading even
as the business community capitalized on the alliance with a machine administration whose loyalty was now beyond question. Editors celebrating the first anniversary of Mayor Capdevielle's victory at the polls were
amazed. "His election was regarded with many misgivings," they reflected,
but thanks to his "resourcefulness in an emergency" and the police reforms since enacted, they were prepared to name him among the greatest chief executives New Orleans had ever seen.[103]

Shortly before Christmas, the city endured one last sensational crime
drama when a white man, unconvincingly disguised in blackface, staged
an audacious train robbery before escaping into the swamps outside
town.[104] Police officers and outraged citizens attempted to follow the trail,
but it ran cold and the excitement was forgotten—until a trapper discovered his bloody corpse. Already badly wounded, the robber had apparently committed suicide by slashing his own throat as the searchers closed
on his location.[105] Hundreds descended on the morgue to view the body
and a reporter from the *Daily Picayune* followed the story to a desolate

grave in the potter's field. As an afterthought, he asked attendants to show him the grave of Robert Charles, which was unmarked and overgrown with weeds. One carnival operator had offered cash for the remains, hoping to display the pickled corpse as an attraction—officials chose a secret burial to frustrate grave robbers. But standing there in the cold and silence, anyone could see that security measures were no longer necessary. Charles was just another "bad negro," rotten and forgotten as white society moved on.[106]

That same afternoon, reporters visited the St. Charles Hotel to interview the general manager of the South's most luxurious property about the booming economy. Only months before, he had mobilized private security to protect black employees as mobs rampaged in the streets. But with his lavish rooms packed with visiting planters and merchants—probably the most reliable measure of a strong business season—the drama was long since forgotten. "We are enjoying phenomenally good times, the best times in memory," he gushed, describing the related booms in cotton and real estate that were prompting capitalists to look southward with newfound enthusiasm. "There is confidence all over the country in the future of New Orleans and a belief among the moneyed class that we are entering a period of progress and prosperity unparalleled in history."[107]

Before commercial elites put the capstone on an extraordinary period, there was one last cause for celebration. In a special session two days after Christmas, councilmen formally accepted a bid for the municipal bond issue that had nearly been torpedoed by the uprising. The transaction promised to raise more than $12 million to finance a long-awaited modern sewerage and drainage system, the missing piece that would safeguard the city's health and guarantee its economic growth.[108] The terms were a bit disappointing, since investors wanted 4 percent annually. Some enviously noted that New York officials had recently accepted a record-breaking bid on somewhat better terms, but most progressive-minded residents were happy to overlook the unfavorable comparison, embrace the future, and, following European custom, welcome 1901 as the *real* beginning of the twentieth century.[109]

Thousands packed into Uptown's First Presbyterian Church on New Year's morning, an unusually diverse crowd, "Methodists, Baptists, Episcopalians, Jews, German Protestants, Lutherans, merchants, scholars, professional men, representatives of the great business and railroad interests, shipping people," and so forth, eager to listen as the South's greatest living orator delivered a sermon titled "The Twentieth Century." Over his four-decade ministry, Reverend Benjamin M. Palmer had witnessed secession, reunion, occupation, and the bloody, interminable struggles in New Orleans ever since, but on such an occasion, the octogenarian clergyman painted a more sweeping vista: human evolution on the grandest possible scale. Masterfully guiding his audience from antediluvian times through antiquity and now into the modern age, Palmer reflected on eternity, mortality, and life's meaning—considering the rise of civilization from its primitive days and imperial conquests throughout history, before finally gesturing toward incredible things yet to come. At each step, God's hand could be discerned, preserving and preparing the white race, the wellspring of European and American genius, to bring light to the world's dark corners as the appointed hour approached, a glorious design sure to be realized in the coming century: white supremacy was paving the way for Christ's millennium. "He looked into the future with prophetic vision and saw a kingdom upon this earth inhabited by men in spiritual bodies," witnesses described, "and the golden city which the prophet described in his vision."[110]

Streaming from the service in awestruck reverence, parishioners had every reason to believe that a Divine Kingdom was fast approaching, that America would play a decisive role in its magnificent dawning, and that New Orleans had been chosen for some unique purpose. It was certainly poised to advance in leaps and bounds at this critical juncture, according to the special New Year's daily editions that hit the streets that morning. Thanks to the unprecedented opening months of the business season, the city had smashed its records for imports and exports, customs duties, bank clearances, postal receipts, and virtually every other financial indicator during the most prosperous calendar year in its boom-bust history. Remembering Thomas Jefferson's famous—and so far infamously misguided—prediction that New Orleans would become the greatest commercial metropolis in America, editors copped to "serious difficulties along the way," but expressed renewed confidence that it would ultimately prove true.[111] After decades of maddening setbacks and fierce political struggles, the city had its soundest mayoral administration in memory, backed wholeheartedly by the business community. Game-changing municipal improvements were funded, and the economy was roaring again. For boosters who had watched in agony as New Orleans shuddered forward in fits and starts, its destiny slipping further beyond the horizon, these were omens confirming a brilliant future, challenges met through resilience and sacrifice. "The new century opens with all these difficulties and obstacles in the way removed," they marveled. Eyes on the Promised Land, it seemed the old slaveholder's prophecy was finally coming true.[112]

Epilogue

MARK JAMES ROBERT ESSEX, KNOWN AS "JIMMY," WAS *born and raised in Emporia, a prairie town settled by abolitionists determined to stop slavery from spreading into Kansas, but one that grew up thanks to its slaughterhouses. The killing business—cattle and pigs—was how his father had become a respected figure in the tiny black community, starting at a packing company and working his way up to foreman. The job allowed him to make a good life for his wife and five children, and his second-born Jimmy had done the rest on his own. He was a happy kid, personable, an all-American boy who joined the Cub Scouts and loved hunting and fishing. Varsity sports were a stretch—he had a delicate frame and stood five feet seven—but he was outgoing, likable, and novel enough in a nearly all-white town that he never ran into serious trouble along racial lines. He was an average student with above-average social skills, making friends easily and dating a few girls—both races, but nothing too serious. Jimmy spoke airily about becoming a preacher one day, but he dropped out after a semester at the local state college and lasted one more at the community college. When he said that he was joining the Navy, his parents were supportive.*

Jimmy seemed to be doing well in the early days. He passed basic training with high marks and earned certification as a dental technician—he wanted a good job, not a warzone experience. He got along with his co-workers and impressed his boss as bright and eager to please, the best assistant he had ever worked with. When his parents visited Imperial Beach, a naval airbase south of San Diego, they were thrilled he was getting along so well. But the honeymoon only lasted a few months. The military was a buzz-saw he never saw coming. A Congressional Black Caucus investigation would later explain that enlistees like him were "victims of discrimination from the time that they enter the services until the time they are discharged," while commanders acknowledged that "systemic racism exists throughout the armed forces." But for a good-hearted kid without the experience to see the punches coming, it was a shock to the core. The base was a hunting ground for any white man with a rank and a racial grudge—and Jimmy was a "cocky nigger," his playfulness and confidence reading as defiance to all the wrong people. The first blows were bewildering: a boss at the military bar where he worked made him ask permission before doing the same jobs that his white co-workers did freely; when he bought a car to escape the base, returning was a thirty-minute ordeal as the guards questioned him and searched the vehicle; after he began dating a Mexican woman and brought her to the canteen, white sailors humiliated the couple by staring them down and muttering racial slurs. By the time Jimmy finally snapped and sucker punched a white petty officer who was harassing him, he already was a marked man.

As the torment worsened, his relationships to other black sailors deepened. They exposed him to the politics he needed to understand what was happening to him, an education in racism that his childhood never really provided: this was what it meant to be a black man in America. They hung out together whenever they could, safety in numbers, but there was only so much they could do to protect each other when race and rank were power and they were on the wrong side of both. White sailors were one thing. Two of them jumped Jimmy in retaliation for the punch, and there was a nightclub scuffle when he was out with friends—the black sailors were the only ones disciplined. But senior officers were the real problem. They wrote him up for the smallest infractions and gave him special duty, always the dirtiest and most demeaning jobs. Complaints went nowhere; they only made things worse. There were disciplinary hearings, then panic attacks and nightmares. He stole sedatives from the dental office to ease the pain and told his parents that Navy life was nothing like what he imagined. "Blacks have trouble getting along here," he wrote home.

Jimmy made it barely eighteen months before he finally cracked, packing a duffel bag and boarding a Greyhound bus to New Orleans. He got off in El Paso and called his parents to send money so that he could return home. Once he made it back to Emporia, they convinced him to report back to the military and deal with the consequences of going absent without leave. His mother was heartbroken. Her son's youthful enthusiasm was gone for good. "That was a happy-go-lucky kid," she concluded. "This was a serious-minded man."

"I just needed time to think," Mark Essex said at his court-martial. "I had to talk to some black people, because I'd begun to hate all white people. I was tired of going to white people and telling them my problems and not getting anything done." The proceedings were a formality. Essex voluntarily pleaded guilty. In exchange, the Navy granted him a general discharge for unsuitability. The agreement was supposed to minimize damage for everyone involved: it allowed a troubled sailor to avoid a worst-case dishonorable discharge, although for official purposes, he was admitting that he was the problem. Essex was free without further discipline, but the reality was more complicated: anything less than an honorable discharge was a glaring red flag for a black veteran, especially when tens of thousands were returning from Vietnam to face the same challenging adjustment to civilian life.

Essex drifted, but not without purpose. His first stop was Harlem, where he tried to connect with the Black Panthers, to continue the revolutionary education other black sailors had provided him in the military. But it was a dead end—the Panthers were compromised by police surveillance and infiltration, crippled by internal squabbles that were moving toward open warfare between factions. He returned home to Emporia after a few weeks, but his childhood home was changed. Everywhere he looked, he saw things he had failed to observe as a kid: segregated neighborhoods and social circles, white bosses and black employees. Sometimes it seemed as though he was back to carefree Jimmy. But whenever politics and race came up, instantly a darkness came over him, one that concerned his parents enough that they asked the family's pastor to intercede. The exorcism went nowhere. "There's nothing I can do," he apologized. "The boy just hates white people."

Essex found work, but keeping it was the problem. Feigning satisfaction and taking orders from white supervisors wore him down and he seemed to cycle through menial jobs every few weeks, mostly doing carpentry and working as a handyman for local businesses. He did a few weeks at the slaughterhouse where his father had worked for almost three decades and managed to last six months at a local factory, but he quit after receiving two late notices. He seemed to enjoy the weekends and nights he spent doing construction on a new church building for his family's congregation, but it was a part-time, short-term gig, and soon he was back to the same grind. He retreated inward as the months passed, disappearing into the country-side for hours. One day, he called a Navy buddy in Louisiana and said that he was coming down. There was nothing left for him at home, plus he needed a fresh start in a place where there were more black people, a real community. It was a two-day drive, eight hundred miles in a beat-up Chevy Impala. Southbound to New Orleans.

* * * *

THE EARLY TWENTIETH century was a hopeful era for the machine and the city it now unquestionably controlled. Although health problems forced Paul Capdevielle to decline a second term despite his widespread popularity, he was replaced by Martin Behrman, an ambitious machine boss who promised to run a "clean business administration" and then surprised the skeptics by mostly sticking to his campaign pledge. Following his predecessor's example, Behrman would build strong relationships with the business community and sidestep the outrageous scandals that plagued the old machine, continuing on the course established during the early months of the Capdevielle administration. And while engineering setbacks and financial troubles continued to delay the greatness and prosperity that every right-minded citizen glimpsed on the horizon, the frustrations did nothing to weaken the nearly unbeatable Choctaw machine and its stranglehold on the mayor's office: nine victories in ten contests, a political dynasty that spanned almost fifty years.[1]

The reasons behind the half-century of dominance were widely recognized, although discreetly. When an Ivy League political scientist visited New Orleans to interview bosses and private citizens midway through the machine's reign, they vaguely described an "understanding" between politicians and businessmen, a "spirit of cooperation" in which unofficial campaign donations were exchanged for unspecified favors. One anonymous state representative from Orleans Parish told him that politicians "agreed to do nothing that would hurt business and that business would be the judge," while an unnamed attorney described how bosses worked "hand in glove with business on everything," which made them "almost invincible." But although the machine had strayed a long way from its rough-and-tumble roots, careful triangulation also guaranteed its dominance, since workers remained part of its coalition. Labor representatives from the skilled trades enjoyed a place at the bargaining table, where machine politicians would be responsible for negotiating agreeable deals. Although the most privileged craftsmen had a voice, the radical possibilities chased by a previous generation during the general strike were gone—an acceptable compromise for business leaders, who better appreciated the stability provided by machine go-betweens and embraced political arrangements they once condemned.[2] The visiting scholar concluded, "To them, these mutually beneficial relationships are normal, necessary, and in the interests of the city."[3]

For those inclined to agree, there was some evidence to support these claims. During the early 1900s, game-changing drainage and sewerage projects started by the Capdevielle administration were completed, helping to eradicate yellow fever and cholera epidemics in the new century. Officials modernized shipping infrastructure by constructing a belt railroad system, allowing the Port of New Orleans to reclaim its status as the second ranking in the country. While merchants predicted that the Panama Canal would "revolutionize the commerce of the world" and elevate New Orleans to global supremacy, others marketed the city with an eye toward the rapidly growing tourism and convention industries. Promoting its reputation as "The City That Care Forgot," they portrayed the metropolis as a playground catering to exotic desires, before eventually rebranding as "America's Most Interesting City" when civic leaders objected to the implied negligence.[4] Despite the short-lived controversy, boosters praised "expansion in every direction," made possible by the machine's relationship with the business community.[5]

But for all this apparent progress, there were worrying signs. Among major American cities, New Orleans ranked near the bottom in per capita appropriations for police and fire protection, hospitals, road maintenance, and recreation—and dead last in education spending.

Some blamed corruption, but government expenses were similarly un-impressive. Truthfully, the source of the trouble was neither a conspir-acy nor a mystery. By the end of the machine's rule, working families in New Orleans spent a greater share of their income on food than counter-parts anywhere else in America.[6] Meanwhile, slumlords with little reason to improve run-down rental properties dominated housing markets, busi-nessmen successfully lobbied for special privileges and tax exemptions, and employers who paid starvation wages and steadily profited from the shipping-dominated economy saw no reason to diversify. Combined, these forces badly—and artificially—depressed municipal funding. Even though its property tax rates were comparable to those of its peers, New Orleans generated the lowest per capita revenue among major Ameri-can cities: 20 percent below the norm.[7] It was a metropolis being stran-gled by its wealthy residents, with help from their friends in high places. "Businessmen have difficulty seeing the difference between their personal profits and the general welfare of the city," an observer noted, cautiously adding, "In some cases, the relationship was something less than benefi-cial to the average citizen."[8]

Yet the regime did not underserve equally. Although bargaining by segregated unions gave W.E.B. Du Bois the impression that "the Negro artisan is gaining, or at least not losing" in the early 1900s, these break-throughs obscured a bleaker reality for the working-class majority.[9] Al-though they represented one-fourth of the male workforce in New Orleans, black men were nearly two-thirds of its lowest-status, unspecial-ized laborers.[10] They carved drainage ditches, cleaned downtown streets, repaired streetcar tracks, disposed of human waste and animal carcasses, and served as porters, doing the "negro jobs" once filled by Robert Charles and tending the city's unending needs for starvation wages.[11] Black women like Virginia Banks were just as critical and no less marginalized. They made up nearly half of working women in New Orleans, disproportion-ately employed as domestic servants and laundresses.[12] Among more than fifty thousand black workers in New Orleans midway through the ma-chine's dynasty, few were represented in the negotiations between ma-chine bosses, union organizers, and business leaders. The majority had only vague promises that progress would trickle down far enough to help them, and cold, unchanging statistics that proved the lie as the years passed.[13]

Countless other measures revealed the structurally produced relationship between race and desperation. Primary school attendance rates were comparable across the color line, a baseline reflecting a community that valued education and fought tenaciously for access during Reconstruction and its aftermath. But illiteracy rates for black men and women were more than seventeen times higher than for native-born white adults, a difference driven by the steady flow of expendable and vulnerable laborers drawn from the countryside.[14] Meanwhile, three-quarters of homes in New Orleans were rental properties, mostly overcrowded rooming houses and cramped apartments that catered to single workers and poor families. Almost nine in ten black-occupied homes were rented, a percentage that compared unfavorably with property ownership rates in the exploitative sharecropping economy. Among the migrants who came to New Orleans to escape crushing poverty in the countryside, the experience was usually continuity rather than opportunity: starvation wages, dismal conditions, no chance of getting ahead.[15]

That was assuming they survived for long. Perhaps most damningly, New Orleans posted higher average mortality rates for black residents than any major urban area in America—nearly double those of white residents.[16] Authorities were eager to emphasize the distinction when they explained the city's unwholesome reputation to outside capitalists and prospective emigrants. They published monthly death tolls and segregated victims by race, proving that New Orleans was perfectly safe "to the white home-seeker," since *black deaths* were the reason for its ghastly mortality rates.[17] It was the closest the ruling class would come to a confession: their forward-looking New Orleans was a place where black workers were critical to progress, yet mostly excluded from its humane possibilities. This was a city whose most vulnerable residents suffered so desperately that they dragged its aggregate statistics to the bottom tranche of possibility for human life in twentieth-century America, cycled through an urban threshing machine that demanded, despised, and destroyed them in its misconceived climb toward a future that was never coming.

* * * *

MARK ESSEX MET *his buddy in Harvey, a downscale Westbank suburb just across the river from New Orleans. Together they found Essex a cheap apartment nearby. A few weeks later he was accepted into a community-based job training program that was funded by LBJ's Great Society to reduce urban poverty and provide economic opportunity. On the application, he selectively listed a few prior jobs and supervisors, wrote down his Navy experience, and misrepresented his discharge as honorable. He told other lies in response to the state-mandated questions: "Within the past 10 years, have you been discharged from a position because your conduct or work was not satisfactory? Have you resigned after being notified that your conduct or work was not satisfactory? Have you been arrested? Have you been charged, indicted, or summoned into court as a defendant? Have you been held by federal, state, or other law enforcement authorities for any violation of any federal law, state law, parish or municipal law, regulation, or ordinance?" No, no, no, no, no. Essex omitted his experience with the military justice system. He claimed to have satisfied a decade's worth of authority figures, all the way back to when he was thirteen, without the slightest exception, without even raising suspicion—and so he was accepted into the program's vending machine repair school. Administrators rejected his Navy buddy, citing his "attitude at the time of the interview."*

The program was structured. Classes ran from 8:00 a.m. to 4:30 p.m. on weekdays. Attendance was mandatory—three absences were cause for expulsion, no exceptions. Weekly pay was fifty dollars, roughly the federal poverty line for a single individual. But he seemed to thrive. Essex was easily the best in his class. He was alert and constantly asked questions, but otherwise kept his head down and got the work done. The instructor noticed his aptitude and pushed him hard to read electrical circuit diagrams, the ones that he only gave to his brightest students to challenge them, privately reaching out to contacts at the phone company to find him a position. Essex noticed and seemed to appreciate the care. One day he gave the white supervisor a drawing to show his gratitude. It was beautifully executed, although the subject seemed a bit strange: a black man, muscle-bound, armored, and wielding a massive sword.

Essex seemed to be building a life for himself in New Orleans, working on a vocation and even finding a girlfriend, whom he dated casually. When he visited his parents back home in Emporia, they were thrilled that he had finally put his troubles behind him. But truthfully, he was struggling. Money was always a problem. The stipend was never enough. He moved into a new place within weeks, then again, and then again, four apartments in five months, sometimes leaving when he fell behind on rent and landlords threatened him with eviction. Daily expenses were a challenge. And there was always the unforeseen. A few weeks after he joined the work program, he was driving a few classmates to police headquarters, where one needed to pay a traffic fine, when he missed a stop sign and struck a car being driven by an NOPD homicide detective. Nobody was injured, but he was taken into custody, the standard procedure for drivers with out-of-state licenses. Bond was twenty dollars, which he posted and then forfeited when he failed to show up for trial. The damage was a few hundred dollars and he was uninsured. He worked out a deal to pay twenty-five dollars a month, but quickly came up short and sent the insurance company an apology, detailing his circumstances and promising to make up the difference as soon as possible.

Personal hardship was one thing, but his broadening perspective was even more troubling. His latest move brought him to Dryades Street in Central City, among the city's most blighted neighborhoods, where police were a regular presence as the homicide rate pushed toward record highs. He saw black suffering everywhere he looked. These were eye-opening scenes for a young man from small-town Kansas, even one disillusioned by his military experience. His classroom performance deteriorated. He seemed distracted and disinterested, missing a class, then a second. When his instructor asked what was happening, Essex was evasive. But he had started to resent the program, seeing it as part of the system that perpetuated the poverty that surrounded and ensnared him. Jumping through hoops, impressing an endless string of white supervisors for an entry-level job that might one day provide something a bit more than subsistence—which could be snatched away at any time, by any mistake.

Essex studied the problem on his own, making few efforts to connect with like-minded people. It was too dangerous, particularly for a newcomer in a city where police informants were everywhere. He made a few friends and gradually expanded his social circle to include classmates and other acquaintances, but none were really close and he mostly stayed away from politics in conversations with them, especially because his thoughts were taking him to dark places. By now, Essex was reading voraciously. He preferred books on Africa, discovering an ancestral homeland and reimagining himself as he did, independently studying Zulu and Swahili and even trying on a new nickname. No more Jimmy—he was Mata. It meant "bow," the chosen weapon of a black marksman.

* * * *

"THE NEGROES ARE better treated and enjoy more peace in New Orleans than in any other city," its longest-serving mayor boasted in the early 1920s.[18] Although there were mountains of evidence to refute the first claim, he could make a limited case for the second, particularly considering the shocking racial violence engulfing American cities. Atlanta was the first to erupt in the early 1900s, when rampaging white mobs killed more than two dozen black residents before authorities came together with businessmen and community leaders to restore the peace.[19] That was only a prelude to a nationwide white uprising as the first waves of the Great Migration began to reshape the racial demographics of American cities starting in the mid-1910s.[20] Storm clouds shadowed a wartime economic boom, underscored by a racial pogrom in East St. Louis: dozens, perhaps even hundreds killed, and more than six thousand refugees, in July 1917.[21] But dark skies were everywhere by decade's end. During the Red Summer of 1919, violence erupted in cities across the country: Charleston, Philadelphia, Baltimore, Washington, Chicago, Knoxville, Omaha, and dozens more, with total casualties approaching one thousand victims.[22] The aftershocks in the early 1920s climaxed in the destruction of Greenwood, the Tulsa neighborhood also known as "Black Wall Street," where prosperous residents had created one of the wealthiest non-white communities in the country—which police officers, among others, firebombed to the ground as white mobs slaughtered up to three hundred civilians and created ten thousand more refugees, the single most destructive act of racial violence in American history.[23]

As cities across America burned, New Orleans experienced heightened tensions and disruptive strikes, but nothing approaching the bloodshed seen elsewhere. For many white observers, the most concerning development was black mobilization unfolding nationwide as targeted residents successfully defended their homes and neighborhoods. Shootouts between white mobs and would-be victims, some of them World War I veterans, forced more conservative black leaders to denounce Bolshevism and radicalism, but they reflected evolving ideologies and self-defense strategies at the grassroots. Militancy dovetailed with black nationalism, as Marcus Garvey embraced Bishop Turner's dream of an African homeland and drove it to unprecedented heights of visibility and controversy. Watching from the sidelines, authorities in New Orleans praised themselves for the progress made in the decades since the Charles crisis, which had transformed the most volatile city in late-nineteenth-century America into an unusually calm one by the twentieth century's bloody standards. After all, they concluded, two decades of peace was "a good record in view of what's happened in other cities."[24]

If the mobs had miraculously disappeared, other forms of violence were underpinning social order in New Orleans. Although the police force was still undersized and underfunded, the department's law enforcement philosophy had evolved dramatically in response to its changing mandate. Officers carried more powerful service weapons and trained at a dedicated shooting range, while precinct commanders organized military-style parades and demanded more aggression from patrolmen. The consequences of the reforms were far-reaching, but the most significant was death: NOPD officers now killed suspects at historically unprecedented rates. During the late 1800s, fatal police shootings had been relatively uncommon, occurring approximately once every eighteen months on average.[25] But more than forty civilians were gunned down between 1900 and 1920—one deadly shooting every five months—and roughly twenty more were killed by private detectives and night watchmen employed by corporations to provide supplemental protection.[26] Although black males represented less than 15 percent of the overall population, they made up more than two-thirds of the victims in fatal police shootings, many of them killed under questionable circumstances: "put his hand to his right breast as if he was going to draw a weapon," "placed his hand on his hip pocket as if to draw a weapon," "put his hand toward his pocket as if to draw a weapon," "the bullet landing in the negro's back," "the bullet lodging in his back," "two shots, one lodging in the left side of the back," "turned around with his hand to his right hip pocket," "no weapons of any kind were found."[27] As authorities in cities across the United States responded to black migration by demanding police occupation in the neighborhoods where they settled, NOPD patrolmen operated from an established template: initiated during slavery, intensified under Jim Crow, and disproportionately shaped by the Charles crisis and its consequences.[28]

The police department had also changed in other ways. Promotional materials would brag about technological developments, including the addition of automobiles and motorcycles, but the disappearance of racial diversity was among the most consequential revolutions to reshape the force.[29] Among a unique cadre spread across a handful of departments in the South, roughly a half-dozen black officers had been serving in New Orleans at the turn of the century, holdovers from a comparatively more liberal era, whose numbers had been reduced from two dozen at the beginning of the 1890s.[30] But the situation deteriorated rapidly for the survivors immediately after the Charles crisis, when two black officers faced dubious administrative charges, one of them for arresting a white man who challenged his authority.[31] White editors and residents demanded a racial purge, but civil service protections required a more gradual process. Over a decade, several black officers were dismissed, others departed voluntarily, and only white applicants were accepted as recruits. When its last black officer finally retired in the early 1910s, the NOPD became a fully segregated force, which it remained through the mid-twentieth century.[32]

Whitening overlapped with a disturbing pattern of escalation by New Orleans police officers, whose mandate to enforce racial order grew even more aggressive over the years. Between the 1920s and 1940s, the average interval between fatal police shootings dropped from five months to less than three—a sixfold increase over the late 1800s—the most serious abuse in a department so violent that the American Civil Liberties Union named it among the worst civil rights violators in the nation by the late

1930s.[33] As officers perfected methods that once threw the city into chaos after a long-forgotten showdown with a workingman named Charles, black men again made up roughly two-thirds of the casualties. Deadly encounters more often began when patrolmen stopped them for disorderly conduct or alleged suspicious behavior than when cops stumbled onto crimes in progress, which preceded fatal shootings involving white victims twice as frequently. Black victims were also three times as likely to be gunned down in one-on-one confrontations, whereas white suspects were more often killed when patrolmen were outnumbered and overwhelmed. Even more telling, less than one-third of black victims were carrying guns. In what had become a catch-all defense for virtually any questionable shooting, unarmed suspects were regularly killed while making gestures that were supposedly misinterpreted as drawing a firearm.[34] Many were shot from behind, legally, since the district attorney's office interpreted the right to use deadly force against escaping felons to include any black man killed while running away, no matter how trivial the alleged offense. In a progressive city where lynch mobs were no longer necessary, police officers committed nearly half the white-on-black homicides in New Orleans.[35]

No matter the circumstances, the common denominator was impunity. Time and time again, police officers faced no legal consequences for racially charged homicides, even in the most egregious cases: a seventeen-year-old inmate serving a thirty-day sentence, killed while escaping from a work gang; an unarmed twenty-one-year-old, shot in the back of the head as he fled a traffic stop for cursing white motorists; a mentally disturbed husband, gunned down for responding angrily when patrolmen called him "boy" and fighting back when one invaded his home; a twenty-year-old, who raised his voice to off-duty officers whose car had struck a young black girl and then resisted when they attempted to arrest him; and so many others.[36] The same impunity extended to private security. When a night watchman spotted two alleged coal thieves and "fired shots which he thought in the air to frighten them," but actually killed unarmed fifteen-year-old John Smith with a bullet through the head, the district attorney's office ruled that it was a justifiable homicide.[37]

On rare occasion, a shooting was so outrageous that it led to charges, for example, when forty-six-year-old George Simmons was murdered while attending his own brother's wake. After a drunken white man in civilian clothes interrupted the mourners and demanded to search them, Simmons failed to respond quickly enough. So the off-duty patrolman called him a "bad nigger," knocked him down, and shot him through the abdomen, mistaking his deafness for defiance. An all-white jury acquitted the murderer anyway.[38]

Despite so many shootings ranging from dubious to cold-blooded homicide, just one police officer would be convicted for killing a black victim during the machine's dynasty: the supernumerary patrolman who drunkenly promised, "I'm going back to kill that goddamn nigger wench," before shooting fourteen-year-old Hattie McCray in the head for resisting his attempted rape. For that crime, he ultimately served one year in prison.[39]

* * * *

Essex withdrew from his classmates and the acquaintances he made in New Orleans as his anger became more focused, sharpened by his reading and reflection. White society was responsible for the suffering and hopelessness he witnessed, but the police were its watchdogs, the ones who drove through the neighborhoods where he lived, harassing and brutalizing, destroying black lives. And they were getting worse. He watched as the NOPD announced the Felony Action Squad to fight surging violent crime, an undercover unit with "shoot to kill" rules of engagement targeting perpetrators that the police chief described as "one step above animals." By the time sheriff's deputies in Baton Rouge killed two unarmed black students at Southern University during protests against the campus administration, he was forming a plot to take revenge, for those crimes and so many others. He was scared to even think about what it was, about what it could become: a retaliatory strike, a revolution, a suicide mission.

Essex began spending hours cleaning his rifle, a Sturm Ruger .44 Magnum that he had purchased before leaving home for the first time, back when he could barely glimpse the mission he now saw clearly. He practiced loading and unloading the high-powered rounds as big as a grown man's thumb.

The nightmares and panic attacks returned worse than before, tormenting his sleep until his waking hours blended into his dreams. In his dingy place on Dryades Street, two blocks from the stoop where two black men were once confronted by NOPD officers, just around the corner from the alley where Robert Charles ambushed a police squad, Essex began painting on the walls. He wrote a manifesto in fragments—ideas, feelings, impulses, a language he barely knew, whispers from ancestors. Black spray painting: AFRICA. MATA. BARAZA. YAMBA. CUSAVA. WATARA. BONYONGA. YACUBA. BABA. CARCOVA. SANA. OCAPA. And dozens more, Swahili words, disconnected and misspelled. And in English, revolution and rage, respectively sprayed in black and red: HATE WHITE PEOPLE. SHOOT THE DEVIL LIKE YOU SHOOT A DOG. BLOND HAIR, BLUE EYES. REVOLUTIONARY JUSTICE IS BLACK JUSTICE. THE QUEST FOR FREEDOM IS DEATH—THEN BY DEATH I SHALL ESCAPE TO FREEDOM. PIG. HATE. BLOOD. MY DESTINY LIES IN THE BLOODY DEATH OF THE RACIST PIGS. And a practical joke on the ceiling, for when they came looking: ONLY A PIG WOULD READ SHIT WRITTEN ON THE CEILING.

Essex missed a third class just before the holidays, triggering an automatic expulsion from his job-training program. But none of that mattered anymore. He was set on a rebel's course now, a showdown that would end in a black revolution or his own death, maybe both. Shortly before Christmas, he mailed a manifesto to a local television station: "Africa greets you. On Dec. 31, 1972, appt. 11 the Downtown New Orleans Police Dept. will be attacked. Reason—many. But the death of two innocent brothers will be avenged. And many others. P.S. The felony action squad ain't shit. MATA."

The letter was sent to the station's mailroom, where it would lay unopened until early January. In the meantime, Essex gave his few valuable possessions to a friend and mailed his mother a brief note, trying to explain the events that were about to take place—and the things her son was about to do. "Africa, this is it mom," he wrote. "It's even bigger than you and I, even bigger than God. I have now decided that the white man is my enemy. I will fight to gain my manhood or die trying. Love, Jimmy."

* * * *

CHANGE CAME TO New Orleans in the mid-1940s, when a charismatic young politician with an LSU law degree, a New Deal pedigree, and fresh ideas about how to revitalize his adopted hometown made a longshot bid for the mayor's office. The machine was on unstable footing by then, weakened by state-level political feuding and a financial crisis that climaxed when city officials unsuccessfully tried to declare bankruptcy during the Great Depression. But despite its troubles, the end came as a surprise to everyone, which included deLesseps "Chep" Morrison, the first-time reform candidate in his early thirties. To build a winning coalition, he courted and convinced enough fed-up businessmen by going back to basics—pledging to patch the city's potholed streets, collect its garbage, unsnarl its traffic jams, and otherwise address the long-standing, embarrassing problems that nearly a half-century of machine rule had been unable to satisfactorily resolve. In many ways, it was the same promise made by a previous generation in its long-forgotten political struggles: to make New Orleans into the progressive, world-class metropolis its most ambitious residents had always dreamed it would become.[40]

If the machine was gone for good, its way of doing business proved far more durable, even when the incoming mayor promised to economize and made waves by cutting patronage jobs and slashing the most egregiously wasteful spending. The conservative alliance between the business community and the reform administration was mostly unchanged, partly thanks to Morrison's focus on projects he described as "the visible evidence of my achievements," including a civic complex and a cutting-edge railroad terminal completed just as air travel began to erode demand for long-distance passenger trains.[41] Although some praised the close relationships between public and private interests for growing the economy and creating jobs, the profits remained concentrated in comparatively few hands, while the benefits were less conclusive than boosters acknowledged. Strong economic growth flashed, then quickly faded, leaving behind debts and budget deficits as the administration refused to raise taxes, selling bonds and borrowing against the future to fund its modernizing vision. Meanwhile, spending on municipal services never seemed to match the problems on the ground, particularly in the city's least-served neighborhoods, where slum clearance—euphemistically known as urban renewal—worsened the housing shortages that disproportionately harmed its most vulnerable residents, including the fifty thousand black families who lived in substandard housing by the early 1960s.[42]

And so, despite the future promised by reformers, the results were mostly uninspiring. Some of the lackluster performance was related to the personality clashes, power struggles, and crooked deals that local political observers tended to blame. But truthfully, New Orleans was facing a particularly extreme version of the social and economic headwinds that were confounding urban policymakers nationwide. Its population grew during the 1950s, although more slowly, peaking at over six hundred thousand residents as the city comfortably retained its status in the American top twenty. Yet short-term growth concealed a far more damaging long-term trend: both locally and nationwide, the white middle classes were fleeing to nearby suburbs, a modest outflow that would soon become a full-scale exodus. During the 1960s, New Orleans recorded its first population decline in history, a pattern that worsened in the coming decades as industry followed and economic stagnation worsened. Ultimately, its white population would decline by two-thirds, more than a quarter-million residents escaping to the outlying suburbs—and to cities, North and South, with better prospects. As white residents packed up and fled, they brought critical tax revenues with them and left behind a metropolis shaped in Jim Crow's image. By 1970, New Orleans was the most impoverished major city in America, a place where three-fourths of black families struggled near or below the poverty line.[43]

Serving and protecting black residents in New Orleans, at least in theory, was a police department that looked nothing like them, despite the community's tenacious efforts to make it otherwise. Civil rights activists made reintegrating the NOPD a top priority beginning in the mid-1940s, organizing petitions, recruiting applicants, and pressuring elected officials to desegregate a department that remained notorious for its unprofessionalism, corruption, and brutality. The breakthrough came in the early 1950s, when New Orleans belatedly joined its peers across the urban South, but the handful of black officers who successfully navigated the hiring gauntlet faced an uphill struggle for legitimacy. Some were relegated to the Juvenile Division, where they focused on black delinquency, while others were assigned to segregated neighborhoods in plainclothes, since there were concerns over the public reaction to putting them in uniform. Although the numbers grew slowly and the restrictions gradually loosened, minimal integration was not enough to bring change to a department with a toxic reputation among black residents, especially after a series of high-profile shootings, brutality charges, and a controversial trial that ended when an all-white jury acquitted three patrolmen for raping a black woman in the late 1950s.[44]

Despite the policing troubles, New Orleans seemed to navigate Jim Crow's demise peacefully, at least compared with its Southern counterparts. Slowly but steadily, black voters registered and returned to the polls during the postwar years, growing the community's political influence while generally avoiding the violent white backlash seen elsewhere in the region. Reintegrating the city's public schools encountered more resistance, including threats to shut down the system and a grassroots movement that claimed twenty-five thousand members, organized to preserve segregation. Just as they had in a previous generation, black leaders in New Orleans countered oppression with protests and lawsuits—but this time, Jim Crow gave way. When federal marshals accompanied four black elementary students in November 1960, the city became the first in the Deep South to desegregate its public schools. Although white teenagers responded with violent demonstrations, the outrage soon passed and desegregation unfolded in relative calm during the years ahead. Sit-ins and protests at segregated lunch counters similarly encountered resistance, including arrests, but quickly produced breakthroughs as proprietors chose desegregation over costly disruptions. As activists gained momentum in the early 1960s, the city's business community belatedly accepted a moderately progressive stance on civil rights, although one reporter explained that they were "more influenced by the slowing of the cash register than by morality." Regardless, Jim Crow's formerly unassailable walls crumbled with surprisingly limited resistance as politicians and businessmen recounted the costs, and white residents, in growing numbers, chose suburban flight rather than fighting for a cause that was finally lost for good.[45]

Despite the demographic changes and structural challenges, by some estimations, New Orleans was on course to becoming a model of cooperative urban race relations by the late 1960s. As ghettos nationwide erupted in the most significant black uprising in American history, New Orleans was the only major city in the country to be spared.[46] During the 1970 mayoral race, a coalition that included the most influential black voting bloc since before the disenfranchising convention elected "Moon" Landrieu, a white progressive who desegregated municipal hiring and appointed black advisers to his administration, setting the city on course to elect its first black mayor before the decade ended. But despite the visible progress, there was an opposing perspective on the streets of New Orleans, one suggesting that long-standing class divisions within the black community were creating widely diverging opportunities. As voter registration, school attendance, and other statistics reflecting participation in public life gradually moved toward equity, grassroots community leaders ranked police harassment and brutality as the most dangerous problem they faced, a concern so dominant that researchers struggled to change subjects. If anything, civil rights breakthroughs made the continuing occupation by Jim Crow's frontline defenders even more glaring as they policed invisible boundaries that should have been destroyed. In a city whose population was quickly approaching a black majority, the police force remained 95 percent white.[47]

* * * *

CROUCHED BEHIND DISCARDED *concrete pipes in a lot overgrown with high weeds and the wrecks of abandoned houses, Mark Essex surveilled the NOPD central lockup facility one hundred yards away, his silhouette ghostly in the light of a waning crescent moon. He could see officers moving inside the building through an open gateway, police cadets who had drawn unpopular duty. It was 10:52 p.m. on New Year's Eve and New Orleans already sounded like a warzone. The exploding fireworks and occasional celebratory gunshots were the perfect cover as Essex aimed his .44 Magnum rifle, inhaled, held the breath, and fired.*

His weapon bucked seven times, the recoil slamming his shoulder with each round. But as he pulled the trigger to fire an eighth round, there was no response. Cursing the jam, Essex retreated, strewing gear and unspent shells as he fled the abortive showdown, likely unaware that his seventh bullet had ripped through the chest of nineteen-year-old Alfred Harrell, one of the department's only black cadets—he died at Charity Hospital at 11:09 p.m., leaving behind a teenaged wife and newborn son. In memoriam, police would mourn the loss of "a young man who resolved any contradiction about being black and a cop."

As responding police officers swarmed the vacant lot across from the lockup facility, Essex sought cover at a warehouse about a half-mile from the scene, wounding himself when a bullet he fired at the locked metal door ricocheted and struck him in the left hand. Reeling backward, he crossed the street and managed to force his way into another warehouse, setting off a burglar alarm in the process. Two officers on their nightly rounds responded. As they approached the warehouse, Essex ambushed them from inside, critically wounding Sergeant Edwin Hosli Sr. before slipping out the back of the building as his partner returned fire and called for backup. Police descended on the second shooting scene, but there was no sign of the gunman. They rushed the wounded sergeant to the hospital, but in the end, nothing could be done. His wife and four children visited his bedside during the two months it took him to die.

Eighteen hours after the gunshots, the reverend of First New St. Mark Baptist Church walked into the sanctuary and was surprised to find a young black man standing inside. The pastor retreated and then reported the break-in, but police officers distracted by the all-hands dragnet saw no reason to connect the suspected burglary to the shootings. A cursory search uncovered nothing suspicious. Two days passed before an anonymous caller directed them back to the church. This time when they searched the chapel, officers discovered bullets, bloody bandages, and a handwritten apology note addressed to the reverend.

As the manhunt intensified, officers encountered predictable challenges. The search areas bordering the crime scenes were impoverished, predominantly black neighborhoods where police-community relations were notoriously tense. Unsurprisingly, residents in the dilapidated projects and slums were less than interested in cooperating with officers who had previously displayed "a pattern of systemic brutality" on those streets. With angry patrol-

men kicking in doors, raiding nightclubs, and shaking them down, locals
retaliated. Some flooded police headquarters with bogus tips, while others
knocked out streetlights. "Kids were having a little fun with the pigs," an
officer complained, seeming to miss the insurrectionary motives behind the
sabotage.

Despite the disruption, the search produced a few promising leads, al-
though even those were frustrating. Police came tantalizingly close when
the owner of Joe's Grocery contacted them, saying a young black man had
come into the convenience store located only a few blocks away from the
church, self-consciously concealing a bandaged left hand as he purchased ra-
zors. By the time the grocer called in the lead, the suspicious customer was
long gone, melted away into Gert Town, a rough neighborhood dotted with
abandoned houses and populated by residents who had no plans to cooper-
ate with a white occupation force. As the days passed and the trail ran cold,
it was as though a neglected and traumatized city within a city was pro-
tecting a killer whose actions gave voice to its unheeded pain.

* * * *

NEW ORLEANS WAS fertile ground when Black Panthers began
organizing there in the summer of 1970, around the same time the FBI
director named them as "the most dangerous and violence prone of all
extremist groups." Their first headquarters was in the St. Thomas Housing Development, a poverty-stricken project sandwiched between the
Central Business District and the mansions of the Lower Garden District, but when the judge who doubled as a slumlord objected and began
eviction proceedings, they relocated to the Desire Projects in the Ninth
Ward.

Constructed in swampland and bounded by railroad tracks, industrial
plants, and a noxious canal connecting the Mississippi River to Lake Pontchartrain, the one-hundred-acre housing development had been
pitched as groundbreaking when it opened in the mid-1950s. But now
fifteen years later it was widely recognized as a "disaster from its incep-
tion," home to more than ten thousand black residents—three-quarters
under twenty-one years old—living in unsanitary and unsafe conditions:
garbage, cockroaches, rats, and open sewage lines. Joining community

groups and militant organizations already on the ground, the Panthers found a desperate need for basic social services they offered: free breakfasts and clothing for schoolchildren, political education programs, and food banks, including goods obtained by pressuring local businesses deemed predatory. They also promised to provide community-based security in a place where residents feared criminals and police officers in equal measure.[48]

As the Panthers gathered supporters in Desire, NOPD commanders primed by the FBI threat assessments responded with immediate hostility. In memos to the mayor's office, they explained how radicals would use the free breakfast program for "propagandizing children with a hate philosophy that poisons the mind against all established authority, and especially the white race."[49] They green-lit surveillance operations and reported that the Panthers were stockpiling weapons—a few shotguns, pistols, and rifles, portrayed as an arsenal—and fortifying the dilapidated building with sandbags.[50] There was little evidence to back up the alarming warnings. Black officers assigned to the Intelligence Unit found nothing to indicate that violent extremists were plotting attacks on police officers or posed any serious threat to the community. "I thought they were good people," one remembered. "They just didn't like police officers."[51]

Despite the reassuring reports, NOPD commanders raised the stakes by authorizing undercover operations targeting the Panthers, a dangerous choice that backfired spectacularly when two black officers were outed during a political education class at party headquarters. Accounts varied on what followed. At the time, authorities described a revolutionary tribunal during which officers were "tortured beyond your imagination and mine."[52] The actual victims remembered things differently, one explaining that there was "just a little scuffle" inside the headquarters before they were thrown outside, where outraged residents attacked them with two-by-fours, pipes, chains, and bottles, seriously injuring them before the cops managed to escape.[53] Later that evening, two black patrolmen were ambushed and several civilians were injured in overnight violence. The next morning, NOPD officers descended on the volatile neighborhood with overwhelming force, supported by a helicopter and multiple armored cars. They put up barriers and evacuated residents before surrounding the Panthers headquarters, where a dozen or so members confronted an es-timated two hundred men armed with automatic rifles. Both sides blamed the other for opening fire, but the thirty-minute gun battle that ensued was indisputably one-sided and miraculously bloodless—the sandbags were a lifesaving decision. The siege ended when the defenders finally sur-rendered, but tensions remained high and the dangerous situation turned deadly after nightfall, when police officers opened fire on a crowd that was allegedly trying to burn down a black-owned grocery store ac-cused of exploiting the community. Four civilians were struck by gun-fire, including twenty-one-year-old Kenneth Borden, whose body lay in the street for more than two hours. Officers charged that he was attempt-ing to firebomb the building. Witnesses questioned the claim, saying the casualties were unarmed when cops opened fire with no warning. One woman bitterly remembered, "Those kids were shot down in cold blood."[54]

For the next two months, both sides waged dueling propaganda cam-paigns, attacking one another by indirect means. As the Panthers moved into a new headquarters in the Desire Projects, continuing to run community-facing programs and using the heavy-handed police response to recruit new members, officials played to the white-dominated main-stream media. The mayor incongruously claimed that the disturbances were "not a civil rights uprising" and denied any racial overtones, but prom-ised to improve conditions in the projects. Less than plausibly, NOPD commanders blamed outside troublemakers for the violence and contended that social services like the breakfast programs were "subterfuges" for radi-cal indoctrination. Black community leaders challenged these accounts, blaming authorities for cracking down on peaceful organizers, but press coverage heavily favored the official narrative. Meanwhile, three women and twelve men were confined in Orleans Parish Prison, waiting to face trial on attempted murder charges and unable to pay bail set twenty times higher than usual by the same judge who evicted them from his St. Thomas slums. "If they stand for what I saw in the news media," he told reporters, "they are certainly anarchistic and revolutionary."[55]

The stalemate lasted until shortly before Thanksgiving, when authorities decided to evict the Panthers on the grounds that they were trespassing, since they were squatting in a vacant apartment that housing authorities refused to lease to them. As rumors spread of an impending raid, the Panthers rallied supporters and circulated fliers, arguing that authorities wanted to "prove to Niggers everywhere that they will not permit any individual, committee, or group to organize and fight for what they call freedom."[56] When 250 NOPD officers armed with M-16s and backed by an armored vehicle nicknamed the "War Wagon" returned to the Desire Projects, most expected a bloodbath, but they faced something even more dangerous: an unruly crowd with an estimated size ranging from hundreds to thousands, defying orders to stay inside. Some threw bottles and rocks. Others stood between the invading force and the hopelessly outgunned defenders. In unison they shouted, "More power to the people!"[57]

The standoff continued for over six hours, but the Panthers refused to give up and the Desire residents refused to move: they had voted democratically and unanimously decided to support the organizers who were supporting them. Forced to choose between a massacre and withdrawing, commanders stood down, supposedly to give the radicals a chance to obtain an injunction to stop the eviction. But the face-saving fooled nobody. Patrolmen boarded buses and retreated, outraged and humiliated, cursing NOPD leadership for its cowardice. As they did, the Desire residents mobbed the Panthers and paraded them through a cheering crowd, countering the official narrative that dangerous outsiders were terrorizing the community.

The uprising in Desire might have been a moment for reconsideration, for recognizing popular support for community-based solutions and the badly misguided police response to radicalism. But things went differently. A few days after the showdown, an NOPD blockade stopped a Panthers convoy as it departed New Orleans to attend the Black Power Conference in Washington, DC, arresting twenty-five activists on dubious trespassing charges. The final blow came before sunrise on Thanksgiving Day, when a man claiming to be a priest with donations for the breakfast program knocked on the apartment door at the Panthers headquarters. When someone answered, disguised officers barged through the door and gunfire erupted, a fierce, short-lived firefight that wounded a young woman before police overpowered the half-dozen members inside. There were angry protests and tensions remained high, but the Panthers were done in New Orleans.

Reactions to the episode were mixed. Establishment leaders in the black community viewed the Panthers as misguided revolutionaries whose belligerence caused more harm than good, even as the scenes in Desire forced them to acknowledge how popular their programs had been among the city's most underserved residents. There was less ambivalence on the streets, only bitterness and outrage. A few weeks after the police raid, someone burned the Panthers headquarters to the ground—a protest targeting municipal authorities. But as the situation calmed down, city officials congratulated themselves on minimizing the violence necessary to eradicate the extremists who tried to bring a revolution to a city that really needed moderate racial progress and economic revitalization, symbolized by its diversifying administration and the cutting-edge construction projects that would make it an international destination. Truthfully, New Orleans was careening toward a shocking tragedy that would bring back memories of the time a lone black gunman waged a one-man war on the NOPD. But for now, they could be satisfied with how far the city had come.[58]

* * * *

AROUND 10:30 A.M. on Sunday morning, January 7, 1973, Mark Essex burst through the door of Joe's Grocery, wearing military fatigues and clutching his Ruger .44 Magnum rifle. He pointed a bandaged hand at the white man who had tipped off police and shouted, "You come here!"

Essex fired once, striking the man in the shoulder before storming out of the store. A few blocks away, he spotted a car and approached, leveling his weapon at the driver and demanding the keys. "I don't want to kill you," he told the black man, "but I'll kill you, too."

Essex floored the '68 Chevelle through an intersection, pinballing off another vehicle and continuing without stopping. He headed toward the Howard Johnson's Motel, a modern skyscraper in the heart of downtown, in the shadow of the Superdome's colossal, unfinished frame. The seventeen-story building comprised ten residential floors—thirty rooms each, divided by a

long hallway—on top of a lobby and six-story parking garage. Essex aban-
doned the car in the garage and entered a nearby stairwell, where he greeted
two maids as "soul sisters" and unsuccessfully propositioned them to open a
locked door and let him onto the residential floors. He climbed the stairs
and eventually found an unlocked door on the top floor of the building. As he
stepped into the narrow hall that ran the floor's length, he encountered
three more black maids, who recoiled at the man wearing military fatigues
and carrying a long gun, but Essex reassured them. "Don't worry, I'm not
going to hurt black people," he said. "I want the whites."

The killing started shortly before 11 a.m., outside the room where Rob-
ert and Betty Steagall, young newlyweds from Virginia, were staying on a
postponed honeymoon. When the groom heard a disturbance and stepped
into the hallway, he unexpectedly encountered an armed man. They locked
in momentary struggle, before Essex knocked him to the ground and fatally
shot the recent medical school graduate through the arm and torso. Betty
was leaning over her dying husband's body, comforting him, when Essex ex-
ecuted her with a gunshot to the head. Then he stepped into their room and
lit a phonebook on fire, placing it under the curtains. As smoke filtered into
the hallway, alarmed guests and employees spread the word that a gunman
was roaming the hotel and starting fires. When managers Walter Collins
and Frank Schneider went to investigate, Essex killed them both. He had
murdered four unarmed civilians in seven minutes.

Police and emergency personnel responded quickly to the gunfire and
flames at the Howard Johnson's, arriving within minutes, but struggling
to get a handle on the situation. Over the next ten hours, Mark Essex would
play a deadly cat-and-mouse game with a law enforcement army: NOPD
officers, Orleans and Jefferson Parish sheriff's deputies, FBI agents, and un-
known sharpshooters, presumably with badges. Some were ordered to the
scene, but many came voluntarily, hundreds of officers eventually position-
ing themselves in the surrounding buildings and establishing a base of op-
erations in the hotel lobby as the siege escalated. Many were armed with
personal weapons, a deadly array of hunting rifles, M1s, fully automatic AR-
15s, and more. Officers put the firepower to good use, relying less on sniping
than spraying down the general vicinity; they turned downtown New Or-
leans into a warzone, eventually firing more than ten thousand rounds. Few

had radios. As police squads painstakingly cleared the hotel rooms and res-
cued guests, the random gunfire pouring into the building was just as dan-
gerous as the carefully placed rounds fired by the sniper inside. "It's amazing
no one was killed," one victim reflected as he recovered from wounds inflicted
by fellow officers.

Further complicating the situation were the television cameras, which had
begun to broadcast the extraordinary scenes both locally and nationwide.
Responding to televised false reports that black gangs were mobilizing down-
town, crowds of white civilians, armed and unarmed, began to descend on
the scene. Authorities later dismissed them as "a large number of morons,
marginal types," who were drawn for questionable reasons. One asked, "It's
supposed to be a nigger, right?"

As officers surrounded the building and police squads probed the smoky
corridors, Essex remained elusive, changing floors and darting from room
to room so unpredictably that officers were certain there were multiple shoot-
ers. He surveyed the scenes below from behind drapes and patiently waited
for the right moment before firing with fearful accuracy. He wounded emer-
gency responders on the neutral ground outside the hotel and then killed
Patrolman Philip Coleman as he attempted to drag them to safety. Motor-
cycle officer Paul Persigo was angling to get a better position when he was
struck in the head, dying instantly. Inside the hotel, officers struggled to lo-
cate the gunman. Essex seemed to anticipate their movements as police re-
took the building, ambushing a squad on the upper floors and mortally
wounding Deputy Superintendent Louis Sirgo, the second-ranking officer
in the NOPD.

Despite the chaos and casualties, police gradually regained control of the
scene. By the early afternoon, multiple fires were mostly under control and
squads had secured the residential floors. Essex retreated to the rooftop, cor-
nered, but undeterred. He positioned himself in a concrete cubicle near the
building's edge, firing potshots and taunting the police as they returned fire
ineffectively. Between exchanges, officers responded to the shooter with pro-
fanities and racial slurs. They covered the rooftop in CS tear gas, but there
was no response. Frustrations mounted. As the hours passed and the siege
wore on, NOPD commanders began to consider extreme measures: dropping
sandbags on the roof to build an improvised parapet for police sharpshooters;

airlifting the War Wagon up there; bombing the cubicle with heavy weights, or even white phosphorus grenades; arming a helicopter with a .50-caliber machine gun and blasting the cubicle to rubble. They reached out to a nearby U.S. Navy airbase and finally settled on a chopper without the heavy artillery.

Just after 6 p.m., a Marine CH-46 transport helicopter powered through the gloomy skies over downtown New Orleans, swooping through fog and freezing rain to make a low pass over the Howard Johnson's. Three police volunteers joined the four-man crew, each armed with a fully automatic AR-15 and hundreds of rounds. As the chopper raced by the cubicle, they pounded the concrete walls with gunfire, but there was no response from the man inside. They repeated the process, then again, then again, drawing wild cheers from the officers and white civilians witnessing the wild scene. The helicopter made dozens of passes over the next two hours, landing three times to refuel and rearm, before returning to the skies. The onslaught was one-sided, mostly. Every now and then, Essex would crack open the cubicle door and fire well-aimed rounds as the helicopter retreated, as if to prove that he was undaunted.

Around 8.50 p.m., as the CH-46 made yet another pass, something finally happened. The helicopter angled toward the rooftop and the police gunmen opened fire, sending bullets skittering across the roof and finally penetrating the cubicle, which was chewed to pieces by the hours-long barrage. Stung by the ricochets, Essex stepped outside, before retreating momentarily. Suddenly he reemerged, hesitated momentarily, then dashed across the rooftop. He shouted in defiance, clutching his rifle and raising his fist in a revolutionary salute. From nearby buildings, police guns opened up simultaneously, continuing for ten minutes as bullets ripped apart the lifeless body on the rooftop. It was a senseless overkill. Medical examiners eventually counted more than two hundred wounds as they documented the gruesome damage. Officers had done everything they could to destroy the body.

Police cleared the Howard Johnson's room by room, but they waited seventeen hours to search the rooftop, convinced that a second gunman was waiting in ambush there. From a dozen or more positions, they fired sporadic bursts toward a "shadowy figure" that multiple officers reported, shouting insults and racial slurs to goad the phantom sniper into attacking: "Power to the people, nigger!" The ghost had a few tricks to play. As the helicopter buzzed overhead during the early morning hours, the gunmen on board inexplicably exchanged fire with a squad covering the rooftop, wounding four officers. When police finally stormed the sniper's position later that afternoon, there was more self-inflicted damage. Someone fired as they prepared to clear a rooftop boiler room, triggering a barrage. Bullets ricocheted wildly off the metal and concrete. Nine officers were wounded by fragments, three of them seriously. When they finally rushed inside, the room was empty and police confronted the unthinkable: the carnage had been caused by a lone gunman, with postmortem assistance from jumpy cops and an unexplained shadow.

In the short term, investigators refused to acknowledge what the evidence showed. Rumors of a black radical conspiracy swirled in the aftermath. Authorities confidently linked Essex to an as-yet-undiscovered cell determined to wage "war on policemen" and demanded protection for officers: state politicians ultimately reinstated the death penalty for cop killers. Mainstream reporters fanned the flames, running stories on the militant groups supposedly operating in New Orleans, ready to strike if they were given the chance. Black leaders lined up to denounce the cop killer and distance the local community from his actions. They described him as "a boy from Kansas who had come here to vent his frustration in a suicide mission," condemning the "senseless violence" that claimed five NOPD officers and asking white residents not to "condemn blacks wholesale" for an outsider's actions. But the mood on the streets was more supportive. During the shooting, many younger black residents had watched from a distance and cheered on the gunman who defied a law enforcement army; one black civic leader explained that the response owed to "years of abuse by police." Another confessed, anonymously, to sympathizing. "I'm not going to condemn or condone what happened," he told reporters. "There's a little of Mark Essex in all of us."

Before the crisis, there had been glimmers of recognition among police commanders in New Orleans, an understanding that they were fighting a losing battle with all the wrong tactics. Just months before he was mortally wounded during the hotel siege, NOPD deputy superintendent Louis Sirgo had spoken at a national police conference in Washington. He condemned structural racism as "the greatest sin of American society," describing militancy as its natural consequence and concluding, "We can no longer hide our problems in prison cages, or in ghetto housing. We must face up to our responsibility. And if we don't then the problem will destroy us."

But those insights seemed to have been lost after his death. Addressing reports that black residents had cheered on the hotel gunman, the NOPD superintendent ventured "that as a result of years of degradation and deprivation, it might somehow be symbolic to some blacks." Detectives conducted the most exhaustive investigation in the department's history, eventually producing a six-hundred-page report that covered every aspect of the shootings and traced the sniper's radicalization back to its source, describing his military experience and "overwhelming hatred of whites and police officers." But they ultimately came up empty when it came to motive, concluding, "What changed Mark Essex into a cold, cunning killer is not known."[59]

* * * *

IF ROBERT CHARLES was a misconceived warning, Mark Essex was a reckoning, a fierce avenger whose search for "manhood" created trauma and loss without disrupting the conditions and structures that transformed him from a happy-go-lucky kid into the twenty-three-year-old gunman who died alone on a hotel rooftop in downtown New Orleans. Charles witnessed and weathered the rise of Jim Crow, before its order destroyed him. Essex survived its legal end, as heroic nonviolent resistance pushed the nation toward a moral awakening, long-awaited and incomplete. Yet as Essex became the hate-filled extremist that white New Orleans once imagined Charles to be, his violent death in a city where race and exploitation remained so inextricably entangled raised troubling questions about Jim Crow's apparent downfall, as did the eerily familiar response by a police force now notorious for its brutality.

By the time Essex died on a hotel rooftop directly across the street from the Louisiana Division archives, where municipal records told the story of another notorious black gunman, cities across the United States were finally catching up to turn-of-the-century New Orleans. Local police expenditures more than doubled during the 1970s, as urban departments across the nation adopted the violently anti-black enforcement strategies it pioneered.[60] But even so, NOPD officers found ways to lead the nation. As social welfare rollbacks and the disastrous escalation of the War on Drugs during the 1980s and early 1990s made New Orleans perhaps the most desperate and dangerous city in America, NOPD officers consistently produced more brutality complaints than any other force in the country, a pattern that continued in the coming years. When investigators from the U.S. Department of Justice Civil Rights Division scrutinized policing in New Orleans during the Obama administration, they found endemic racist practices and brutality, reporting a "pattern of discriminatory policing" and concluding that "officers in the NOPD routinely use unnecessary and unreasonable force in violation of the Constitution." Of the twenty-seven police shootings reported over an eighteen-month period, police targeted black residents in every single one.[61]

Investigators explained that the problems had "developed over a long period of time," but never bothered to trace them to the origin. With every passing decade, even as the city's leadership and law enforcement better reflected its diversity, politicians and police officers were perpetuating and adapting tactics established by a long-ago generation as it stamped out the revolutionary promise of black freedom and interracial solidarity and gave rise to Jim Crow's deadly and persisting regime. Legitimizing the regime were simple narratives presented as common sense, stories told about predators and innocents, about law-abiding citizens and the brave men who protected them from desperadoes, hoodlums, outlaws, criminals, and thugs. When the abuses were too obvious to ignore, there were other stories, told about reasonable suspicions, furtive gestures, and hands that reached for weapons that never existed, over and over again, down through the generations. The stories focused on individuals, concealing power structures and protecting those who profited from them. They were brutally effective.

But there were always counternarratives, more complicated stories of resistance, retribution, and rage that defied simple distinctions between perpetrators and victims and implicated the structures of exploitation and injustice. Those stories also belong to the tragic record of those destroyed by an American poison, haunting the regime's own archives and passed down, in defiance, by those who endured.

Note on Methodology

This book is about how stories compete to shape community-building projects. It also participates in those same conversations. Reconstructing ambiguous events as they happened in turn-of-the-century New Orleans and transforming them into a historical narrative involved challenges, some common, others more unique to the genre and source base. Attempting to do so responsibly, I have carefully considered my choices relating to the author's voice and the norms of historical writing.

Period newspapers are particularly useful sources, providing detailed, real-time accounts of unfolding events and windows into the concerns shared by the reading publics through which these stories circulated. Yet these and other sources are also riddled with minor factual inaccuracies, grammatical errors, clunky phrasing, and other issues that I have directly addressed. Throughout this narrative, I have edited quoted sources for clarity, grammar, style, and conciseness without using ellipses, brackets, and other punctuation marks that draw attention to the editing process. Examples of these choices include correcting wrong names, restructuring and shortening unclear sentences, and other superficial issues. I have been careful not to make substantive changes to meaning—perspective, tone, and intensity—with these decisions, or to otherwise give a misleading impression of the quoted sources.

Accepting the biases and limitations of historical sources, this narrative is presented as authoritative whenever possible. Doing so, I have primarily relied upon historical source evidence, along with some extrapolation and subjective interpretation. When relevant and substantial, I discuss conflicting sources explicitly, for example, when there are discrepancies between eyewitness accounts. Other choices are noted in the footnotes, along with the rationale behind significant interventions, for example, where I make claims about mind states and thought processes that are unverifiable on the basis of existing sources. Beyond these needed clarifications, I have minimized qualifiers and disclaimers, prioritizing narrative flow and presenting the most plausible sequences while forgoing commentary on comparatively minor controversies, inconsistencies, and uncertainties. Like its source base—and other histories—this book uses verifiable facts and interpretive analysis to make arguments, telling a story about the world as it was. While told responsibly, this story and its underlying assumptions can, and should, be questioned.

Acknowledgments

There is never a moment when you're writing history alone. It draws you, completely, into relationships with other people, dead and living. I've had more help than usual from both.

This project took shape over many days spent in the New Orleans Public Library's Louisiana Division. Without the work its archivists do, against the odds, to preserve a history as rich and vibrant as the city deserves, none of this would have been possible. The credit goes to Christina Bryant, Greg Osborn, Amanda Fallis, Stephen Khuehling, Yvonne Loiselle, Cheryl Picou, and Nancy Aloise. My gratitude also goes to archivists and staff members at Tulane University's Louisiana Research Collection and the Historic New Orleans Collection, and the many libraries from New England to the Deep South where this research developed.

My first class in graduate school was co-taught by Maya Jasanoff and Erez Manela, who became supportive mentors throughout every step of the process. Along the way, Nancy Cott, Laurel Thatcher Ulrich, Lisa McGirr, and Rachel St. John showed me how to study American history and made me feel as though I belonged in academia.

The first iteration of this book was a dissertation, which benefited immensely from the insight of the scholars on my committee. Adam Green read a version of this project on a weekend's notice and provided thoughtful and rigorous commentary. It was one of the most intellectually generous things I've seen in academia. Elizabeth Hinton had so many more important things to do than be on my committee, but never made me feel that way for a second.

Vincent Brown supported me, materially and morally, and always looked out for me. He made me believe that I could get through the program. I don't know if academics are supposed to have role models, but he's definitely one of mine, despite his dubious hip hop rankings.

When I first met my advisor, Walter Johnson, I was disappointed that he was a white guy and not the person I imagined when his first book set my undergraduate brain on fire. That was pretty much the only time he disappointed me. He's uncompromisingly ethical and he helped me to make sense of the world, which is really more than you can ask from anyone—and he's also the best historian in America.

There was no obvious reason for Alison Frank Johnson to care about me and my family as much as she has, aside from the fact that she's such a remarkable person.

My colleagues in History and Africana at Bates College have created a welcoming and vibrant space for a young scholar to do more learning than teaching. I'm especially grateful to share a lunch table with Patrick Otim and Wesley Chaney; the most encouraging and supportive hallway in academia with Karen Melvin, Joseph Hall, and Caroline Shaw; and a sustaining community with Charles Nero, Therí Pickens, Sue Houchins, Marcus Bruce, and Hilmar Jensen, among many others.

Elise Capron was the first person to believe in what my proposal could become. She's a powerful advocate and her vision and dedication made this possible. Marc Favreau took a chance on a first-time author and sharpened this book immeasurably with his guidance and expertise. And at the end of a long road, Emily Albarillo and many others made this look and read so much better than I could have imagined.

Some contributions are harder to adequately explain. Eva Wilson cared for me through everything and I'll never forget what she did.

Nicholas Paskert has been a generous friend in every sense and his presence created new possibilities for my life. Sara Gothard is equally wonderful and frighteningly talented.

Geetha Krishnamurthy was the first person to read this without any professional or personal obligation—I'm fortunate to have, as my mother-in-law, a dedicated scholar with a heart for justice. My in-laws, the Krishnamurthy and

Mandava families, and their friends, have supported me from the beginning and welcomed me into their homes across the diaspora.

Through a dozen moves in two countries, no matter where I've called home, I've had the unconditional love of the Baker and Richard families. Their strength and resilience have always been my greatest advantages.

My parents, Huguette and Anthony, brought me to the library before I knew how to read. Ma never got to see this, but her empathy and integrity are the foundation for everything good in my life. Dad taught me to endure—and endured a ridiculous number of conversations about this book and everything else I find interesting without showing anything other than enthusiasm and pride.

My brother Michael has sharper ethical sensibilities than anyone I know—I've tried not to let him down. Before this project was even an idea, I was inspired by my sister's work in New Orleans. I continue to be energized by everything Jessica Céleste is doing to give children in the city, including her daughter Evangeline, a better world than what came before.

This book started on a spontaneous 1,500-mile road trip with a stranger who became everything to me. Amulya Mandava was my guidelight in a darkness that I couldn't see my way through. I've been following her ever since. Her brilliance and compassion brighten the community she creates, and I'm blessed to be in her family.

Notes

PROLOGUE

1. Robert Charles was not named in news coverage as the second Charles brother who participated in the shootout that followed, but he was working with Henry for the same railroad company. After the New Orleans riots, rumors would circulate that he had killed a brakeman in Rolling Fork, which supports the probability that he had participated in the altercation and told acquaintances about the experience. See William Ivy Hair, *Carnival of Fury: Robert Charles and the New Orleans Race Riot of 1900* (Baton Rouge: Louisiana State University Press, 1973), 53–56.

2. "Rolling Fork," New Orleans *Daily Picayune*, May 20, 1892, 6. On the original coverage of the killing, see "Vicksburg," New Orleans *Daily Picayune*, November 7, 1891, 2.

3. Local reporters described the shootout ambiguously, writing, "The negroes turned upon the flagman and he began emptying his pistol at them." See Hair, *Carnival of Fury*, 53–56.

4. Three of the city's four daily newspapers during the period have survived, each with archives containing extensive yet highly problematic coverage of Robert Charles and the riots. Critical readings of the *Daily Picayune*, *Daily States*, and *Times-Democrat* form the core of the narrative sequences in this book. Supplementing these mainstream dailies, the *Southwestern Christian Advocate* was a staple for middle-class black residents in New Orleans. It was operated by black editors and affiliated with the Methodist Episcopal Church, generally taking a moderate stance in advocating for racial justice. The *Advocate* covered the riots in a relatively understated way and did not challenge mainstream characterizations of Robert Charles.

5. The only contemporary account that challenged white depictions of Robert Charles was authored by Ida B. Wells, who had become a nationally significant anti-lynching activist during the 1890s. Although occasionally problematic, her account offers an extraordinarily valuable counterpoint to one-sided characterizations of Charles, including uniquely sympathetic descriptions from several acquaintances. See Ida B. Wells-Barnett, *Mob Rule in New Orleans: Robert Charles and His Fight to the Death* (Chicago, IL: n.p., 1900). On her life and work, see Patricia A. Schechter, *Ida B. Wells and American Reform, 1880–1930* (Chapel Hill: University of North Carolina Press, 2001); Paula J. Giddings, *A Sword Among Lions: Ida B. Wells and the Campaign Against Lynching* (New York: Amistad, 2008); Mia Bay, *To Tell the Truth Freely: The Life of Ida B. Wells* (New York: Hill and Wang, 2010).

6. Beyond the work of Ida B. Wells, Charles has been the central figure in one scholarly book, William Ivy Hair's *Carnival of Fury*, which was published in the 1970s. While the book represents an extraordinary act of recovery in piecing together Charles's biography, it has some deficiencies regarding both interpreting evidence and providing broader historical context, particularly in relation to New Orleans. Although Charles has appeared as a secondary figure in numerous scholarly books, those authors have relied almost exclusively upon the work of Wells and Hair in presenting him to modern audiences. For example, see Bryan Wagner, *Disturbing the Peace: Black Culture and the Police Power After Slavery* (Cambridge, MA: Harvard University Press, 2009), 25–57.

7. There is conflicting information about the birth date and place of Robert Charles. The U.S. Census of 1870 states that he was born in Marion County, Mississippi, around 1864, while the U.S. Census of 1880 states that he was born in Copiah County, Mississippi, in 1865, where the Charles family was living at that time. See U.S. Census of 1870, Mississippi, Marion County, Roll M593_739, 309B; U.S. Census of 1880, Mississippi, Copiah County, Roll 646, 192C.

8. On Charles's childhood and adolescence, see Hair, *Carnival of Fury*, 1–13. On the history of Copiah County, see LaTricia M. Nelson-Easley, *Images of America: Copiah County* (Charleston, SC: Arcadia Publishing, 2007); Works Progress Administration, *Copiah County* (n.p.: Works Progress Administration of Mississippi, 1938); Economic Research Department, Mississippi Power and Light, *Mississippi Statistical Survey of Population, 1800–1980* (Jackson, MS: Mississippi Power and Light Company, 1983).

9. U.S. Senate, *Report of Committees of the Senate of the United States for the First Session of the Forty-Fourth Congress*, vol. 1 (Washington, DC: Government Printing Office, 1876), 259–71.

10. U.S. Senate, *Report of the Special Committee to Inquire into the Mississippi Election of 1883*, 48th Congress, 1st Session, no. 512 (Washington, DC: Government Printing Office, 1884).

11. U.S. Department of the Treasury, *Report on the Internal Commerce of the United States*, vol. 2 (Washington, DC: Government Printing Office, 1888), 170. On Charles in Copiah County, see Hair, *Carnival of Fury*, 1–40.

12. On the economic development of Vicksburg, see Hair, *Carnival of Fury*, 57–68.

13. Hair, *Carnival of Fury*, 46. On the confrontation, see "News Items," Vicksburg *Daily Commercial Herald*, March 18, 1891, 4.

14. For physical descriptions of Charles, see especially "Robert Charles, Murderer," New Orleans *Times-Democrat*, July 25, 1900, 1. On his adult life before New Orleans, see Hair, *Carnival of Fury*, 33–68.

15. On public life in New Orleans, see Mary Ryan, *Civic Wars: Democracy and Public Life in the American City During the Nineteenth Century* (Berkeley: University of California Press, 1997); Reid Mitchell, *All on a Mardi Gras Day: Episodes in the History of New Orleans Carnival* (Cambridge, MA: Harvard University Press, 1995); James Gill, *Lords of Misrule: Mardi Gras and the Politics of Race in New Orleans* (Jackson, MS: University Press of Mississippi, 1997).

16. On the remarkable historical geography of New Orleans, see especially Ari Kelman, *A River and Its City: The Nature of Landscape in New Orleans* (Berkeley: University of California Press, 2003); Craig E. Colten, *An Unnatural Metropolis: Wresting New Orleans from Nature* (Baton Rouge: Louisiana State University Press, 2005); Richard Campanella, *Bienville's Dilemma: A Historical Geography of New Orleans* (Baton Rouge: Louisiana State University Press, 2008); Richard Campanella, *Geographies of New Orleans: Urban Fabrics Before the*

Storm (Lafayette, LA: Center for Louisiana Studies, 2008); Richard Campanella, *Time and Place in New Orleans: Past Geographies in the Present Day* (Gretna, LA: Pelican Publishing, 2002); Peirce F. Lewis, *New Orleans: The Making of an Urban Landscape* (Cambridge, MA: Blackwell, 1992).

17. On the history of antebellum New Orleans in economic and political context, see especially Walter Johnson, *River of Dark Dreams: Slavery and Empire in the Cotton Kingdom* (Cambridge, MA: Harvard University Press, 2013); Scott P. Marler, *The Merchants' Capital: New Orleans and the Political Economy of the Nineteenth-Century South* (New York: Cambridge University Press, 2013); Adam Rothman, *Slave Country: American Expansion and the Origins of the Deep South* (Cambridge, MA: Harvard University Press, 2005); Robert Gudmestad, *Steamboats and the Rise of the Cotton Kingdom* (Baton Rouge: Louisiana State University Press, 2011). See also Stephen A. Caldwell, *A Banking History of Louisiana* (Baton Rouge: Louisiana State University Press, 1935).

18. On railroad construction in Louisiana, which was delayed by the severe economic depression beginning in the late 1830s, see Merl E. Reed, *New Orleans and the Railroads: The Struggle for Commercial Empire* (Baton Rouge: Louisiana State University Press, 1966). On the city's political history and ambivalent relationship to secession, see Frank Towers, *The Urban South and the Coming of the Civil War* (Charlottesville, VA: University of Virginia Press, 2004); Donald E. Reynolds, *Editors Make War: Southern Newspapers in the Secession Crisis* (Carbondale, IL: Southern Illinois University Press, 2006). On the political outlooks shared by merchants in New York and New Orleans, see Philip S. Foner, *Business and Slavery: New York Merchants and the Irrepressible Conflict* (Chapel Hill: University of North Carolina Press, 1941).

19. On New Orleans during the Civil War, see Chester G. Hearn, *The Capture of New Orleans, 1862* (Baton Rouge: Louisiana State University Press, 1995); Michael D. Pierson, *Mutiny at Fort Jackson: The Untold Story of the Fall of New Orleans* (Chapel Hill: University of North Carolina Press, 2009); Chester G. Hearn, *When the Devil Came Down to Dixie: Ben Butler in New Orleans* (Baton Rouge: Louisiana State University Press, 1997); Gerald M. Capers, *Occupied City: New Orleans Under the Federals, 1862–1865* (Lexington, KY: University of Kentucky Press, 1965); Stephen J. Ochs, *A Black Patriot and a White Priest: André Caillout and Claude Paschal Maistre in Civil War New Orleans* (Baton Rouge: Louisiana State University Press, 2000); Elliott Ashkenazi, ed., *The Civil War Diary of Clara Solomon: Growing Up in New Orleans, 1861–1862* (Baton Rouge: Louisiana State University Press, 1995).

20. On the city's literary traditions of the late nineteenth century, see Rien Fertel, *Imagining the Creole City: The Rise of Literary Culture in Nineteenth-Century New Orleans* (Baton Rouge: Louisiana State University Press, 2014); James Nagen, *Race and Culture in New Orleans Stories: Kate Chopin, Grace King, Alice Dunbar-Nelson, and George Washington Cable* (Tuscaloosa, AL: University of Alabama Press, 2014); Violet Harrington Bryan, *The Myth of New Orleans in Literature: Dialogues of Race and Gender* (Knoxville, TN: University of Tennessee Press, 1993); Barbara Eckstein, *Sustaining New Orleans: Literature, Local Memory, and the Fate of a City* (New York: Routledge, 2006). On Southern Progressivism, see especially George B. Tindall, *The Emergence of the New South, 1913–1945* (Baton Rouge: Louisiana State University Press, 1967); Jack Temple Kirby, *Darkness at the Dawning: Race and Reform in the Progressive South* (Philadelphia, PA: Lippincott, 1972); J. Morgan Kousser, *The Shaping of Southern Politics: Suffrage Restriction and the Establishment of the One-Party South, 1880–1910* (New Haven, CT: Yale University Press, 1974); Dewey W.

Grantham, *Southern Progressivism: The Reconciliation of Progress and Tradition* (Knoxville, TN: University of Tennessee Press, 1983); Edward L. Ayers, *The Promise of the New South: Life After Reconstruction* (New York: Oxford University Press, 1992); William A. Link, *The Paradox of Southern Progressivism, 1880–1930* (Chapel Hill: University of North Carolina Press, 1992). See also Lawrence W. Larsen, *The Rise of the Urban South* (Lexington, KY: University Press of Kentucky, 1985); Don H. Doyle, *New Men, New Cities, New South: Atlanta, Nashville, Charleston, Mobile: 1860–1910* (Chapel Hill: University of North Carolina Press, 1990); David Goldfield, *Region, Race, and Cities: Interpreting the Urban South* (Baton Rouge: Louisiana State University Press, 1997).

21. See especially Henry C. Castellanos, *New Orleans as It Was: Episodes of Louisiana Life* (New York: L. Graham & Son, 1895); Grace King, *New Orleans: The Place and the People* (New York: Macmillan & Co., 1895). For later iterations of this approach, see Lyle Saxon, *Fabulous New Orleans* (New York: D. Appleton-Century Company, 1939) and Robert Tallant, *Voodoo in New Orleans* (New York: The Macmillan Company, 1946), among many others. On the relationship between production of history and tourism in New Orleans, see Kevin Fox Gotham, *Authentic New Orleans: Tourism, Culture, and Race in the Big Easy* (New York: New York University Press, 2007); Anthony J. Stanonis, *Creating the Big Easy: New Orleans and the Emergence of Modern Tourism, 1918–1945* (Athens, GA: University of Georgia Press, 2006).

22. On the formulation of the South's "negro problem," see especially K. Stephen Prince, *Stories of the South: Race and the Reconstruction of Southern Identity, 1865–1915* (Chapel Hill: University of North Carolina Press, 2014), 207–46.

23. On New Orleans and the slave trade, see especially Walter Johnson, *Soul by Soul: Life Inside the Antebellum Slave Market* (Cambridge, MA: Harvard University Press, 1999); Steven Deyle, *Carry Me Back: The Domestic Slave Trade in American Life* (New York: Oxford University Press, 2005); Robert H. Gudmestad, *A Troublesome Commerce: The Transformation of the Interstate Slave Trade* (Baton Rouge: Louisiana State University Press, 2003); Michael Tadman, *Speculators and Slaves: Masters, Traders, and Slaves in the Old South* (Madison, WI: University of Wisconsin Press, 1989).

24. Harry Smith, *Fifty Years of Slavery in the United States of America* (Grand Rapids, MI: West Michigan Printing Co., 1891), 15.

25. On urban slavery in New Orleans, see Richard C. Wade, *Slavery in the Cities: The South, 1820–1860* (New York: Oxford University Press, 1964).

26. See Thomas N. Ingersoll, *Mammon and Manon in Early New Orleans: The First Slave Society in the Deep South, 1718–1819* (Knoxville, TN: University of Tennessee Press, 1999), 207–9, 221–39. See also Kenneth R. Aslakson, *Making Race in the Courtroom: The Legal Construction of Three Races in New Orleans* (New York: New York University Press, 2014); Gwendolyn Midlo Hall, *Africans in Colonial Louisiana: The Development of Afro-Creole Culture in the Eighteenth Century* (Baton Rouge: Louisiana State University Press, 1992); Jay Gitlin, *The Bourgeois Frontier: French Towns, French Traders, and American Expansion* (New Haven, CT: Yale University Press, 2010); Gilbert C. Din, *Spaniards, Planters, and Slaves: The Spanish Regulation of Slavery in Louisiana, 1763–1803* (College Station, TX: Texas A&M University Press, 1999); Caryn Cossé Bell, *Revolution, Romanticism, and the Afro-Creole Protest Tradition in Louisiana, 1718–1868* (Baton Rouge: Louisiana State University Press, 1997).

27. Colonists in Louisiana originally used the term *créole* to distinguish native-born Louisianans, both European and African-origin, from immigrants and transported slaves. By the late 1800s, "Creoles" and "Creoles of color" were increasingly used interchangeably to describe Louisiana's sizable multiracial population. On race during the antebellum period, see especially Nathalie Dessens, *From Saint-Domingue to New Orleans: Migration and Influences* (Gainesville, FL: University of Florida Press, 2007); Judith Kelleher Schafer, *Becoming Free, Remaining Free: Manumission and Enslavement in New Orleans, 1846–1862* (Baton Rouge: Louisiana State University Press, 2003); Judith Kelleher Schafer, *Slavery, the Civil Law, and the Supreme Court of Louisiana* (Baton Rouge: Louisiana State University Press, 1994); Judith Kelleher Schafer, *Brothels, Depravity, and Abandoned Women: Illicit Sex in Antebellum New Orleans* (Baton Rouge: Louisiana State University Press, 2009); Emily Clark, *The Strange History of the American Quadroon: Free Women of Color in the Revolutionary Atlantic World* (Chapel Hill: University of North Carolina Press, 2013).

28. On free blacks in comparative perspective, see Leonard P. Curry, *In the Shadow of the Dream: The Free Black in Urban America, 1800–1850* (Chicago: University of Chicago Press, 1981).

29. On violence in New Orleans during Reconstruction, see James K. Hogue, *Uncivil War: Five New Orleans Street Battles and the Rise and Fall of Radical Reconstruction* (Baton Rouge: Louisiana State University Press, 2011); James G. Hollandsworth Jr., *An Absolute Massacre: The New Orleans Race Riot of July 30, 1866* (Baton Rouge: Louisiana State University Press, 2001).

30. On race and politics in New Orleans during Reconstruction, see Justin A. Nystrom, *New Orleans After the Civil War: Race, Politics, and a New Birth of Freedom* (Baltimore: Johns Hopkins University Press, 2010). On Reconstruction in Louisiana, see Ted Tunnell, *Crucible of Reconstruction: War, Radicalism, and Race in Louisiana, 1862–1877* (Baton Rouge: Louisiana State University Press, 1992).

31. See especially John Blassingame, *Black New Orleans, 1860–1880* (Chicago: University of Chicago Press, 1973).

32. On the integration of public transportation in New Orleans, see Roger A. Fischer, "A Pioneer Protest: The New Orleans Street-Car Controversy of 1867," *Journal of Negro History* 53, no. 3 (July 1968): 219–33. On segregation in public schools, Walter Stern, *Race and Education in New Orleans: Creating the Segregated City, 1764–1960* (Baton Rouge: Louisiana State University Press, 2018). See also Donald E. DeVore and Joseph Logsdon, *Crescent City Schools: Public Education in New Orleans, 1841–1991* (Lafayette, LA: Center for Louisiana Studies, 1991), 40–119; Blassingame, *Black New Orleans*, 107–37.

33. On colored elites in late nineteenth-century New Orleans, see Kim M. Carey, "Straddling the Color Line: Political and Social Power of African American Elites in Charleston, New Orleans and Cleveland, 1880–1920" (PhD diss., Kent State University, 2013). See also Blassingame, *Black New Orleans*, 139–71.

34. Among thirty-two American cities with populations above fifty thousand in 1880, New Orleans ranked seventh in debt per capita ($82.08) and eighth in property tax rates ($2.63 per $100 of assessed property). Excluding the unique financial situation of the nation's capital, New Orleans had the second highest ratio of total municipal debt to annual property tax income of any major American city ($7.35 per $1.00), trailing only Jersey City, NJ ($8.61 per $1.00). Population and debt calculations are based on statistics reported in George E. Waring Jr., comp., *Report on the Social Statistics of Cities*, vols. 1 and 2 (Washington, DC: Government Printing Office, 1887).

35. Michael A. Ross has convincingly argued that New Orleans experienced comparatively slow growth vis-à-vis other Southern cities because of a combination of geographical challenges and ideology-driven resistance to Northern investors. See Michael A. Ross, "Resisting the New South: Commercial Crisis and Decline in New Orleans, 1865–85," *American Nineteenth Century History* 4, no. 1 (Spring 2003): 59–76. See also Marler, *The Merchants' Capital*, 206–30.

36. Illinois Central Railroad Company, *The Commercial, Industrial, and Financial Outlook for New Orleans* (Cedar Rapids, IA: Republican Printing Company, 1894), 8. See also Andrew Morrison, *New Orleans and the New South* (New Orleans: Metropolitan Publishing Company, 1888). On river improvements, see especially Kelman, *A River and Its City*, 119–56. On the Cotton Exposition, see especially Samuel C. Shepherd Jr., "A Glimmer of Hope: The World's Industrial and Cotton Centennial Exposition, New Orleans, 1884–1885," *Louisiana History* 26, no. 3 (Summer 1985): 271–90; Thomas D. Watson, "Staging the 'Crowning Achievement of the Age': Major Edward A. Burke, New Orleans, and the Cotton Centennial Exposition," *Louisiana History* 25, no. 3 (Summer 1984): 229–57; Miki Pfeffer, "'My Chairman and Fellow American Citizens': African American Agency at the World's Industrial and Cotton Centennial Exposition in New Orleans, 1884–1885," *Louisiana History* 51, no. 4 (Fall 2010): 442–62.

37. On the New Orleans Cotton Exchange, see L. Tuffly Ellis, "The New Orleans Cotton Exchange: The Formative Years, 1871–1880," *Southern History* 39, no. 4 (November 1973): 545–64. On the emergence of bourgeois identity in the United States, see especially Karen Halttunen, *Confidence Men and Painted Women: A Study of Middle-Class Culture in America, 1830–1870* (New Haven, CT: Yale University Press, 1982); Stuart M. Blumin, *The Emergence of the Middle Class: Social Experience in the American City, 1760–1900* (New York: Cambridge University Press, 1989); Sven Beckert, *The Monied Metropolis: New York City and the Consolidation of the American Bourgeoisie, 1850–1896* (New York: Cambridge University Press, 2001); Thomas Augst, *The Clerk's Tale: Young Men and Moral Life in Nineteenth-Century America* (Chicago: University of Chicago Press, 2003); Sven Beckert and Julia B. Rosenbaum, eds., *The American Bourgeoisie: Distinction and Identity in the Nineteenth Century* (New York: Palgrave Macmillan, 2010). On the early development of a Southern middle class, see Jonathan Daniel Wells, *The Origins of the Southern Middle Class, 1800–1861* (Chapel Hill: University of North Carolina Press, 2004); Jennifer R. Green, *Military Education and the Emerging Middle Class of the Old South* (New York: Cambridge University Press, 2008); Jonathan Daniel Wells and Jennifer R. Green, eds., *The Southern Middle Class in the Long Nineteenth Century* (Baton Rouge: Louisiana State University Press, 2011).

38. On the founding of the Board of Trade, see H.S. Herring, *A Brief History of a Commercial Exchange: The New Orleans Board of Trade and Some of Its Important Activities* (New Orleans: New Orleans Board of Trade, 1917).

39. Joy J. Jackson, *New Orleans in the Gilded Age: Politics and Urban Progress, 1880–1896*, 2nd ed. (Lafayette, LA: Center for Louisiana Studies, 1997), 123–44. On antebellum politics in New Orleans, see John M. Sacher, *A Perfect War of Politics: Parties, Politicians, and Democracy in Louisiana, 1824–1861* (Baton Rouge: Louisiana State University Press, 2003).

40. On politics in Gilded Age New Orleans, see Jackson, *New Orleans in the Gilded Age*, 1–72. See also Edward F. Haas, *Political Leadership in a Southern City: New Orleans in the Progressive Era, 1896–1902* (Ruston, LA: Louisiana Tech University, 1988), 1–11.

41. Jackson, *New Orleans in the Gilded Age*, 1–72.

42. On municipal politics during the period, see especially Jackson, *New Orleans in the Gilded Age*, 1–94. On Populism in Louisiana, see especially Donna A. Barnes, *The Populist Movement in Louisiana, 1881–1900* (Baton Rouge: Louisiana State University Press, 2011), and

William Ivy Hair, *Bourbonism and Agrarian Protest: Louisiana Politics, 1877–1900* (Baton Rouge: Louisiana State University Press, 1969). See also Roger Shugg, *Origins of Class Struggle in Louisiana: A History of White Farmers and Laborers During Slavery and After, 1840–1875* (Baton Rouge: Louisiana State University Press, 1939); on Southern Populism, see Omar H. Ali, *In the Lion's Mouth: Black Populism in the New South, 1886–1900* (Jackson, MS: University Press of Mississippi, 2010); Joseph Gerteis, *Class and the Color Line: Interracial Class Coalition in the Knights of Labor and the Populist Movement* (Durham, NC: Duke University Press, 2007); Matthew Hild, *Greenbackers, Knights of Labor, and Populists: Farm-Labor Insurgency in the Late-Nineteenth-Century South* (Athens, GA: University of Georgia Press, 2007); James M. Beeby, ed., *Populism in the South Revisited: New Interpretations and New Departures* (Jackson, MS: University Press of Mississippi, 2012). See also Charles Postel, *The Populist Vision* (New York: Oxford University Press, 2009), and Lawrence Goodwyn, *Democratic Promise: The Populist Movement in America* (New York: Oxford University Press, 1976).

43. On the Deep South during the emergence of Jim Crow, see especially Glenn Feldman, *The Disfranchisement Myth: Poor Whites and Suffrage Restriction in Alabama* (Athens, GA: University of Georgia Press, 2004); Stephen Cresswell, *Rednecks, Redeemers, and Race: Mississippi After Reconstruction, 1877–1917* (Jackson, MS: University Press of Mississippi, 2006); William Gillette, *Retreat from Reconstruction* (Baton Rouge: Louisiana State University Press, 1979); Albert D. Kirwin, *Revolt of the Rednecks: Mississippi Politics, 1876–1925* (Lexington, KY: University of Kentucky Press, 1951). See also Stephen Kantrowitz, *Ben Tillman and the Reconstruction of White Supremacy* (Chapel Hill: University of North Carolina Press, 2000).

44. In 1900, the Port of New Orleans ranked second in the nation in export values. Globally, it ranked twenty-seventh in terms of vessel calls in 1890. See "Mapping Global Urban Interactions: Maritime Flows and Port Hierarchies Since the Late Nineteenth Century," http://www.lboro.ac.uk/gawc/rb/rb429.html.

45. In New Orleans, the U.S. Census was conducted during the summer months, when many residents traditionally departed to avoid epidemic diseases, escape sweltering temperatures, and attend to business matters. For example, the U.S. Census of 1840 showed Baltimore with a slightly larger population, but the population of New Orleans increased by tens of thousands during the winter business season, giving it a much higher *de facto* population. According to figures from the U.S. Census of 1900, accounting for winter growth rates of up to 40 percent, New Orleans would have ranked among the top ten cities during its business season.

46. Compared with these manufacturing centers, New Orleans had a smaller population of first-generation immigrants and a larger population of second-generation immigrants, whose parents had arrived during the antebellum period. For demographic and occupational comparisons, see *Report of the Population of the United States at the Eleventh Census: 1890*, vol. 2 (Washington, DC: Government Printing Office, 1897), 631–743. On white racial formation during this period, see especially Nell Irvin Painter, *The History of White People* (New York: Norton, 2010) and Matthew Frye Jacobson, *Whiteness of a Different Color: European Immigrants and the Alchemy of Race* (Cambridge, MA: Harvard University Press, 1999).

47. The only comparable black community in the country in 1900 was in Washington, DC, where federal positions had provided opportunities for roughly eighty thousand black residents. Of the fifteen largest American cities, Washington, DC, had the largest black population by percentage (31.1), followed by New Orleans (27.1), Baltimore (15.6), St. Louis (6.2), Pittsburgh (5.3), and Philadelphia (4.8). In terms of size and demographic composition, the only city approximating New Orleans during this period was Louisville, Kentucky, with just over two hundred thousand residents, of whom roughly 20 percent were classified as "negro." While boasting significant black populations, New South cities such as Atlanta (39.8) and Memphis (48.8) had considerably smaller populations of roughly one hundred thousand residents, creating significant differences of scale in relation to urban law enforcement and municipal services. For demographic statistics, see U.S. Bureau of the Census, *Abstract of the Twelfth Census of the United States* (Washington, DC: Government Printing Office, 1904), 103–5.

48. The black populations in many American cities spiked between 1950 and 1960, finally beginning to resemble the demographic composition of turn-of-the-century New Orleans. For example, Chicago (13.6 to 22.9), Detroit (16.2 to 28.9), Cleveland (16.2 to 28.6), Philadelphia (18.2 to 26.4), and St. Louis (17.9 to 28.6). For comprehensive statistics on population and demographic shifts, see U.S. Bureau of the Census, *U.S. Census of Population: 1960*, vol. 1 (Washington, DC: Government Printing Office, 1964). Historians have recently explored the racialization of urban crime during the late nineteenth and early twentieth centuries, but studies have primarily focused on cities in the North. See especially Khalil Gibran Muhammad, *The Condemnation of Blackness: Race, Crime, and the Making of Modern Urban America* (Cambridge, MA: Harvard University Press, 2010); Kali N. Gross, *Colored Amazons: Crime, Violence, and Black Women in the City of Brotherly Love, 1880–1910* (Durham, NC: Duke University Press, 2006).

1. FORTUNES

1. Porter was not specifically named in press accounts of the Sunday meeting, but his status as a member of the union committee was noted in earlier coverage. See "Still General," New Orleans *Daily Picayune*, November 4, 1892, 6.

2. Although various sources disagree regarding Porter's age, see Orleans Parish Marriage Records, vol. 10, 383. See also U.S. Census of 1910, Louisiana, Orleans Parish, Roll T624_524, 11A. On his background, see Daniel Rosenberg, *New Orleans Dockworkers: Race, Labor and Unionism, 1892–1923* (Albany: State University of New York, 1988), 30. See also Stuart B. Kaufman, Peter J. Albert, and Grace Palladino, eds., *The Samuel Gompers Papers*, vol. 4 (Urbana: University of Illinois Press, 1986), 545.

3. On the Workingman's Amalgamated Council and the New Orleans General Strike of 1892, see Roger Shugg, "The New Orleans General Strike of 1892," *Louisiana Historical Quarterly* 21, no. 2 (April 1938): 547–60.

4. "The Status of the Labor Trouble," New Orleans *Daily Picayune*, November 6, 1892, 4.

5. "Merchants to Resist," New Orleans *Times-Democrat*, October 23, 1892, 6. On the negotiations preceding the strike, see especially David Paul Bennetts, "Black and White Workers: New Orleans, 1880–1900 (PhD diss., University of Illinois at Urbana-Champaign, 1972), 393–414.

6. "Strikers Weakening," New Orleans *Times-Democrat*, October 28, 1892, 3.

7. The committee's reference to Chief Justice Roger B. Taney's infamous assertion in the U.S. Supreme Court decision in *Dred Scott v. Sandford* is notable and likely intentional, as both sides invoked specters of slavery in making their case. On the committee's message, see "A General Strike," New Orleans *Daily Picayune*, November 5, 1892, 1.

8. "The Pressure," New Orleans *Times-Democrat*, November 7, 1892, 3.

9. "The Strike," New Orleans *Daily Picayune*, November 8, 1892, 1.

10. "To the Public," New Orleans *Daily Picayune*, November 8, 1892, 1. On the ambivalence of the New Orleans Typographical Union during the general strike, see Bernard A. Cook, "The Typographical Union and the New Orleans General Strike of 1892," *Louisiana History* 24, no. 4 (Autumn 1983): 377–88.

11. "The Strike," New Orleans *Times-Democrat*, Friday, October 28, 1892, 3.

12. Letter of J. Simon to John Fitzpatrick on November 8, 1892, reprinted in the New Orleans *Times-Democrat*, November 9, 1892, 2.

13. For Page M. Baker's image and obituary, see "The Last Roll," *Confederate Veteran* 18, no. 7 (July 1910): 338. On his service with the Washington Artillery, see William M. Owen, *In Camp and Battle with the Washington Artillery of New Orleans* (Baton Rouge: Louisiana State University Press, 1999).

14. R.H. Henry, *Editors I Have Known Since the Civil War* (Jackson, MS: n.p., 1922), 302. See also Henry Rightor, *Standard History of New Orleans* (Chicago: Lewis Publishing Company, 1900), 282–83.

15. "The Strike," New Orleans *Times-Democrat*, November 4, 1892, 4.

16. "The Strike," New Orleans *Times-Democrat*, November 4, 1892, 4. On the connection between Senegambia and Louisiana, see Hall, *Africans in Colonial Louisiana*.

17. "The Situation," New Orleans *Times-Democrat*, November 9, 1892, 4.

18. "The Strike," New Orleans *Daily Picayune*, November 9, 1982, 1.

19. Statement of Mayor John Fitzpatrick to the New Orleans City Council on November 9, 1892, reprinted as "The City Council," New Orleans *Daily Picayune*, November 9, 1892, 1.

20. John Smith Kendall, *History of New Orleans*, vol. 2 (Chicago: Lewis Publishing Company, 1922), 516. On Fitzpatrick's life, career, and mayoral tenure, see Brian Gary Ettinger, "John Fitzpatrick and the Limits of Working-Class Politics in New Orleans, 1892–1896," *Louisiana History* 26, no. 4 (Autumn 1985): 341–67.

21. On New Orleans politics during the period, see especially Jackson, *New Orleans in the Gilded Age*, 35–72.

22. Jackson, *New Orleans in the Gilded Age*, 23.

23. Ettinger, "John Fitzpatrick," 341–67.

24. "Election of the Regular City Ticket," New Orleans *Times-Democrat*, April 23, 1892, 4.

25. "The Mayor Acts," New Orleans *Daily Picayune*, May 24, 1892, 3.

26. "Arguments Fail," New Orleans *Times-Democrat*, November 8, 1892, 3.

27. Bennetts, "Black and White Workers," 415. See also Shugg, "New Orleans General Strike of 1892," 555.

28. "The Strike," New Orleans *Daily Picayune*, November 10, 1892, 1. See also "Governor to Act," New Orleans *Times-Democrat*, November 10, 1892, 1.

29. Bennetts, "Black and White Workers," 422–23.

30. Shugg, "New Orleans General Strike of 1892," 547.

31. "The Situation," New Orleans *Times-Democrat*, November 10, 1892, 4.

32. "Among the Strikers," New Orleans *Times-Democrat*, November 11, 1892, 3.

33. "Settled," New Orleans *Daily Picayune*, November 11, 1892, 1. See also Shugg, "New Orleans General Strike of 1892," 558.

34. Letter of Samuel Gompers to John M. Callahan on November 21, 1892, quoted in Philip S. Foner, *History of the Labor Movement in the United States*, vol. 2, *From the Founding of the American Federation of Labor to the Emergence of American Imperialism* (New York: International Publishers, 1955), 203.

35. On the Homestead Strike, which served as the backdrop for the New Orleans General Strike of 1892, see Paul Krause, *The Battle for Homestead, 1880–1892: Politics, Culture, and Steel* (Pittsburgh, PA: University of Pittsburgh Press, 1992).

36. "City Council," New Orleans *Daily Picayune*, November 16, 1892, 6.

37. "Concerning Our Recent Editions," New Orleans *Times-Democrat*, November 12, 1892, 4.

38. "Let the Mayor Be Impeached," New Orleans *Times-Democrat*, November 12, 1892, 4.

39. "The Impeachment Proceedings Against the Mayor," New Orleans *Times-Democrat*, September 15, 1894, 4.

40. "The Picayune's Telephone," New Orleans *Daily Picayune*, May 9, 1894, 2. On the garbage controversy, see Jackson, *New Orleans in the Gilded Age*, 91.

41. "Belt Railroad," New Orleans *Times-Democrat*, May 16, 1894, 1. On the history of the Garden District, see especially S. Frederick Starr, *Southern Comfort: The Garden District of New Orleans* (Princeton, NJ: Princeton Architectural Press, 2005).

42. "Municipal Misrule," New Orleans *Times-Democrat*, May 26, 1894, 3.

43. "The Beginning of the End," New Orleans *Times-Democrat*, May 30, 1894, 4; "An Uprising of the People," New Orleans *Daily Picayune*, May 30, 1894, 4.

44. "What Public Opinion Can Do," New Orleans *Times-Democrat*, August 29, 1894, 4.

45. "The Impeachment Proceedings Against the Mayor," New Orleans *Times-Democrat*, September 15, 1894, 4.

46. "The Influx of Newcomers to Cease," New Orleans *Times-Democrat*, November 25, 1893, 4.

47. For the juxtaposition of the injunction and the mayor's trial, see "Federal Power," and "The Mayor," New Orleans *Times-Democrat*, November 9, 1894, 1, 3. For Baker's editorial, see "An Appeal to the Federal Courts," New Orleans *Times-Democrat*, November 9, 1894, 4.

48. "The Situation on the Levee," New Orleans *Times-Democrat*, November 10, 1894, 4.

49. Accepting testimony from a white shopkeeper in July 1900 at face value, historian William Ivy Hair concluded that Charles had adopted the alias "Curtis Robertson" and faced charges of illegal alcohol sales in October 1894, although these claims are highly unlikely. In Copiah County, Curtis Robertson was "a noted negro of the town" who was apparently known for running an illegal saloon. He appeared in court several times between 1894 and 1896, and was sentenced to serve three months in jail in December 1896 in a trial that drew "an immense crowd to the courthouse to witness the proceedings." By that time, Charles had already moved to New Orleans. None of his black acquaintances described any legal troubles or unexplained absences that corresponded with this period, while a recommendation letter from a white supervisor in May 1896 was made out to "R. Charles," suggesting he was known by that name locally. Finally, reports from Copiah County in July 1900 specifically questioned any connection between Charles and Robertson. Under the circumstances, it seems likely that the white man who claimed that Charles was "Curtis Robertson" confused him with another notorious black man from Copiah County who shared a superficially similar name. See Hair, *Carnival of Fury*, 57–68. On the description of Charles as "Curtis Robertson," see "He Knew Charles," New Orleans *Daily States*, July 29, 1900, 8. On Robertson's arrest, see "A Tiger Hunt and Big Game Was Bagged," New Orleans *Daily Picayune*, December 30, 1896, 12. On reports from Copiah County following Charles's death, see "Charles' Mississippi Record," New Orleans *Daily Picayune*, July 30, 1900, 3.

50. On the New Orleans labor movement during the 1880s, see Eric Arnesen, *Waterfront Workers of New Orleans: Race, Class, and Politics, 1863–1923* (Urbana: University of Illinois Press, 1994), 74–118.

51. Rosenberg, *New Orleans Dockworkers*, 52–53. See also Arnesen, *Waterfront Workers of New Orleans*, 121–22.

52. Rosenberg, *New Orleans Dockworkers*, 54–55.

53. "The Delano and the Screwmen," New Orleans *Daily Picayune*, October 10, 1894, 3.

54. "Novel Hold-Up," New Orleans *Times-Democrat*, October 27, 1894, 2. See also "Masked Men Raid Ships," New Orleans *Daily Picayune*, October 27, 1894, 1.

55. Letter of Charles Stoddart to John Fitzpatrick on October 28, 1894, reprinted in "Details of the Riot," New Orleans *Daily Picayune*, October 28, 1894, 10.

56. "An Armed Mob on the Levee," New Orleans *Daily Picayune*, October 28, 1894, 10.

57. On the discovery of Taylor's body, see "The Police Describe Their Part in Yesterday's Events," New Orleans *Daily Picayune*, November 2, 1894, 11. On the foreman's family and property, see Civil District Court, Orleans Parish, Case Nos. 50,989 and 51,250, New Orleans Public Library, Louisiana Division (NOPL).

58. "Labor Lines Still Drawn," New Orleans *Daily Picayune*, November 2, 1894, 11.

59. "Colored Screwmen," New Orleans *Daily Picayune*, November 2, 1894, 11.

60. "Federal Power," New Orleans *Times-Democrat*, November 9, 1894, 1.

61. "The Colored Men Cut the Rates," New Orleans *Daily Picayune*, December 16, 1894, 24. On the continuing tensions during the autumn of 1894, see Arnesen, *Waterfront Workers of New Orleans*, 128–32.

62. British Foreign Office, *Diplomatic and Consular Reports on Trade and Finance, No. 1551, United States, New Orleans* (London: Harrison and Sons, 1895), 17.

63. "Longshoremen Join in Reductions," New Orleans *Daily Picayune*, March 3, 1895, 11. See also Arnesen, *Waterfront Workers of New Orleans*, 135–39.

64. "Laborers Arrive," New Orleans *Times-Democrat*, March 10, 1895, 11.

65. "Another Mob," New Orleans *Times-Democrat*, March 10, 1895, 2.

66. "Lawlessness," New Orleans *Times-Democrat*, March 12, 1895, 1.

67. "Talk with Capt. Journee," New Orleans *Times-Democrat*, March 12, 1895, 3.

68. "Mayor Fitzpatrick Responsible," New Orleans *Times-Democrat*, March 12, 1895, 4.

69. Homicide Report for Morris Mitchell, March 12, 1895, NOPL.

70. Officers reported that they had run toward the sound of the first volley, which had come from St. Ann Street, when they heard a second volley coming from St. Philip Street. Other witnesses reported that the officers had quickly taken shelter in a nearby shed, which is consistent with their apparent inactivity during a massacre that took place over at least ten minutes. For competing versions, see Homicide Report for Morris Mitchell, March 12, 1895, NOPL; "Murder on the Levee," New Orleans *Times-Democrat*, March 13, 1895, 1; "Murder Stains the City Wharves," New Orleans *Daily Picayune*, March 13, 1895, 1.

71. "Murder on the Levee," New Orleans *Times-Democrat*, March 13, 1895, 1. See also "Murder on the Wharves," New Orleans *Daily Picayune*, March 13, 1895, 1.

72. "Disgusted with the Mayor," New Orleans *Times-Democrat*, March 13, 1895, 3.

73. Homicide Report for Henry James, March 12, 1895, NOPL.

74. Homicide Report for Morris Mitchell, March 12, 1895, NOPL.

75. "Policemen Filed on Top of One Another," New Orleans *Times-Democrat*, March 13, 1895, 1.

76. "The Killing of Lopez," New Orleans *Daily Picayune*, March 13, 1895, 2. See also Homicide Report for Fred Lopez, March 12, 1895, NOPL.

77. "A Definite Pursuit," New Orleans *Daily Picayune*, March 13, 1895, 1. On Alfred J. Lopez's full name and profession, see *Soards' New Orleans Directory for 1900* (New Orleans: Soards' Directory Co., n.d.), 579.

78. Homicide Report for Leon Maillard, March 12, 1895, NOPL.

79. "The Mallard Murder," New Orleans *Times-Democrat*, March 13, 1895, 3. See also "Ran Behind the Cars," New Orleans *Daily Picayune*, March 13, 1895, 1.

80. Homicide Report for Henry James, March 12, 1895, NOPL.

81. "The Up Town Mob," New Orleans *Times-Democrat*, March 13, 1895, 3.

82. On these events, see also "Murderers Up Town Too," New Orleans *Daily Picayune*, March 13, 1895, 2.

83. Homicide Report for Jules Payne, March 12, 1895, NOPL.

84. "The Official Responsible for the Rioting and Lawlessness of Yesterday," New Orleans *Times-Democrat*, March 13, 1895, 6.

85. "Governor Foster in Charge," New Orleans *Daily Picayune*, March 13, 1895, 3.

86. "Citizens Meet," New Orleans *Times-Democrat*, March 13, 1895, 7.

87. "Appearance of the Levee," New Orleans *Times-Democrat*, March 14, 1895, 1.

88. "Will Support the Governor," New Orleans *Times-Democrat*, March 14, 1895, 3.

89. "The Law on the Levee," New Orleans *Daily Picayune*, March 15, 1895, 1.

90. "Levee Guarded," New Orleans *Times-Democrat*, March 15, 1895, 1.

91. "Disturbance at Gretna," New Orleans *Daily Picayune*, May 17, 1895, 4. See also Arnesen, *Waterfront Workers of New Orleans*, 142.

92. "Minor Items," *The Cultivator and Country Gentleman*, 60, no. 2203 (April 18, 1895): 315.

93. "Our Recreant Mayor," New Orleans *Times-Democrat*, March 13, 1895, 4.

94. "Judge King's Decision," New Orleans *Times-Democrat*, March 15, 1895, 4; "Mayor Fitzpatrick's Vindication," New Orleans *Daily Picayune*, March 15, 1895, 4.

95. "Mayor Fitzpatrick's Vindication," New Orleans *Daily Picayune*, March 15, 1895, 4.

96. Ettinger, "John Fitzpatrick," 349–50.

97. "The Commerce of a Great City in the Hands of 'Hoodlums,'" *Southwestern Christian Advocate*, March 14, 1895, 1.

98. *The Citizens' League; A History of the Great Reform Movement in New Orleans, April 21, 1896* (New Orleans: S.W. Taylor, n.d.).

99. "For Good City Government," New Orleans *Daily Picayune*, November 9, 1895, 1.

100. "Platform of the Citizens' League," in *The Citizens' League*.

101. "The Citizens' League in the Third Ward," New Orleans *Daily Picayune*, February 1, 1896, 9.

102. See "Mayor Walter C. Flower," in *The Citizens' League*.

103. "Citizens' League Names a Leader," New Orleans *Daily Picayune*, March 22, 1896, 11. See also "Flower Says He Will Run," New Orleans *Daily Picayune*, March 31, 1896, 1.

104. "The Regulars and Their City Ticket," New Orleans *Times-Democrat*, February 14, 1896, 2. On Fitzpatrick's refusal to run, see "City and State Politics," New Orleans *Times-Democrat*, February 18, 1896, 7.

105. In advance of the state and municipal elections in April 1896, colored men were recorded as numbering 14,177 of 60,084 registered voters in Orleans Parish (23.6 percent), roughly approximating their percentage of the total population. See *Report of the Secretary of State to*

His Excellency W.W. Heard, Governor of the State of Louisiana, May 12, 1902 (Baton Rouge, LA: Baton Rouge News Publishing Company, 1902), 554. On Fitzpatrick's address, see "The Louisiana Conference," *Southwestern Christian Advocate*, January 30, 1896, 1.

106. "The League in the Third," New Orleans *Times-Democrat*, March 21, 1896, 7. On Citizens' League organizer Dennis Mahoney's profession, see *Soards' New Orleans City Directory for 1895*, 613.

107. "Mr. Buck Nominated by the Ring," New Orleans *Daily Picayune*, April 8, 1896, 4.

108. "Republicans Who Reason," New Orleans *Daily Picayune*, April 19, 1896, 12.

109. "Colored Labor," New Orleans *Daily Picayune*, April 14, 1896, 7. On the attack, see "Screwmen in Trouble," New Orleans *Times-Democrat*, February 9, 1895, 2.

110. "A Glorious Uprising of the People," New Orleans *Daily Picayune*, April 22, 1896, 4; "Citizens' League Landslide," New Orleans *Times-Democrat*, April 22, 1896, 1.

111. "Governor Foster and New Orleans," New Orleans *Times-Democrat*, April 22, 1896, 4.

112. "The Citizens' League," New Orleans *Times-Democrat*, April 22, 1896, 4.

113. "Analysis of the City Vote," New Orleans *Times-Democrat*, April 26, 1896, 4.

114. "The Negro at His Post—a Glorious Victory," *Southwestern Christian Advocate*, April 30, 1896, 1.

2. Visions

1. On the recommendation, see "Two Policemen Foully Murdered," New Orleans *Daily States*, July 24, 1900, 8.

2. For a fragmentary account of Charles's stay in New Orleans, see Hair, *Carnival of Fury*, 94–113.

3. "Two Policemen Foully Murdered," New Orleans *Daily States*, July 24, 1900, 2.

4. "Laurada Sails," New Orleans *Times-Democrat*, March 2, 1896, 2.

5. "Untitled," New Orleans *Daily Picayune*, April 4, 1896, 4.

6. On emigration during the post-Reconstruction period, see Kenneth C. Barnes, *A Journey of Hope: The Back-to-Africa Movement in Arkansas During the Late 1800s* (Chapel Hill: University of North Carolina Press, 2004), and Edwin S. Redkey, *Black Exodus: Black Nationalist and Back-to-Africa Movements, 1890–1910* (New Haven, CT: Yale University Press, 1969). On the African Colonization Society, see David Brion Davis, *The Problem of Slavery in the Age of Emancipation* (New York: Knopf, 2014); Ousmane K. Power-Greene, *Against Wind and Tide: The African American Struggle Against the Colonization Movement* (New York: New York University Press, 2014); Eric Burin, *Slavery and the Peculiar Solution: A History of the American Colonization Society* (Gainesville: University Press of Florida, 2005).

7. On the failure of the ACS during the 1890s, see Redkey, *Black Exodus*, 73–149.

8. "Emancipation Oration," *Southwestern Christian Advocate*, January 30, 1890, 5.

9. "Should the Afro-American Emigrate? If So, Why?" *Southwestern Christian Advocate*, April 18, 1895, 3.

10. "Liberia," *Voice of Missions* 4, no. 1 (January 1895): 4.

11. "The Local Agents," New Orleans *Times-Democrat*, August 4, 1900, 6.

12. "Immigration of Negroes to Liberia," *Southwestern Christian Advocate*, June 6, 1895, 4.

13. William Royal was listed as a laborer in the city directory from 1895, although in later years he was listed as an agent and an evangelist. See *Soards' New Orleans Directory for 1895*,

800. On Royal's age, see U.S. Census of 1900, Louisiana, Orleans Parish, Roll 574, 11B. See also "The Local Agents," New Orleans *Times-Democrat*, August 4, 1900, 6.

14. "At the Home Office," New Orleans *Times-Democrat*, August 4, 1900, 3, 6.

15. "Experience of a Party of Negroes Shipped to Liberia a Year Ago," *Southwestern Christian Advocate*, October 15, 1896, 5.

16. "At the Home Office," New Orleans *Times-Democrat*, August 4, 1900, 3, 6.

17. Letter from Daniel J. Flummer to Mrs. Ida B. Wells-Barnett on August 21, 1900, reprinted in Wells-Barnett, *Mob Rule in New Orleans*, 46–47.

18. Anonymous letter to Mrs. Ida B. Wells-Barnett on August 23, 1900, reprinted in Wells-Barnett, *Mob Rule in New Orleans*, 47.

19. On Janvier's speech, see National Municipal League, *Proceedings of the Louisville Conference for Good City Government and the Third Annual Meeting of the National Municipal League* (Philadelphia, PA: National Municipal League), 211–17. On the functions of the Board of Civil Service Commissioners, see *Charter of the City of New Orleans of 1896* (New Orleans: L. Graham and Son, 1896), 30–38. See also George M. Reynolds, *Machine Politics in New Orleans, 1897–1926* (New York: Columbia University Press, 1936), 58–61.

20. "The Choctaw Club Wigwam Wide Open," New Orleans *Daily Picayune*, May 2, 1897, 12.

21. "Choctaw Club," New Orleans *Times-Democrat*, May 2, 1897, 7. See also "The Choctaw Club Wigwam Wide Open," New Orleans *Daily Picayune*, May 2, 1897, 12.

22. On both measures, see *Acts Passed by the General Assembly of the State of Louisiana at the Regular Session Begun and Held in the City of Baton Rouge on the Eleventh Day of May, 1896* (Baton Rouge, LA: Advocate, 1896), 46–81, 85–87.

23. "Franchise Limitations," New Orleans *Daily Picayune*, August 29, 1897, 15.

24. "The Constitutional Convention," New Orleans *Daily Picayune*, August 29, 1897, 4.

25. "Register," New Orleans *Times-Democrat*, November 9, 1897, 4.

26. "It Will Be Stamped Out," New Orleans *Daily Picayune*, September 15, 1897, 4.

27. "The Torch Applied," New Orleans *Daily Picayune*, September 24, 1897, 1. See also "Ten Cases, Four Deaths," New Orleans *Daily Picayune*, September 25, 1897, 1.

28. On the opening of the building as the Bercegeay School, see "The Bercegeay Public School," New Orleans *Daily Picayune*, July 7, 1893, 8. On the school's renaming, see "Teachers Assigned to Their Places," New Orleans *Daily Picayune*, September 29, 1893, 8.

29. "A Panic Results," New Orleans *Daily Picayune*, September 24, 1897, 1.

30. "The Torch Applied," New Orleans *Daily Picayune*, September 24, 1897, 1.

31. "The Fire Started," New Orleans *Daily Picayune*, September 24, 1897, 2. See also "Mob Applies the Torch," New Orleans *Times-Democrat*, September 24, 1897, 7.

32. "Mob Applies the Torch," New Orleans *Times-Democrat*, September 24, 1897, 7.

33. "Reforming the Police Force," New Orleans *Daily Picayune*, September 23, 1897, 4.

34. "The Fire Started," New Orleans *Daily Picayune*, September 24, 1897, 2.

35. "Mob Applies the Torch," New Orleans *Times-Democrat*, September 24, 1897, 7.

36. "The Mayor Stands Firm," New Orleans *Daily Picayune*, September 25, 1897, 1.

37. "The Mob of Arsonists," New Orleans *Times-Democrat*, September 25, 1897, 3.

38. On the yellow fever epidemic of 1897, see especially Jo Ann Carrigan, *The Saffron Scourge: A History of Yellow Fever in Louisiana, 1796–1905* (Lafayette, LA: Center for Louisiana Studies, Southwestern Louisiana University, 1994), 141–66.

39. See Campanella, *Time and Place in New Orleans*, 59–60; Ari Kelman, "'The Cat Became the Companion of the Crawfish': Struggling to Drain New Orleans' Wetlands," *Historical Geography* 32 (2004), 157–80.

40. Letter of "K" to the New Orleans *Times-Democrat* on December 17, 1897, reprinted as "Concerning the Sanitary Needs of the City," New Orleans *Times-Democrat*, December 18, 1897, 10.

41. "Superintendent Gaster," New Orleans *Times-Democrat*, October 1, 1897, 3.

42. "Mayor Flower Says Just Why He Voted," New Orleans *Daily Picayune*, October 29, 1897, 6. On Gaster's resignation, see "Supt. Gaster Resigns," New Orleans *Times-Democrat*, October 2, 1897, 3. For a positive spin on his failed resignation, see "He Called 'Checkmate,'" New Orleans *Times-Democrat*, October 14, 1897, 3.

43. The budget of the Reconstruction-era Metropolitan Police had peaked at $840,000, but during the early 1880s, the budget for the renamed Crescent City Police shrunk below $200,000. By comparison, the police appropriation had been above $230,000 as early as the 1850s—without factoring inflation. See Dennis Charles Rousey, *Policing the Southern City: 1805–1889* (Baton Rouge: Louisiana State University Press, 1996), 161–62. See also "Plea for the Finest Sent to the Council," New Orleans *Daily Picayune*, January 4, 1899, 4.

44. *Annual Report of the Board of Police Commissioners and the Superintendent of Police of the City of New Orleans for the Year 1899* (New Orleans: n.p., 1900), 35.

45. By ordinance, overtime pay was reduced from $3.50 to $2.50 per day. See *Annual Report of the Board of Police Commissioners for the Year 1898*, 11. On comparative salaries, see "Plea for the Finest Sent to the Council," New Orleans *Daily Picayune*, January 4, 1899, 4.

46. Waring Jr., comp., *Report on the Social Statistics of Cities*, vol. 2, 292.

47. *Annual Report of the Board of Police Commissioners for 1898*, 6.

48. On Boylan's Detective Agency, see *Biographical and Historical Memoirs of Louisiana*, vol. 1 (Chicago: Goodspeed Publishing Company, 1892), 310–11.

49. "Mr. Howard's Plain Talk," New Orleans *Times-Democrat*, December 12, 1897, 3.

50. "Urged to Register," New Orleans *Times-Democrat*, November 9, 1897, 6.

51. On the outcome, see "Yesterday's Election," New Orleans *Times-Democrat*, January 12, 1898, 4. On advance registration, see "Thirty Thousand Voters Enrolled," New Orleans *Daily Picayune*, December 25, 1897, 12.

52. The clergyman, Benjamin M. Palmer, had declared that "the abolition spirit is undeniably atheistic," exhorting his congregation to defend slavery as a "duty to ourselves, to our slaves, to the world, and to Almighty God . . . to preserve and transmit our existing system of domestic servitude, with the right, unchallenged by man, to go and root itself wherever Providence and nature may carry it." See Thomas Cary Johnson, *The Life and Letters of Benjamin Morgan Palmer* (Richmond, VA: Presbyterian Committee of Publication, 1906), 213.

53. "The Convention and the Suffrage Qualification," New Orleans *Daily Picayune*, February 9, 1898, 4.

54. On the chairman's opening speech, see *The Convention of '98: A Complete Work on the Greatest Political Event in Louisiana's History* (New Orleans: William E. Myers, 1898), 14–16.

55. On the political situation in Louisiana preceding the convention, see Michael Perman, *Struggle for Mastery: Disenfranchisement in the South, 1898–1908* (Chapel Hill: University of North Carolina Press, 2001), 124–47. See also William Ivy Hair, *Bourbonism and Agrarian Protest*, 268–79.

56. John R. Kemp, ed., *Martin Behrman of New Orleans: Memoirs of a City Boss* (Baton Rouge: Louisiana State University Press), 43–44.

57. Rightor, *Standard History of New Orleans*, 281.

58. "Suffrage," New Orleans *Daily States*, February 15, 1898, 4.

59. "Fitness vs. Justice," New Orleans *Daily States*, February 25, 1898, 4. On Hearsey's opposition to the grandfather clause, see "The Suffrage Plan," New Orleans *Daily States*, March 3, 1898, 4.

60. On the lengthy negotiations throughout the convention, see *Official Journal of the Proceedings of the Constitutional Convention of the State of Louisiana* (New Orleans: H.J. Hearsey, 1898).

61. "The Poll Tax Again," New Orleans *Daily States*, March 5, 1898, 4. On the attitudes of rural delegates toward the poll tax, see Perman, *Struggle for Mastery*, 142–44. On the New Orleans business community's support for the poll tax, see "The Poll Tax Plan," New Orleans *Daily States*, March 8, 1898, 4.

62. "The Suffrage Plan," New Orleans *Daily States*, March 3, 1898, 4.

63. On the passage and implementation of the Sunday Law, see Nystrom, *New Orleans After the Civil War*, 211.

64. "Adjournment of the Convention," New Orleans *Daily States*, May 10, 1898, 4.

65. On the chairman's address, see *Official Journal of the Proceedings of the Constitutional Convention of the State of Louisiana*, 379–84.

66. "The Convention and Its Work," New Orleans *Daily Picayune*, May 13, 1898, 4.

67. On the introduction of the measure and the debate surrounding the issue, see *Official Journal of the Proceedings of the Constitutional Convention of the State of Louisiana*, 357–66.

68. "The Convention," New Orleans *Times-Democrat*, May 11, 1898, 4.

69. "The Bond Issue," New Orleans *Daily States*, May 10, 1898, 4.

70. Kemp, *Martin Behrman of New Orleans*, 50.

71. The proposed tax increase was two mills, meaning two dollars for every thousand dollars of assessed property (0.2 percent), levied over a period of forty-three years. The proposal raised the annual property tax rate to 2.2 percent. By comparison, local tax rates reached postwar highs of 3.175 percent in 1882, during the height of the city's debt crisis. On historical property tax rates, see *Comptroller's Report of the City of New Orleans from July 1, 1900 to December 31, 1900* (New Orleans: Boucher & Fuxan, 1901), 200–211.

72. "The Grandest Opportunity New Orleans Ever Had," New Orleans *Daily Picayune*, June 6, 1899, 4.

73. "Hats Off to Our Patriotic Women!" New Orleans *Daily Picayune*, June 7, 1899, 1.

74. The property tax measure passed with a vote of 6,272 to 394, while the issue of mayoral appointments won by a total of 3,850 to 2,695. Voters supporting the appointment of commissioners had a combined assessed value of $27.1 million, averaging $7,034 per voter, whereas those supporting election of commissioners had a combined assessed value of $10.4 million, averaging $3,863 per individual. See "Sewerage and Drainage: Official Figures, Giving the Result of Tuesday's Election," New Orleans *Times-Democrat*, June 8, 1899, 6.

75. "New Orleans Takes a Great Step Forward," New Orleans *Daily Picayune*, June 7, 1899, 4.

76. On the legislation, see *Acts Passed by the General Assembly of the State of Louisiana at the Extra Session Begun and Held in the City of Baton Rouge on the Eighth Day of August, 1899* (Baton Rouge, LA: Printed by the Advocate, 1899).

77. Clinton Rogers Woodruff, "A Year's Municipal Development," *Proceedings of the Milwaukee Conference for Good City Government and Sixth Annual Meeting of the National Municipal League* (Philadelphia, PA: National Municipal League, 1900), 68.

78. Martin Behrman memorably summed up the problems facing reformers, saying, "In those days, the words 'silk stocking' were used to point out a type of citizen who knew about municipal government because he read magazines and books. The high-class silk stocking always

knew what led to the fall of the Roman Empire, but he didn't seem to know that the bulk of voters were more interested in schools, police, firemen, hospitals, parks, and squares, and labor troubles." See Kemp, *Martin Behrman of New Orleans*, 108.

79. In 1896, Orleans Parish counted 45,907 white voters (76.4 percent) and 14,177 colored voters (23.6 percent) in the electorate. By the spring of 1900, it counted 38,407 white voters (96.3 percent) and 1,493 colored voters (3.7 percent). White voters in the parish suffered an overall reduction of 16.3 percent between 1896 and 1900, whereas the statewide reduction rate of white voters was 18.1 percent. By comparison, black voters in Orleans parish suffered an 89.5 percent overall reduction between 1896 and 1900, compared with a statewide reduction rate of black voters of 95.8, showing the limited, though demonstrable, capability of urban black elites in resisting disenfranchisement. For voter registration statistics, see *Report of the Secretary to His Excellency W.W. Heard, Governor of the State of Louisiana* (Baton Rouge, LA: Baton Rouge News Publishing Co., 1902), 554–57.

80. "Fourteenth Ward," New Orleans *Daily Picayune*, August 16, 1899, 12.

81. "Mr. Janvier's Views," New Orleans *Times-Democrat*, August 25, 1899, 9. On Janvier's nomination, see "The Mayor Names Seven Citizens," New Orleans *Daily Picayune*, August 23, 1899, 8.

82. "Mr. Janvier's Views," New Orleans *Times-Democrat*, August 25, 1899, 9.

83. "The Primaries Yesterday," *Daily Picayune*, September 9, 1899, 4. For a strong analysis of the New Orleans municipal elections, see Robert L. Dupont, "Progressive Civic Development and Political Conflict: Regular Democrats and Reformers in New Orleans" (PhD diss., Louisiana State University, 1999), 74–89.

84. "Politicians Confabulating," New Orleans *Daily Picayune*, September 11, 1899, 4.

85. "The Ticket," New Orleans *Times-Democrat*, September 12, 1899, 4.

86. "The City Ticket, So Far," New Orleans *Daily Picayune*, September 12, 1899, 4.

87. *The Picayune's Guide to New Orleans*, 6th ed. (New Orleans: Picayune Job Print, 1904), 58.

88. "Evening Session," New Orleans *Times-Democrat*, September 12, 1899, 2. See also "Night Session," New Orleans *Daily Picayune*, September 12, 1899, 9.

89. "Evening Session," New Orleans *Times-Democrat*, September 12, 1899, 2.

90. "Nominated Paul Capdevielle," New Orleans *Daily Picayune*, September 12, 1899, 9.

91. "Evening Session," New Orleans *Times-Democrat*, September 12, 1899, 2.

92. "Mr. Capdevielle Received Another Ovation," New Orleans *Daily Picayune*, September 12, 1899, 9.

93. "Evening Session," New Orleans *Times-Democrat*, September 12, 1899, 2. On Martin Behrman's recollection of the convention, see Kemp, *Martin Behrman of New Orleans*, 63.

94. *The Picayune's Guide to New Orleans*, 6th ed., 58. On Capdevielle's background, see *Biographical and Historical Memoirs of Louisiana*, vol. 1, 340.

95. On this more skeptical perspective, see "The Ticket," New Orleans *Times-Democrat*, September 12, 1899, 4.

96. "The City Ticket, So Far," New Orleans *Daily Picayune*, September 12, 1899, 4.

97. On Capdevielle's dealings with the New Orleans Street Railway Employees' Union, see "Answer Asked," New Orleans *Times-Democrat*, February 21, 1895, 3. On the park controversy, see "The City Campaign," New Orleans *Daily Picayune*, September 17, 1899, 4.

98. "Regular Caucus," New Orleans *Times-Democrat*, September 16, 1899, 7.

99. "The Tenth Ward Shows Its Hand," New Orleans *Daily Picayune*, September 22, 1899, 9.

100. Dupont, "Progressive Civic Development and Political Conflict," 77.

101. "The Jacksonian Ticket," New Orleans *Daily Picayune*, September 26, 1899, 4.

102. "The Sixth Ward for Capdevielle," New Orleans *Daily Picayune*, October 1, 1899, 10.

103. "Kicking at One of the Finest Names, at That," *Harlequin* 1, no. 13 (September 13, 1899): 4.

104. "Capdevielle Says Where He Stands," New Orleans *Daily Picayune*, October 15, 1899, 10.

105. J. Pemberton Baldwin, "New Orleans Under a Partisan Administration," *Proceedings of the Chicago Conference for Good City Government and the Tenth Annual Meeting of the National Municipal League* (Philadelphia, PA: National Municipal League, 1904), 149.

106. Kemp, *Martin Behrman of New Orleans*, 64.

107. "Count the Vote as Cast," New Orleans *Daily Picayune*, November 7, 1899, 4.

108. On straight-ticket voting, see "Vote the Straight Ticket," New Orleans *Times-Democrat*, November 7, 1899, 4. See also "Stamp the Rooster," New Orleans *Daily Picayune*, November 7, 1899, 4.

109. "A Most Decisive Victory," New Orleans *Daily Picayune*, November 8, 1899, 4. On the complete election results, see "Regulars Carry the Election," New Orleans *Times-Democrat*, November 8, 1899, 4.

110. "The Negro at His Post—A Glorious Victory," *Southwestern Christian Advocate*, April 30, 1896, 1.

111. "A Charge and a Plea," *Southwestern Christian Advocate*, November 30, 1899, 1. On Booker T. Washington's article, see "The Case of the Negro," *Atlantic Monthly* 84, no. 505 (November 1899): 577–87.

112. "The City Election," New Orleans *Times-Democrat*, November 8, 1899, 4.

113. At the beginning of 1900, the New Orleans Police Department employed 193 patrolmen and a few dozen part-time "supernumeraries." National reformers calculated the ratio of population to policemen in New Orleans as 800:1, although limiting the number to beat cops increased the ratio to over 1,500:1, while further reducing it to the number of patrolmen available on any given shift increased the ratio to more than 3,000:1. See "Seattle's Police Force," *City Government* 8, no. 4 (April 1900): 94. See also *Annual Report of the Board of Police Commissioners for the Year 1899*, 35.

114. *Annual Report of the Board of Police Commissioners for 1899*, 35–36.

115. "Old Out, The New In," New Orleans *Daily States*, May 7, 1900, 3.

116. "Capdevielle and Council," New Orleans *Daily Picayune*, May 8, 1900, 1, 9.

117. "New Administration," New Orleans *Times-Democrat*, May 8, 1900, 3.

118. "Mayor Capdevielle's Address," New Orleans *Times-Democrat*, May 8, 1900, 3.

119. "Mr. Capdevielle's Inaugural Address," New Orleans *Times-Democrat*, May 9, 1900, 4.

120. "White Men Barred," New Orleans *Daily States*, May 8, 1900, 1.

121. "An Outrage on White Labor," New Orleans *Daily States*, May 8, 1900, 4.

122. "White Men Barred," New Orleans *Daily States*, May 8, 1900, 1.

3. ECLIPSE

1. "At Break of Day," New Orleans *Times-Democrat*, May 29, 1900, 3. On Professor Brown Ayres, who headed the scientific observations and would later become president of the University of Tennessee, see Tulane University of Louisiana, *Catalogue of Academic Students, 1900–1901* (New Orleans: Published by the University, 1901), 27.

2. "Tulane University Planning for the Eclipse," New Orleans *Daily Picayune*, May 9, 1900, 3; "Sun's Total Eclipse," New Orleans *Daily Picayune*, May 13, 1900, 5; "In Advance of the Eclipse of the Sun," New Orleans *Daily Picayune*, May 23, 1900, 6; "Prof. Ayres on the Coming Eclipse," New Orleans *Daily Picayune*, May 24, 1900, 12; "Eclipse To-Morrow," New Orleans *Times-Democrat*, May 27, 1900, 12; "The Eclipse," New Orleans *Times-Democrat*, May 28, 1900, 3.

3. "New Orleans Saw It All," New Orleans *Daily Picayune*, May 29, 1900, 1.

4. "Sol's Visage Hidden for an Instant," New Orleans *Times-Democrat*, May 29, 1900, 1.

5. "Sol's Visage Hidden for an Instant," New Orleans *Times-Democrat*, May 29, 1900, 1; "New Orleans Saw It All," New Orleans *Daily Picayune*, May 29, 1900, 1.

6. "Creeping Shadow of the Moon," New Orleans *Times-Democrat*, May 29, 1900, 3.

7. "The Tiny Crescent Shadows," New Orleans *Daily Picayune*, May 29, 1900, 3.

8. "Sol's Visage Hidden for an Instant," New Orleans *Times-Democrat*, May 29, 1900, 1.

9. "On the Electric Cars," New Orleans *Daily Picayune*, May 29, 1900, 3.

10. "Among the Negroes," New Orleans *Times-Democrat*, May 29, 1900, 7.

11. "Introduction of Bills," New Orleans *Times-Democrat*, May 29, 1900, 8.

12. On the unfavorable comparison between the capitol building and the asylum, see William Russell Howard, *My Diary, North and South*, vol. 1 (Boston: T.O.H.P. Burnham, 1863), 290. See also Mark Twain, *Life on the Mississippi* (New York: Harper & Brothers, 1901), 290–91.

13. On the state legislature, see *Membership in the Louisiana House of Representatives, 1812–2012*, David R. Poynter Legislative Research Library. Early in the session, state representatives had affirmed the ascendance of white supremacy with symbolic legislation, endorsing the repeal of the Fifteenth Amendment and passing along a petition celebrating Confederate president Jefferson Davis to the Committee on Militia, Pensions, and Artificial Limbs. See *Official Journal of the Proceedings of the House of Representatives of the State of Louisiana at the First Regular Session of the First General Assembly, Under the Adoption of the Constitution of 1898, Begun and Held in the City of Baton Rouge, May 14, 1900* (Baton Rouge, LA: The Advocate, 1900), 39, 53, 64.

14. "Inaugural Address," New Orleans *Daily Picayune*, May 22, 1900, 1. On Governor William W. Heard's inaugural speech, see also Sidney J. Romero, ed., *"My fellow citizens . . .": The Inaugural Addresses of Louisiana's Governors* (Lafayette, LA: Center for Louisiana Studies, University of Southwestern Louisiana, 1980).

15. *Official Journal of the House of Representatives*, 22.

16. On Harry Wilson's age, listed as "Henry D. Wilson," see U.S. Census of 1900, Louisiana, Tangipahoa Parish, Roll 583, Page 16A. On the origins of the nickname "Bloody Tangipahoa," see Michael Pfeifer, *Rough Justice: Lynching and American Society, 1874–1947* (Urbana: University of Illinois Press, 2004), 83.

17. White men in Louisiana's Florida parishes had seen their electoral share increase from 60 percent to over 90 percent between 1896 and 1900. In 1900, when Heard ran as the Democratic gubernatorial candidate, Tangipahoa Parish voters gave him more than 80 percent of their support. See Perry H. Howard, *Political Tendencies in Louisiana* (Baton Rouge: Louisiana State University Press, 1971), 440, 447.

18. *Official Journal of the House of Representatives for 1900*, 60.

19. *Official Journal of the House of Representatives for 1900*, 75.

20. "The Separate Car Law," New Orleans *Times-Democrat*, July 4, 1900, 4.

21. "New and Notables at Local Hotels," New Orleans *Daily Picayune*, October 15, 1900, 6.

22. On the history and significance of the *Southwestern Christian Advocate*, see John M. Giggie, "The African American Press," in Diane Winston, ed., *The Oxford Handbook of Religion and the American News Media* (New York: Oxford University Press, 2012), 579–90. On the location of the newspaper office, see "The Book Concern Building in New Orleans," *The Christian Advocate* 84, no. 40 (October 7, 1909): 1582–83. On the surrounding neighborhood, see Sanborn-Perris Map Co., *Insurance Maps of New Orleans, Louisiana* (1896), vol. 2, 104.

23. I. Garland Penn, *The Afro-American Press and Its Editors* (Springfield, MA: Wiley & Co., 1891), 226.

24. "Why 'Home Missions'?" *The Christian Advocate* 75, no. 46 (November 15, 1900): 1845.

25. Scott won the editorial election by a wide margin, earning 635 of 655 ballots cast. See "Elections by the General Conference at Chicago," *The Christian Advocate* 75, no. 22 (May 31, 1900): 888. See also "The Editor Re-Elected," *Southwestern Christian Advocate*, May 31, 1900, 8. On the timing of the election, see "Proceedings of the General Conference," *The Christian Advocate* 75, no. 23 (June 7, 1900): 923.

26. "Why the Failure to Elect a Bishop?" *Southwestern Christian Advocate*, July 12, 1900, 1. On Scott's spirited campaign for the election of a colored bishop, see "Will the General Conference Elect a Colored Bishop?" *Southwestern Christian Advocate*, April 26, 1900, 2; "We Should Have a Colored Bishop," *Southwestern Christian Advocate*, April 19, 1900, 2; "Give Us a Bishop of African Descent," *Southwestern Christian Advocate*, April 26, 1900, 2; "A Colored Bishop," *Southwestern Christian Advocate*, May 2, 1900, 2; "The Necessity for a Colored Bishop in the M.E. Church," *Southwestern Christian Advocate*, May 2, 1900, 3.

27. "Editorial Comments," *Southwestern Christian Advocate*, June 25, 1896, 1.

28. "Race Identity in New Orleans," *Southwestern Christian Advocate*, July 19, 1900, 8.

29. Letter of J.N. Kinchen to New Orleans *Times-Democrat* on June 23, 1900, printed as "The Separate Car Bill," New Orleans *Times-Democrat*, June 25, 1900, 11. On Kinchen's occupation, see *Soards' New Orleans Directory for 1900*, 492.

30. Letter of Harold Arthur Griffin to New Orleans *Times-Democrat* on June 27, 1900, printed as "Against the Separate Car Law," New Orleans *Times-Democrat*, June 28, 1900, 11.

31. "Editorial Notes," *Southwestern Christian Advocate*, June 28, 1900, 1.

32. "Prisoners Tumble," New Orleans *Daily Picayune*, May 29, 1900, 9.

33. Letter of Frank Bishop to R.M. Walmsley on June 4, 1900, Department of Police and Public Buildings Letterbooks, NOPL.

34. Letter of W.J. Hardee to Paul Capdevielle on May 23, 1900, Records of Mayor Paul Capdevielle, NOPL; Letter of W.J. Hardee to Paul Capdevielle on May 19, 1900, Records of Paul Capdevielle, NOPL; Letter of Jules S. Dreyfous to Paul Capdevielle on May 25, 1900, Records of Paul Capdevielle, NOPL; Letter of Arthur McGuirk to James T. Harris on May 29, 1900, Mayor's Letterbooks, NOPL.

35. Letter from Columbus H. Allen to New Orleans *Times-Democrat* on June 27, 1900, printed as "Favors the Wilson Bill," New Orleans *Times-Democrat*, June 29, 1900, 6. On Allen's profession, see *Soards' New Orleans Directory for 1900*, 71.

36. Letter from R.D. Wilde to New Orleans *Times-Democrat* on June 26, 1900, printed as "The Separate Car Bill," New Orleans *Times-Democrat*, June 27, 1900, 11. On Old Southwest humor, see Hennig Cohen, and William B. Dillingham, eds., *Humor of the Old Southwest*, 3rd ed. (Athens: University of Georgia Press, 1994); M. Thomas Inge and Ed Piacentino, eds., *Southern Frontier Humor: An Anthology* (Columbia: University of Missouri Press, 2010); Ed Piacentino, ed., *Southern Frontier Humor: New Approaches* (Jackson: University Press of Mississippi, 2013).

37. "Startled Railway Officials," New Orleans *Times-Democrat*, June 20, 1900, 3.

38. The street railroad scheme combined business, pleasure, and politics, helping the investors to improve their position vis-à-vis Francophone rivals by boosting the property values of the upriver real estate collectively known as the American Quarter. See Albert E. Fossier, *New Orleans, the Glamour Period, 1800–1840* (New Orleans: Pelican Publishing Co., 1957), 40–44. See also Lake Douglas, *Public Spaces, Private Gardens: A History of Designed Landscapes in New Orleans* (Baton Rouge: Louisiana State University Press, 2011), 82–87.

39. Charter of the New-Orleans and Carrollton Rail Road Company (New Orleans: E. Johns & Co., 1837).

40. On the history of streetcars in nineteenth-century New Orleans, see Louis C. Hennick and E. Harper Charlton, *The Streetcars of New Orleans* (Gretna, LA: Jackson Square Press, 2005), 4–22.

41. Rightor, *Standard History of New Orleans*, 311, 314–15.

42. Rightor, *Standard History of New Orleans*, 312. See also "The System of the New Orleans & Carrollton Railroad Company," *Street Railway Journal* 18, no. 5 (November 1901): 393; "Heavy Track Construction in New Orleans," *Street Railway Journal* 16, no. 21 (June 2, 1900): 532–34.

43. For a late nineteenth-century map showing New Orleans streetcar lines, see "New Orleans," *Rand McNally & Co.'s Indexed Atlas of the World* (Chicago: Rand McNally, 1897), 325. On the conversion to electric vehicles, see New Orleans *Daily Picayune*, February 2, 1893.

44. The Picayune's Guide to New Orleans, 6th ed., 201.

45. Rightor, *Standard History of New Orleans, Louisiana*, 314–15. Streetcars remain a key feature of the modern urban landscape of New Orleans, evoking the sense of Old World luxury that has become central to the city's tourist industry.

46. Fischer, "The New Orleans Street-Car Controversy of 1867," 219–20.

47. "The Colored People and Their Friends," New Orleans *Tribune*, April 21, 1867, 3.

48. "The Street Cars and the Reserved Rights," New Orleans *Times*, May 1, 1867, 10. The former slave who forced his way onto the segregated vehicle was named William Nichols. On his age and origins, see U.S. Census of 1870, Louisiana, Orleans Parish, Roll M593_520, 493B.

49. "Disturbance Down Town," New Orleans *Daily Picayune*, May 5, 1867, 8. See also Fischer, "The New Orleans Street-Car Controversy," 223–24.

50. Letter of D.M. Reid to Edward Heath on May 5, 1867, G.T. Beauregard Papers, Louisiana State University.

51. Letter from Thomas E. Adams to Lieutenant Ramel on May 6, 1867, reprinted in New Orleans *Daily Crescent*, May 7, 1867.

52. "Becoming Serious," New Orleans *Daily Picayune*, May 7, 1867, 8.

53. "The Public Schools," New Orleans *Tribune*, May 9, 1867, 4.

54. Railways Oppose Separate Car Laws," New Orleans *Times-Democrat*, October 20, 1900, 3.

55. "Consolidation of New Orleans Companies," *Street Railway Journal* 16, no. 3 (January 20, 1900): 80. See also "New Orleans Deal Declared Off," *Street Railway Journal* 17, no. 2 (January 12, 1901): 89–90.

56. In fact, the New Orleans Street Railway Union would be organized in 1902 and would stage a series of work stoppages in the ensuing years. For the union's comprehensive records, see New Orleans Street Railway Union, 1902–1948, Louisiana Research Collection, Tulane University.

57. Samuel Gompers, *Seventy Years of Life and Labor*, vol. 1 (New York: E.P. Dutton & Co., 1925), 350.

58. Report of the Industrial Commission on the Relations and Conditions of Capital and Labor, vol. 7 (Washington, DC: Government Printing Office, 1901), 200–208.

59. Motorman and Conductor 1, no. 3 (May 1895): 3.

60. Motorman and Conductor 1, no. 3 (May 1895): 8.

61. "The Arbitrators Give a Verdict," New Orleans *Daily Picayune,* August 11, 1895; "Louisiana Ten-Hour Law," *Motorman and Conductor* 2, no. 4 (July 1896): 9. On the reported betrayal, see *Motorman and Conductor* 2, no. 6 (September 1896): 6. On the progress of the bill through the house, see House Bill No. 272, *Official Journal of the House of Representatives of the State of Louisiana* (Baton Rouge, LA: Printed by the Advocate, 1896).

62. Division No. 2 apparently dissolved sometime after the spring of 1897, evidenced by the reemergence of a reorganized union, Division No. 194, in the fall of 1901. For the last appearance of Division No. 2 in *Motorman and Conductor,* see "Secretaries of Local Divisions," *Motorman and Conductor* 3, no. 3 (March 1897): 2. For the first appearance of Division No. 194, see "President's Report," *Motorman and Conductor* 8, no. 7 (September 1901): 2–3.

63. "A Unique Strike and Boycott, with Its Results and Lessons," *Street Railway Journal* 12, no. 7 (July 1896): 442–43.

64. Emerson P. Schmidt, *Industrial Relations in Urban Transportation* (Minneapolis: University of Minnesota Press, 1937), 128–52.

65. George H. Morgan, *Annual Statement of the Trade and Commerce of St. Louis, Reported to the Merchants' Exchange of St. Louis* (St. Louis, MO: R.P. Studley & Co., 1900), 34, 51.

66. The St. Louis and Suburban Railway Company survived the 1898 merger and operated forty miles of track, but the United Railways Company of St. Louis, which operated under the name St. Louis Transit Company, dominated the industry, with almost three hundred miles of track and $25 million capitalization. See John Moody, ed., *Moody's Manual of Corporation Securities,* 2nd ed. (New York: John Moody & Co., 1901), 455–58, and *The Mayor's Message to the Municipal Assembly of the City of St. Louis* (St. Louis, MO: Nixon-Jones Printing Co., 1901), 598.

67. "St. Louis Swings into Line," *Motorman and Conductor* 6, no. 3 (April 1900): 1–3, 6.

68. Motorman and Conductor 6, no. 4 (May 1900): 6.

69. Letter of W.J. Stone to Thomas P. Rixey on May 29, 1900, reprinted in Thomas P. Rixey, ed., *Twenty-Second Annual Report of the Missouri Bureau of Labor Statistics* (Jefferson City, MO: Tribune Printing Company, 1900), 429–31.

70. "Step Toward an Adjustment," St. Louis *Republic,* May 31, 1900, 3.

71. "Three Strikers Killed and One Wounded by the Possemen," St. Louis *Republic,* June 11, 1900, 1.

72. "Song of the St. Louis Posse Comitatus," *Motorman and Conductor* 6, no. 7 (August 1900): 1.

73. On the strike, see Walter Johnson, *The Broken Heart of America: St. Louis and the Violent History of the United States* (New York: Basic Books, 2020), 177–79. See also James Neal Primm, *Lion of the Valley: St. Louis, Missouri, 1764–1980,* 3rd ed. (St. Louis, MO: Missouri Historical Society Press, 1998), 358–62.

74. Rev. Frank Foster, "The Street-Car Strike at St. Louis," *The Independent* 52, no. 2695 (July 26, 1900): 1782–84.

75. In fact, the estimated cost of the strike to the St. Louis Transit Company was higher than the stock capital of the New Orleans & Carrollton Railroad Company and two of the city's three remaining streetcar companies. See *Moody's Manual of Railroads and Corporation Securities,* vol. 2 (New York: J. Moody & Co., 1901), 396.

76. "New Orleans and the Gas Belt Swing in Line," *Motorman and Conductor* 8, no. 5 (July 1901): 2.

77. "The System of the New Orleans & Carrollton Railroad Company," *Street Railway Journal* 18, no. 5 (November 1901): 395.

78. "New Orleans and the Gas Belt Swing in Line," *Motorman and Conductor* 8, no. 5 (July 1901): 2.

79. Journal of the Proceedings of the House of Representatives for 1900, 249–50.

80. "Railways Oppose Separate Car Laws," New Orleans *Times-Democrat*, October 20, 1900, 3.

81. "The Separate Car Bill," New Orleans *Daily Picayune*, July 3, 1900, 4.

82. Letter from Observer to New Orleans *Times-Democrat* on June 28, 1900, printed as "Separate Cars," New Orleans *Times-Democrat*, June 29, 1900, 6.

83. "Railways Oppose Separate Car Laws," New Orleans *Times-Democrat*, October 20, 1900, 3.

84. "No Change in the St. Louis Strike," New Orleans *Daily Picayune*, May 11, 1900, 2.

85. "The Separate Car Bill," New Orleans *Daily Picayune*, July 3, 1900, 4. See also "Separate Street Cars," New Orleans *Times-Democrat*, July 9, 1900, 4.

86. "Separate Car Question," New Orleans *Times-Democrat*, July 4, 1900, 4.

87. "Defeat the Street Car Bill," New Orleans *Daily Picayune*, July 9, 1900, 4.

88. "Allowed to Die," New Orleans *Daily Picayune*, July 11, 1900, 4.

89. "Race Identity in New Orleans," *Southwestern Christian Advocate*, July 19, 1900, 1.

90. DeVore and Logsdon, *Crescent City Schools*, 118.

91. "The School Board's Annual Farce," *Southwestern Christian Advocate*, July 26, 1900, 1.

92. On the composition of the New Orleans School Board, see "School Board," New Orleans *Daily Picayune*, September 15, 1900, 3.

93. DeVore and Logsdon, *Crescent City Schools*, 118–19.

94. "Some Lessons from the Outbreak Last Week," *Southwestern Christian Advocate*, August 2, 1900, 1.

95. On the structures comprising the neighborhood, see Sanborn-Perris Map Co., *Insurance Maps of New Orleans, Louisiana* (1896), vol. 3.

96. On Charles's employment history, see Hair, *Carnival of Fury*, 94–95.

97. In the aftermath of violence, press observers would document the items found in Charles's room in detail. See "The Murderer, Charles," New Orleans *Times-Democrat*, July 25, 1900, 7, 9.

98. "Making of a Monster," New Orleans *Times-Democrat*, July 29, 1900, 5. See also "Two Policemen Foully Murdered," New Orleans *Daily States*, July 24, 1900, 5.

99. William J. Simmons, *Men of Mark: Eminent, Progressive, and Rising* (Cleveland, OH: Geo. M. Rewell & Co., 1887), 805–10.

100. "Wayward Dots and Jots," *Christian Recorder* 16, no. 76 (September 19, 1878): 2.

101. On Turner's life and evolving ideology, see Stephen Ward Angell, *Bishop Henry McNeal Turner and African-American Religion in the South* (Knoxville: University of Tennessee Press, 1992), 123–56.

102. Address of Bishop Henry McNeal Turner on November 28, 1874, reprinted in *African Repository* 51, no. 2 (April 1875): 39.

103. "Africa," *Voice of Missions* 2, no. 1 (January 1894): 1. On Bishop Turner's interest in African emigration during the 1890s, see Angell, *Bishop Henry McNeal Turner and African-American Religion in the South*, 215–37.

104. "American Negro," *Voice of Missions* 7, no. 1 (January 1899): 1.

105. "Home of the Blacks," *Washington Post*, February 2, 1895, 9.

106. "Official Circular No. 3," *Voice of Missions* 4, no. 2 (February 1896): 1; "Ho! For Africa," *Voice of Missions* 3, no. 3 (March 1895): 1; "Homesick and Destitute," *Voice of Missions* 3, no. 9 (September 1895): 2; "A White Man on Liberia," *Voice of Missions* 4, no. 10 (October 1895): 1.

107. "Untitled," *Voice of Missions* 1, no. 8 (August 1893): 2.

108. On the structure and activities of the International Migration Society in New Orleans, see "At the Home Office," New Orleans *Times-Democrat*, August 4, 1900, 3, 6.

109. Wells-Barnett, *Mob Rule in New Orleans*, 48.

110. "Bishop Turner's African Scheme," *Southwestern Christian Advocate*, September 14, 1899, 1.

111. "Two Policemen Foully Murdered," New Orleans *Daily States*, July 25, 1900, 8.

112. Anonymous letter to Ida B. Wells-Barnett on August 23, 1900, reprinted in Wells-Barnett, *Mob Rule in New Orleans*, 47.

113. "The Murderer, Charles," New Orleans *Times-Democrat*, July 25, 1900, 8.

114. Sanborn-Perris Map Co., *Insurance Maps of New Orleans, Louisiana* (1909), vol. 4, 393.

115. See NOPD Arrest Records, Sixth Precinct, July 4–5, 1900, NOPL. This characterization of the neighborhood comes from a review of NOPD arrest records for the Sixth Precinct between May and September of 1900, along with relevant press coverage.

116. "Our Picayunes," New Orleans *Daily Picayune*, February 16, 1900, 4.

117. Cocaine had multiple uses as a stimulant, appetite suppressant, painkiller, and anti-inflammatory. For example, one railroad official estimated that three-fourths of engineers used cocaine "to facilitate the removal of cinders from their eyes." See "By and By!" New Orleans *Times-Democrat*, May 3, 1900, 4.

118. "Cocaine," New Orleans *Times-Democrat*, April 26, 1900, 3, 7.

119. "To Carry Blacks to Africa," Atlanta *Constitution*, July 27, 1900, 6.

120. D.J. Flummer, *The Negro in Liberia* (Birmingham, AL: International Migration Society, 1897), 7.

121. Letter of Daniel J. Flummer to Ida B. Wells-Barnett, reprinted in Wells-Barnett, *Mob Rule in New Orleans*, 46–47.

4. SPECTERS

1. "Pierce Tells Little," New Orleans *Daily Picayune*, July 25, 1900, 9.

2. "'Sweating' the Accomplice," New Orleans *Times-Democrat*, July 25, 1900, 3.

3. "Pierce Still Firm," New Orleans *Daily Picayune*, July 26, 1900, 7.

4. "'Sweating' the Accomplice," New Orleans *Times-Democrat*, July 25, 1900, 3.

5. "Pierce Tells Little," New Orleans *Daily Picayune*, July 25, 1900, 9. On the weather, see "The Picayune's Weather Prophet," New Orleans *Daily Picayune*, July 24, 1900, 2; "Temperature du Juillet 23," New Orleans *L'Abeille*, July 24, 1900, 2.

6. "'Sweating' the Accomplice," New Orleans *Times-Democrat*, July 25, 1900, 3.

7. "'Sweating' the Accomplice," New Orleans *Times-Democrat*, July 25, 1900, 3.

8. "Bent on Murder," New Orleans *Times-Democrat*, July 24, 1900, 3.

9. "Negro Kills Bluecoats and Escapes," New Orleans *Times-Democrat*, July 25, 1900, 1.

10. See New Orleans *Daily Picayune*, "Investigating Police Sergeants," March 14, 1893, 4; "Aucoin's Cases Did Not Come Up," September 10, 1896, 3; "One Man Holds Out for an Acquittal," March 2, 1898, 13; "Sergeant Aucoin Fined 10 Days' Pay," November 6, 1896, 9; "Sergeant Aucoin's Case Continued," July 12, 1894, 7; "Teaching Police How to Behave," May 13, 1897, 10.

11. Letter of J.H.M. to the New Orleans *Times-Democrat* on July 2, 1900, reprinted in "Get Rid of This Taint," New Orleans *Times-Democrat*, July 3, 1900, 6.

12. "The Menace of the Negro," New Orleans *Times-Democrat*, July 5, 1900, 4.

13. For example, of 17,609 arrests made in 1899, 7,359 (41.7 percent) were related to nonviolent drinking and disturbing the peace charges, while 4,792 (27.2 percent) were for violations of city ordinances. Offenses comprising threats to public safety, ranging from threats to reckless driving to murders, represented less than 20 percent of total arrests. While the "colored" population of New Orleans comprised 27 percent of the city's total population according to the Twelfth U.S. Census, black men and women represented 38.8 percent of arrests in 1899, proportions that were approximated throughout the 1890s. Based on these numbers, black residents were arrested at rates roughly 1.45 times their population proportion, whereas whites were arrested at roughly 0.85 times. For arrest statistics in 1899, see *Annual Report of the Board of Police Commissioners for the Year 1900*, 38–48. See also Rousey, *Policing the Southern City*, 159–99.

14. "Morris Park Toughs," New Orleans *Daily Picayune*, July 5, 1900, 11.

15. NOPD Arrest Records, Sixth Precinct, July 23, 1900, NOPL.

16. "Thieves Busy," New Orleans *Times-Democrat*, May 26, 1900, 7.

17. Clark did not admit to reporters that she had reported the men to police, but Patrolman Mora and Supernumerary Cantrelle claimed that the three women had spoken with Sergeant Aucoin. See "Duel in the Street," New Orleans *Times-Democrat*, July 25, 1900, 7; "Police Pistols," New Orleans *Daily Picayune*, July 24, 1900, 8.

18. Along with five other officers, Supernumerary Joseph D. Cantrelle had been appointed to the New Orleans Police Department on April 11, 1900. See *Annual Report of the Board of Police Commissioners for 1900*, 22.

19. "Two Police Victims of an Assassin's Weapon," New Orleans *Daily Picayune*, July 25, 1900, 1.

20. "Bent on Murder," New Orleans *Times-Democrat*, July 25, 1900, 3.

21. "Duel in the Street," New Orleans *Times-Democrat*, July 25, 1900, 7. See also "Officer Mora's Story," New Orleans *Daily Picayune*, July 24, 1900, 8.

22. "Sergeant Aucoin's Statement," New Orleans *Times-Democrat*, July 25, 1900, 7.

23. "Duel in the Street," New Orleans *Times-Democrat*, July 25, 1900, 7.

24. Conflicting versions of the sequence of events would emerge, but the most consistent and comprehensive version was recorded during Sergeant Aucoin's subsequent trial. See "Police Board Tries Sergeant Aucoin," New Orleans *Daily Picayune*, September 27, 1900, 7.

25. "'Sweating' the Accomplice," New Orleans *Times-Democrat*, July 25, 1900, 3.

26. This vague sequence represents the only version of the story matching the multiple accounts told by each participant in the confrontation.

27. "Duel in the Street," New Orleans *Times-Democrat*, July 25, 1900, 7.

28. "Aucoin Said Not To," New Orleans *Times-Democrat*, July 27, 1900, 7.

29. "Sergeant Aucoin's Statement," New Orleans *Times-Democrat*, July 26, 1900, 7.

30. "Neader's Statement," New Orleans *Times-Democrat*, July 26, 1900, 3. On Neader's age and occupation, see U.S. Census of 1900, Louisiana, Orleans Parish, Roll 574, 25A.

31. "Aucoin and Trenchard," New Orleans *Times-Democrat*, July 26, 1900, 3.

32. "'Sweating' the Accomplice," New Orleans *Times-Democrat*, July 25, 1900, 3.

33. "Police Pistols," New Orleans *Daily Picayune*, July 24, 1900, 8. See also "Aucoin Said Not To," New Orleans *Times-Democrat*, July 27, 1900, 7; "At the Charity Hospital," New Orleans *Daily Picayune*, July 27, 1900, 7.

34. "Duel in the Street," New Orleans *Times-Democrat*, July 25, 1900, 7; Sanborn-Perris Map Co., *Insurance Maps of New Orleans, Louisiana* (1896), vol. 3, 234; *The Era Druggists' Directory*, 11th ed. (New York: D.O. Haynes & Co., 1905), 88.

35. See *Annual Report of Board of Police Commissioners for the Year 1898*, 58–60. On the frequency and variety of problems with the police call boxes, see Fire Alarm and Police Telegraph Complaint Books, NOPL. For complaints from police administrators, see *Annual Report of the Board of Police Commissioners for 1900*, 78–79. See also Hair, *Carnival of Fury*, 129.

36. "Duel in the Street," New Orleans *Times-Democrat*, July 25, 1900, 7.

37. "Duel in the Street," New Orleans *Times-Democrat*, July 25, 1900, 7.

38. Day had recently moved to be closer to the Sixth Precinct Station, as city directories for 1900 listed his address as Tchoupitoulas Street, whereas newspapers cited his address as Jackson Avenue. See *Soards' New Orleans Directory for 1900*, 251.

39. "Captain John T. Day," New Orleans *Daily States*, July 24, 1900, 8. "Day, Boyle, and Walsh," New Orleans *Daily Picayune*, October 12, 1895, 1.

40. See New Orleans *Daily Picayune*, "Dennis Corcoran Shoots at a Sergeant," July 6, 1895, 12; "A Trip to Chinatown," February 6, 1898, 8; "Sergeant Day Captures Catoire's Would-Be Assassin," December 29, 1894, 8; "Bullets More Potent Than Ballots," September 22, 1893, 2; "The Tree Cutters Arrested," January 17, 1891, 3.

41. New Orleans *Daily Picayune*, "Four Lives Lost in the Great Fire," April 30, 1894, 1; "The Mayor Teaches the Commissioners," October 10, 1895, 7.

42. "Day, Boyle, and Walsh," New Orleans *Daily Picayune*, October 12, 1895, 1.

43. U.S. Census of 1900, Louisiana, Orleans Parish, Roll 574, 9A; Orleans Parish Marriage Records, vol. 12, 948; "Sketches of the Martyrs," New Orleans *Daily Picayune*, July 25, 1900, 8.

44. On the description of the New Orleans Police Department's "don't care" approach, see "Investigated Police Departments," *City Government* 1, no. 4 (November 1896): 117.

45. "Tracking Mora's Assailant," New Orleans *Times-Democrat*, July 25, 1900, 3.

46. "Two Police Victims of an Assassin's Weapon," New Orleans *Daily Picayune*, July 25, 1900, 1, 8.

47. *Annual Report of Board of Police Commissioners for the Year 1896*, 54. On the station, see *History of the New Orleans Police Department* (New Orleans: L. Graham & Son, 1900), 123. See also Richard G. Carrott, *The Egyptian Revival: Its Sources, Monuments, and Meanings, 1808–1858* (Berkeley: University of California Press, 1978), 119.

48. "The Grand Jury Completes Its Work," New Orleans *Daily Picayune*, March 3, 1900, 11.

49. Letter of J.M. Ferguson to D.S. Gaster, November 21, 1900, Department of Police and Public Records Letterbooks, NOPL.

50. *Annual Report of the Board of Police Commissioners for 1898*, 13.

51. On the history of "sweating," also known as the "third degree," see George C. Thomas and Richard A. Leo, *Confessions of Guilt: From Torture to Miranda and Beyond* (New York: Oxford University Press, 2012), 112–42.

52. "The Detectives' 'Third Degree,'" *The Public* 9, no. 3 (September 29, 1906): 604–5.

53. "The Third Degree," *Everybody's Magazine* 3, no. 15 (November 1900): 406.

54. "Sergeant Day's Muscle Gives Him a Grip on Suspicious Characters," New Orleans *Daily Picayune*, July 30, 1895, 6.

55. "'Sweating' the Accomplice," New Orleans *Times-Democrat*, July 25, 1900, 3.

56. "Pierce Still Firm," New Orleans *Daily Picayune*, July 26, 1900, 7.

57. "'Sweating' the Accomplice," New Orleans *Times-Democrat*, July 25, 1900, 3.

58. "The Police Witnesses," New Orleans *Daily Picayune*, July 25, 1900, 8.

59. On the officers involved, including their length of service, see *History of the New Orleans Police Department*, 43, 85, 87, 107, 111.

60. "Two Police Victims of an Assassin's Weapon," New Orleans *Daily Picayune*, July 25, 1900, 8.

61. "Two Police Victims of an Assassin's Weapon," New Orleans *Daily Picayune*, July 25, 1900, 8; "'Sweating' the Accomplice," New Orleans *Times-Democrat*, July 25, 1900, 3; "The Police Witnesses," New Orleans *Daily Picayune*, July 25, 1900, 8.

62. "Two Police Victims of an Assassin's Weapon," New Orleans *Daily Picayune*, July 25, 1900, 8.

63. "The Police Witnesses," New Orleans *Daily Picayune*, July 25, 1900, 8.

64. "Police Board Tries Sergeant Aucoin," New Orleans *Daily Picayune*, September 27, 1900, 7. On Merritt's residence, see *Soards' New Orleans Directory for 1900*, 608. On his approximate age, see Orleans Parish Death Records, vol. 181, 503. Charles Merritt did eventually join the New Orleans Police Department, where he was involved in his own confrontation with black suspects five years after the crisis, firing and missing a fleeing man who "made a motion as if to draw a pistol out of his pocket." No firearm was recovered at the scene. See "Negroes Acted Suspiciously," New Orleans *Times-Democrat*, July 3, 1905, 4.

65. "There's the Place," New Orleans *Daily Picayune*, July 25, 1900, 8. The detailed Sanborn Fire Insurance Maps suggest that the building had been recently constructed. Published in 1896, an earlier map shows a building at the site that does not match the description given by local newspapers, while the 1909 version of the map shows a narrow building marked "Negro Tenements" that matches contemporary descriptions of the house where Charles lived. Given the frequency of fires, the strong possibility exists that the earlier building had been destroyed between 1896 and 1900. For example, fires destroyed homes on the 1900 and 2100 blocks of Fourth Street in the years before Charles lived in the 2000 block. See "A Fourth Street Fire Starts While the Occupants of a Cottage Were at Church," New Orleans *Daily Picayune*, February 10, 1896, 6; "A Morning Fire Destroys a Number of Cottages on Fourth Street," New Orleans *Daily Picayune*, February 14, 1899, 10. For comparison, see Sanborn-Perris Map Co., *Insurance Maps of New Orleans, Louisiana* (1896), vol. 3, 234, and Sanborn Map Company, *Insurance Maps of New Orleans, Louisiana* (1909), vol. 4, 392.

66. "The Fatal Alley," New Orleans *Times-Democrat*, July 25, 1900, 7.

67. "Negro Kills Bluecoats and Escapes," New Orleans *Times-Democrat*, July 25, 1900, 1.

68. "Sergeant Aucoin's Statement," New Orleans *Times-Democrat*, July 25, 1900, 7.

69. "Two Policemen Foully Murdered," New Orleans *Daily States*, July 24, 1900, 8. On Cryder's age, see U.S. Census of 1900, Louisiana, Orleans Parish, Roll 574, 8B.

70. "Had a Poor Weapon," New Orleans *Times-Democrat*, July 25, 1900, 7.

71. "Two Police Victims of an Assassin's Weapon," New Orleans *Daily Picayune*, July 25, 1900, 8.

72. After Charles's death, the Orleans Parish Coroner's Office examined his body and noted the presence of "one flesh wound upper 3rd of right thigh bandage green gauze." Charles would not have had time to dress this wound during the shootout that claimed his life, corroborating the eyewitness reports and blood evidence suggesting that he had been shot during the Dryades Street shootout. See Coroner's Inquest for Robert Charles, July 27, 1900, NOPL. On Charles's movements after the shooting, see "Two Policemen Foully Murdered," New Orleans *Daily States*, July 24, 1900, 1.

73. Given the lack of reliable witness accounts, this version of these events relies on subjective interpretation of available evidence. William Ivy Hair offers a somewhat different version of events, suggesting that Robert Charles had been preparing to leave the room when police arrived. This seems highly unlikely, however, since Charles would have most likely been at the apartment for a considerable amount of time despite the obvious risk of being discovered, even accounting for slow movement caused by his injuries. No reliable witnesses placed him elsewhere during the four-hour interval between the first and second shootouts, and as subsequent events demonstrated, he was mobile and had close friends in New Orleans. Therefore, the most likely version of events is that Charles waited at the apartment in anticipation of the officers arriving. For Hair's alternative narrative, see *Carnival of Fury*, 123–24.

74. "The Dual Murder," New Orleans *Times-Democrat*, July 25, 1900, 3; "The Police Witnesses," New Orleans *Daily Picayune*, July 25, 1900, 8. Hair claimed that Day was killed instantly, which is contradicted by the testimony of the surviving police witnesses.

75. "Two Police Victims of an Assassin's Weapon," New Orleans *Daily Picayune*, July 25, 1900, 8.

76. Coroner's Inquest for Peter J. Lamb, July 24, 1900, NOPL; "At the Morgue," New Orleans *Daily States*, July 24, 1900, 8; "With the Dead," New Orleans *Daily Picayune*, July 25, 1900, 8; "Removing the Dead," New Orleans *Times-Democrat*, July 25, 1900, 7.

77. "Defective Police Pistols," New Orleans *Times-Democrat*, July 25, 1900, 9; "Aucoin and Trenchard," New Orleans *Times-Democrat*, July 26, 1900, 3.

78. "Aucoin and Trenchard," New Orleans *Times-Democrat*, July 26, 1900, 3.

79. "The Police Witnesses," New Orleans *Daily Picayune*, July 25, 1900, 8.

80. For the officers' varying accounts in the immediate aftermath of the shooting, see "The Police Witnesses," New Orleans *Daily Picayune*, July 25, 1900, 8; "Sergeant Aucoin's Statement," New Orleans *Times-Democrat*, July 25, 1900, 7; "Had a Poor Weapon," New Orleans *Times-Democrat*, July 25, 1900, 7; "Aucoin and Trenchard," New Orleans *Times-Democrat*, July 26, 1900, 3.

81. "The Women's Story," New Orleans *Times-Democrat*, July 26, 1900, 3.

82. "Two Police Victims of an Assassin's Weapon," New Orleans *Daily Picayune*, July 25, 1900, 8.

83. "Two Policemen Foully Murdered," New Orleans *Daily States*, July 24, 1900, 8.

84. Coroner's Inquest for John T. Day, July 24, 1900, NOPL; "At the Morgue," New Orleans *Daily States*, July 24, 1900, 8; "With the Dead," New Orleans *Daily Picayune*, July 25, 1900, 8; "Removing the Dead," New Orleans *Times-Democrat*, July 25, 1900, 7; "The Women's Story," New Orleans *Times-Democrat*, July 26, 1900, 3.

85. "Aucoin and Trenchard," New Orleans *Times-Democrat*, July 26, 1900, 3.

86. "The Women's Story," New Orleans *Times-Democrat*, July 26, 1900, 3.

87. "The Police Witnesses," New Orleans *Daily Picayune*, July 25, 1900, 8.

88. "Sergeant Aucoin's Statement," New Orleans *Times-Democrat*, July 25, 1900, 7.

89. "Aucoin and Trenchard," New Orleans *Times-Democrat*, July 26, 1900, 3.

90. Investigators would find clothes in an abandoned house behind Charles's apartment, leading them to conclude that he had changed in an attempt to disguise himself. See "Hounds on the Scent," New Orleans *Daily States*, July 24, 1900, 8.

91. "Assassin's Flight," New Orleans *Times-Democrat*, July 25, 1900, 3, 7.

92. "Hounds on the Scent," New Orleans *Daily States*, July 24, 1900, 8.

93. "Had a Poor Weapon," New Orleans *Times-Democrat*, July 25, 1900, 7.

94. Contemporary newspapers recorded that the shot was taken from seventy-five yards, but measuring from where the building stood to the corner of Fourth and Rampart suggests a slightly shorter distance. See "His Deadly Aim," New Orleans *Times-Democrat*, July 25, 1900, 7.

95. "Cowardice Charged," New Orleans *Times-Democrat*, July 26, 1900, 3.

96. "Two Police Victims of an Assassin's Weapon," New Orleans *Daily Picayune*, July 25, 1900, 8.

97. "Giving the Alarm," New Orleans *Times-Democrat*, July 25, 1900, 7.

98. "Two Policemen Foully Murdered," *Daily States*, July 24, 1900, 1.

99. Hair, *Carnival of Fury*, 130.

100. "'There's the Place,'" New Orleans *Daily Picayune*, July 25, 1900, 8.

101. "The Murderer, Charles," New Orleans *Times-Democrat*, July 25, 1900, 8.

102. "The Murderer, Charles," New Orleans *Times-Democrat*, July 25, 1900, 7, 9.

103. Wells-Barnett, *Mob Rule in New Orleans*, 44.

104. Wells-Barnett, *Mob Rule in New Orleans*, 44–45.

105. Wells-Barnett, *Mob Rule in New Orleans*, 48.

106. "He Knew Charles," New Orleans *Sunday States*, July 29, 1900, 8. On Levy's age, see U.S. Census of 1900, Louisiana, Orleans Parish, Roll 571, 5B.

107. "Making of a Monster," New Orleans *Times-Democrat*, July 29, 1900, 3.

108. "Making of a Monster," New Orleans *Times-Democrat*, July 29, 1900, 3.

109. "Other Police Murders," New Orleans *Daily Picayune*, July 25, 1900, 9.

110. "Woman in the Case," New Orleans *Times-Democrat*, July 25, 1900, 7. On Banks's approximate age, see U.S. Census of 1880, Louisiana, Orleans Parish, Roll 463, 442A. See also Orleans Parish Marriage Records, vol. 43, 67. For her image, see "Virginia Banks," New Orleans *Times-Democrat*, July 25, 1900, 3.

111. "Charles' Old Mistress," New Orleans *Daily Picayune*, July 25, 1900, 9.

112. Banks spoke to several newspapers in the wake of the killings, offering various stories of her relationship with Charles. See "Woman in the Case," New Orleans *Times-Democrat*, July 25, 1900, 7; "Charles' Old Mistress," New Orleans *Daily Picayune*, July 25, 1900, 9; "Two Police Foully Murdered," New Orleans *Daily States*, July 24, 1900, 8.

113. "Police Pistols," New Orleans *Daily Picayune*, July 24, 1900, 8.

114. "Two Police Victims of an Assassin's Weapon," New Orleans *Daily Picayune*, July 25, 1900, 8. See also "Two Policemen Foully Murdered," New Orleans *Daily States*, July 24, 1900, 8, and "Bent on Murder," New Orleans *Times-Democrat*, July 25, 1900, 3.

115. "At the Hospital," New Orleans *Daily Picayune*, July 30, 1900, 3.

116. "Captain John T. Day," New Orleans *Daily States*, July 24, 1900, 8; "The Dual Murder," New Orleans *Times-Democrat*, July 25, 1900, 3.

117. "With the Dead," New Orleans *Daily Picayune*, July 25, 1900, 8. On the scene outside the morgue, see also "Removing the Dead," New Orleans *Times-Democrat*, July 25, 1900, 7, and "At the Morgue," New Orleans *Daily States*, July 24, 1900, 8.

118. "Negro Murderers," New Orleans *Daily States*, July 25, 1900, 4.

119. "Defective Police Pistols," New Orleans *Times-Democrat*, July 25, 1900, 9.

120. "Aucoin Said Not To," New Orleans *Times-Democrat*, July 27, 1900, 7.

121. "Negro Murderers," New Orleans *Daily States*, July 25, 1900, 4.

5. FLAMBEAUX

1. "Two Police Victims of an Assassin's Weapon," New Orleans *Daily Picayune*, July 25, 1900, 8.
2. "Citizens Inflamed," New Orleans *Times-Democrat*, July 25, 1900, 7.
3. "Two Police Victims of an Assassin's Weapon," New Orleans *Daily Picayune*, July 25, 1900, 8.
4. "During the Day," New Orleans *Daily Picayune*, July 25, 1900, 9. See also NOPD Arrest Records, Sixth Precinct, July 24, 1900, NOPL.
5. "Citizens Inflamed," New Orleans *Times-Democrat*, July 25, 1900, 7.
6. "Arrests Made," New Orleans *Times-Democrat*, July 25, 1900, 7.
7. "Negroes in Trouble," New Orleans *Daily States*, July 25, 1900, 8. See also NOPD Arrest Records, Sixth Precinct, July 24, 1900, NOPL.
8. "Arrests Made," New Orleans *Times-Democrat*, July 25, 1900, 7. See also NOPD Arrest Records, Sixth Precinct, July 24, 1900, NOPL.
9. Letter of Edwin L. Reynolds to Paul Capdevielle on August 20, 1900, Council Records, NOPL. On McCarthy's age, see NOPD Arrest Records, Sixth Precinct, July 24, 1900, NOPL.
10. "Negroes in Trouble," New Orleans *Daily States*, July 25, 1900, 8.
11. "White Man's Escape," New Orleans *Daily States*, July 24, 1900, 8. See also NOPD Arrest Records, Sixth Precinct, July 24, 1900, NOPL.
12. "Negroes in Trouble," New Orleans *Daily States*, July 25, 1900, 8.
13. "White Man's Escape," New Orleans *Daily States*, July 24, 1900, 8. The following month, the New Orleans mayor's office received a handwritten letter from a partner in a New York–based insurance firm, which explained that he had been solicited by McCarthy's parents. The letter emphasized McCarthy's military service during the Spanish-American War and attempted a possible explanation for his behavior at the scene, saying that McCarthy had suffered a serious head injury while in the military. "Within a short time of his arrival home, his actions became so eccentric, his manner towards his family so strange, and his thinking so uncertain that his parents became alarmed," the author described, "and he was confined as apparently insane." Letter of Edwin L. Reynolds to Paul Capdevielle on August 20, 1900, Council Records, NOPL.
14. "Arrests Made," New Orleans *Times-Democrat*, July 25, 1900, 7. On Meyers's age and residence, see NOPD Arrest Records, Sixth Precinct, July 24, 1900, NOPL.
15. On Supernumerary Sam Exnicios's appointment, see *History of the New Orleans Police Department*, 127.
16. "Arrests Made," New Orleans *Times-Democrat*, July 25, 1900, 7.
17. "Shielded the Blacks," New Orleans *Daily Picayune*, July 25, 1900, 8.
18. "Many Scents," New Orleans *Times-Democrat*, July 25, 1900, 9.
19. "Still at Large," New Orleans *Daily States*, July 25, 1900, 1.
20. On antebellum crime in New Orleans, see Dennis Rousey, "Cops and Guns: Police Use of Deadly Force in Nineteenth-Century New Orleans," *American Journal of Legal History* 28, no. 1 (January 1984), 41–66; Fossier, *New Orleans*, 161–74; Robert C. Reinders, *End of an Era: 1850–1860* (Gretna, LA: Pelican Publishing, 1964), 63–71, Schafer, *Brothels, Depravity, and Abandoned Women*, 5–7; Thomas C. Buchanan, *Black Life on the Mississippi: Slaves, Free Blacks, and the Western Steamboat World* (Chapel Hill: University of North Carolina Press, 2004), 122–47. For nineteenth-century depictions of crime, see, among many examples, James Silk Buckingham, *The Slave States of America*, vol. 1 (London: Fisher, Son &

Co., 1842), 351–52; Amos Andrew Parker, *Trip to the West and Texas* (Concord, NH: White & Fisher, 1835), 191–92; Henry A. Ashworth, *Tour of the United States, Cuba and Canada* (London: A.W. Bennett, 1861), 79–80; Robert Everest, *A Journey Through the United States and Part of Canada* (London: John Chapman, 1855), 108–10; J. Benwell, *An Englishman's Travels in America* (London: Binns and Goodwin, 1853), 115–16.

21. "Police Pursuit," New Orleans *Daily Picayune*, July 25, 1900, 8; "Still at Large," New Orleans *Daily States*, July 25, 1900, 1.

22. On the swamps surrounding the city, see especially Colten, *An Unnatural Metropolis*; Kelman, *A River and Its City*; Campanella, *Time and Place in New Orleans*.

23. Castellanos, *New Orleans as It Was*, 209–10.

24. Castellanos, *New Orleans as It Was*, 218, 258.

25. On Bras-Coupé, see Castellanos, *New Orleans as It Was*, 209–16. See also Bryan Wagner, "Disarmed and Dangerous," *Representations* 92, no. 1 (Fall 2005): 117–51.

26. Castellanos, *New Orleans as It Was*, 164, 211.

27. On the link between Reconstruction and post-Reconstruction violence, see especially Michael J. Pfeifer, "The Origins of Postbellum Lynching: Collective Violence in Reconstruction Louisiana," *Louisiana History* 50, no. 2 (Spring 2009): 189–201.

28. Leading databases show at least 105 executions of black men in Louisiana between 1877 and 1900, compared to 278 lynchings, although historical records are incomplete and both figures are certainly underestimated. On capital punishment in Louisiana, see "Executions in the United States, 1608–2002: The ESPY File," accessible online at https://www.icpsr.umich.edu/icpsrweb/NACJD/studies/8451. On lynching, see "Monroe Work Today Data Set," accessible online at http://archive.tuskegee.edu/archive/handle/12345 6789/984.

29. During the 1890s, fourteen black persons (all men) were lynched in Bossier Parish, Louisiana, while twelve were killed in both Jefferson Parish, Louisiana (eleven men and one woman), and Monroe County, Alabama (nine men and three women). Eleven black men were killed in Shelby County, Tennessee; ten black persons (seven men and three women) were killed in Butler County, Alabama; ten black men were killed in Chilton County, Alabama, Marion County, Florida, and Columbia County, Florida, respectively. Reflecting the ubiquity of racial violence in the area, Jefferson Parish suffered eight deadly lynching incidents during the period (some including multiple victims), which also ranked second in the nation compared with the eleven deadly incidents in Bossier Parish.

30. Mary Elizabeth Hines, "Death at the Hands of Persons Unknown: The Geography of Lynching in the Deep South, 1882–1910" (PhD diss., Louisiana State University, 1992), 20.

31. On the lynching of James Hawkins, see "A Lynching Near Gretna," New Orleans *Daily Picayune*, September 24, 1896, 1; "The Gretna Lynching," New Orleans *Times-Democrat*, September 25, 1896, 9; "Gagged and Tied," New Orleans *Times-Democrat*, September 28, 1900, 3.

32. "Negroes Frightened," New Orleans *Times-Democrat*, September 27, 1896, 8.

33. "Still at Large," New Orleans *Daily States*, July 25, 1900, 1; "Suspects at Kenner," New Orleans *Daily Picayune*, July 25, 1900, 9.

34. For comparison, see "Robert Charles," New Orleans *Daily States*, July 24, 1900, 1. "Robert Charles, Murderer," New Orleans *Times-Democrat*, July 25, 1900, 1. "Description of Charles," New Orleans *Times-Picayune*, July 25, 1900, 8; "L'assassin Robert Charles," *L'Abeille de la Nouvelle Orléans*, July 25, 1900, 1.

35. "Many Scents," New Orleans *Times-Democrat*, July 25, 1900, 9. For a slightly different version of events, see "Suspects at Kenner," New Orleans *Daily Picayune*, July 25, 1900, 9, and "Ricks Released," New Orleans *Times-Democrat*, July 26, 1900, 3; "Still at Large," New Orleans *Daily States*, July 25, 1900, 1.

36. "Many Scents," New Orleans *Times-Democrat*, July 25, 1900, 9.

37. "Gretna Excited," New Orleans *Daily Picayune*, July 25, 1900, 9.

38. "Still at Large," New Orleans *Daily States*, July 25, 1900, 1, 8. See also "An Innocent Negro," New Orleans *Times-Democrat*, July 26, 1900, 3.

39. "A Mob's Fearful Work," New Orleans *Times-Democrat*, January 13, 1896, 1. See also "Two Lives Taken in Defiance of the Law," New Orleans *Daily Picayune*, January 13, 1896, 1.

40. "Still at Large," New Orleans *Daily States*, July 25, 1900, 1.

41. "Citizens Inflamed," New Orleans *Times-Democrat*, July 25, 1900, 7.

42. "The Mob at Night," New Orleans *Daily Picayune*, July 25, 1900, 9.

43. "The Mob at Night," New Orleans *Daily Picayune*, July 25, 1900, 9.

44. "The Mob at Night," New Orleans *Daily Picayune*, July 25, 1900, 9.

45. "The Mob at Night," New Orleans *Daily Picayune*, July 25, 1900, 9.

46. "Citizens Inflamed," New Orleans *Times-Democrat*, July 25, 1900, 7.

47. "Police Pursuit," New Orleans *Daily Picayune*, July 25, 1900, 8, 9.

48. "The Mob at Night," New Orleans *Daily Picayune*, July 25, 1900, 9.

49. "Mob Anger Is Vented at Random," New Orleans *Times-Democrat*, July 26, 1900, 1.

50. "Pierce Remanded," New Orleans *Times-Democrat*, July 26, 1900, 3.

51. "Pierson Arraigned," New Orleans *Daily States*, July 25, 1900, 8.

52. "Pierce Still Firm," New Orleans *Daily Picayune*, July 26, 1900, 7.

53. "The Burial of the Victims," New Orleans *Daily Picayune*, July 26, 1900, 7.

54. "The Funerals," New Orleans *Daily States*, July 25, 1900, 8.

55. "The Burial of the Victims," New Orleans *Daily Picayune*, July 26, 1900, 7.

56. See Tom Smith, *Crescent City Lynchings: The Murder of Chief Hennessy, the New Orleans "Mafia" Trials, and the Parish Prison Mob* (New York: Lyons Press, 2007); Richard Gambino, *Vendetta: A True Story of the Worst Lynching in America* (Garden City, NY: Doubleday, 1977); Marco Rimanelli and Sheryl L. Postman, eds., *The 1891 New Orleans Lynchings and U.S.-Italian Relations: A Look Back* (New York: P. Lang, 1992); Joseph Masselli, *Italians in New Orleans* (Charleston, SC: Arcadia Publishing, 2004).

57. Biographical and Historical Memoirs of Louisiana, vol. 1, 439.

58. Gambino, *Vendetta*, 80.

59. Edwin L. Jewell, comp., *Jewell's Digest of the City Ordinances, Together with the Constitutional Provisions, Acts of the General Assembly and Decisions of the Courts Relative to the Government of the City of New Orleans* (New Orleans: Edwin L. Jewell, 1882), 291.

60. B.A.C. Emerson, comp., *Historic Southern Monuments* (New York: Neale Publishing Company, 1911), 153–56. On the dedication, see also "Ceremonies Connected with the Unveiling of the Statue of General Robert E. Lee," *Southern Historical Society Papers*, vol. 14 (Richmond, VA: William Ellis Jones, 1886), 62–102. On the purpose of Lee's positioning, see *Fodor's New Orleans 2013* (New York: Random House, 2013), 93.

61. "The Mob Forms," New Orleans *Times-Democrat*, July 26, 1900, 9.

62. "Mob Anger Is Vented at Random," New Orleans *Times-Democrat*, July 26, 1900, 1.

63. "The March of the Mob," New Orleans *Daily Picayune*, July 26, 1900, 1.

64. "With the Dead," New Orleans *Daily Picayune*, July 28, 1900, 3.

65. "Murdered Sergeant Porteous," New Orleans *Times-Democrat*, July 28, 1900, 7.

66. "The Burial of the Victims," New Orleans *Daily Picayune*, July 26, 1900, 7.

67. On the connection between Porteous and Trenchard, see U.S. Census of 1870, Louisiana, Orleans Parish, Roll M593_534, 366A, and Orleans Parish Marriage Records, vol. 11, 818.

68. "Murdered Sergeant Porteous," New Orleans *Times-Democrat*, July 28, 1900, 7.

69. "The March of the Mob," New Orleans *Daily Picayune*, July 26, 1900, 1.

70. "The Mob Forms," New Orleans *Times-Democrat*, July 26, 1900, 9.

71. "Youthful Jurists," New Orleans *Times-Democrat*, May 22, 1900, 13; "Tulane's Law Class," New Orleans *Daily Picayune*, November 25, 1899, 5.

72. "The March of the Mob," New Orleans *Daily Picayune*, July 26, 1900, 1.

73. "The March of the Mob," New Orleans *Daily Picayune*, July 26, 1900, 1. For a somewhat different sequence of events, see "'To the Parish Prison,'" New Orleans *Times-Democrat*, July 26, 1900, 9.

74. "In Douglas Square," New Orleans *Times-Democrat*, July 26, 1900, 9. For Samuel M. Cowen's age, full name, and occupation, see U.S. Census of 1900. For his election as councilman and tenure as mayor *pro tempore*, see "Kenner," New Orleans *Daily Picayune*, September 15, 1899, 12.

75. "In Douglas Square," New Orleans *Times-Democrat*, July 26, 1900, 9. On the lynching spree in Jefferson Parish in the 1890s, see Pfeifer, *Rough Justice*, 67–93.

76. "The First Victim," New Orleans *Times-Democrat*, July 26, 1900, 9; "The March of the Mob," New Orleans *Daily Picayune*, July 26, 1900, 1. The *Daily Picayune* claimed that Sanders had been wounded outside his home, but was likely unaware that he had been carried there after the attack. A *Times-Democrat* reporter claimed to have spoken with Sanders, making that account more credible. See also "At the Hospital," New Orleans *Daily Picayune*, July 26, 1900, 7.

77. "At the Hospital," New Orleans *Daily Picayune*, July 26, 1900, 7. On the railroad journey between Chicago and New Orleans, see *Appleton's General Guide to the United States and Canada*, vol. 2 (New York: D. Appleton and Company, 1898), 369–72.

78. Letter of Meek, Meek, Cochrane & Munsell to Mayor Paul Capdevielle on September 4, 1900, Records of Mayor Paul Capdevielle, NOPL.

79. "Looting a Store," New Orleans *Times-Democrat*, July 26, 1900, 9.

80. "The March of the Mob," New Orleans *Daily Picayune*, July 26, 1900, 1.

81. "'To the Parish Prison,'" New Orleans *Times-Democrat*, July 26, 1900, 9.

82. "Halted at the Prison," New Orleans *Daily Picayune*, July 26, 1900, 7.

83. "When the Ministers of the Law Fail," New Orleans *Daily Picayune*, March 15, 1891, 4.

84. Telegram of James G. Blaine to Francis T. Nicholls on March 15, 1891, reprinted in *Correspondence in Relation to the Killing of the Prisoners in New Orleans*, 16–17. On Nicholls, see Garnie W. McGinty, "Francis Tillou Redding Nicholls," *North Louisiana History* 15, no. 1 (Winter 1984): 30–39. For coverage of the diplomatic fallout, see "Fava's Recall," New Orleans *Daily Picayune*, April 2, 1891, 1. On the grand jury, see "Report of Grand Jury as to Killing in New Orleans Parish Prison of Certain Persons Charged with the Murder of Chief of Police Hennessy," reprinted in U.S. Department of State, *Papers Relating to the Foreign Relations of the United States* (Washington, DC: Government Printing Office, 1892), 714–22.

85. Rev. S.J. Barrows, "The Orleans Parish Prison," *The Christian Union* 43, no. 14 (April 2, 1891): 436–37. Days before the massacre, Judge James G. Clark had petitioned councilmen to authorize the construction of a new prison, citing the "largely dilapidated" and "ruinous condition" of the old facility. See "The Criminal Courts and Prisons," New Orleans *Daily Picayune*, March 6, 1891, 4.

86. "City Council," New Orleans *Daily Picayune*, November 4, 1891, 3.

87. On the design flaws, see "City Hall," New Orleans *Daily Picayune*, August 30, 1892, 10. On the aftermath, see "New Orleans," *American Architect and Building News* 38, no. 882 (November 19, 1892): 115–16. On the building, see also Richard Campanella, "'Ominous': New Orleans' Old Criminal Courts Building and a Brief History of Penal Architecture," *Preservation in Print* (April 2016): 12–13. On the facility opening, see "Parish Prisoners in the New Jail," New Orleans *Daily Picayune*, January 22, 1895, 8.

88. Illinois Central Railroad Company, *The Commercial, Industrial, and Financial Outlook for New Orleans*, 89–91. For the physical layout of the facility, see Sanborn-Perris Map Co., *Insurance Maps of New Orleans* (1896), vol. 2, 106.

89. *The Picayune's Guide to New Orleans*, 5th ed. (New Orleans: Picayune Job Print, 1903), 89. See also "From the Old Prison to the New Jail," New Orleans *Daily Picayune*, January 18, 1895, 3.

90. "At the Parish Prison," New Orleans *Times-Democrat*, July 26, 1900, 9.

91. "Halted at the Prison," New Orleans *Daily Picayune*, July 26, 1900, 7.

92. "The Prison Protected," New Orleans *Daily Picayune*, July 26, 1900, 9.

93. "The First Murder," New Orleans *Daily Picayune*, July 26, 1900, 7.

94. "The Gathering," New Orleans *Times-Democrat*, July 26, 1900, 9; "The Victim," July 26, 1900, 9.

95. Alan Lomax, *Mister Jelly Roll: The Fortunes of Jelly Roll Morton, New Orleans Creole and "Inventor of Jazz"* (Berkeley: University of California Press, 2001), 89. On the early history of jazz in New Orleans, see especially Donald Marquis, *In Search of Buddy Bolden: First Man of Jazz* (Baton Rouge: Louisiana State University Press, 1978); Grace Lichtenstein, *Musical Gumbo: The Music of New Orleans* (New York: W.W. Norton, 1993); R. Collins, *New Orleans Jazz: A Revised History* (New York: Vantage Press, 1996); Samuel Charters, *A Trumpet Around the Corner: The Story of New Orleans Jazz* (Jackson: University Press of Mississippi, 2008); Charles Hersch, *Subversive Sounds: Race and the Birth of Jazz in New Orleans* (Chicago: University of Chicago Press, 2007); John McCusker, *Creole Trombone: Kid Ory and the Early Years of Jazz* (Jackson: University Press of Mississippi, 2012).

96. Lomax, *Mister Jelly Roll*, 91.

97. "The Dancers Dusted," New Orleans *Times-Democrat*, July 27, 1900, 6.

98. "The Dancers Dusted," New Orleans *Times-Democrat*, July 27, 1900, 6, 7. See also "Gaster's Report," New Orleans *Times-Democrat*, August 31, 1900, 11.

99. Lomax, *Mister Jelly Roll*, 91.

100. Lomax, *Mister Jelly Roll*, 91.

101. "The First Murder," New Orleans *Daily Picayune*, July 26, 1900, 7.

102. "In the Tenderloin," New Orleans *Times-Democrat*, July 26, 1900, 9.

103. "The First Murder," New Orleans *Daily Picayune*, July 26, 1900, 7.

104. "In the Tenderloin," New Orleans *Times-Democrat*, July 26, 1900, 9.

105. "The Inmates Were Terrified," New Orleans *Daily Picayune*, July 26, 1900, 7. A decade later, while working as a night watchman for Boylan's Detective Agency, Wallace Sabatier and his partner would kill two unarmed black burglars under suspicious circumstances. See Homicide Report for Charles Croghan, April 5, 1911, NOPL.

106. "The Victim," New Orleans *Times-Democrat*, July 26, 1900, 9.

107. "The Homicide," New Orleans *Times-Democrat*, July 26, 1900, 9.

108. Coroner's Inquest for Unknown, July 25, 1900, NOPL.

109. "Mob's Fury Checked by the Mayor," New Orleans *Times-Democrat*, July 27, 1900, 3.

110. "August Thomas," New Orleans *Daily States*, July 27, 1900, 1.

111. "Wednesday Night Victims," New Orleans *Daily Picayune*, July 27, 1900, 7.

112. "At the Hospital," New Orleans *Daily Picayune*, July 26, 1900, 7.

113. "At the Hospital," New Orleans *Daily Picayune*, July 26, 1900, 7.

114. Joel Cook, *America: Picturesque & Descriptive*, vol. 3 (New York: P.F. Collier & Son, 1900), 419.

115. Newspapers gave estimates of Taylor's age ranging from twenty-six to thirty, but Charity Hospital records listed him as twenty-six years old. See Charity Hospital Record of Deaths, NOPL. On the history of the French Market, see Helen Tangires, *Public Markets and Civic Culture in Nineteenth-Century America* (Baltimore: Johns Hopkins University Press, 2003).

116. Charity Hospital Record of Deaths, July 1900, and Coroner's Inquest for Louis Taylor, July 27, 1900, NOPL. See also "At the Charity Hospital," New Orleans *Daily Picayune*, July 27, 1900, 7.

117. "Taylor Dead," New Orleans *Daily States*, July 27, 1900, 1.

118. "The Third Victim," New Orleans *Daily Picayune*, July 26, 1900, 7.

119. "Philo Fatally Shot," New Orleans *Times-Democrat*, July 26, 1900, 9.

120. "At the Hospital," New Orleans *Times-Democrat*, July 26, 1900, 7; "Injuries and Casualties," New Orleans *Times-Democrat*, July 27, 1900, 6; "Wednesday Night Victims," New Orleans *Daily Picayune*, July 27, 1900, 7. The preceding day, the *Picayune* had erroneously reported that the unnamed victim had been shot. See "A Fourth Body Found," New Orleans *Daily Picayune*, July 26, 1900, 7. The victim was named as Joseph Nelson. On Nelson's age, see Orleans Parish Death Records, vol. 122, 1125.

121. Lomax, *Mister Jelly Roll*, 92.

122. "Not an Arrest," New Orleans *Daily States*, July 26, 1900, 3.

123. Lomax, *Mister Jelly Roll*, 92.

6. REVELATIONS

1. "During the Day," New Orleans *Daily Picayune*, July 27, 1900, 7. See also "Stop to Business," New Orleans *Daily States*, July 26, 1900, 3. For a contemporary description of the New Orleans and Western Terminal and Port Chalmette, see "Picturesque New Orleans," *Frank Leslie's Popular Monthly* 45, no. 3 (March 1898): 325–30.

2. "Narrow Escape," New Orleans *Times-Democrat*, July 27, 1900, 7. On Columbus's age and marriage, see Orleans Parish Marriage Records, vol. 22, 271.

3. "Incidents and Casualties," New Orleans *Times-Democrat*, July 27, 1900, 6; "At the Hall," New Orleans *Daily States*, July 26, 1900, 1.

4. "Attacked the Jesuit Church," New Orleans *Daily Picayune*, July 27, 1900, 7.

5. "Labor Intimidated," New Orleans *Times-Democrat*, July 27, 1900, 6.

6. "A Dastardly Attack," New Orleans *Daily Picayune*, July 27, 1900, 7.

7. Born in Virginia around 1840, Washington was likely a slave who was transported and sold in the Deep South. See U.S. Census of 1880, Louisiana, Orleans Parish, Roll 464, 482C.

8. New Orleans *Times-Democrat*, "The Casualties," July 27, 1900, 7.

9. "On the Levee," New Orleans *Daily Picayune*, July 27, 1900, 7.

10. "Labor Intimidated," New Orleans *Times-Democrat*, July 27, 1900, 6.

11. "Mob's Fury Checked by the Mayor," New Orleans *Times-Democrat*, July 27, 1900, 1.

12. "On Poydras Street," New Orleans *Daily Picayune*, July 27, 1900, 7.

13. "Protecting Negroes," New Orleans *Times-Democrat*, July 27, 1900, 6. On the long history of black draymen in another major American city, see Graham R. Hodges, *New York City Cartmen, 1667–1850* (New York: New York University Press, 1986).

14. "On Poydras Street," New Orleans *Daily Picayune*, July 27, 1900, 7.

15. "Exchanges Take Action," New Orleans *Times-Democrat*, July 27, 1900, 3.

16. "Praise Capdevielle," New Orleans *Daily States*, July 27, 1900, 8.

17. On the terms of the bond issue, see "Notice to Capitalists and Investors," New Orleans *Daily States*, July 23, 1900, 3.

18. "At the Board of Trade," New Orleans *Daily States*, July 26, 1900, 1.

19. "City Hall," New Orleans *Daily Picayune*, July 17, 1900, 12.

20. See New Orleans *Times-Democrat*, "Mob's Fury Checked by the Mayor," July 27, 1900, 1; "Mayor Rises to the Occasion," July 27, 1900, 3. See also "At the Mayor's Office," New Orleans *Daily Picayune*, July 27, 1900, 1.

21. Letter of Paul Capdevielle to D.S. Gaster on July 26, 1900, Mayor's Letterbooks, NOPL.

22. "Mayor Issues Call," New Orleans *Daily States*, July 26, 1900, 7.

23. Proclamation of Mayor Paul Capdevielle on July 26, 1900, Mayor's Letterbooks, NOPL.

24. "Exchanges Take Action," New Orleans *Times-Democrat*, July 27, 1900, 3.

25. For an image of the New Orleans Cotton Exchange Building, see Leonard V. Huber, *New Orleans: A Pictorial History* (New York: Crown, 1971).

26. "Exchanges Take Action," New Orleans *Times-Democrat*, July 27, 1900, 3.

27. "Mass Meeting!" New Orleans *Daily Picayune*, March 14, 1891, 4.

28. "At the Feet of Clay," New Orleans *Daily Picayune*, March 14, 1891, 4.

29. On the economic and political motives behind the massacre, see especially Gambino, *Vendetta*.

30. "The New Orleans Mafia Case," *American Law Review* 25 (May–June 1891): 430.

31. "Mayor Rises to the Occasion," New Orleans *Times-Democrat*, July 27, 1900, 3.

32. "Mob's Fury Checked by the Mayor," New Orleans *Times-Democrat*, July 27, 1900, 1.

33. On Wood's sale of a stern-wheel steamboat to the U.S. government, see *Annual Reports of the War Department for the Fiscal Year Ended June 30, 1900, Report of the Chief of Engineers, Part 3* (Washington, DC: Government Printing Office, 1900), 2270–71.

34. Elmer E. Wood Papers, NOPL. The selected quotes are located on page 3 of Wood's untitled typescript. On Wood's age and birthplace, see his Louisiana Sons of the American Revolution membership application.

35. Elmer E. Wood Papers, NOPL. The selected quotes are located on page 34 of Wood's untitled typescript.

36. On B.D. Wood, see *Twenty-Ninth Annual Meeting of the National Board of Trade* (Philadelphia, PA: Burk & McFetridge Co., 1899), 18.

37. "Mob's Fury Checked by the Mayor," New Orleans *Times-Democrat*, July 27, 1900, 1.

38. "At the Mayor's Office," New Orleans *Daily Picayune*, July 27, 1900, 3.

39. "Arming the Citizen Police," New Orleans *Times-Democrat*, July 27, 1900, 3.

40. See images titled "Arming the Volunteer Police" and "Special Volunteer Force," published in the New Orleans *Times-Democrat*, July 27, 1900, 3.

41. "The Citizen Police," New Orleans *Daily Picayune*, July 27, 1900, 3.

42. "At the Mayor's Office," New Orleans *Daily Picayune*, July 27, 1900, 3.

43. Letter of William L. Hughes to Paul Capdevielle on July 31, 1900, Council Records, NOPL. On dinner at the St. Charles Hotel, see "Feeding the Peace Guardians," New Orleans *Daily Picayune*, July 27, 1900, 6.

44. "Street Railroads," New Orleans *Daily Picayune*, July 27, 1900, 7. See also "Motorman Shot," New Orleans *Times-Democrat*, July 27, 1900, 7.

45. "Street Railroads," New Orleans *Daily Picayune*, July 27, 1900, 7. See also "Mayor Rises to the Occasion," New Orleans *Times-Democrat*, July 27, 1900, 1, 3.

46. Letter of Arthur McGuirk to American Express Co. on July 26, 1900, Mayor's Letterbooks, NOPL.

47. Letter of N.T. Brown to Arthur McGuirk on July 26, 1900, reprinted in "The Pleasant Nay," New Orleans *Times-Democrat*, July 27, 1900, 3.

48. Letter of J. Stuart to Paul Capdevielle on July 26, 1900, Council Records, NOPL.

49. Letter of Paul Capdevielle to Colonel Elmer Wood on July 26, 1900, Council Records, NOPL. On the story, see "Mayor Rises to the Occasion," New Orleans *Times-Democrat*, July 27, 1900, 3.

50. Morrison, *New Orleans and the New South*, 108.

51. "At Baldwin's and Eshleman's," New Orleans *Daily Picayune*, July 26, 1900, 7.

52. Letter of W.L. Hughes to Colonel Elmer E. Wood on August 2, 1900, Council Records, NOPL. See also "Arming the Citizen Police," New Orleans *Times-Democrat*, July 27, 1900, 3, and "At Baldwin's Store," New Orleans *Daily Picayune*, July 27, 1900, 7. On the closure of J. Dutrey's store, see "Closes Gun Store," New Orleans *Daily States*, July 26, 1900, 1.

53. "Mob's Fury Checked by the Mayor," New Orleans *Times-Democrat*, July 27, 1900, 1, 3.

54. Circulating in the morning, other New Orleans dailies had already gone to print by the time word of the murders began to spread. On the newspaper's masthead and the initial story, see "Two Policemen Foully Murdered," New Orleans *Daily States*, July 24, 1900, 1.

55. Hair, *Carnival of Fury*, 142.

56. "Murder of Police Officers," New Orleans *Daily Picayune*, July 25, 1900, 4.

57. "Negro Criminals," New Orleans *Times-Democrat*, July 25, 1900, 4.

58. "Colored Aid Proffered," New Orleans *Times-Democrat*, July 25, 1900, 9. See also "Negroes Offer Aid," New Orleans *Daily Picayune*, July 25, 1900, 9.

59. "Negro Condemnation," New Orleans *Times-Democrat*, July 26, 1900, 3.

60. "The Negro Population," New Orleans *Daily States*, July 25, 1900, 4.

61. "Negro Murderers," New Orleans *Daily States*, July 25, 1900, 4.

62. "Anent the Riot and the Millennium," *Harlequin* 2, no. 8 (August 18, 1900): 2.

63. "No Race War," New Orleans *Daily Picayune*, July 26, 1900, 4.

64. "Negroes Hunted All Night by Mobs Made Out of Boys," New Orleans *Daily Picayune*, July 26, 1900, 1.

65. On the professions and ages of the arrestees, see NOPD Arrest Records, especially July 26 and 27, 1900, NOPL.

66. "Pepe Roses Denies," New Orleans *Daily Picayune*, July 27, 1900, 4. On Roses and his criminal history, see Christopher Joseph Cook, "'An Utter Disregard for the Law': Law, Order, and the Criminal Element in the Robert Charles Riot of 1900," *Louisiana History* 60, no. 1 (Winter 2019): 29–34.

67. "A Hoodlum Fireman," New Orleans *Daily Picayune*, July 27, 1900, 4; "Hughes' Big Docket," New Orleans *Daily States*, July 27, 1900, 8. On Blanque's background and employment history, see Thomas O'Connor, ed., *History of the Fire Department of New Orleans* (New Orleans: n.p., 1895), 471.

68. "City Council and the Departments," New Orleans *Daily Picayune*, August 2, 1900, 3. On Blanque's unsuccessful appeal of his dismissal, see "Two Council Committees Meet," New Orleans *Daily Picayune*, August 18, 1900, 3.

69. On the race riots as a form of protest regarding sexual politics, see especially Alecia P. Long, *The Great Southern Babylon: Sex, Race, and Respectability in New Orleans, 1865–1920* (Baton Rouge: Louisiana State University Press, 2005).

70. "Separate Street Car Law," New Orleans *Times-Democrat*, July 2, 1900, 4.

71. "In the Path of the Storm," New Orleans *Times-Democrat*, July 27, 1900, 4.

72. "In the Path of the Storm," New Orleans *Times-Democrat*, July 27, 1900, 4.

73. "Our Police," New Orleans *Daily States*, July 26, 1900, 4; "Colored Baptists," New Orleans *Daily Picayune*, July 25, 1900, 3.

74. "Order Reigns in the City," New Orleans *Daily Picayune*, July 27, 1900, 4.

75. "Praise Capdevielle," New Orleans *Daily States*, July 27, 1900, 8.

76. "Clubs Are Trumps," New Orleans *Daily Picayune*, July 27, 1900, 7.

77. James S. Zacharie, *New Orleans Guide* (New Orleans: F.F. Hansell & Bros., 1902), 164. On the history and social significance of the Boston Club, see Stuart O. Landry, *History of the Boston Club* (New Orleans: Pelican Publishing Company, 1938). On the Pickwick Club, see Augusto P. Miceli, *The Pickwick Club of New Orleans* (New Orleans: Pickwick Press, 1964).

78. "Clubs Are Trumps," New Orleans *Daily Picayune*, July 27, 1900, 7.

79. "Clubs Are Trumps," New Orleans *Daily Picayune*, July 27, 1900, 7.

80. "Arming the Squads," New Orleans *Daily States*, July 26, 1900, 1.

81. "Mob's Fury Checked by the Mayor," New Orleans *Times-Democrat*, July 27, 1900, 1.

82. On the layout of the Mabry residence, see Sanborn-Perris Map Co., *Insurance Maps of New Orleans, Louisiana* (1896), vol. 2, 130. The Orleans Parish Coroner cited "life" under the entry for Hannah Mabry's "time in the city." See Coroner's Record of Views for Hannah Mabry, July 27, 1900, NOPL.

83. The New Orleans *Daily States* gave the names David and Anna, but U.S. Census data indicates that the elder couple was Douglas and Hannah Mabry. See U.S. Census of 1900, Louisiana, Orleans Parish, Roll 574, 18B. On the marriage of Harry Mabry and Nancy Watkins, see Orleans Parish Marriage Records, vol. 20, 265.

84. "Woman Shot While She Slept," New Orleans *Times-Democrat*, July 27, 1900, 1. For testimony about the events of that evening, see "The Jury Hears Some Witnesses," New Orleans *Daily Picayune*, October, 26, 1900, 11.

85. "Hoodlums' Last Rally," New Orleans *Daily Picayune*, July 27, 1900, 7. See also Coroner's Inquest for Hannah Mabry, July 27, 1900, NOPL.

86. "The Special Police," New Orleans *Daily States*, July 27, 1900, 8. On the makeup of the squad, see "The Citizen Police," New Orleans *Daily Picayune*, July 27, 1900, 3.

87. "Woman Shot While She Slept," New Orleans *Times-Democrat*, July 27, 1900, 6.

88. "Hoodlums' Last Rally," New Orleans *Daily Picayune*, July 27, 1900, 7. City directories listed Clinton Murray as a physician living nearby on Magazine Street. See *Soards' New Orleans Directory for 1899*, 610.

89. "Woman Shot While She Slept," New Orleans *Times-Democrat*, July 27, 1900, 6.

90. "Here to Stay," New Orleans *Daily Picayune*, July 27, 1900, 3.

91. "Mayor Reviews Situation," New Orleans *Times-Democrat*, July 27, 1900, 7.

92. This is an abbreviation of the Death Certificate for Hannah Mabry, July 27, 1900; see also Coroner's Inquest for Hannah Mabry, July 27, 1900, NOPL; Coroner's Record of Views for Hannah Mabry, July 27, 1900, NOPL; Charity Hospital Record of Deaths, July 1900, NOPL.

93. "Peace and Order Reign," New Orleans *Daily States*, July 27, 1900, 1.
94. "A Foul Murder," New Orleans *Daily States*, July 27, 1900, 1.
95. "Total Arrests of the Day," New Orleans *Daily Picayune*, July 27, 1900, 4. See also "Hughes' Big Docket," New Orleans *Daily States*, July 27, 1900, 8.
96. "A Cowardly Affair," New Orleans *Daily States*, July 27, 1900, 1.
97. "Citizen Police Work Day and Night," New Orleans *Daily Picayune*, July 28, 1900, 6.
98. "Financial and Commercial," New Orleans *Daily States*, July 27, 1900, 7.
99. "A False Alarm," New Orleans *Daily Picayune*, July 27, 1900, 4.
100. "Short-Lived Hope," New Orleans *Times-Democrat*, July 27, 1900, 6. See also "Rumors of Arrest," New Orleans *Daily Picayune*, July 27, 1900, 4.
101. "Where is Charles?" New Orleans *Daily States*, July 27, 1900, 1.

7. CRUCIBLE

1. For a visual representation of the neighborhood surrounding the crime scene, see Sanborn-Perris Map Co., *Insurance Maps of New Orleans, Louisiana* (1896), vol. 2.
2. "Negro Murder," New Orleans *Daily Picayune*, September 3, 1900, 6.
3. "The Mission of Death," New Orleans *Times-Democrat*, July 28, 1900, 3.
4. "Corporal Lally," New Orleans *Times-Democrat*, July 28, 1900, 7.
5. "Talk with Gaster," New Orleans *Daily States*, July 29, 1900, 1.
6. "Martha Williams' Story," New Orleans *Daily States*, August 4, 1900, 1.
7. "Martha Williams' Story," New Orleans *Daily States*, August 4, 1900, 1.
8. New Orleans newspapers described the Saratoga Street property in detail, printing illustrated floor plans and highlighting points of interest. For a map, see "Scene of Friday's Battle," New Orleans *Times-Democrat*, July 30, 1900, 3. For written descriptions of the property, see "The House of Death," New Orleans *Times-Democrat*, July 29, 1900, 3. See also "Charles' Castle of Death," New Orleans *Daily Picayune*, July 29, 1900, 1.
9. "Talk with Joyce," New Orleans *Daily States*, July 28, 1900, 2; "Mr. Joyce," New Orleans *Daily Picayune*, May 15, 1901, 13. On the marriage of John Joyce and Margaret Smith, see Orleans Parish Marriage Records, vol. 19, 328. On the Joyce family, see U.S. Census of 1920, Louisiana, Orleans Parish, Roll T625_623, 4A. On Joyce's profession, see *Soards' New Orleans Directory for 1900*, 475.
10. Hair, *Carnival of Fury*, 156–58.
11. Silas Jackson's landlord, F.S. Salter testified regarding their relationship during his tenant's subsequent trial. See "Testimony of F.S. Salter" and "Testimony of Mr. Joyce," New Orleans *Daily Picayune*, May 15, 1901, 13.
12. Hair, *Carnival of Fury*, 156–58.
13. "Testimony of Silas Jackson," New Orleans *Daily Picayune*, May 15, 1901, 13.
14. "The Mission of Death," New Orleans *Times-Democrat*, July 28, 1900, 3.
15. For a detailed illustration of the apartment's interior layout and furnishings, see "Scene of Friday's Battle," New Orleans *Times-Democrat*, July 30, 1900, 3.
16. "Testimony of Silas Jackson," New Orleans *Daily Picayune*, May 15, 1901, 13.
17. "With the Prisoners," New Orleans *Daily Picayune*, July 29, 1900, 3.
18. On the department's uniform regulations, see *Manual of the City Police for 1890*, 32–36.
19. "The House of Death," New Orleans *Times-Democrat*, July 29, 1900, 3.

20. Sergeant Porteous suffered four gunshot wounds. Whereas the first three bullets passed directly through his body from front to back, indicating that he was standing and facing Charles, the bullet that pierced his heart entered his right side at an upward and forward angle, suggesting that he was lying on his stomach when a standing gunman inflicted the fatal wound from moderate range. On his wounds, see Coroner's Inquest for Gabriel Porteous, July 27, 1900, NOPL. On the position of his body, see "Scene of Friday's Battle," New Orleans *Times-Democrat*, July 30, 1900, 3.

21. Coroner's Inquest for John F. Lally, July 28, 1900, NOPL.

22. "Scene of Friday's Battle," New Orleans *Times-Democrat*, July 30, 1900, 3.

23. "Testimony of Silas Jackson," New Orleans *Daily Picayune*, May 15, 1901, 13.

24. "In Mortal Terror of Him," New Orleans *Times-Democrat*, July 28, 1900, 7.

25. "With the Prisoners," New Orleans *Daily Picayune*, July 28, 1900, 3.

26. "Testimony of Officer Esser," New Orleans *Daily Picayune*, May 15, 1901, 13.

27. "Officer Seigel's Story," New Orleans *Daily Picayune*, July 28, 1900, 3.

28. "Testimony of Patrolman Finney," New Orleans *Daily Picayune*, May 15, 1901, 13. See also "Testimony of Officer Price" and "Testimony of Officer John Kerwin," New Orleans *Daily Picayune*, May 15, 1901, 13.

29. "Charles Kills His Fifth Man," New Orleans *Times-Democrat*, July 28, 1900, 3.

30. For Brumfield's age and birthplace, see Death Certificate for Albert Brumfield, July 27, 1900, NOPL.

31. "The Brumfield Funeral," New Orleans *Times-Democrat*, July 31, 1900, 3. See also "Albert L. Brumfield," New Orleans *Daily Picayune*, July 28, 1900, 8.

32. Hair, *Carnival of Fury*, 166.

33. "Testimony of Rev. Father Fitzgerald," New Orleans *Daily Picayune*, May 15, 1901, 13.

34. "Charles Is No More," New Orleans *Times-Democrat*, July 28, 1900, 3.

35. "How Brunfield Was Killed," New Orleans *Times-Democrat*, July 29, 1900, 8. On eyewitness Charles A. Kent's occupation, see *Soards' New Orleans Directory for 1900*, 488.

36. Coroner's Inquest for Albert Brumfield, July 27, 1900, NOPL.

37. "How Brunfield Was Killed," New Orleans *Times-Democrat*, July 29, 1900, 8.

38. "St. Charles Hotel, New Orleans," *Successful American* 5, no. 5 (May 1902): 301.

39. "At the City Hall," New Orleans *Times-Democrat*, July 28, 1900, 7.

40. Letter of W.L Hughes to Colonel Elmer E. Wood on August 2, 1900, Council Records, NOPL.

41. "The City Stirred," New Orleans *Times-Democrat*, July 28, 1900, 6.

42. "Bloody Riot Up Town," New Orleans *Daily States*, July 27, 1900, 1.

43. "Longshoremen and Dagoes," New Orleans *Times-Democrat*, July 28, 1900, 11.

44. Coroner's Inquest for Unknown, July 27, 1900, NOPL. The inquest specified four bullet wounds, but cited two additional wounds to the thigh and buttocks without indicating the cause. The inquest cited the unknown victim's residence as "Gallatin and Hospital," which was actually the location where he was murdered.

45. "Longshoremen and Dagoes," New Orleans *Times-Democrat*, July 28, 1900, 11.

46. "Testimony of Father Fitzgerald," New Orleans *Daily Picayune*, May 15, 1901, 13. See also "A Man and a Boy Saw Biri Shoot," New Orleans *Daily Picayune*, December 15, 1900, 3, and "Well Under Way," New Orleans *Times-Democrat*, December 15, 1900, 3.

47. "How Brunfield Was Killed," New Orleans *Times-Democrat*, July 29, 1900, 8.

48. "From Rear of the Building," New Orleans *Times-Democrat*, July 28, 1900, 3.

49. "Charles Kills Fifth Man," New Orleans *Times-Democrat*, July 28, 1900, 3.

50. "The Work of Brave Men," New Orleans *Daily States,* July 28, 1900, 3. On the professions of the rescuers, William Ball and Vic Mauberret, see *Soards' New Orleans City Directory for 1900,* 94, 600.

51. "Made of Hero Stuff," New Orleans *Times-Democrat,* July 28, 1900, 6.

52. On the layouts of neighborhood properties, see Sanborn-Perris Map Co., *Insurance Maps of New Orleans* (1896), vol. 2, 166. See also "Charles Is No More," New Orleans *Times-Democrat,* July 28, 1900, 3.

53. "Charles Is No More," New Orleans *Times-Democrat,* July 28, 1900, 3.

54. "Holds Them at Bay," New Orleans *Times-Democrat,* July 28, 1900, 6; "Charles Is No More," New Orleans *Times-Democrat,* July 28, 1900, 3.

55. "From Rear of the Building," New Orleans *Times-Democrat,* July 28, 1900, 3, 6. On Van Kuren's wounds, see Coroner's Inquest for Andrew Van Kuren, July 27, 1900, and Death Certificate for Andrew Van Kuren, July 28, 1900, NOPL.

56. "The Shooting Begins," New Orleans *Daily States,* July 29, 1900, 1. On Batte's age and profession, see U.S. Census of 1900, State of Louisiana, Orleans Parish, Roll 571, 7B. On his cause of death, see Coroner's Inquest for H.H. Batte, July 31, 1900, NOPL.

57. "At the Charity Hospital," New Orleans *Times-Democrat,* July 28, 1900, 7. On LeClerc's appointment as a convention delegate, see *The Convention of '98,* 39–40. On his appointment to the police board, see *Annual Report of the Board of Police Commissioners for 1903,* 10.

58. "At the Scene Today," New Orleans *Daily States,* July 28, 1900, 1. On the injuries suffered by the besiegers, see "At the Charity Hospital," New Orleans *Times-Democrat,* July 28, 1900, 7.

59. "Holds Them at Bay" and "Charles Is No More," New Orleans *Times-Democrat,* July 28, 1900, 3, 6.

60. "Reading the Bulletins," New Orleans *Times-Democrat,* July 28, 1900, 11. On the location of the *Times-Democrat* office, on Camp Street between Gravier and Natchez, see Sanborn-Perris Map Co., *Insurance Maps of New Orleans, Louisiana* (1896), vol. 2, 102.

61. "The Mayor's Hand Keeps a Firm Hold," New Orleans *Daily Picayune,* July 28, 1900, 9.

62. On the Great New Orleans Fires of 1788 and 1794 and the history of the city's fire department, see O'Connor, ed., *History of the Fire Department of New Orleans.* See also Cindy Ermus, "Reduced to Ashes: The Good Friday Fire of 1788 in Spanish Colonial New Orleans," *Louisiana History* 54, no. 3 (Summer 2013): 292–331.

63. "Smoked Out of Hiding Place," New Orleans *Times-Democrat,* July 28, 1900, 6. New Orleans ranked first of forty-two American cities with populations above 100,000 in multiyear per capita losses due to fire during the 1890s, although New York's unreported rate was likely higher overall. See "Statistics of Fires in American Cities Having a Population of 20,000 and Upward," *City Government* 9, no. 4 (October 1900): 100.

64. "Smoked Out of Hiding Place," New Orleans *Times-Democrat,* July 28, 1900, 6.

65. "Smoked Out of Hiding Place," New Orleans *Times-Democrat,* July 28, 1900, 6.

66. "Charles Shot to Pieces," New Orleans *Daily States,* July 27, 1900, 1.

67. "Smoked Out of Hiding Place," New Orleans *Times-Democrat,* July 28, 1900, 6.

68. Newspapers reported Noiret's age as twenty-four, although state records listed him as two years younger. See Orleans Parish Death Records, vol. 189, 293. On Special Police Squad No. 1, see "The First Squad," New Orleans *Daily Picayune,* July 29, 1900, 10.

69. "How Charles Met Death," New Orleans *Times-Democrat,* July 29, 1900, 3.

70. For example, see "Who Killed Charles?" New Orleans *Times-Democrat,* October 15, 1900, 3.

71. "Run to Cover and Killed," New Orleans *Times-Democrat,* July 28, 1900, 3.

72. On the outcome of arbitration, see "Noiret Wins," New Orleans *Times-Democrat*, October 16, 1900, 3.

73. Noiret's initial account of the shooting was corroborated by at least one other eyewitness and published in the *Daily Picayune* and the *Times-Democrat*, despite the fact that two other men claimed credit for killing Charles. The events depicted are reconstructed from multiple accounts, with the quotes taken from both of Noiret's initial interviews. See "How Charles Met Death," New Orleans *Times-Democrat*, July 29, 1900, 3; "The Killing of Charles," New Orleans *Daily Picayune*, July 28, 1900, 2. See also "Who Killed Him?" New Orleans *Daily States*, July 29, 1900, 8. For Noiret's testimony during the arbitration proceedings, see "One Third Through," New Orleans *Times-Democrat*, October 10, 1900, 3.

74. "The Killing of Charles," New Orleans *Daily Picayune*, July 28, 1900, 2.

75. "How Charles Met Death," New Orleans *Times-Democrat*, July 29, 1900, 3. For corroborating testimony, see "Hawkins Tells How," New Orleans *Daily Picayune*, July 30, 1900, 3. See also "One Third Through," New Orleans *Times-Democrat*, October 10, 1900, 3.

76. "Run to Cover and Killed," New Orleans *Times-Democrat*, July 28, 1900, 3.

77. "From the Rear of the Building," New Orleans *Times-Democrat*, July 28, 1900, 3.

78. "Dead Body in Mob's Hands," New Orleans *Times-Democrat*, July 28, 1900, 6.

79. "Pour Lead into the Prostrate Form," New Orleans *Daily Picayune*, July 28, 1900, 2.

80. "Carrying the Corpse Off," New Orleans *Daily States*, July 27, 1900, 1. On Porteous's age, see U.S. Census of 1900, Louisiana, Orleans Parish, Roll 571, 5B. On his profession, see *Soards' New Orleans Directory for 1900*, 74.

81. "Removed to the Morgue," New Orleans *Times-Democrat*, July 28, 1900, 6.

82. "Dead Body in Mob's Hands," New Orleans *Times-Democrat*, July 28, 1900, 6.

83. Coroner's Inquest for "Unknown, supposed to be Jackson," July 27, 1900, NOPL.

84. "Another Negro," New Orleans *Daily Picayune*, July 28, 1900, 2.

85. "Exciting Scenes at Headquarters," New Orleans *Times-Democrat*, July 28, 1900, 6, 7.

86. "At the Morgue," New Orleans *Times-Democrat*, July 28, 1900, 6.

87. Coroner's Inquest for Robert Charles, July 27, 1900, NOPL.

88. "A Haunt for Desperate Blacks," New Orleans *Daily Picayune*, July 29, 1900, 2.

89. "Annie Gant's Story," New Orleans *Times-Democrat*, July 28, 1900, 7.

90. Newspapers published conflicting accounts of where George Ford was discovered, listing both the main building and the rear annex as locations. Given the fact that Ford was in the main building when the first shots were fired, it seems implausible that he fled to the rear building and remained undetected throughout the shootout, and equally unlikely that he would have survived the gunshots and fire that destroyed significant portions of the structure unscathed. The more plausible version of events is that he was in the front upstairs room of the main building, which was connected by staircase to the room where he had been playing cards when the shooting began. This room had no view of the courtyard or rear building and therefore likely remained relatively undisturbed during the shootout. For an account of his capture, see "Ford's Own Words" and "Ford's Arrest," New Orleans *Daily Picayune*, July 28, 1900, 6.

91. "Ford's Arrest," New Orleans *Daily Picayune*, July 28, 1900, 6.

92. "Ford's Own Words," New Orleans *Daily Picayune*, July 28, 1900, 6.

93. "At the Scene Today," New Orleans *Daily States*, July 28, 1900, 1.

94. "In Mortal Terror of Him," New Orleans *Times-Democrat*, July 28, 1900, 7.

95. "Silas Jackson's Statement," New Orleans *Times-Democrat*, July 28, 1900, 7.

96. "With the Prisoners," New Orleans *Daily Picayune*, July 28, 1900, 3.

97. "Quiet at Midnight," New Orleans *Daily Picayune*, July 28, 1900, 6.

98. "The Thomy Lafon School," New Orleans *Daily Picayune*, January 22, 1898, 3. On Lafon's remarkable life, see Frederick D. Smith, "Thomy Lafon," in Jessie Carney Smith, ed., *Encyclopedia of African American Business*, vol. 2 (Westport, CT: Greenwood Press, 2006), 447–49.

99. "Negro Schoolhouse Burned," New Orleans *Times-Democrat*, July 28, 1900, 7.

100. "Thomy Lafon School Burned to the Ground," New Orleans *Daily Picayune*, July 28, 1900, 8.

101. "Brutal Attack," New Orleans *Times-Democrat*, July 29, 1900, 3.

102. "Charles Identified," New Orleans *Daily Picayune*, July 29, 1900, 1.

103. "Positive Identification," New Orleans *Times-Democrat*, July 29, 1900, 3.

104. For slightly differing accounts of the identification, see "Charles Identified," New Orleans *Daily Picayune*, July 29, 1900, 1; "Positive Identification," New Orleans *Times-Democrat*, July 29, 1900, 1.

105. "Positive Identification," New Orleans *Times-Democrat*, July 29, 1900, 1.

106. "End of a Desperado," New Orleans *Daily Picayune*, July 28, 1900, 4.

107. "Storm and Stress," New Orleans *Times-Democrat*, July 28, 1900, 4.

108. Letter of M.J. Sanders to Paul Capdevielle on July 28, 1900, Council Records, NOPL.

109. "At the City Hall," New Orleans *Daily States*, July 29, 1900, 1.

110. "City Resumes Its Usual Quietude," New Orleans *Times-Democrat*, July 29, 1900, 1.

111. "Burial of Charles," New Orleans *Times-Democrat*, July 30, 1900, 1.

112. "Charles' Body Buried," New Orleans *Daily Picayune*, July 30, 1900, 1. See also "Burial of Charles," New Orleans *Times-Democrat*, July 30, 1900, 1.

113. Leonard V. Huber, *New Orleans Architecture: The Cemeteries*, vol. 3 (Gretna, LA: Pelican Publishing Company, 1974), 60. See also Rightor, *Standard History of New Orleans*, 266.

114. Based on the author's personal observation of Holt Cemetery in New Orleans, Louisiana. See also Shannon Lee Dawdy, "Holt Cemetery, New Orleans, Louisiana," in Paul Graves-Brown et al., eds., *The Oxford Handbook of the Archaeology of the Contemporary World* (New York: Oxford University Press, 2013), 452–55.

115. "At the Morgue," New Orleans *Times-Democrat*, July 29, 1900, 8.

116. "Charles' Body Buried," New Orleans *Daily Picayune*, July 30, 1900, 1.

117. "In the Churches," New Orleans *Times-Democrat*, July 30, 1900, 3.

118. Proclamation of Paul Capdevielle on July 29, 1900, Mayor's Letterbooks, NOPL.

119. "New Orleans Is Peaceful Once Again," New Orleans *Daily Picayune*, July 30, 1900, 1, 3.

8. REDEMPTION

1. "A Busy Night," New Orleans *Times-Democrat*, August 1, 1900, 6. See also "Riot Echoes at the City Council," New Orleans *Daily Picayune*, August 1, 1900, 3, and Motion of the New Orleans City Council on July 31, 1900, Council Records, NOPL.

2. "Storm and Stress," New Orleans *Times-Democrat*, July 28, 1900, 4.

3. Resolution of the New Orleans Board of Trade on August 2, 1900, Council Records, NOPL.

4. Letter of Achille Blais to Paul Capdevielle on August 1, 1900, Council Records, NOPL. On Blais's biography, see *Who's Who in Louisiana and Mississippi: Biographical Sketches of Prominent Men and Women of Louisiana and Mississippi* (New Orleans: Times-Picayune, 1918), 25.

5. "Special Police Medals," New Orleans *Times-Democrat*, September 19, 1900, 3.

6. Letter of James C. Simpson to Paul Capdevielle on September 19, 1900, Records of Mayor Paul Capdevielle, NOPL.

7. Letter of Edgar F. Pilie to Paul Capdevielle on September 18, 1900, Records of Mayor Paul Capdevielle, NOPL. On Pilie's age, see U.S. Census of 1900, Louisiana, Orleans Parish, Roll 572, 22A. On his occupation, see *Soards' New Orleans Directory for 1900*, 698. On these letters, see especially Records of Mayor Paul Capdevielle and Mayor's Letter Books, NOPL.

8. "The Families of the Dead Officers," New Orleans *Times-Democrat*, July 30, 1900, 4.

9. "Lift the Mortgage!" New Orleans *Times-Democrat*, August 2, 1900, 3.

10. Annual pensions of $150 were provided to the dependents of deceased NOPD officers by the Police Mutual Benefit Association, representing three months' salary for patrolmen. See *Annual Report of the Board of Police Commissioners for 1900*, 35–36.

11. "Fund for the Widows of Policemen," New Orleans *Times-Democrat*, August 2, 1900, 3; "The Mayor's Fund," New Orleans *Times-Democrat*, August 3, 1900, 3. On the lawsuit filed by Brumfield's mother against the Sun Mutual Insurance Company, see "Gist of the News," New Orleans *Times-Democrat*, November 22, 1900, 1.

12. "The Times-Democrat Fund," New Orleans *Times-Democrat*, August 3, 1900, 3.

13. For example, the *Times-Democrat* cited a one-dollar donation by Joseph Basile and several other men listed as laborers in Soards' directory. See "The Times-Democrat Fund," New Orleans *Times-Democrat*, August 3, 1900, 3. See also *Soards' New Orleans Directory for 1900*, 103.

14. See Mayor's Letterbooks, NOPL.

15. Letter of Henry H. Smith to Paul Capdevielle on August 10, 1900, Council Records, NOPL.

16. Letter of Thomas C. Anderson to Paul Capdevielle on August 2, 1900, Council Records, NOPL.

17. "Mayor's List in Detail," New Orleans *Daily States*, August 2, 1900, 8.

18. Telegraph of Klaw & Erlanger to Paul Capdevielle on August 2, 1900, Council Records, NOPL. See also Letter of Paul Capdevielle to Klaw & Erlanger Syndication on August 1, 1900, Mayor's Letterbooks, NOPL; "Swelling the Fund" and "The Mayor's Fund," New Orleans *Times-Democrat*, August 3, 1900, 3.

19. Letter of Arthur C. McGuirk on August 5, 1900, Mayor's Letterbooks, NOPL. Letter of F. Bishop to S.F. Walmsley on August 17, 1900, Department of Police and Public Buildings Letterbooks, NOPL; Letter of F. Bishop to S.F. Walmsley on August 17, 1900, Department of Police and Public Buildings Letterbooks, NOPL. See also Letter of F. Bishop to J. Garlick on August 15, 1900, Department of Police and Public Buildings Letterbooks, NOPL.

20. For example, see Letter from C.H. Lavillebeuvre to R.M. Walmsley on September 18, 1900, Mayor's Letterbooks, NOPL.

21. "The Fund for the Families of the Murdered Police Officers," New Orleans *Daily Picayune*, September 20, 1900, 4.

22. On the indictment, see Criminal District Court, Orleans Parish, Case No. 30,035, NOPL.

23. "John Willis Strangled," New Orleans *Daily Picayune*, August 5, 1900, 11.

24. "Strangled to Death," New Orleans *Times-Democrat*, August 5, 1900, 3.

25. "John Willis Strangled," New Orleans *Daily Picayune*, August 5, 1900, 11.

26. "Strangled to Death," New Orleans *Times-Democrat*, August 5, 1900, 3.

27. "People Fled," Boston *Daily Globe*, July 31, 1900, 12.

28. "The Green Turtle Club," New Orleans *Daily Picayune*, August 5, 1900, 11. The earliest mention of the Green Turtle Club in New Orleans newspapers was in an article published in April 1900, which listed James Clavin as vice-president of the organization. See "Green Turtle Club," New Orleans *Times-Democrat*, April 30, 1900, 10. On Clavin's position with the police department, see *Annual Report of the Board of Police Commissioners for 1900*, 96. See also *Soards' New Orleans Directory for 1900*, 208.

29. "New Orleans Negroes Want No Outside Help," New Orleans *Times-Democrat*, August 5, 1900, 7.

30. "Incendiary Literature," New Orleans *Times-Democrat*, August 5, 1900, 7.

31. "New Orleans Negroes Want No Outside Help," New Orleans *Times-Democrat*, August 5, 1900, 7.

32. "An Enemy of the Race," New Orleans *Times-Democrat*, August 5, 1900, 7.

33. "New Orleans Negroes Want No Outside Help," New Orleans *Times-Democrat*, August 5, 1900, 7.

34. "Incendiary Literature," New Orleans *Times-Democrat*, August 5, 1900, 7.

35. "Negroes Organize," New Orleans *Daily States*, August 5, 1900, 8.

36. "Propaganda of Discord," New Orleans *Times-Democrat*, August 4, 1900, 6.

37. "Mayor Capdevielle Will Act," New Orleans *Times-Democrat*, August 5, 1900, 7.

38. "Superintendent Gaster Investigating," New Orleans *Times-Democrat*, August 5, 1900, 7.

39. "Some Lessons from the Outbreak of Last Week," *Southwestern Christian Advocate*, August 2, 1900, 1; "Editorial Notes," *Southwestern Christian Advocate*, August 2, 1900, 1.

40. "Some Lessons from the Outbreak of Last Week," *Southwestern Christian Advocate*, August 2, 1900, 1.

41. "Editorial Notes," *Southwestern Christian Advocate*, August 9, 1900, 1.

42. "Trembling Wretches Before the Bar," New Orleans *Daily Picayune*, August 8, 1900, 3.

43. "More Indictments," New Orleans *Times-Democrat*, August 9, 1900, 3. On the professions of Foley and Flanagan, see *Soards' New Orleans Directory for 1900*, 328, 332.

44. "Mabry Locked Up," New Orleans *Daily Picayune*, August 5, 1900, 11.

45. "More Indictments," New Orleans *Times-Democrat*, August 9, 1900, 3. On the indictments of the murderers of August Thomas, see also Criminal District Court, Orleans Parish, No. 30,074 and No. 30,061, NOPL.

46. "Editorial Notes," *Southwestern Christian Advocate*, August 23, 1900, 1.

47. Letter of Arthur McGuirk to D.S. Gaster on August 2, 1900, Mayor's Letterbooks, NOPL.

48. Letter from Arthur McGuirk to D.S. Gaster on July 31, 1900, Mayor's Letterbooks, NOPL.

49. While the mayor's office fielded a variety of requests from residents, letters regarding the behavior of black men are rare in correspondence in the months preceding the uprising, suggesting that this was a unique response connected to the Robert Charles crisis. For the mayor's comprehensive correspondence, see Mayor's Letterbooks, NOPL.

50. Letter of J.L. Lammoureux to Paul Capdevielle, undated, Council Records, NOPL.

51. Letter of Arthur McGuirk to D.S. Gaster on August 21, 1900, Mayor's Letterbooks, NOPL.

52. Letter of Arthur McGuirk to D.S. Gaster in August 1900, Mayor's Letterbooks, NOPL.

53. Letter of J. Falk to Paul Capdevielle on August 9, 1900, Council Records, NOPL. Falk would run into his own legal troubles in the ensuing years, facing charges for carrying a concealed weapon and obtaining goods by false pretenses. See "Before Judge Aucoin," New Orleans *Times-Democrat*, July 6, 1905, 4; "Two Big Damage Suits Are Filed," New Orleans *Times-Democrat*, January 15, 1911, 29.

54. Letter of Secretary Arthur C. McGuirk to J. Falk on August 9, 1900, Mayor's Letter-books, NOPL.

55. "Northern Papers and the Negro Question," New Orleans *Times-Democrat*, August 14, 1900, 4.

56. "Race Riot of the West Side," *New York Times*, August 16, 1900, 1; "Almost a Riot at Thorpe's Funeral," New York *Evening World*, August 16, 1900, 1; "West Side Race Riot," New York *Tribune*, August 16, 1900, 1.

57. "Anti-Negro Riots North and South," New Orleans *Times-Democrat*, August 17, 1900, 4.

58. Telegram of New York *Evening World* to Mayor W.C. Flower on August 16, 1900, Council Records, NOPL.

59. Response of Paul Capdevielle to New York *Evening World*, undated, Mayor's Letterbooks, NOPL. See also "New York Riots," New Orleans *Times-Democrat*, August 17, 1900, 3.

60. "Police Guilty of Cowardice," New Orleans *Daily Picayune*, August 9, 1900, 3. See also "Dismissed in Disgrace," New Orleans *Times-Democrat*, August 9, 1900, 3, and "Fired All Four," New Orleans *Daily States*, August 9, 1900, 2.

61. "Police Guilty of Cowardice," New Orleans *Daily Picayune*, August 9, 1900, 3.

62. "Dismissed from the Force," New Orleans *Times-Democrat*, August 9, 1900, 4. See also "Before the Police Board," New Orleans *Times-Democrat*, July 31, 1900, 4. On the dismissals, see Memo of the Office of the Superintendent of Police on August 9, 1900, Council Records, NOPL.

63. "The Police Board," New Orleans *Times-Democrat*, August 8, 1900, 4. See also "Now That Order Has Been Restored," New Orleans *Daily Picayune*, July 31, 1900, 4.

64. "Grand Jury Report," New Orleans *Times-Democrat*, August 30, 1900, 6. See also "The Grand Jury's Record Report," New Orleans *Daily Picayune*, August 30, 1900, 3.

65. Letter of Frank T. Smith on August 4, 1900, reprinted in the New Orleans *Daily States*, August 5, 1900, 8.

66. "The Police Board," New Orleans *Times-Democrat*, August 31, 1900, 4. See also "The New Police Commissioners," New Orleans *Daily Picayune*, August 31, 1900, 4. On the appointments of John McGraw and John McCloskey, see "Police Board," New Orleans *Times-Democrat*, August 31, 1900, 11. A third police board member would resign at the beginning of 1901 and be replaced by Adolph S. Leclerc, one of the men wounded by Charles during the Saratoga Street siege. See *Annual Report of the Board of Police Commissioners for 1901*, 10–11.

67. Fourteen officers had been dismissed during the first seven months of 1900. See *Annual Report of the Board of Police Commissioners for 1900*, 24–27. A total of thirty-two officers would be dismissed in 1900, about 50 percent more terminations than any other year since the reorganization of the police board in the early 1890s. During the first seven months of 1900, commissioners issued fines amounting to $145.05 to city police officers. In the five months following the riots, fines spiked to $309.95. In 1900, total fines for city and harbor police officers reached a three-year high of $542.75. In 1901, officers were fined $900.25, more than twice the total annual average of $362.72 during the 1890s. See *Annual Report of the Board of Police Commissioners for 1900,* 46, and *Annual Report of the Board of Police Commissioners for 1901*, 29–30.

68. On the budget and changes to manpower, see *Annual Report of the Board of Police Commissioners for 1900* and *Annual Report of the Board of Police Commissioners for 1902*.

69. "The Police Board Does Business," New Orleans *Daily Picayune*, September 11, 1900, 16.

70. "Police Board," New Orleans *Times-Democrat*, August 31, 1900, 11.

71. "Place to Shoot," New Orleans *Daily Picayune*, September 8, 1900, 3.

72. *Annual Report of the Board of Police Commissioners for 1898*, 11.

73. "The Police Board Does Business," New Orleans *Daily Picayune*, September 11, 1900, 16; "Unusual Trials by the Police Board," New Orleans *Daily Picayune*, November 15, 1900, 7. On the adoption of the new weapons, see Letter of John Journeé to Paul Capdevielle on September 13, 1901, Records of Mayor Paul Capdevielle, NOPL.

74. "The Police Board Does Business," New Orleans *Daily Picayune*, September 11, 1900, 16. See also "Blame Yourself and Not Your Police, O New Orleans," *Harlequin* 2, no. 7 (August 11, 1900): 2–3.

75. "The Police Board," New Orleans *Times-Democrat*, April 5, 1901, 4.

76. On the contrasting stories, see "Negroes Resist Arrest," New Orleans *Times-Democrat*, August 17, 1900, 9, and "A Bad Negro," New Orleans *Daily Picayune*, August 17, 1900, 9.

77. "A Bad Negro," New Orleans *Daily Picayune*, August 17, 1900, 9.

78. "Negroes Resist Arrest," New Orleans *Times-Democrat*, August 17, 1900, 9. On Harris's age, see U.S. Census of 1900, Louisiana, Orleans Parish, Roll 575, 6A. As a fourteen-year-old boy, Harris had been arrested after striking an older man on the head, but he avoided prison for the man's death when the coroner declared his death to be the result of heart disease. See "When a Boy He Killed a Man," New Orleans *Times-Democrat*, July 4, 1896, 8. On his sentencing, see "Criminal District Court," New Orleans *Times-Democrat*, November 10, 1900, 11.

79. On Morton's unedited recollections, see Alan Lomax's original recorded interviews with Jelly Roll Morton, particularly the tracks beginning with "The Story of Aaron Harris" on *Jelly Roll Morton: The Complete Library of Congress Recordings* (2005).

80. On Harris's death, see "Negro Kills Enemy Who Threatened Him," New Orleans *Times-Picayune*, July 15, 1915, 12. Author Cecil Brown situates Aaron Harris within the broad cultural tradition of African American folk legend, although he wrongly identifies him as the alleged snitch. See Cecil Brown, *Stagolee Shot Billy* (Cambridge, MA: Harvard University Press, 2003), 97–98.

81. Lomax, *Mister Jelly Roll*, 56.

82. Lomax, *Mister Jelly Roll*, 57.

83. "Negro Murder," New Orleans *Daily Picayune*, September 3, 1900, 6. See also "Shot on His Doorstep," New Orleans *Times-Democrat*, September 3, 1900, 7. On Clark's age, see Orleans Parish Death Records, vol. 123, 158.

84. See especially Ida B. Wells, *Southern Horrors: Lynch Law in All Its Phases* (New York: New York Age Print, 1892), and *The Red Record: Tabulated Statistics and Alleged Cause of Lynching* (n.p., 1895).

85. Wells-Barnett, *Mob Rule in New Orleans*, 48.

86. "Mabry Murder Trial," New Orleans *Times-Democrat*, October 26, 1900, 7; "The Jury Hears Some Witnesses," New Orleans *Daily Picayune*, October 26, 1900, 11.

87. "Mabry Swears He Swore to Lies," New Orleans *Daily Picayune*, October 27, 1900, 11.

88. "Sensation Promised," New Orleans *Times-Democrat*, May 21, 1901, 3.

89. "The Grand Jury Meeting at Night," New Orleans *Daily Picayune*, May 25, 1901, 13.

90. Murder charges against six accused murderers would be dropped by the late spring of 1901. For the adjudication of the cases, see Criminal District Court, Orleans Parish, Case Nos. 30061, 30062, 30074, and 30076, NOPL.

91. On the outcome, see "Riot Cases All Dropped," New Orleans *Times-Democrat*, May 23, 1901, 3.

92. "Death of Major H.J. Hearsey," New Orleans *Daily States*, October 30, 1900, 1.

93. "Death of Major Hearsey," New Orleans *Daily Picayune*, October 31, 1900, 7.

94. Letter of Paul Capdevielle to the Editors of the *Daily States* on October 30, 1900, Mayor's Letterbooks, NOPL. See also Letter of Paul Capdevielle to Mrs. H.J. Hearsey on October 30, 1900; Letter of Paul Capdevielle to Hon. Robert Ewing on October 30, 1900, Mayor's Letterbooks, NOPL.

95. "Major Hearsey," New Orleans *Times-Democrat*, October 31, 1900, 4.

96. "The Negro Problem and Its Final Solution," New Orleans *Daily States*, August 7, 1900, 4.

97. "He Spoke as He Thought" from the New Orleans *German Gazette*, reprinted in New Orleans *Daily States*, October 31, 1900, 10.

98. "Major Hearsey Buried," New Orleans *Times-Democrat*, November 1, 1900, 10.

99. On the waterfront activity, see, for example, "Miles of Wharfage Crowded with Cotton," New Orleans *Times-Democrat*, October 5, 1900, 3.

100. "Good Business," New Orleans *Times-Democrat*, November 1, 1900, 4.

101. On the dispute, see, for example, "Reached the Limit," New Orleans *Times-Democrat*, October 23, 1900, 3, and "Striking Roustabouts' Demands Are Ignored," New Orleans *Times-Democrat*, October 31, 1900, 3.

102. "The Roustabout Trouble," New Orleans *Times-Democrat*, October 31, 1900, 4. On the role played by colored leaders, see "Idle Negroes," New Orleans *Daily Picayune*, October 21, 1900, 4.

103. "An Ovation to the Mayor," New Orleans *Daily Picayune*, November 8, 1900, 4.

104. "A Train Held Up at the City Line, Robbers Escaping," New Orleans *Daily Picayune*, December 14, 1900, 1.

105. On the career and death of Channing B. Barnes, alias Jack Nelson, see "Death Tells the Secret of the Train Robbery," New Orleans *Times-Picayune*, December 19, 1900, 1.

106. "Channing B. Barnes Lies in Potter's Field," New Orleans *Daily Picayune*, December 22, 1900, 3.

107. "Blakely's Plain Talk," New Orleans *Times-Democrat*, December 22, 1900, 9.

108. "Sewerage, Drainage, and Water Bonds," New Orleans *Times-Democrat*, December 28, 1900, 4.

109. "Municipal Bonds," New Orleans *Times-Democrat*, December 30, 1900, 4.

110. "Dr. Palmer on 'The 20th Century,'" New Orleans *Times-Democrat*, January 2, 1901, 1, 6.

111. "Wonderful Prosperity of the Crescent City," New Orleans *Times-Democrat*, January 1, 1901, 3.

112. "New Orleans During the Century," New Orleans *Times-Democrat*, January 1, 1901, 4.

EPILOGUE

1. Martin Behrman won mayoral elections in 1904, 1908, 1912, and 1916, before suffering a shock defeat in 1920 to a statewide reform movement headed by John M. Parker, the New Orleans businessman who played a major role in the Charles crisis, but later broke with the machine. Behrman would return to office in 1925, although he would die less than a year into his unprecedented fifth term. On Behrman in his own words, see especially Kemp, *Martin Behrman of New Orleans*. On Parker's political career and ideology, see Matthew James Schott, "John M. Parker of Louisiana and the Varieties of American Progressivism" (PhD dissertation, Vanderbilt University, 1969).

2. Most significantly, waterfront workers reestablished interracial cooperation during the early twentieth century, founding the Dock and Cotton Council in 1901 and collectively bargaining with employers for nearly two decades. See Arnesen, *Waterfront Workers of New Orleans.* For an in-depth analysis of civic progress and municipal governance during this period, see Dupont, "Progressive Civic Development and Political Conflict."

3. Reynolds, *Machine Politics in New Orleans*, 138–41.

4. William Allen, *New Orleans Old and New* (New Orleans: New Orleans Association of Commerce Convention and Tourism Bureau, 1914); Alfred S. Amer, *Souvenir of New Orleans, "The City That Care Forgot"* (New Orleans: Compliments of the St. Charles, 1917). On the controversy, see Emily Epstein Landau, *Spectacular Wickedness: Sex, Race, and Memory in Storyville, New Orleans* (Baton Rouge: Louisiana State University Press, 2013), 177–91.

5. For a concise history of New Orleans under the Behrman administration, including the cited quotation, see Kendall, *History of New Orleans*, vol. 2, 547–64.

6. U.S. Bureau of Labor Statistics, *Handbook of Labor Statistics: 1941 Edition*, vol. 1, no. 694 (Washington, DC: Government Printing Office, 1942), 91–93.

7. Per capita tax revenue in New Orleans was $17.54, the lowest among twenty-one American cities with populations above 300,000 residents. Among the fifty largest American cities, only Birmingham, Alabama ($16.49) posted a lower rate. See U.S. Bureau of the Census, *Financial Statistics of Cities Having a Population of Over 30,000: 1919* (Washington, DC, Government Printing Office, 1921), 51.

8. Reynolds, *Machine Politics in New Orleans*, 140.

9. W.E.B. Du Bois, ed., *The Negro Artisan: A Social Study* (Atlanta, GA: Atlanta University Press, 1902), 127. Between 1910 and 1920, weekly wage scales for union members rose considerably for bricklayers ($27.50 to $44.00), carpenters ($19.20 to $36.00), and plasterers ($24.00 to $45.00). See U.S. Bureau of Labor Statistics, *Union Scale of Wages and Hours of Labor, May 15, 1921* (Washington, DC: Government Printing Office, 1922), 39–41.

10. According to census statistics, 13,066 of 32,695 black male workers were classified as "laborers" in 1920, compared with 2,647 longshoremen, 1,309 teamsters, and 1,048 carpenters. See U.S. Census Bureau, *Fourteenth Census of the United States*, vol. 4 (Washington, DC: Government Printing Office, 1923), 1154–57.

11. During the early 1920s, the average hourly wages of bricklayers ($1.00) and carpenters ($0.88) were three times higher than those of common laborers ($0.30). See "Labor Rates and Conditions Throughout the Country," *Engineering News-Record* 88, no. 5 (February 22, 1922): 215.

12. In 1920, census officials classified 18,073 of 22,305 black female workers under "domestic and personal service," with almost 90 percent of them designated as either servants or laundresses. The average rate of workforce participation between 1900 and 1920 was 54.5 percent among black women, compared with 23.8 percent among native-born white women. On occupations by race in New Orleans during 1920, see U.S. Bureau of the Census, *Fourteenth Census of the United States*, vol. 4, 1154–57. On workforce participation by race, see U.S. Bureau of the Census, *Women in Gainful Occupations, 1870–1920* (Washington, DC: Government Printing Office, 1929), 269–76.

13. For employment statistics in New Orleans in 1930, see U.S Bureau of the Census, *Fifteenth Census of the United States*, vol. 4 (Washington, DC: Government Printing Office, 1933), 628–30. For employment statistics in New Orleans in 1940, see U.S. Bureau of the Census, *Sixteenth Census of the United States*, vol. 3, no. 3 (Washington, DC: Government Printing Office, 1943), 241–46.

14. The overall illiteracy rates in New Orleans were 15.7 percent for black residents, compared with 13.9 percent among foreign-born residents and 0.9 percent among native-born white residents. These rates were partially reduced by the traditional strength of the local public school system and compared favorably with Birmingham (18.4) and Atlanta (17.8) and similarly with Memphis (15.6) and Richmond (14.9), but they were significantly higher than Baltimore (12.9) and Washington, DC (8.6). See U.S. Bureau of the Census, *Fourteenth Census of the United States*, vol. 2, 1097, 1184.

15. Across the state, 81.3 percent of black families rented their homes as opposed to owning them, a number that had decreased only slightly from the turn of the century (84.2). By comparison, 55.1 percent of white families rented their homes in 1920. In New Orleans, roughly three-quarters of all homes were rented rather than owned. Although comparative rates between white and black residents are unavailable for 1920, statistics for 1930 show that 84.4 percent of black-occupied homes in New Orleans were rented in 1930. See U.S. Bureau of the Census, *Fourteenth Census of the United States*, vol. 2 (Washington, DC: Government Printing Office, 1922), 1285–86; U.S. Bureau of the Census, *Negroes in the United States, 1920–1932* (Washington, DC: Government Printing Office, 1935), 277.

16. From 1911 to 1920, the average mortality rate in New Orleans was 31.4 per 1,000 black residents, compared with 16.4 for white residents. By comparison, death rates in Atlanta were 16 percent lower for white residents (13.8) and 22 percent lower for black residents (24.6). Memphis ranked second with an average death rate of 29.9 per 1,000 black residents, ahead of Baltimore (28.3), Richmond (26.5), Birmingham (26.4), Louisville (26.1), Washington, DC (24.7), and other major cities with large black populations. See U.S. Bureau of the Census, *Mortality Statistics: 1920* (Washington, DC: Government Printing Office, 1922), 12–13. On black populations in American cities from 1910 to 1930, see U.S. Bureau of the Census, *Negroes in the United States, 1920–1932*, 55.

17. This was a claim that appeared in monthly publications from the New Orleans Health Department during the early twentieth century. For example, see "Monthly Report of Health Department of the City of New Orleans, Month of September, 1920."

18. Kemp, *Martin Behrman of New Orleans*, 51–53.

19. See David Fort Godshalk, *Veiled Visions: The 1906 Atlanta Race Riot and the Reshaping of American Race Relations* (Chapel Hill: University of North Carolina Press, 2005).

20. See especially Isabel Wilkerson, *The Warmth of Other Suns: The Epic Story of America's Great Migration* (New York: Vintage, 2011); James N. Gregory, *The Southern Diaspora: How the Great Migrations of Black and White Southerners Transformed America* (Chapel Hill: University of North Carolina Press, 2005); Davarian L. Baldwin, *Chicago's New Negroes: Modernity, the Great Migration, and Black Urban Life* (Chapel Hill: University of North Carolina Press, 2007); James R. Grossman, *Land of Hope: Chicago, Black Southerners, and the Great Migration* (Chicago: University of Chicago Press, 1991); Nicholas Lemann, *The Promised Land: The Great Migration and How It Changed America* (New York: Knopf, 1991).

21. On the East St. Louis Riot, see Charles L. Lumpkins, *American Pogrom: The East St. Louis Riot and Black Politics* (Athens: Ohio University Press, 2008).

22. See especially David F. Krugler, *1919, The Year of Racial Violence: How African Americans Fought Back* (New York: Cambridge University Press, 2015); Barbara Foley, *Spectres of 1919: Class and Nation in the Making of the New Negro* (Urbana: University of Illinois Press, 2003); Jan Voogd, *Race Riots and Resistance: The Red Summer of 1919* (New York: Peter Lang, 2008).

23. On the Tulsa riots, see especially Alfred L. Brophy, *Reconstructing the Dreamland: The Tulsa Riot of 1921* (New York: Oxford University Press, 2002).

24. Kemp, *Martin Behrman of New Orleans*, 71.

25. Historian Dennis Rousey counted seventeen targeted civilians killed by police officers between 1863 and 1889, a period of twenty-seven years. Police records from the 1890s are spotty, but they suggest a general continuation of this pattern. On police killings during the late nineteenth century, see Rousey, *Policing the Southern City*, 173-88.

26. Available homicide records from 1900 to 1920 contain reports on suspects killed by police officers, although five years are unavailable (1900, 1904, 1907, 1908, 1920), suggesting the total number of police killings in the period is likely more than fifty. The forty-one documented fatal shootings involve twenty-eight black victims and thirteen white victims. The records for the period also contain at least seventeen deadly shootings involving watchmen and private detectives. For homicide records on many years between the 1890s and 1945, see NOPD Homicide Records, NOPL.

27. Between 1900 and 1920, the proportion of black residents in New Orleans declined slightly from 27.1 to 26.1 percent. See U.S. Bureau of the Census, *Abstract of the Twelfth Census of the United States* (Washington, DC: Government Printing Office, 1904), 104; U.S. Bureau of the Census, *Abstract of the Fourteenth Census of the United States* (Washington, DC: Government Printing Office, 1923), 110. These quotes come from the police report detailing these killings, each taking place under questionable circumstances. See Homicide Report of Jim Badger, April 10, 1909; Homicide Report of Frank Loeper, January 8, 1911; Homicide Report of Charles Croghan, April 15, 1911; Homicide Report of Sam Johnson, April 1, 1912; Homicide Report of John Ball, July 18, 1915; Homicide Report of William Wallace, May 4, 1916; Homicide Report of Henry Johnson, June 26, 1916; Homicide Report of Abraham Price, May 26, 1918, NOPL.

28. On policing in New Orleans during the 1920s, see Jeffrey S. Adler, *Murder in New Orleans: The Creation of Jim Crow Policing* (Chicago: University of Chicago Press, 2019). On policing in black communities during the early twentieth century, see especially Simon Balto, *Occupied Territory: Policing Black Chicago from the Red Summer to Black Power* (Chapel Hill: University of North Carolina Press, 2019).

29. On the mechanization of the force, see New Orleans Police Department, *Fifty Years of Progress, 1900-1950* (New Orleans: Franklin Publishing Co., n.d.), 11.

30. See W. Marvin Dulaney, *Black Police in America* (Bloomington: Indiana University Press, 1996), 8-18. On black officers in New Orleans during the period, see also Vanessa Flores-Roberts, "Black Policemen in Jim Crow New Orleans" (master's thesis, University of New Orleans, 2011).

31. See "A Proud Peeler," New Orleans *Times-Democrat*, August 2, 1900, 2, and "Charged with False Imprisonment," New Orleans *Times-Democrat*, August 3, 1900, 3.

32. On black police officers in the South, see Dulaney, *Black Police in America*, 8-46.

33. Homicide records denoting police shooting of civilians between 1925 and 1945 are incomplete, but available in full for fourteen years. For analysis of these records, see Jeffrey S. Adler, "The Killer Behind the Badge: Race and Police Homicide in New Orleans, 1925-1945," *Law and History Review* 30, no. 2 (May 2012): 495-531. On the ACLU report, see William V. Moore, "Civil Liberties in Louisiana: The Louisiana League for the Preservation of Constitutional Rights," *Louisiana History* 31, no. 1 (Winter 1990): 59.

34. Only 31 percent of black victims were armed with guns compared with 53 percent of white victims; 60 percent were killed in one-on-one confrontations with officers compared with

17 percent of white victims; and black victims were 50 percent less likely to have criminal records. See Adler, "The Killer Behind the Badge," 510–11.

35. Adler, "The Killer Behind the Badge," 501–2, 505.

36. Homicide Report of John Williams, April 11, 1932; Homicide Report of Milton Batisse, June 29, 1930; Homicide of Felton Robinson, June 17, 1943; Homicide of Edward Sanders, March 4, 1930, NOPL. For more details on some of these shootings, see Adler, "The Killer Behind the Badge."

37. Homicide Report of John Smith, February 2, 1935, NOPL.

38. Homicide Report of George Simmons, January 10, 1931, NOPL. See also Adler, "The Killer Behind the Badge," 514.

39. Homicide Report of Hattie McCray, February 10, 1930, NOPL. After a highly celebrated trial, Charles Guerand was convicted and sentenced to death, but later declared insane and spared execution. After five years of hospitalization, he pled guilty to manslaughter and received a three-year sentence, although he was released after serving just one year in jail. See "Policeman Given Three Year Sentence," New Orleans *Times-Democrat*, March 3, 1937, 1, 9; "Charles Guerand Is Freed from Angola After Year of Slaying Term Served," New Orleans *Times-Democrat*, April 14, 1938. See also Adler, "The Killer Behind the Badge," 502–3.

40. On municipal politics during the 1930s, see especially Garry Boulard, *Huey Long Invades New Orleans: The Siege of a City, 1934–36* (Gretna, LA: Pelican Publishing, 1998). On de-Lesseps S. Morrison and his administration, see Edward F. Haas, *DeLesseps S. Morrison and the Image of Reform: New Orleans Politics, 1946–1961* (Baton Rouge: Louisiana State University Press, 1974).

41. Haas, *DeLesseps S. Morrison and the Image of Reform*, 41–66, 82–97.

42. Haas, *DeLesseps S. Morrison and the Image of Reform*, 50–51, 67–81, 232–33. On housing, see Kent B. Germany, *New Orleans After the Promises: Poverty, Citizenship, and the Search for the Great Society* (Athens: University of Georgia Press, 2007), 32–33.

43. On these demographic changes, see especially Germany, *New Orleans After the Promises*, 1–8. See also Haas, *DeLesseps S. Morrison and the Image of Reform*, 232–33. Among the fifty largest American cities according to the U.S. Census of 1970, New Orleans had the highest percentage of families living in poverty. See James K. Glassman, "New Orleans: I Have Seen the Future, and It's Houston," *The Atlantic* (July 1978).

44. On policing in New Orleans during this era, see especially Leonard N. Moore, *Black Rage in New Orleans: Police Brutality and African American Activism from World War II to Hurricane Katrina* (Baton Rouge: Louisiana State University Press, 2010), 17–42.

45. For a comprehensive account of civil rights in Louisiana during the twentieth century, see Adam Fairclough, *Race and Democracy: The Civil Rights Struggle in Louisiana* (Athens: University of Georgia Press, 1995). On the struggle to desegregate schools in New Orleans, see Liva Baker, *The Second Battle of New Orleans: The Hundred-Year Struggle to Integrate the Schools* (New York: HarperCollins, 1996).

46. Fairclough, *Race and Democracy*, 427.

47. By the end of the 1960s, there were 74 black NOPD officers on a total force of 1,320. See Moore, *Black Rage in New Orleans*, 62. On the survey of black community leaders, see Fairclough, *Race and Democracy*, 426.

48. Orissa Arend, *Showdown in Desire: The Black Panthers Take a Stand in New Orleans* (Fayetteville: University of Arkansas Press, 2009), 1–12.

49. Memo of Joseph Giarrusso to Moon Landrieu on August 20, 1970, Records of Mayor Moon Landrieu, NOPL.

50. Memo of Joseph Giarrusso to Moon Landrieu on August 5, 1970, Records of Mayor Moon Landrieu, NOPL.

51. Arend, *Showdown in Desire*, 32–33.

52. Germany, *New Orleans After the Promises*, 276.

53. Arend, *Showdown in Desire*, 62–63.

54. Arend, *Showdown in Desire*, 79–81.

55. Moore, *Black Rage in New Orleans*, 80.

56. Germany, *New Orleans After the Promises*, 282.

57. Arend, *Showdown in Desire*, 102.

58. For the most comprehensive coverage of these events, including interviews with key participants, see Arend, *Showdown in Desire*. Additional scholarly accounts include Moore, *Black Rage in New Orleans*, 70–87, and Germany, *New Orleans After the Promises*, 271–87.

59. The narrative presented in these sections intentionally avoids endnotes, in order to relate the story and its eerie parallels without drawing attention to its academic construction. These events have been reconstructed primarily using the New Orleans Police Department's comprehensive report on the Essex investigation. It is available in the Louisiana Division of the New Orleans Public Library's main branch, which is located directly across the street from the former Downtown Howard Johnson's Hotel. This account also relies heavily on the only book published on the shootings, Peter Herndon's *A Terrible Thunder: The Story of the New Orleans Sniper* (1978; repr. New Orleans: Garrett County Press, 2010). Select quotations are also drawn from contemporary news coverage, particularly multiple stories by the *Washington Post* and *New York Times*. On Alfred Harrell's obituary and an informal police version of events, see the NOPD's *Our Beat* magazine, available at Tulane University's Louisiana Research Collection. All other quotes come from the sources cited above.

60. Moore, *Black Rage in New Orleans*, 115. On the rise of mass incarceration from the 1960s through the present day, see especially Elizabeth Hinton, *From the War on Poverty to the War on Crime: The Making of Mass Incarceration in America* (Cambridge, MA: Harvard University Press, 2016). See also Michelle Alexander, *The New Jim Crow: Mass Incarceration in the Age of Colorblindness* (New York: The New Press, 2010).

61. Multiple studies by the U.S. Justice Department from the early 1980s through the mid-1990s recorded more citizen brutality complaints against the NOPD than any other department in the nation. For example, see U.S. Department of Justice, *Study on Police Department Complaints: 1984–1990* (Washington, DC: U.S. Government Printing Office, 1992). See also Moore, *Black Rage in New Orleans*, 5–7, and Christina Metcalf, *Race Relations and the New Orleans Police Department: 1900–1972* (honors thesis, Tulane University, 1985). On the Obama administration's investigation, see U.S. Department of Justice, Civil Rights Division, *Investigation of the New Orleans Police Department* (March 2011).

Index

About the Author

Andrew Baker earned his PhD in history from Harvard University and is currently a faculty member in the Bates College History Department. He lives in Maine.

Publishing in the Public Interest

Thank you for reading this book published by The New Press. The New Press is a nonprofit, public interest publisher. New Press books and authors play a crucial role in sparking conversations about the key political and social issues of our day.

We hope you enjoyed this book and that you will stay in touch with The New Press. Here are a few ways to stay up to date with our books, events, and the issues we cover:

- Sign up at www.thenewpress.com/subscribe to receive updates on New Press authors and issues and to be notified about local events

- Like us on Facebook: www.facebook.com/newpressbooks

- Follow us on Twitter: www.twitter.com/thenewpress

- Follow us on Instagram: www.instagram.com/thenewpress

Please consider buying New Press books for yourself; for friends and family; or to donate to schools, libraries, community centers, prison libraries, and other organizations involved with the issues our authors write about.

The New Press is a 501(c)(3) nonprofit organization. You can also support our work with a tax-deductible gift by visiting www.thenewpress.com/donate.